From Sea-Bathing
to Beach-Going

Diálogos Series KRIS LANE / SERIES EDITOR

Understanding Latin America demands dialogue, deep exploration, and frank discussion of key topics. Founded by Lyman L. Johnson in 1992 and edited since 2013 by Kris Lane, the Diálogos Series focuses on innovative scholarship in Latin American history and related fields. The series, the most successful of its type, includes specialist works accessible to a wide readership and a variety of thematic titles, all ideally suited for classroom adoption by university and college teachers.

ALSO AVAILABLE IN THE DIÁLOGOS SERIES:

Gamboa's World: Justice, Silver Mining, and Imperial Reform in New Spain by Christopher Albi

The Conquest of the Desert: Argentina's Indigenous Peoples and the Battle for History edited by Carolyne R. Larson

From the Galleons to the Highlands: Slave Trade Routes in the Spanish Americas edited by Alex Borucki, David Eltis, and David Wheat

A Troubled Marriage: Indigenous Elites of the Colonial Americas by Sean F. McEnroe

Staging Frontiers: The Making of Modern Popular Culture in Argentina and Uruguay by William Garrett Acree Jr.

A Woman, a Man, a Nation: Mariquita Sánchez, Juan Manuel de Rosas, and the Beginnings of Argentina by Jeffrey M. Shumway

The Origins of Macho: Men and Masculinity in Colonial Mexico by Sonya Lipsett-Rivera

Mexico in the Time of Cholera by Donald Fithian Stevens

Tides of Revolution: Information, Insurgencies, and the Crisis of Colonial Rule in Venezuela by Cristina Soriano

Mexico City, 1808: Power, Sovereignty, and Silver in an Age of War and Revolution by John Tutino

For additional titles in the Diálogos Series, please visit unmpress.com.

From Sea-Bathing to Beach-Going

A Social History of the Beach in Rio de Janeiro, Brazil

B. J. Barickman EDITED BY HENDRIK KRAAY AND BRYAN MCCANN

University of New Mexico Press Albuquerque

Printed in the United States of America

Library of Congress Cataloging-in-Publication Data

Names: Barickman, B. J. (Bert Jude), 1958– author. | Kraay, Hendrik, 1964– editor. | McCann, Bryan, 1968– editor.

Title: From sea-bathing to beach-going: a social history of the beach in Rio de Janeiro, Brazil / B. J. Barickman, edited by Hendrik Kraay and Bryan McCann.

Other titles: Diálogos (Albuquerque, N.M.)

Description: Albuquerque: University of New Mexico Press, 2022. | Series: Diálogos series | Includes bibliographical references and index.

Identifiers: LCCN 2021048482 (print) | LCCN 2021048483 (e-book) | ISBN 9780826363626 (cloth) | ISBN 9780826363633 (paper) | ISBN 9780826363640 (e-book)

Subjects: LCSH: Bathing beaches—Brazil—Rio de Janeiro—History. | Beachgoers—Brazil—Rio de Janeiro—History. | Rio de Janeiro (Brazil)—Social life and customs—History.

Classification: LCC F2646.2. B38 2022 (print) | LCC F2646.2 (e-book) | DDC 981.5300946—dc23

LC record available at https://lccn.loc.gov/2021048482

LC e-book record available at https://lccn.loc.gov/2021048483

Founded in 1889, the University of New Mexico sits on the traditional homelands of the Pueblo of Sandia. The original peoples of New Mexico—Pueblo, Navajo, and Apache—since time immemorial have deep connections to the land and have made significant contributions to the broader community statewide. We honor the land itself and those who remain stewards of this land throughout the generations and also acknowledge our committed relationship to Indigenous peoples. We gratefully recognize our history.

Cover illustration: Lifesaving Post, Mid-1930s. Fuss, *Brasilien*, plate 76. Arquivo Images2You.

Designed by Mindy Basinger Hill

Composed in 11/14 pt Garamond Premier Pro and Caniste Regular

To all Bert's friends, colleagues, and especially his students,
we offer our hearts and our gratitude
for your every gift to him.

To Hendrik Kraay and Bryan McCann,
we extend our profound appreciation
for bringing Bert's work to life.

With deep and abiding love for our brother,
we dedicate this book, as he dedicated all his work,
to our parents.

JUDY BARICKMAN & NANCY BARICKMAN FOREBAUGH

Contents

Illustrations

Maps

Figures

Tables

Preface

AT THE TIME OF HIS PREMATURE DEATH in November 2016, our friend and colleague Bert J. Barickman left an unfinished manuscript with the working title of "A Social History of the Beach in Rio de Janeiro: Sea-Bathing and Beach-Going in the Nineteenth and Twentieth Centuries." In 2015, he had shared the first four chapters with a large number of colleagues in North America and Brazil, all of whom were deeply impressed with his research and the argument that he crafted from it on the transition from sea-bathing to beach-going in the Brazilian capital. Those who had seen the manuscript agreed that Barickman's work should see the light of day. With the enthusiastic support of Judy Barickman and Nancy J. Barickman-Forebaugh, Bert's sisters and heirs, Hendrik Kraay and Bryan McCann began to reconstruct what he had had in mind for his book. The "Homenagem a Bert Barickman" panel held at the July 2018 Brazilian Studies Association Congress in Rio de Janeiro, organized by McCann, with participation from Martha Santos, Kraay, and Marcus J. M. Carvalho, provided added impetus to this work.

In the course of our editing, we have striven to remain true to Barickman's distinctive voice and his vision for this book. Kraay and McCann edited chapters 1–4, while Kraay translated and edited the article that is the basis for chapter 5. McCann authored the epilogue, in part drawing on the notes that Barickman left for his final chapters and on some of the material referring to the post-1950 period in the chapters that he had drafted, while Kraay wrote the introduction. We are highly conscious that this is not the book that Barickman would have written—as Kraay explains in the introduction, he had in fact, planned an eight-chapter work that would have carried the story to the end of the twentieth century—but we hope that the following pages give readers an indication of what he might have done.

We have benefited from comments on the 2015 version of chapters 1–4 from Jeff Garmany, João José Reis, Marc Hertzman, Mary Karasch, Paulo Donadio, and Thomas H. Holloway, as well as from Richard Graham's and Sandra Lauderdale Graham's comments on an earlier version of chapter 5. In the published version of this chapter, Barickman also thanked Kátia Bezerra, Jeff Garmany, Rafael Fortes, Victor Andrade de Melo, Jim Freeman, Maurício de Almeida, David Ortiz, Elizabeth Moreira dos Santos, Álvaro Vicente G. Truppel P. do Cabo, and Ana Carvalho. Barickman's original research was funded in part by a 2004 National Endowment for the Humanities (NEH) research grant for a project titled "A Social History of Public Space in Rio de Janeiro, 1850s–1960s." He delighted in telling that the dry social-scientific title was an imposition by the NEH, which thought it impolitic to publicize that it was paying for a US scholar to study Brazilian beaches. Kevin Gosner assisted with obtaining material from Bert's computer. Pedro Falk, PhD candidate at the University of Calgary, compiled the bibliography from the original manuscript's footnotes. João Rabello Sodré obtained an important source for us in Rio de Janeiro. During part of the editing process, Kraay held the inaugural Naomi Lacey Annual Resident Fellowship at the Calgary Institute for the Humanities. Funding for the images was provided by the University of Arizona's Department of History and the Center for Latin American Studies; special thanks to Department Head Alison Futrell (History) and Director Marcela Vásquez (CLAS). The maps were created by William Gillies, history undergraduate student at the University of Calgary, from data in *imagineRio* (www.imaginerio.org). We thank Alida C. Metcalf for making these data available. Thanks also to Zubin Meer for his careful copyediting of the manuscript.

Portions of chapter 3 appeared as "Not Many Flew Down to Rio: The History of Beach-Going in Twentieth-Century Rio de Janeiro," *Journal of Tourism History* 6, nos. 2–3 (2009): 223–41. The last section of chapter 4 appeared as parts of "'Passarão por mestiços': o bronzeamento nas praias cariocas, noções de cor e raça e ideologia racial, 1920–1950," *Afro-Ásia*, no. 40 (2009): 173–221. Chapter 5 is a translated and revised version of "Medindo maiôs e correndo atrás de homens sem camisa: a polícia e as praias cariocas, 1920–1950," *Recorde* 9, no. 1 (Jan.–June 2016): 1–66.

Hendrik Kraay
CALGARY, AB, CANADA

Bryan McCann
WASHINGTON, DC, UNITED STATES

Introduction

HENDRIK KRAAY

THIS BOOK TELLS THE STORY OF HOW a long and narrow ocean beachfront neighborhood and the distinctive practice of beach-going invented by its residents came to symbolize a city and, indeed, a nation. Today, of course, Copacabana and the other nearby ocean beaches of Ipanema and Leblon are instantly recognizable around the world as Rio de Janeiro's and as quintessentially Brazilian, integral to the culture of the city and the country. Few fail to recognize Tom Jobim's hit song "The Girl from Ipanema" or photographs of Copacabana's sweeping arc of sand jammed with people on a hot summer weekend. One striking element of these photographs is how few people can be found in the water. This is not just because the South Atlantic waters off Rio de Janeiro are relatively cold and can have dangerous waves and undertows. Rather, it is because people are "going to the beach," which does not necessarily imply swimming or bathing, or even a quick dip in the water to cool off. How this practice developed is this book's main focus.

The five chapters that constitute this book were all that Bert J. Barickman had completed of a projected eight-chapter book on the history of sea-bathing and beach-going in Rio de Janeiro before his untimely death in 2016. While this is not the book that he would have written, *From Sea-Bathing to Beach-Going* analyzes the core changes that took place in the 1920s, when the long-standing custom of sea-bathing gave way to beach-going (and the closely related suntanning), especially in the rapidly developing elite neighborhood of Copacabana. Barickman's focus is on the social and cultural implications of these transformations for the city of Rio de Janeiro and its residents, known as Cariocas, from the early nineteenth to the mid-twentieth century.

Because this is not a conventional monograph but the editors' effort to create a book out the chapters that the author had been able to draft, I begin this introduction unconventionally, by outlining the five chapters that follow and then turning to some of the broader themes and issues that emerge from Barickman's arguments. Chapter 1 introduces nineteenth-century Rio de Janeiro and documents the nineteenth-century practice of sea-bathing, demonstrating that it was common for Cariocas to go for an early morning bath in Guanabara Bay. Neither trash nor sewage nor lack of changing facilities deterred them. Evidence for the growing prominence of sea-bathing comes from diverse sources, including advertising for bathing wear, police reports on drownings, and the increasing number of establishments devoted to sea-bathing, which all came to constitute a veritable "bathing industry." Already in the 1810s, bathing barges offered conveniences to those who could pay for their services; more barges are documented over the course of the century. Land-based bathing establishments, located alongside Rio de Janeiro's downtown, offered changerooms, lifeguards, diving docks, and other services to their clientele. By 1900, some ten such establishments operated along the city's bayshore, with most concentrated at Boqueirão do Passeio and Santa Luzia beaches, located at the south end of today's Avenida Rio Branco in an area that was landfilled in the early twentieth century. Of course, most Cariocas could not afford these establishments' services and went bathing when and where they could. Indeed, Cariocas of all classes bathed in the bay: slaves, the free poor, foreign visitors, and members of the city's middle and upper classes. Even the three monarchs who governed from Rio de Janeiro, and their families, bathed, sometimes publicly in the case of Pedro I. In short, as early twentieth-century Rio de Janeiro's chronicler João do Rio (Paulo Barreto) put it in 1904, sea-bathing was a "Carioca custom."

Chapter 2 takes on the questions of why Cariocas bathed and what this says about nineteenth-century society. A long-standing tradition in Rio de Janeiro today holds that, in the nineteenth-century, sea-bathing served primarily (even exclusively) medicinal purposes. To be sure, many Cariocas took to the bay's waters to cure an enormous variety of real or imagined ailments, and Brazilian doctors were well versed in the European medical thinking about thalassotherapy (the therapeutic uses of seawater). But to argue that Cariocas only bathed on their doctors' orders misrepresents the motives for sea-bathing. As in Europe and North America, sea-bathing was a way to get some relief from the summer heat and increasingly became an important leisure activity. Hygienists also promoted sea-bathing as healthful exercise for children and adults alike. This, in turn, was linked to the growing prominence of aquatic sports, especially rowing, Rio de Janeiro's most popular sport before the advent of football (soccer) in the twentieth century (rowing clubs were closely connected to bathing houses). African and Indigenous cultural traditions, as well as European lower-class customs, may also have influenced the development of what João do Rio described as the "Carioca custom." Moreover, by the end of the century, sea-bathing had become fashionable in Rio de Janeiro, just as it was in Europe and North America, and the bathing establishments became places of middle- and upper-class sociability.

At the same time, sea-bathing raised questions about proper comportment, dress, and relations between the sexes, and chapter 2 introduces this issue, which would dominate discussions about sea-bathing (and later beach-going) until the mid-twentieth century and later. Men and women of all classes in states of partial undress bathed together, and Rio de Janeiro's most popular beaches around 1900 were located adjacent to the city's center. All of this prompted concerns about the appropriate use of public space, police campaigns against bathing in the nude, and efforts to impose "decent" attire on Carioca bathers; "families"—coded language for "respectable" members of society—demanded that the police "moralize" bathing practices, even as they themselves claimed to be exempt from the police oversight. Out of these conflicts emerged distinctive (and often still-contested) codes for acceptable uses of public space.

Chapter 3 begins with the economic and social changes in early twentieth-century Rio de Janeiro that turned the Brazilian capital into a major metropolis of over three million inhabitants by 1960. It examines the increasing social and spatial segregation that came to characterize the city after 1900, as government efforts to remodel and "civilize" the capital displaced many of the poor from their former downtown homes. It describes the city's expansion northward as poor suburbs spread along the railway lines and its southward growth toward Copacabana and the other oceanfront neighborhoods. These were the years that favelas (shantytowns) expanded and racial segregation became relatively more pronounced, though it remained (and remains) far from complete. Downtown renovations did away with Boqueirão do Passeio beach in 1905 (and later landfills eliminated Santa Luzia and Calabouço beaches in the 1920s). While some worried that there would be no place to bathe, other downtown and suburban beaches remained popular locations for lower-class bathers. By the 1910s, Flamengo emerged as the preferred beach for middle- and upper-class bathers; this chapter concludes with a discussion of elite sociability in Flamengo during this beach's heyday as the Carioca elite's preferred location for bathing. Alongside these changes in the "Carioca custom," others began to look to Copacabana, Ipanema, and Leblon as sites for the development of new bathing resorts. Accessible by streetcar after 1892, Copacabana soon attracted real estate developers and speculators, some of whom sought to develop this neighborhood into a bathing resort that would attract foreign tourists and cater to a Carioca elite determined to distance itself from the rest of the population. Ultimately, however, the dreams of creating a Brazilian Biarritz failed to materialize, for few foreign tourists made it to the distant Brazilian capital and few Brazilians from elsewhere in the country needed to go to Rio de Janeiro to find beaches (and even fewer could afford the trip). In short, tourism played no significant role in the development of Rio de Janeiro's oceanfront beaches, unlike so many other cities famous for their sun-dappled sandy beaches.

Instead, domestic trends primarily shaped the creation of Carioca beach-going culture. Chapter 4 focuses on the development of Copacabana and the invention of beach-going. This out-of-the-way district became much more accessible in the 1890s, when a tramway company bored a tunnel through the low but steep hills that separated it from the rest of the city (another tunnel opened in the first decade of the twentieth century). These changes opened the area to development, and with considerable government support, Copacabana soon became an elite residential district; by the 1930s, houses and mansions gave way to often spectacular art-deco apartment buildings that enabled greater population density but also signaled social distinction. Automobiles, owned by the privileged few until midcentury, made Copacabana beach accessible to the well-off who lived elsewhere in the city. The establishment of a lifeguard service in the 1910s made bathing in the open ocean safer and gave Copacabana its distinctive geography marked by numbered lifeguard posts. In the 1920s, tanning quickly became the fashion in Rio de Janeiro, and Copacabana residents were at the forefront of those who adopted this custom on their relatively wide beach. In the context of a racially divided society, tanning raised numerous questions about the significance of dark and darkened skin, and in the concluding section of this chapter, Barickman shows how the discourse about tanning nevertheless reinforced existing hierarchies. Cariocas ultimately distinguished between color acquired through exposure to the sun and natural color, thus preserving the line between whites and nonwhites.

Chapter 5 turns to police efforts to moralize sea-bathing and beach-going from the 1910s to the 1940s. Since the nineteenth century, the police had concerned themselves with public decency and enforcing norms of conduct, and, in the twentieth century, periodic campaigns sought to restrict bathing dress to prevent "nudism" and to prevent people from walking on city streets in bathing attire, even if they were merely going from their homes to a nearby beach. They had to wear a robe or a jacket to cover their bathing attire. The sporadic campaigns that, after the 1920s, targeted Copacabana especially prompted intense debate in the press that suggests the gradual emergence of an elite Copacabana identity oriented around its residents' comfortable self-image as paragons of civilization and modernity.

The epilogue to this book, written by Bryan McCann and incorporating some material originally by Barickman, briefly surveys the history of beach-going to the end of the twentieth century. In the original outline for this book, Barickman contemplated writing two additional chapters about the period from about 1950 to the 1990s, and this epilogue addresses some of the issues that he intended to explore in them.

As editors, McCann and I are acutely conscious of a missing chapter in this book. The chapter 5 that I constructed from Barickman's previously published Portuguese-language article was originally intended to serve as the basis for chapter 6. The chapter 5 that Barickman intended to write would treat the full range of activities that Cariocas have come to associate with beach-going. To the best of our knowledge, all that he had written for this chapter was a rough outline in which he noted some of the topics that he proposed to address. These included what people did on the beach (everything from sports like football, shuttlecock, and gymnastics to sociability), what they wore (women, increasingly the maillot, and men, ever briefer swimming trunks), how they behaved, and how beach-going became integrated into daily life. Other topics slated for this chapter included the barriers that kept lower-class Cariocas from the Zona Norte (North Zone) or suburbs from coming to Copacabana, everything from trams and buses that banned riders in bathing attire, to circuitous routes that did not directly connect the Zona Norte to the ocean beaches, to the lack of changing facilities. He also planned to map the microgeography of the ocean beaches, marked by lifeguard posts. Beach-going at Copacabana, and later also Ipanema and Leblon, was considered a modern and cosmopolitan activity, and Carioca beach-goers frequently looked to Europe and the United States for models to emulate. In short, this chapter would have thoroughly documented the mid-twentieth-century culture of beach-going that Cariocas invented, much in the same way that chapter 1 documents the nineteenth-century practices of sea-bathing (that continued into the early twentieth century). To be sure, both chapters 4 and 5 contain numerous references to these activities, but they do not offer a systematic analysis of them.

In correspondence with colleagues, Barickman repeatedly emphasized that he was writing a book about sea-bathing and beach-going, not a history of the beach. The latter would have to include topics scarcely mentioned in the following pages, such as the use of the beach by fishers, seaside Candomblé and Umbanda ceremonies, environmental degradation, suicide by drowning, the smuggling of slaves and goods, and many more; he sometimes touches on them, but only insofar as they speak to the issues raised by sea-bathing and beach-going.[1] Barickman also avoided structuring his book around the political history of the period, for the social and cultural changes that he analyzes neither resulted directly from political changes nor mapped neatly onto them. Readers familiar with twentieth-century Brazilian history will note, for example, that there is no mention of the abortive 6 July 1922 junior-officer revolt at Copacabana Fort that ultimately launched the politico-military movement known as *Tenentismo*. The 1922 revolt ended in a bloody shootout on the beachfront Avenida Atlântica, halfway up Copacabana beach at what is today Siqueira Campos Street (named after one of the two survivors of the eighteen civilian and military rebels who had walked up the beach in protest against the government of President Artur Bernardes). It was, of course, winter, so there were few people on the beach at the time, but one photograph shows a baffled beach-goer looking on from the sand as the rebels walk by.[2] Antônio de Siqueira Campos, incidentally, was a strong swimmer who reportedly swam from one end of Copacabana to the other for his morning exercise while stationed at the fort.[3]

A (very) brief political overview of the century and a half covered by this book would emphasize that Rio de Janeiro was the capital of the Portuguese Empire from 1808 to 1821, of the Brazilian Empire from 1822 to 1889, and of the Brazilian Republic from 1889 to 1960, when the seat of government was transferred to Brasília. For almost all of this time, Rio de Janeiro enjoyed a distinct legal status, formalized as the Neutral Municipality (1835–1889) and the Federal District (by the terms of the 1891 republican constitution). During the empire, it was often known as the Corte (Court or seat of the monarchy). Some aspects of city government were directly run or closely monitored by the imperial or republican national governments, while in other areas the city government had the same responsibilities that other municipalities had.

Rio de Janeiro became the Portuguese Empire's capital in 1808, when Queen Maria I and Prince Regent João (the future King João VI) fled there to escape the Napoleonic invasion of Portugal. The court's arrival and the subsequent opening of the ports to trade with friendly nations effectively ended much of Brazil's colonial status, laid the foundations for the city's political hegemony over the rest of Brazil, and turned it into an increasingly cosmopolitan city. Independence came in 1822 in the form of a centralized constitutional monarchy that lasted until 1889 under Emperors Pedro I (1822–1831) and Pedro II (1831–1889); the latter was overthrown by a military coup that proclaimed a republic on 15 November 1889. Slavery, the foundation of colonial and imperial Brazilian economy and society, lasted until 1888. A decentralized republican regime institutionalized in the early 1890s, today known as the Old or the First Republic, lasted until 1930, when it was overthrown in the so-called Revolution of 1930, that brought Getúlio Vargas to power. Vargas initially presided over a period of political liberalization and increasingly partisan politics. Over time, he strengthened the national government and significantly expanded state power in the economy and in society, especially during his Estado Novo (New State) dictatorship from 1937 to 1945. A military coup overthrew Vargas and instituted a limited democratic regime that would last until the military dictatorship of 1964 to 1985. Many of these regime changes had no impact on the social, economic, and cultural changes that Barickman traces in the following chapters, but they sometimes shaped the sources. Periods of press censorship in the twentieth century constrained discussions about certain topics (particularly criticisms of government actions). The first elected president of the new republic, General Eurico Gaspar Dutra (1946–1951), a social conservative, set the tone for the last great police effort to moralize beach-going, discussed in chapter 5.

Barickman focused his research on the summer months, roughly November to March, which eventually came to be recognized as the bathing or beach-going season. He worked extensively with Rio de Janeiro's rich periodical record, since 2012 mostly available through the Biblioteca Nacional's massive open-access database, the Hemeroteca Digital Brasileira. For most of the time that he worked on this book, however, he had to struggle with the library's microfilm collection. He combed through the mainstream press but also examined magazines and illustrated periodicals; Copacabana neighborhood newspapers reveal the *mentalités* of this district's residents from the 1920s to the 1940s. He carefully mined the hundreds of travelers' descriptions of nineteenth- and early twentieth-century Rio de Janeiro for their comments about sea-bathing and beach-going, and he followed medical opinion about these practices through the theses that aspiring doctors had to write before receiving their degrees and through other medical literature. Municipal regulation of sea-bathing and beach-going left archival trails that Barickman followed, as did contemporary policing. Literary sources also reveal aspects of sea-bathing and beach-going cultures. Barickman constantly dialogues with the chroniclers, folklorists, and local historians who have done much to shape Cariocas' understandings of themselves.

The images reproduced in this book are but a small selection of the voluminous iconographic record that exists for these late nineteenth- and twentieth-century Carioca customs. While painters and early photographers focused their brushes and lenses on landscapes or buildings, and generally portrayed beaches and waterfronts devoid of people, the illustrated press that emerged in the 1860s provides a rich record of sea-bathing. Advances in photography and printing technologies enabled, as of the 1910s, newspapers and magazines to feature photo spreads that documented daily life, especially that of the elite; only some of them are sufficiently clear that they can be reproduced in chapters 3–5. Foreign photographers like Peter Fuss and Geneviève Naylor captured remarkably candid images of life on Flamengo and Copacabana beaches in the 1930s and 1940s. In his chapter drafts, Barickman indicated some of the images that he wished to include and cited many more in the notes; we have done our best to follow these indications for the photographs included in this book.

Several themes run through following pages. Barickman draws extensively on the historical literature on Rio de Janeiro, as well as the international customs of sea-bathing and beach-going, which enables him to highlight what was distinctive about the Brazilian capital, particularly the deep integration of sea-bathing and beach-going into urban life in a national capital that became a major metropolis by the middle of the twentieth century. *From Sea-Bathing to Beach-Going* is deeply informed by social-scientific and historical writing about race, class, and gender; civilization and modernity; space; the body; and the role of the state in shaping and fostering certain kinds of urban development. Barickman develops his arguments and analysis over the course of his chapters, with occasional theoretical and methodological commentaries in the footnotes. Rather than extract all of this material and rework it into a conventional introduction, we let Barickman's analysis speak for itself in the following chapters. They present a fascinating tale of social and cultural change and the origins of some of the quintessentially Carioca and, by extension, Brazilian cultural practices.

Abbreviations

ACM — *Annaes do Conselho Municipal* (Rio de Janeiro)

AGCRJ — Arquivo Geral da Cidade do Rio de Janeiro

- FGP, HD — Fundo do Gabinete do Prefeito—D.F., Documentos da administração de Henrique Dodsworth
- Icon. — Divisão de Iconografia

AL — *Almanak Laemmert* (title varies)

- I — Indicador
- N — Notabilidades

AN — Arquivo Nacional

- ASDPA, PT — Arquivos da Segunda Delegacia de Polícia Auxiliar, Peças Teatrais
- DPE — Decretos do Poder Executivo
- PI — Privilégios industriais

APERJ, FDPPS — Arquivo Público do Estado do Rio de Janeiro, Fundo da Divisão de Polícia Política e Social

Aurélio — Aurélio Buarque de Holanda Ferreira, *Dicionário Aurélio eletrônico século XXI*, version 3.0, CD-ROM (Rio: Nova Fronteira, 1999)

BICM — *Boletim da Illustrissima Camara Municipal da Côrte* (Rio de Janeiro)

BIM — *Boletim da Intendencia Municipal* (Rio de Janeiro)

"Bin" — "Binoculo"

BM — *Beira-Mar*

BN — Biblioteca Nacional

BPDF — *Boletim da Prefeitura do Distrito Federal*

BS — *Boletim de Serviço* (of the Polícia Civil do Distrito Federal and, later, of the Departamento Federal de Segurança Pública)

"Cc" — "Cousas da cidade" (later, "Coisas da cidade")

cad. — caderno

CLMV	*Collecção das leis municipaes vigentes. . . .* 4 vols. Rio de Janeiro: various publishers, 1922–1932.
CMa	*Correio da Manhã*
CMe	*Correio Mercantil*
cód(s).	códice(s)
Cop M	*Copacabana Magazine*
Copacabana	*O Copacabana*
CP	*Codigo de Posturas*
Crz	*O Cruzeiro*
CS	*A Comedia Social*
cx	caixa
D de N	*Diário de Notícias*
D de Not	*Diario de Noticias* (1885–1886)
DC	*Diário Carioca*
dec.	Decreto
DN	*Diário da Noite*
DRJ	*Diario do Rio de Janeiro*
"EN"	"Ecos e Notícias" or "Écos e Noticias"
FF	*Fon-Fon!*
FL	*Folhinha Laemmert* (title varies)
GB	*Gazeta do Banho*
GN	*Gazeta de Notícias*
GRJ	*Gazeta do Rio de Janeiro*
GT	*Gazeta da Tarde*
Houaiss	Instituto Antônio Houaiss, *Dicionário eletrônico Houaiss da língua portuguesa*, version 1.0, CD-ROM (São Paulo: Objetiva, 2001)
IBGE	Instituto Brasileiro de Geografia e Estatística
JC	*Jornal do Commercio*
JB	*Jornal do Brasil*
Dom	*Domingo* (supplement of the *Jornal do Brasil*)
Malho	*O Malho*
Mequetrefe	*O Mequetrefe*
Mosquito	*O Mosquito*
"Ns"	"Notas sociaes" or "Notas sociais"
OG	*O Globo*
ZS	Caderno *Zona Sul* (supplement of *O Globo*)

OI	*O Imparcial*
OJ	*O Jornal*
OP	*O Paiz*
"P&R"	"Pingos & Respingos"
PCRJ	Prefeitura da Cidade do Rio de Janeiro
PDF	Prefeitura do Distrito Federal
pref	prefeito do Distrito Federal
pres	president
PT	*Para Todos*
RC	*Revista de Copacabana*
req(s).	requerimento(s)
RI	*Revista Illustrada*
RN	*Rio Nú*
RS	*Revista da Semana*
SI	*Semana Illustrada*
sup.	suplemento
"T&N"	"Tópicos & Notícias"
UH	*Última Hora*
VF	*A Vida Fluminense* (1868–1875)

An asterisk indicates an online edition. Page numbers for articles published in newspapers refer to the first section (caderno or seção) unless otherwise noted. Likewise, all citations of articles from evening papers are from the first editions of those papers except where the note refers to a later edition. Dates for articles are provided in the following format: (day.month.year). Unless otherwise indicated, all of the newspapers cited were published in Rio de Janeiro.

A Note on Orthography and Currency

THE SPELLING OF PORTUGUESE TERMS and names always presents problems for historians of Brazil. No single standardized orthography existed in the country in the nineteenth and early twentieth centuries. Standardization came only with the orthographic reform of 1943. A second orthographic reform, approved in 1971, introduced mainly minor changes in the 1943 spelling rules. It was followed by a third reform that took effect in January 2009. I have adopted two main conventions in dealing with the changing orthography. On the one hand, in the main text, I have modernized all spellings. On the other, as is common practice, I have retained, in the notes and the bibliography, original spellings in citing manuscript sources and in supplying author-title information of printed sources. I have, however, made two main exceptions. First, for periodicals that ceased publication before the 1943 orthographic reform, I have retained in the main text the original spelling; for example, *Mephistopheles* rather than *Mefistófeles*. Second, the *Jornal do Commercio* continued to be published as the *Jornal do Commercio* (even in its online edition) and not as the *Jornal do Comércio*, until its demise in 2016. I therefore cite it as such.

This book includes references to the various currencies that have circulated in Brazil since the nineteenth century.[1] Inflation, especially in the second half of the twentieth century, led the Brazilian government to make repeated changes in the country's currency. The longest-lasting currency in Brazil's history was the *mil-réis* (or one thousand *réis*), which dated from the colonial period. One mil-réis was generally written as Rs.1$000. A smaller sum, such as 500 réis, was written as Rs.$500. One thousand mil-réis equaled one *conto de réis*, or simply one *conto*, expressed in writing as Rs.1:000$000. Thus, the sum Rs.9:500$400 should be read as nine contos and five thousand four hundred réis. In 1942, the *cruzeiro* replaced the mil-réis. One cruzeiro, which equaled one mil-réis, was written as Cr$1.00.[2] Whenever possible, in the text or in the notes, I provide equivalents to prices and wages in pounds sterling or US dollars. I have, in other cases, measured those prices against the prices of basic foodstuffs or the value of the official minimum wage (first instituted in 1943).[3]

From Sea-Bathing to Beach-Going

1

"A Carioca Custom"

Sea-Bathing in the Nineteenth and Early Twentieth Centuries

RIO DE JANEIRO IN THE 1870S OR 1880S: It is December, or it could be February or any other month in the hot season. The clock has just struck four in the morning. Most Cariocas (residents of the city) take advantage of the last hour or so before dawn to sleep a bit more. Many of them, given the occasionally stifling heat of a tropical summer, have spent much of the previous night tossing and turning before finally falling asleep. Outside their houses, an almost complete silence reigns on the dimly lit streets. But a careful observer, still awake, would see sleepy denizens walking down those shadowy city streets. They are lone individuals, small groups of friends, couples, and entire families with yawning children in tow. Some are, at first view, strangely dressed and wrapped in sheets or large towels; others wear normal clothes. All make their way to the shores of Guanabara Bay, where they will bathe in its salty waters. As the sun rises over the bay, more will join them.

This chapter takes a first step in investigating those predawn and early morning bathers. More specifically, after supplying a description of nineteenth-century Rio de Janeiro, it discusses the preferred times and locations for sea-bathing in the city. Nineteenth-century Cariocas bathed at all of the city's bayshore beaches, especially those close to the populous downtown, undeterred by the trash and filth that accumulated on city beaches and sometimes bobbed in the water around them. Early in the century, travelers regularly noted Cariocas' bathing customs, and as newspapers expanded, advertisements for bathing attire and houses located close to the beaches reveal the breadth of the sea-bathing customs. Sadly, though, police reports on accidental drownings frequently note that victims were regular bathers. After midcentury, commercial bathing barges and land-based bathing houses proliferated along the city's bayshore beaches, catering to thousands of well-off bathers who could afford their services, while many more Cariocas bathed on their own. This chapter demonstrates that sea-bathing became an increasingly common practice in Rio de Janeiro during the nineteenth century and documents the material culture of sea-bathing. Why residents of the city went bathing in the nineteenth and early twentieth centuries is considered in the next chapter.

A Tropical Capital

Most of Rio de Janeiro lies on the western shore of Guanabara Bay, a vast and nearly landlocked expanse of more than four hundred square kilometers of water dotted with islands that seldom failed to win praise from foreign travelers in the nineteenth century and in the first half of the twentieth. Herman Melville called it "the Bay of All Beauties" in 1850. Eighty-three years later, the *South American Handbook* proclaimed that Rio de Janeiro's bay, "with its superb brilliance of colouring, is the most admired in the world." "The entry" into the bay, it added, "is an unequalled spectacle." For her part, Cecile Hulse Matschat, an American traveler, wrote in 1939 of "Guanabara Bay, [as being] so startling[ly] beautiful that is like nothing else in the world."[1] The city's setting was, and is, indeed stunning. Encircling the bay are hills and mountains of the most diverse shapes and heights, many of which arise abruptly from the otherwise generally flat and low-lying terrain occupied by the city itself. Tropical forests cover some of the mountains and hills; other outcrops display bare granite faces. On clear days, it is possible to see the jagged peaks of the Serra dos Órgãos (Organs Mountains), more than one hundred kilometers north of the city.

As table 1.1 shows, the city grew considerably in the nineteenth century. A 1799 count registered fewer than 44,000 free and enslaved men, women, and children in Rio de Janeiro's urban parishes.[2] The arrival of the Portuguese Court in 1808 encouraged greater immigration from Portugal, a new flow of immigrants from elsewhere in Europe, and an increase in the forced migration of Africans through the transatlantic slave trade.[3] The population surpassed 79,000 by 1821, on the eve of independence; Rio de Janeiro then already ranked as Brazil's largest city, and its population continued to grow. In 1849, the city could claim nearly 206,000 inhabitants—an increase of roughly 180 percent since 1821. Growth seems to have slowed in the 1850s and 1860s, only to accelerate again in the last quarter of the century. The population

TABLE 1.1. *Population of Rio de Janeiro, 1799–1906. Urban parishes only.*

YEAR	TOTAL	FREE AND FREED		SLAVES	
		Number	*Percent*	*Number*	*Percent*
1799	43,376	28,390	66	14,986	34
1821	79,321	43,139	54	36,182	46
1838	97,162	60,025	62	37,137	38
1849	205,906	127,051	62	78,855	38
1872	228,743	191,176	84	37,567	16
1890	422,756	422,756	100	0	0
1906	621,933	621,933	100	0	0

SOURCES: Lobo, *História*, 1:135; "Mappa da população do Municipio da Corte," in Brazil, *Relatorio* . . . (1838), n.p.; Karasch, *Slave Life*, 61–66; Brazil, *Recenseamento* (1872), 21; Soares, "*Povo*," 381.

increased by 85 percent in the eighteen years after 1872, growing from 228,743 to 422,756 in 1890, and the city gained another nearly 200,000 residents by 1906 to reach 621,933.

Major changes in the composition of the city's population accompanied this growth. In 1849, 78,855 slaves accounted for 38 percent of all inhabitants, which made Rio de Janeiro the largest slaveholding city in the Americas.[4] Slaveholding was, in fact, so widespread in the Brazilian capital that nearly anyone who could afford to do so owned at least one slave; even freed people sometimes possessed slaves. Men and women held in slavery worked as not only household servants but also in almost every imaginable unskilled occupation and in many skilled trades. The majority of those enslaved men and women in the first half of the nineteenth century were African by birth. Although most African-born slaves hailed from Central Africa, the city's slave population included much smaller but still sizeable numbers of East and West Africans.

After 1850, when the transatlantic slave trade to Brazil ended, the slave population declined steadily. A negative rate of natural reproduction contributed to that decline; so, too, did the repeated outbreaks of yellow fever, cholera, and other diseases. Sales to coffee planters in the city's hinterland also diminished the slave population; urban slaveholders could not resist the ever-higher prices that planters were willing to pay for enslaved workers. Manumissions further reduced the slave population. Indeed, the 1872 national census reveals that the number of slaves living and working in Rio de Janeiro had decreased by more than 50 percent in the two decades after the country ceased importing enslaved Africans. The slave population dwindled from 37,567 in 1872 to fewer than 7,500 by 1886–1887, less than two full years before Brazil finally abolished slavery in May 1888.[5]

The 1872 census also reveals that freeborn and freed Blacks and *pardos* (individuals of mixed African and European ancestry) had come to outnumber slaves by a wide margin. The 53,509 free men and women of color enumerated in the census made up more than one-fifth (23 percent) of the city's inhabitants. In turn, native- and foreign-born individuals classified as white accounted for approximately 60 percent of the population. Partly as a result of continuing immigration from Europe, the proportion of whites increased to nearly 67 percent by 1890.

Whatever their color, place of birth, or legal status, Rio de Janeiro's inhabitants made their home in a city that was an administrative and military center and thus a seat of political power. The city served as the de facto capital of the Portuguese Empire between 1808 and 1821, while Prince Regent João (King João VI after 1816) and the court resided there, and then as Brazil's national capital from 1822 to 1960. Consequently, both before and after independence, hundreds of government employees as well as a large contingent of military officers, soldiers, and sailors lived in the city. John Luccock, an Englishman who lived in Rio de Janeiro shortly after the arrival of the Portuguese Court, estimated that the city's population already included around a thousand men employed "in public offices," another thousand inhabitants "connected in various ways with the Court," and about one thousand "soldiers of the line."[6] The number of government employees, it is safe to say, grew over the course of the nineteenth century.

Rio de Janeiro, however, was much more than an administrative center and garrison town. It ranked as Brazil's chief port for overseas trade.[7] Between 1796 and 1807, the city already handled more exports by value than any other coastal city in Brazil. From its harbor flowed sugar, gold, cotton, coffee, hides, sugarcane brandy, indigo, and other commodities produced in the city's far-flung hinterlands. Arriving ships unloaded manufactures and foodstuffs such as olive oil, salt cod, and wine, from Europe, as well as enslaved Africans, all destined for sale in the city itself and elsewhere in colonial Portuguese America. Rio de Janeiro gained even greater commercial importance in later years as coffee overtook sugar as Brazil's most valuable export and as the country emerged as the largest supplier of coffee to the world market. The bulk of that coffee came from plantations in the Paraíba Valley, located for the most part in the province of Rio de Janeiro and, hence, within the city's immediate hinterland. There, planters relied on the labor of tens of thousands of mainly African-born slaves to clear the forests and to produce ever-larger quantities of coffee. The volume of coffee exported from Rio de Janeiro rose from a mere 7,762 tons in 1820 to more than 46,000 tons in 1835 and then to an annual average of approximately 140,000 tons in the 1850s. By the end of the previous decade, the value of all the goods shipped overseas from the city had already come to account for nearly half of the country's entire export trade. Exports of coffee through Rio de Janeiro peaked in the early 1880s at roughly 263,000 tons and thereafter declined, but not by any means to insignificant levels. In the 1890s, the western districts of São Paulo replaced the Paraíba Valley as Brazil's most important coffee-producing region, and, in turn, Santos eventually replaced Rio de Janeiro as the country's main port for the coffee trade. The Brazilian capital nevertheless remained a major hub for international and coastal commerce. It also continued to hold an unrivaled position as Brazil's financial capital. After 1870, light manufacturing, albeit on a small scale, began to contribute to the city's economic development.[8]

Rio de Janeiro's long-term economic growth certainly enriched the city's upper class, especially import and export merchants (including, before 1850, those engaged in the transatlantic slave trade), bankers, coffee factors, and officials at the highest levels of the national government. To that list should be added those coffee planters who preferred to live the better part of the year in Rio de Janeiro rather than on their estates, and also, in some cases, the representatives of foreign firms with operations in Brazil. But the benefits of economic growth did not accrue only to a narrow upper-class elite. Zephyr Frank has shown that early nineteenth-century Rio de Janeiro witnessed the expansion of a middle-ranking population, composed of better-off shop owners, artisans, and tavern-keepers, as well as their families, who advanced economically through investment in slaves. It would, as Frank himself notes, be misleading to equate those families as a group with a middle class in any modern sense of the term. Indeed, his study takes as its central example a middling property owner José Antônio Dutra, a freed former slave born in Africa and a barber by trade. Even though Dutra owned thirteen slaves at the time of his death in 1849, he was, nonetheless, still a barber who sullied his hands when he shaved his customers, pulled their teeth, or bled them with leeches. While working, he wore a "barbering smock," not a frock coat and tie, and he had little or no formal education. Many families, such as Dutra's, who had built their fortunes by investing in slaves, saw those fortunes diminish in the second half of the century with the decline of slavery both as a labor regime and as an institution.

Something along the lines of a modern white-collar middle class, however, gradually took shape in nineteenth-century Rio de Janeiro. Its members, who were predominantly white, included mid-level government employees, office workers in private firms, journalists, senior clerks in larger stores, liberal professionals such as lawyers, doctors, and engineers, and also, of course, their families. Yet, that fledgling middle class accounted for only a small share of the city's population. Most of Rio de Janeiro's free inhabitants, both before and after abolition in 1888, lived in poverty and sometimes in miserable poverty. In fact, the ranks of the free poor seem to have grown both in absolute numbers and as a proportion of the entire population after the midcentury mark.[9]

In addition to experiencing demographic and economic growth, the Brazilian capital also expanded geographically (map 1.1). At the end of the eighteenth century, it was a cramped city of narrow streets that spread out in a rough grid from its main square, the Largo do Paço (Palace Square, the current Praça XV de Novembro), which faced the port. Marshes and hills at the time confined its urbanized area to a few square kilometers. That area, however, expanded greatly to accommodate a population that underwent a nearly tenfold increase between 1799 and 1890. The drainage of marshes on the city's western edges, along with landfills, allowed after 1810 for the rapid occupation of the neighborhood still known as the Cidade Nova (New City). From the Cidade Nova, the city spread further west into areas that became the neighborhoods of Estácio (called at the time Mata-Porcos), Rio Comprido, Catumbi, Engenho Velho, Tijuca, and São Cristóvão. The city also expanded southward with the development of a string of neighborhoods along or near the bayshore: Glória, Santa Teresa, Catete, Flamengo, Laranjeiras, and Botafogo. To be sure, late nineteenth-century Rio de Janeiro was far from the sprawling metropolis that it would become in the twentieth century, but, because of its topography, it was hardly a compact city. A chain of mountains and steep hills, the Serra da Carioca, made it impossible to travel directly from neighborhoods such as Tijuca, Rio Comprido, or Estácio to those located along the southern bayshore. Residents of, say, Estácio or Rio Comprido with businesses in Flamengo or Botafogo had to go there by way of a long circuitous route that took them through the city's center, unless they wished to follow trails up and down the steep slopes of the forested Serra da Carioca. Rio de Janeiro was, in any event, sufficiently spread out to impress Ulick Ralph Burke, an English businessman entrepreneur who visited the city in 1882; he described it as "an enormously straggling town," where "everything" seemed to be "about six miles from everything else."[10]

To move around their ever-more "straggling town," most Cariocas came to depend on collective transportation. The first buses, drawn by four mules, began to circulate in the city in 1836. Known as *gôndolas*, they could carry as many as fourteen passengers. By the 1840s, small steam ferries linked São Cristóvão

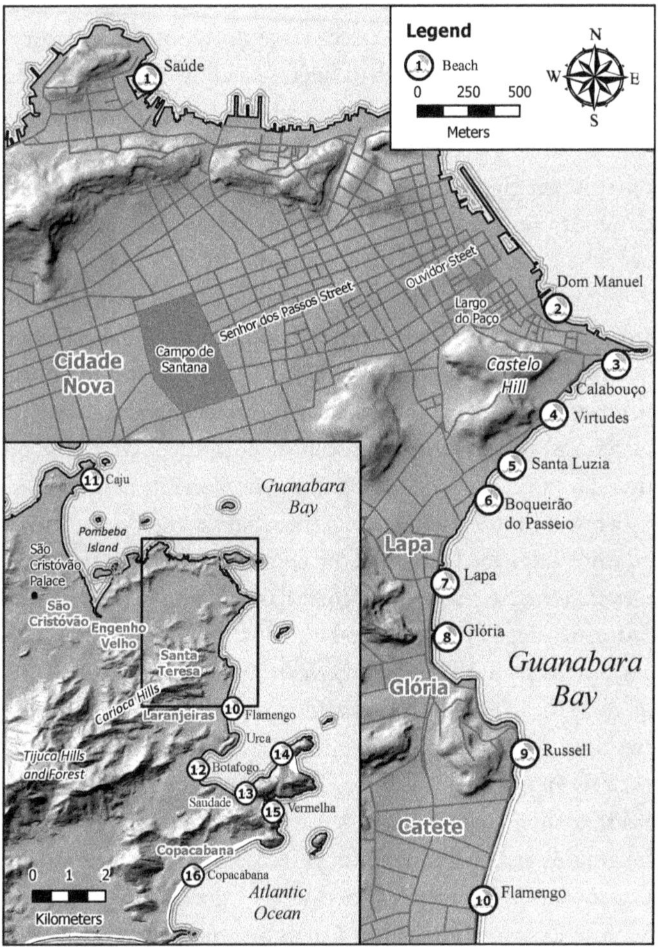

MAP 1.1. Rio de Janeiro in the Second Half of the Nineteenth Century. Street grid of 1875.

and Botafogo with the city's center and also Rio de Janeiro with Niterói on the other side of the bay. Even so, as Maurício de Almeida Abreu points out, easy "spatial mobility" within the city remained a "privilege of the few." That, however, began to change in the late 1860s with the establishment of regular tram service. Starting in 1868, foreign- and locally owned companies laid miles and miles of track spreading out in all directions from the city's center. The trams, initially drawn by donkeys and, after 1890, by electricity, proved immensely successful; they transported nearly 73 million passengers in 1896 alone, and by 1907, the city boasted two hundred and ninety kilometers of tracks. Their success, in fact, drove out of business the buses and the ferries (except those that crossed the bay to Niterói). By the last decades of the nineteenth century, moreover, daily passenger train service had begun to allow for the further expansion of the city, and, along the rail lines, in what were outlying and still largely rural parishes, Rio de Janeiro's first suburbs developed.[11]

Nevertheless, despite geographic expansion, the parishes that corresponded to the colonial city continued to serve as Rio de Janeiro's political, economic, and cultural heart. The ministries, other government offices, and the parliament (which became a congress after 1889) were all located there; so, too, were the most important trading houses, the banks, the offices of many liberal professionals, the best shops, the newspapers, all the theaters, and the most fashionable *confeitarias* (pastry-shop cafés that also served ice cream and alcohol). Numerous artisan workshops and small-scale manufacturers could also be found in the center. From those workshops and the fashionable confeitarias, it might take only a few minutes' walk to reach the wharves and docks, where stevedores loaded onto ships the bulk of all the coffee that Brazil exported.[12]

Furthermore, even as late as 1890, more than half (54 percent) of all Cariocas still resided in the city's central parishes. Most inhabitants of those parishes were poor, and many lived in squalid, overcrowded tenements known as *cortiços*, or *estalagens*, or in equally overcrowded rooming houses (*casas de cômodos*).[13] The wealthy, for their part, had gradually abandoned the central parishes as places of residence after the 1810s. They built villas (*chácaras*) and mansions in areas that then lay on the city's outskirts, but that would over time become thoroughly urbanized neighborhoods. Among those neighborhoods, São Cristóvão, situated to the northwest of the city's center, held a special draw because Emperor Pedro I and then his son, Pedro II, resided there. Yet, by the 1880s, Flamengo, Laranjeiras, and especially Botafogo, all of which were located along or near the southern bayshore, clearly stood out as the city's most fashionable neighborhoods. It would, however, be less than accurate to claim that Rio de Janeiro had any exclusively upper-class residential districts. Tenements existed in not only the city's core but also all parts of Rio de Janeiro and even in Botafogo, the most "aristocratic" neighborhood at the time. Indeed, Aluísio Azevedo (1857–1913) set his 1890 naturalistic novel *O cortiço* (The Tenement) in Botafogo.[14]

Beyond geographic expansion and demographic growth, Rio de Janeiro underwent still other changes. When João and the court arrived, they found a colonial city with few public amenities and with a large and highly visible slave population. It was, in their view, scarcely fit to serve as the seat of a European monarchy in exile. Not surprising, the authorities appointed by the prince regent wasted little time in trying to "Europeanize" and "civilize" the city. They immediately banned the almost Moorish latticework that covered the windows of most houses. Paulo Fernandes Viana, holding the new post of police intendant, and a new full-time police force (the Guarda Real de Polícia), sought to discipline and "civilize" the behavior of Rio de Janeiro's inhabitants. Often using brutal methods, the new police force targeted primarily slaves and the free poor. The thirteen years that the Portuguese Court remained in Rio de Janeiro also saw the establishment of a public library; an academy of fine arts; a royal press that published the *Gazeta do Rio de Janeiro*, Brazil's first newspaper; a museum; a medical school; and a military academy, as well as the construction of a new theater and a merchant's exchange.[15]

Efforts to "civilize" and "Europeanize" Rio de Janeiro continued after independence but proved slow-moving. In the late nineteenth century, Cariocas could, it is true, point to various improvements in the city's infrastructure, such as the expanding tramlines, the introduction of gas street-lighting in 1854, piped running water for at least some privileged residences by 1860, and even a public telephone service by the early 1880s. They could also point to a lively daily and weekly press, to the sophisticated shops that sold imported luxury items to those who could afford them, to several impressive private mansions, and to the large Campo de Santana with its more than fifteen hectares of attractive gardens laid out between 1873 and 1880 by a French landscape artist. But they had to admit that Rio de Janeiro ended the century with only a handful of modestly imposing public buildings and without any thoroughfare remotely comparable to London's Regent Street, Paris's Rue de Rivoli, or Berlin's Unter den Linden, not to mention Buenos Aires' Avenida de Mayo or Mexico City's Paseo de la Reforma. Indeed, most streets in the city's center were, just as in colonial times, so narrow that a carriage could barely pass through them. Cariocas would have to wait until after 1900 for any far-reaching attempt to make their city into a "civilized" "European" capital in the tropics.[16]

Times, Locations, Trash, and Sewage

In this city of contrasts, sea-bathing was primarily a predawn or early morning activity. The first bathers began arriving at the city's beaches at three or four o'clock in the morning; most of them would be out of the water and on their way home or to work before six or seven o'clock, and by nine thirty, the beaches were largely empty of bathers.[17] This early morning custom fit well with Cariocas' sleeping habits. Not surprising, bathers sought out beaches close to their residences, but this meant that they shared the sand and the water with much of the city's trash and sewage normally disposed there.

Most Cariocas then went to bed early; after all, it was not cheap to keep a house lit late into the night. Outside their houses, those residents found few attractions after dark other than the theaters, which did draw large audiences. But, once the performances ended, most theatergoers, for lack of anything else to do, quickly made their way home. After 1825, the police very selectively enforced a 10:00 p.m. curfew; at that hour, all taverns, eateries, and the like had to expel their last customers and close their doors. Indeed, some foreign visitors to Rio de Janeiro were surprised by how quiet the city was after ten o'clock. It was only in 1873 that the police made an exception to the curfew for hotel restaurants, confeitarias, and corner stands that sold coffee, cheap wine, and sugarcane brandy, as well as newspapers, tobacco, and snacks. Such kiosks could stay open until one in the morning. Five years later, authorities finally abolished the curfew, which allowed for the greater development of nightlife. Men, or at least better-off men, increasingly stayed out late, spending their time at cafés, restaurants, cabarets, beer gardens, and confeitarias, where they might be accompanied by women who, precisely because they were out at night in public, were regarded as less than "respectable." Yet, as late as the 1880s, Cariocas typically took lunch at ten or eleven in the morning and had dinner at four or five in the afternoon. Those who could afford a third daily meal ate a light supper (*ceia*) before retiring. Even formal dinners were routinely scheduled for four o'clock. In the 1890s, the standard time for such dinners was only a bit later: six in the evening.[18]

Going to bed early, most of Rio de Janeiro's residents also woke early. The traveler Ernst Ebel, for example, complained in the 1820s about the noise that prevented him from sleeping after six in the morning. That noise began at five with a cannon shot; a half hour later, a police cornet sounded, and then church bells began to ring. Creaking ox carts filled the streets before seven in the morning, and street vendors were already shouting their wares. More than forty years later, two North American travelers noted that, in many households, everyone was "astir" "at early dawn." Photographs from 1903, taken at half past five, reveal that, by that hour, sellers and customers had already begun to haggle at Rio de Janeiro's main market. Thus, leaving home for a predawn or early morning sea bath would not have upset the sleeping habits of a population that retired and rose early.[19]

The preference for predawn and early morning bathing, beyond fitting into those habits, also stemmed from racial considerations. At the time, a white complexion represented the aesthetic ideal. It might be a rosy whiteness, which, in contrast to pallor, could suggest good health. Even so, the ideal was a fair complexion. The same, of course, was true in Europe. In Brazil, however, the value assigned to a fair complexion represented more than just an imported European standard of beauty. It reflected hierarchies of color and race based on more than three centuries on slave labor and widespread miscegenation. For the dominant class, a fair complexion—and the fairer the better—distinguished them, before 1888, from the slaves whom they owned, and both before and after 1888, from the free population of color more generally. After all, the line separating someone regarded as white from someone recognized as having some degree of African ancestry and hence as being a descendant of slaves could be tenuous. In turn, for free men and women known to be of mixed background, a lighter complexion translated into a higher rank in the prevailing color and racial hierarchies.[20] It should then come as little surprise that newspapers and magazines regularly carried advertisements for skin-lightening cosmetic products, which could help mask signs of a a racially mixed ancestry. To cite merely one of many examples, Crème da la Mèque, sold in Rio de Janeiro in the 1860s, promised "to whiten instantaneously the darkest skin."[21]

The value assigned to whiteness had other consequences. For instance, it resulted in a desire to avoid, as much as possible, direct exposure to the sun because a tanned complexion might raise doubts about racial ancestry even in the case of those Brazilians regarded as white. In turn, among (free) people of acknowledged mixed racial background, a complexion darkened by the sun would only highlight that background. Free women and men who could afford to do so, therefore, often used parasols and umbrellas to protect themselves from the sun.[22] Bathing before dawn or in the early morning was, obviously, another way to avoid the sun and, hence, tanning. In 1884, Frank De Yeaux Carpenter, a North American author, reported that, when, contrary to common practice, Cariocas went bathing "in the middle of the day," they used "umbrellas" in the water to shade themselves from the sun's rays.[23] The Cariocas mentioned by Carpenter were, presumably, white and of higher social standing, or at least better-off free pardos. The free poor (of whatever color) may very well have also worried about exposure to the sun. Nevertheless, like slaves, they went bathing at any hour of the day or night when they had a bit of spare time and felt like doing so. Daniel P. Kidder and James C. Fletcher, two North American Protestant missionaries who spent time in Rio de Janeiro in the 1850s, noted that, by seven in the morning, when "the sun is high," "all the busy white throng" of bathers had left the beach in Flamengo. "Here and there, however," they added, "may be seen a curly head popping up and down among the waves, its wooly covering defying the fear of *coup de soleil*."[24]

In the nineteenth century and in the first years of the twentieth, the preferred locations for bathing were the bayshore beaches in or near the city's center, which often had only a very narrow stretch of sand. Over time, embankments further narrowed those beaches, almost entirely eliminating, in some cases, the sand.[25] The practice of "mining" beaches for their sand to make cement and for other purposes also reduced their width. The 1830 code of municipal ordinances prohibited the removal of sand between the Saco do Alferes and Glória because it could render streets lining the shore and even buildings on those streets more vulnerable to the destructive force of storm tides. In the 1850s, the city council extended the prohibition to encompass Flamengo's beach. But municipal ordinances did not put an end to the "abuse" of mining the city's beaches. In the 1880s, even the fire department disobeyed the legislation and extracted sand from Flamengo beach.[26]

The absence of any broad stretch of sand in no way, however, interfered with sea-bathing, an activity practiced in the water. This is clear from the "system" to create "artificial beaches for sea-bathing at those points along the shore lacking natural beaches" that Francisco Filinto de Almeida and João Gateli de Solá tried to patent in 1907. Instead of landfills to create wider expanses of sand at a stretch of shoreline, their system sought to make bathing possible at locations next to quays where the water was too deep for bathers to stand by raising the sea floor. The result would have not been a sandy beach, but, rather, an area of shallow water where bathers could stand with their heads above the surface.[27]

For that reason, the sandless quay in front of the Largo do Paço in the city's center served as a "public bathing-space." Throughout the nineteenth and well into the twentieth centuries, the poor and (until 1888) slaves would go bathing at any spot, with or without sand, that allowed access to the bay: the quays near the Largo do Paço, the small stretches of shore between wharves, the wharves themselves, and even the Dom Pedro II Dock.[28] However, after the mid-nineteenth century, the preferred locations for bathing were Boqueirão do Passeio and Santa Luzia beaches, which, in the first half of the twentieth century, landfills eliminated and which were located just east and west, respectively, of the current southern end of the Avenida Rio Branco in the city's center. Lapa, Glória, Russell, and Flamengo also attracted bathers.[29] Other beaches also saw use, including Botafogo, Caju, and Saudade (near what is today the neighborhood of Urca).[30]

Those beaches were not necessarily clean. Indeed, in the first half of the nineteenth century, they sometimes served as dumping grounds for rubbish and dead animals.[31] An 1876 ordinance prohibited depositing trash and dead animals in any public space, including the city's beaches, and a succession of private firms, under official contract, began to take responsibility for cleaning the city's streets and beaches and for collecting trash. In the 1860s, these firms constructed "stations" at various points along the bayshore to receive trash and dead animals, which would then be shipped to Sapucaia Island in the middle of the bay. In October 1879 alone, the island received more than five and a half thousand tons (meticulously recorded by the company as 5,553,811 kilograms) of trash, including an impressive number of dead animals: 1,540 dogs, 27 horses, 3 oxen, 166 sheep, and 142 pigs as well as 4,600 birds and other small creatures. But the service provided by the trash companies often fell short. Thus, in 1874, the *Diario do Rio de Janeiro* complained that employees of the firm then responsible for trash collection sometimes left "a large number of dead animals" for five or more days at Boqueirão do Passeio beach. Six years later, the *Jornal do Commercio* called authorities' attention to a "pile of straw, leaves, and other materials" that had been "fermenting" for several days at a stretch of Flamengo's beach regularly used by bathers. The fermenting vegetable matter covered a dead animal already in a state of decomposition, and the pile could easily transform itself into "a source of disease."[32]

Although Guanabara Bay was undoubtedly far less polluted than it is today,

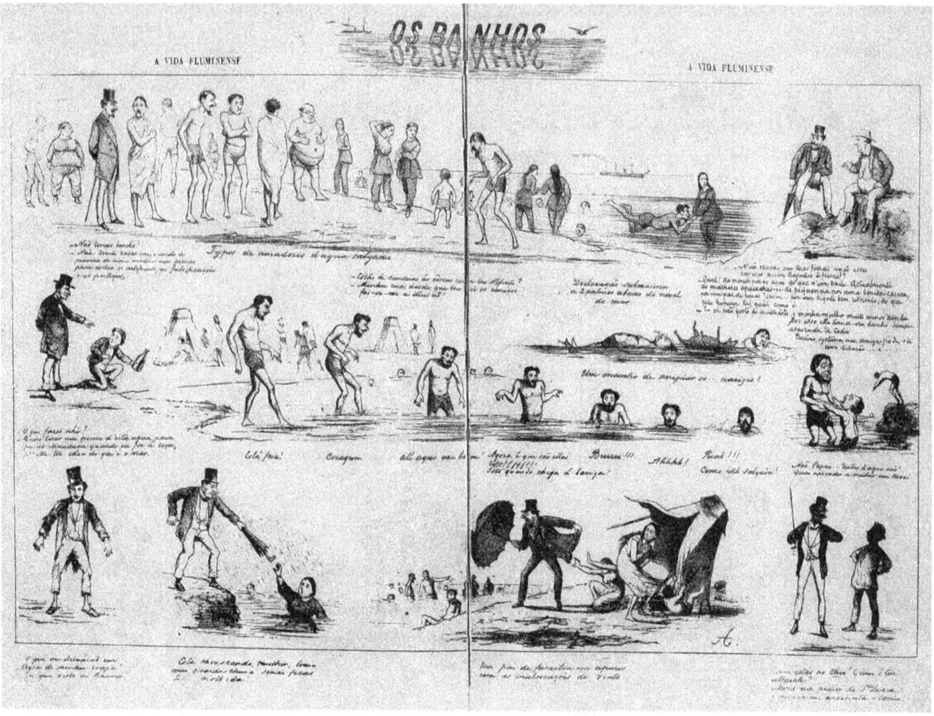

FIGURE 1.1. Bathing Customs, 1870. *VF* (22.1.1870), 28–29.

the city's beaches did not always present the best conditions for bathing. Bathers sometimes found trash not only on the sand but also in the water. In 1855, *O Brasil Illustrado* published a cartoon showing a bather in the water; around him float barrels, trash, and what appears to be a chamber pot. In another cartoon, drawn by Angelo Agostini in 1870 for *A Vida Fluminense,* a bather swims into a dead pig floating in the water alongside another bather (figure 1.1). An article in the *Revista Illustrada* took up the matter six years later. It noted that recent heavy rains had carried all the city's "filth" to its beaches and, from there, to the waters of the bay. Nevertheless, amid that filth, a whole "flock of bathers" dove or waded into the bay. The article's author went on to ask where those bathers were going to wash themselves after having "dis-washed" themselves in the bay.[33]

The trash certainly bothered bathers but not enough for most of them to give up sea-bathing. They tolerated it (at least up to a point) just as they also tolerated—sometimes using a perfumed handkerchief—the foul smells and the lack of cleanliness that they encountered on city streets. Filth and foul smells were part of everyday urban life at the time not only in Rio de Janeiro but also, to a greater or lesser extent, in other large cities elsewhere in the world. It would take local officials (sometimes reliant on authoritarian laws) and physicians concerned with public hygiene decades to create new attitudes toward urban cleanliness and to impose—with varying degrees of success—a new sanitary discipline on the Brazilian capital's population.[34]

The trash that bathers could easily see was not the only health risk that they faced when they waded or plunged into Guanabara Bay. A greater risk might come from what they could not see. In the first half of the nineteenth century, Rio de Janeiro lacked a system of sanitary sewers. As a result, every night (between nine in the evening and six in the morning, according to the 1830 bylaws), slaves had to go down to points on the city's bayshore designated by the municipality, where they emptied barrels filled with human excrement (*tigres*) so that the tides would disperse the filth.[35] At the time, the bacteriological revolution had not yet transformed medicine, and scientists lacked any means to measure the presence of fecal coliforms in the water. Perhaps more important, water itself, according to a belief dating back to antiquity, cleansed and purified. Thus, if on the following morning, the water did not smell bad (or at least not too bad), and, if it was not visibly contaminated, bathers did not hesitate to dive in. For instance, Kidder and Fletcher, who lived in a house facing Flamengo beach in the early 1850s, noted that, on some nights, depending on the direction of the wind, an unbearable stench invaded their house from the tigres that the slaves carried to the beach. The two missionaries resorted to smelling salts, bottles of cologne, and anything else that could relieve their "olfactories." Nevertheless, they were not at all surprised to see, on the following mornings, men, women, and children bathing at the same beach, with—in their words—its "clear salt water."[36]

In 1857, work began on installing sewer lines in Rio de Janeiro. The Brazilian capital thus became one of the first cities in the world to have a system of underground sanitary sewers. But the sewage handled by the system received only minimal treatment before City Improvements (the British-owned sewer company) pumped it into the bay. By the 1890s, if not before, that sewage was causing serious pollution problems in Botafogo Cove.[37] The sewer network, moreover, did not encompass the entire city; even some buildings in the city's center lacked connections to it. Among them was the Hospital da Santa Casa de Misericórdia, the city's main charity hospital, located less than a hundred meters from one of City Improvements' sewage treatment facilities. As late as 1912, the hospital discharged "the waste water, urine, and feces" of hundreds of patients directly into the bay by way of an open-air trench, "a major threat to public health." Even worse, the trench emptied its contents into the waters of Santa Luzia beach, where a "large number of people" "carelessly" bathed near this "disease-producing factory."[38] They did so no doubt because generally they did not see or smell the contamination. Even when they did perceive the pollution or ran up against raw human waste in the water, the disgust that they no doubt felt would not have necessarily reflected an awareness informed by medical science.

That should not surprise us. In the early 1910s, the scientific community had already begun to recognize that untreated sewage might represent a danger to bathers' health. Nevertheless, scientists and other experts would for decades continue to insist that the sea absorbed and purified sewage and thus minimized that danger. In the early 1970s, for instance, authorities in Rio de Janeiro suspected that bathing in water polluted by raw sewage might spread diseases such as hepatitis and typhoid. They therefore requested the opinion of a prominent British expert. He informed them that, though bathing in water contaminated by untreated human excrement might be disagreeable, it posed no health risk to beach-goers. Indeed, it was only in the late 1970s that scientists provided conclusive proof of the risks that bathers braved at beaches polluted by untreated sewage. Yet, even in recent times, thoroughly polluted beaches in Rio de Janeiro and in other coastal cities in Brazil continue to attract bathers who apparently assign little importance to official warnings about health risks.[39]

An Ever-More Common Practice

Pollution and trash did not prevent sea-bathing from becoming a popular practice in Rio de Janeiro and a well-established habit among many residents of the city. That habit, according to historiographical tradition, had its beginnings in 1817, when João VI supposedly became the first person to go sea-bathing in Rio de Janeiro. As the story goes, a tick bit his leg and the bite became infected. His doctors recommended sea baths as a treatment, but the newly crowned king feared that crabs would nibble at his toes. Therefore, a special contraption was built for him at Caju beach; it consisted of a large basin, punctured by numerous small holes to let the salt water in, and a small hoist to lower the basin, with João in it, into the water.[40] Sea baths were, by then, a standard treatment that European-trained doctors prescribed.

Although it is true that João bathed at Caju to treat the infected tick bite, he was certainly not the first resident of the city to go sea-bathing. Nireu Cavalcanti cites the example of Bernardo Francisco de Brito, a wealthy merchant who owned a villa in Botafogo where he and his family went bathing in the first decade of the nineteenth century. There is no reason to suppose that Bernardo Francisco and his family were the only Cariocas at the time to wade or dive into the bay's waters. In 1812, five years before João first entered his perforated basin at Caju beach, one of Bernardo Francisco's neighbors, Diogo Gambier, put his Botafogo villa up for sale. In the advertisement, he touted the property's various attractions, including its location: "Being very close to Botafogo Cove," it was "convenient for sea-bathing."[41] The year before, the *Gazeta* had already informed its readers that a bathing barge was anchored just off the Largo do Paço. Known as the Flutuante (Floater, a name later assigned generically to other bathing barges), it offered sea baths for both "men and ladies" with "complete convenience, safety, and decency." It also provided its customers with a free boat service to transport them from the Largo do Paço. Such customers, it is safe to assume, did not hail from those poorer ranks of free Carioca society that could not afford the Rs.$160 that the barge charged in 1815 for a half-hour saltwater bath; with this sum, a Carioca could also have purchased about a week's worth of cassava flour, a basic foodstuff at the time.[42]

It is unclear how long the Flutuante continued to operate. But, along with the Botafogo villas, its mere existence as a commercial enterprise suggests that sea-bathing was already a familiar practice in the 1810s. Travelers' accounts confirm this. Luccock, for example, mentioned the practice in his "notes" on Rio de Janeiro in 1808 and again in 1813, when he described Botafogo as a beach frequented by "sea-bathers." Carl Schlichthorst, a German mercenary who lived in the city between 1824 and 1826, did more than mention the practice. He recounted his own early morning bathing experiences in Catete (Flamengo). He further noted that women, accompanied by their slave maids, bathed at the same beach. During an 1828 visit, Charles Brand saw "hundreds" of bathers, including the Emperor Pedro I, who crowded the waters just off the Largo do Paço. Brand's observations match those of William Gore Ouseley, who held a post in the British legation in the mid-1830s and again between 1838 and 1841 and who, like Schlichthorst, went bathing. Ouseley also reported that "people [were] constantly bathing" in the bay.[43]

Sea-bathing became even more common after midcentury. The evidence on the matter is, however, often scattered and fragmentary. Sometimes it comes from passing references to the practice made by foreign travelers who visited the city.[44] In other cases, it comes from advertisements placed in the local press. A men's clothing store, for instance, advertised in 1848 that it had "bathing drawers [*ceroulas de banho*]" for sale. The same store in the 1860s continued to supply its customers with "a wide selection" of such drawers, including boys' sizes. Other stores already sold "bathing tents [*barracas para banhos*]" for changing at the beach (such tents appear in figures 1.1, 1.2, 2.6, and 2.7). Women's bathing costumes, in turn, inspired the publication in 1867 of a cartoon in *O Arlequim*. According to the cartoon's caption, "the latest fashions" in such costumes include "designs for every taste, for those who wish to show a great deal as well as for those who wish to remain incognito [while bathing], for the best nourished [and] for those with the skinniest legs" (figure 1.2). Women who were interested in "the latest fashions" might find them at Au Gagne Petit, described in an 1872 advertisement as a "store specializing in stockings and bathing attire." Or they could buy them at À la Ville de Bruxelles; located on Ouvidor Street, the city's most fashionable high street at the time, this store sold bathing attire as early as the 1870s. In 1882, its seamstress owner informed her clients that she had just received from Europe a complete stock of women's articles for sea-bathing: costumes, towels, caps, and peignoirs (robes). She also sold custom-made bathing costumes. Other seamstresses no doubt did the same. Women interested in a made-to-measure costume could, in the early 1880s, purchase "superior baize for bathing apparel" at Au Parc Royal, which later became one of Rio de Janeiro's main department stores; it also sold ready-made bathing costumes in the first years of the twentieth century.[45]

Clothing stores were not alone in targeting bathers. Owners of houses along or near the shore did the same; in rental advertisements, they noted that their properties were conveniently located for tenants who wished to go bathing. Some of those property owners wished to let out entire houses; others offered for rent only rooms where bathers could change.[46] Likewise, hotels began referring to sea-bathing in their advertisements. In 1842, M. Hahn offered "furnished rooms for people who wish to go sea-bathing" at his hotel facing Botafogo beach. Eight years later, Flamengo's Hotel dos Estrangeiros informed prospective guests that it offered "a magnificent view of the sea" and "every convenience for bathing." Other hotels located near the bayshore followed

FIGURE 1.2. Female Bathing Dress, 1867. *O Arlequim* (8.12.1867), 5.

the example, and in 1882, a physician, Dr. Manoel Joaquim Fernandes Eiras, who owned a private hospital overlooking Botafogo beach, opened the Grande Hotel Balneário (Grand Bathing Hotel) at the same beach. For a "reasonable" price, the hotel allowed nonguests to use its bathing service.[47]

Newspapers also routinely reported on bathers who drowned at the city's beaches and sometimes pointed out that the victims were in the habit of bathing every day. For instance, in reporting on the 1875 death of Francisco Rodrigues Chaves, a post office employee, at Boqueirão do Passeio beach, the *Diario do Rio de Janeiro* observed that he went sea-bathing "every morning." The *Jornal do Commercio* added that he did so as a "curative means" to treat a malady that afflicted him. Other bathers who perished held occupations as diverse as bookkeeper, foundry worker, commercial employee, factory watchman, salesclerk, clog-maker, plumber or firefighter (*bombeiro*), hospital janitor, clerk at a bakery, and police soldier. Drowning victims also included free foreign-born residents of Rio de Janeiro as well as slaves, such as José, who lost his life in Botafogo in 1868. Another slave named Alberto Furtado Chevalier (who, unusually for slaves, had two surnames) suffered the same fate in 1879 when he went bathing in Flamengo. At the time of his tragic death, he was about to make the last payments needed to purchase his freedom from his owner.[48]

Despite their varied backgrounds and occupations, nearly all the victims who appear in the drowning reports were male. That in part reflects the fact that men and boys seem to have made up the majority of bathers at Rio de Janeiro's beaches in the nineteenth and early twentieth centuries. It must also have reflected other gender differences. Minimally "respectable" women were expected to behave daintily, especially in public. Most female bathers, therefore, tended to be cautious while in the water. By contrast, men, especially younger men, often sought to show off their manliness to impress not only friends but also young women at the beach. That, in turn, led them to adopt risky and even more reckless behavior while bathing, an enduring pattern, to judge by lifeguards' reports from the second half of the twentieth century.[49]

What is unclear from the published drowning reports is whether many Cariocas knew how to swim. The press sometimes noted that the victim did not know how to swim; in other cases, the reports stated that the victim had got into trouble while swimming. But, more often than not, they did not mention the matter. The other available sources provide contradictory information. For example, in 1808, Luccock observed that "a few Brazilians" learned to swim, but only those whose occupations or health required them to do so. Nearly eighty years later, in commenting on the death of a shipwrecked sailor in the bay, *O Paiz* claimed that "*70 percent* of the personnel in our navy completely lack any knowledge of how to swim." The paper, therefore, urged the imperial government to set up a swimming school (the government, in fact, had contracted for such a facility in 1876, but it was never built).[50] If more than two-thirds of all sailors could not swim at the time, then, surely, an even larger share of the general population would not have known how to swim.

In the 1850s, however, Kidder and Fletcher noted that the slaves who went bathing in Flamengo "all" swam "remarkably well."[51] And it was not just slaves. Some private boys' schools began to include swimming lessons in their curricula after the mid-nineteenth century. Of course, it is impossible to say how many boys at those schools did in fact learn how to swim (and a reluctant lad in figure 1.1 beseeches his father to give him swimming lessons at home). But, in the 1860s, Michel Calógeras practiced swimming while bathing. In the novel *Dom Casmurro* (1899), written by Joaquim Maria Machado de Assis (1839–1908) and set in the early 1870s, Escobar does the same. So, too, does

Luís Fontagra in *A vida* (The Life, 1911), a novel by Tomás Lopes (1879–1913); in scenes that Lopes situated in the 1890s, Fontagra "[throws] himself into the water" in Flamengo, near Barão do Flamengo Street, and swims as far as the Morro da Viúva (Widow's Hill) and back, a distance of roughly fourteen hundred meters. Marcelina, the main female character in an 1878–1879 short story by Machado de Assis "dove, swam . . . and floated like a 'naiad.'"[52] In 1881, a few years after the story's publication, the *Revista Illustrada* called on its readers to see how, while bathing, "Cariocas exercise themselves gracefully in the art of swimming." At the time, a swimming club already existed in Botafogo. Some of its members may have taken part in the public swimming races that were held in the bay's waters starting in the mid-1880s. Such examples and others suggest that a knowledge of swimming was not especially unusual.[53] However, it is worth remembering that even those who know how to swim may die by drowning. *Dom Casmurro*'s Escobar drowns despite being an experienced swimmer.

In any case, residents of Rio de Janeiro did not need to know how to swim to go sea-bathing and to take part in an increasingly more common activity in the city. The *Folhinha Laemmert*, an illustrated almanac published annually for decades after 1839, provides further evidence that regularly wading or plunging into the sea was becoming a widespread habit among Cariocas. Already in its 1855 edition, the *Folhinha* included a brief discussion of sea-bathing. Four years later, it again mentioned the practice and published a cartoon depicting sea-bathers. Other cartoons and references to bathing appeared in the *Folhinha* in later years. For instance, the edition for 1888 included a cartoon and observed that, "every morning," the city's beaches swarmed with bathers.[54] The cartoons in the *Folhinha* were not the first to appear (as we have seen, *O Brasil Illustrado* had printed a cartoon showing a bather in 1855). Rio de Janeiro's other illustrated magazines subsequently also published cartoons dealing with sea-bathing. Henrique Fleiüss's *Semana Illustrada* portrayed sea-bathing on various occasions between 1868 and 1876. Cartoons depicting bathing also appeared in Angelo Agostini's *Revista Illustrada*, which ranked as perhaps Rio de Janeiro's most important illustrated magazine in the late nineteenth century (see figures 1.1, 1.2, 2.1, 2.2, 2.6, and 2.7).

Sea-bathing inspired not only cartoonists but also inventors. Between 1870 and 1910, the Brazilian government received more than a dozen patent requests for inventions related to sea-bathing, mainly from residents of Rio de Janeiro. Several of the applications were for bathing systems that floated. José Matoso

Duque Estrada Carneiro, for instance, patented in 1876 a "floating bathing pool [*banheiro flutuante*]," which, he claimed, would allow people to bathe safely. Safety also concerned Antônio Augusto dos Santos Luzes, who, in 1890, sought to patent his own "banheiro flutuante." His version consisted of two floating docks with dressing rooms and "galvanized iron baskets" to drop bathers into the water for the purpose of "shock immersions, which doctors recommended for those too sick to move about on their own." An overhead "network of cables or wires" would link the two docks; hanging from that network would be a series of ropes for bathers to hold while in the water and, thereby, avoid "disasters."[55]

One year after Santos Luzes submitted his patent request, João Gonçalves Ferreira Tito attempted to patent an invention that he called the *Salva-vidas Misterioso* (Mysterious Lifesaver). Consisting of a hollow canvas-covered cylinder, with head and foot harnesses, as well as small wooden planks, a set of ropes, and "folding metal fins," the contraption apparently would allow a bather to float standing up in the water. If, by chance, currents carried the bather out to sea, there was no need to worry, for the Mysterious Lifesaver also included a three-day supply of food and fresh water, a compass, a searchlight, matches, and a horn. Tito's invention furthermore had the advantage of weighing a mere twenty kilograms. Far less complicated and certainly far more practical was the "*vestimenta flutuante* [floating vestment]" that André Cateysson, a French "industrialist" who lived in Rio de Janeiro, tried to patent in 1904. The "vestment" could be made of any type of fabric and according to any design. In that regard, it did not differ from common bathing costumes. The difference lay in the tubes filled with either air or cork that Cateysson inserted into the "vestment." He attached to his patent request a photograph of bathers wearing different versions of his invention; they vaguely resemble the Michelin Man.[56] The two women in the center of figure 1.2 are wearing what appear to be simpler flotation devices.

The Business of Bathing

The best evidence of sea-bathing's increasing importance in city life comes from the growing number of commercial establishments devoted directly to bathing. Another *flutuante* (bathing barge), anchored off the Largo do Paço, began to operate in 1848. In 1851, José Maria da Silva Paranhos, the future Viscount of Rio Branco, praised it "as an excellent convenience." On board, customers found "thirty-two cabins" in two galleries, one for men and another for women. The cabins had clean rectangular bathtubs, measuring "ten *palmos* in length and six in width"; that is, 2.2 by 1.3 meters. Each cabin had its own independent door and a window looking out onto the bay, as well as everything that a bather needed to undress, dress, and rest—"a wicker chair, a foot mat, and a hanger." From the viscount's point of view, the barge offered a great advantage: "to take salt-water baths," he stated, it was no longer "necessary . . . to set up a tent at the beach or expose oneself to others." The barge also had a "discreetly stocked bar [*botequim*]" and a large awning, under which were benches "where three hundred people can be at ease, breathing the fresh air, enjoying a view of the port, and hearing the harmonious sounds of a piano." The only thing lacking, in Paranhos's opinion, was a bit of decoration; he suggested placing pots with dried flowers on the barge's deck.[57]

A lack of flowers did not, however, prevent the barge from achieving commercial success, which led its owner, Cândido José de Carvalho, to request a fifteen-year exclusive privilege for operating other bathing barges. Carvalho received that privilege in 1852 and opened another barge. But it ran into problems soon after it was inaugurated in 1854 and does not seem to have lasted long. By contrast, Carvalho's original barge continued to operate well into the 1860s. According to letters sent to the *Correio Mercantil* in 1862 by one of its customers, it attracted an "extraordinary" number of bathers—so many, in fact, that they dangerously overcrowded the small boat that ferried them from the quay in front of the Largo do Paço to the barge. Nearly all of them had to make the short trip standing up in the boat and "grabbing on to each other." "Many families," as a result, preferred to charter a boat to take them to the barge.[58] The last barge to operate in the city opened in 1873 and enjoyed commercial success until the mid-1880s. Owned by a company called Salubridade (Healthfulness), it was apparently larger and more elaborately outfitted than any previous flutuante. It boasted "a thirty-meter-long [covered] bathing pool [*banheiro*] for men as well as twenty-eight bathing rooms for ladies and families, completely separated from and on the opposite side of the men's pool."[59]

In the early 1870s, when Salubridade opened its barge, a firm called Banhos Populares Fluminenses (Fluminense [i.e., Rio de Janeiro] Popular Baths) began operating at Boqueirão do Passeio and Russell beaches. Advertisements published in 1873 claimed that it offered its customers "the greatest conveniences": "clean and comfortable tents" for undressing and dressing "according to the system adopted at the most frequented beaches in Europe" and a small dock for "shock baths," diving or jumping directly into the water. The firm had also hired a team of "swimming bathers [*banheiros nadadores*]." Banheiros nadadores, more commonly called in Rio de Janeiro *banhistas nadadores* (which can also be translated as swimming bathers) or even simply *banhistas* (bathers), were roughly the equivalent of the bathing masters and *maîtres baigneurs* at English and French beaches. They accompanied the timid into the water and, in practice, also served as lifeguards. Thus, the banheiros nadadores hired by the firm were "ready to enter the water with bathers who need such help and . . . to come to their aid in the case of any disaster." In competing with the barge, Banhos Populares Fluminenses had at least two advantages. First, to go bathing, its customers did not need to wait at a quay to have themselves ferried into the middle of the bay in a small and sometimes overcrowded boat. Second, its prices were cheaper: whereas "a simple bath" on the barge cost Rs.$500, Banhos Populares Fluminenses charged only Rs.$200 for "a single bath" (i.e., for the rental of a changing tent).[60]

In the 1870s, a French immigrant, François Alphonse Cot d'Ordan, opened the first *casa de banhos de mar* (sea-bathing house) in Rio de Janeiro: the Boqueirão, located at the beach of the same name. Just as elsewhere, Rio de Janeiro's *casas de banhos*, which were also known as *estabelecimentos de banhos* (bathing establishments), rented out small rooms, where their customers could change from street clothes into bathing attire. They sometimes provided other services, such as washing bathing costumes or renting towels, and they almost always employed one or more banhistas nadadores to accompany bathers into the water and to serve as lifeguards. The Boqueirão also maintained a diving dock. The house prospered, so much so that d'Ordan published in 1881 a small newspaper, the *Gazeta do Banho* (Bathing Gazette), to entertain his customers.[61] When he died in 1886, the French immigrant left a fortune worth more than 96 contos de réis (Rs.96:760$000; equivalent to £7,536 at the time); this placed him among the wealthiest 12 or 13 percent of the city's residents whose estates were inventoried between 1885 and 1889.[62] The establishment was still offering its services to bathers in 1904. In that year, João do Rio (Paulo Barreto), who through his articles became the best-known chronicler of daily life, customs, and fashions in early twentieth-century Rio de Janeiro, reported that, after d'Ordan's death, his widow, "many times over a millionaire," had rented out the establishment and moved to Paris.[63]

D'Ordan soon had competition. Already in November 1879, another bathing house, the Banhos Fluminenses (with forty-seven changerooms) opened at

Boqueirão do Passeio beach. "Everything" at the establishment, according to an advertisement published that summer, had been "prepared with the greatest care"; customers could expect "cleanliness and order." More than twenty years later, the establishment, by then considerably enlarged, continued to attract bathers.[64] Other entrepreneurs also sought profit in sea-bathing. Between 1870 and 1905, Rio de Janeiro's municipal council received more than thirty requests for licenses to open sea-bathing establishments.[65] Some of the requests involved ambitious proposals. Thus, in 1877, Guilherme de Castro sought permission to open three bathing houses: one to be located at Boqueirão do Passeio beach, the second at Russell beach, and the third in Botafogo. Other proposals submitted to Rio de Janeiro's city council might seem a bit odd today. Alfredo Marques de Souza, for instance, requested in 1884 permission to set up sentry box–style cabanas (*guaritas*) along the shore for use by shoe-shiners and bathers. His request, which was apparently denied, did not clarify what shining shoes had to do with sea-bathing or how bathers would share the sentry boxes with shoe-shiners. Four years later, Teódulo Pupo de Morais and Teófilo Rufino Bezerra de Menezes sought permission to build a "vast floating bathing pool," which would be enclosed by iron bars, facing Boqueirão do Passeio beach. The bars would allow waves to enter the pool, but they would also prevent "voracious fish" from attacking bathers, an unusual concern, for I have found only one reference to shark attacks on bathers (from 1819). The council rejected their request.[66]

It did, however, approve a much more modest request submitted in 1885 by Eugênio Carrier, who wanted to install at Santa Luzia beach what he called "rolling tents [*barracas rolantes*]" for use by bathers. His request did not explain what those "rolling tents" were and how they differed from the changing tents that others rented to bathers.[67] Carrier's "rolling tents" could have been bathing machines; that is, small carriages pulled by donkeys or horses that allowed bathers to change and then hauled them into the sea, where they could bathe more or less discreetly. Bathing machines were common at European beaches in the nineteenth century and in Montevideo even as late as the 1910s. Likewise, bathers at Guarujá, São Paulo's first luxury seaside resort, could also hire them in the early twentieth century. Yet, with the possible exception of Carrier's "rolling tents," bathing machines were apparently never used in Rio de Janeiro. Ouseley in the 1830s and early 1840s and Isabel Burton, who was in Rio de Janeiro in the second half of the 1860s, both commented on their absence.[68] The explanation for this may well lie in the narrowness of the main bayshore beaches, which would have made it difficult to park and maneuver bathing machines.[69]

In any event, by about 1900, more than ten casas de banhos were operating along the city's bayshore. At least seven of them were located at Boqueirão do Passeio beach. They included the Boqueirão, founded by d'Ordan, and three houses owned by families of Italian immigrants: the Salitures, the Provenzanos, and the Amendolas. Bathers who preferred Santa Luzia could turn to the establishments at that beach. Flamengo, in turn, could claim two casas de banhos. Yet another house functioned at Saudade beach.[70]

The multiplication of such establishments led Rio de Janeiro's municipal council to pass legislation governing their operations. Thus, an 1896 law required bathing establishments to have a room for providing first aid to drowning victims as well as a lifesaving boat. It further required them to install a cable with floats in the water for bathers to hold on to. The establishments also needed to employ "at least three banhistas skilled in swimming."[71] A later law, approved in 1908, expanded those requirements. This law and the 1909 decree that regulated its implementation required that bathing houses hire not only three banhistas but also two other employees to man a lifesaving boat.[72] Nicolau Sevcenko has asserted that, according to this law, "young women [*moças*] could enter the water only if accompanied by a banhista."[73] It is true that banhistas nadadores did sometimes go into the water with timid bathers—both younger and older women as well as men. But neither the 1908 law nor the 1909 decree said anything about a prohibition against young women bathing unaccompanied by a banhista nadador. Nor did the legislation even mention accompanying young women or other bathers into the water as one of the duties of banhistas nadadores. From the law and the decree, it is clear that, for the authorities, banhistas nadadores were above all else supposed to serve as lifeguards. The concern with drownings also shows up in the twelfth article of the 1909 decree, which required bathing establishments to hire a nurse and to keep on hand various types of surgical equipment and medicines to revive drowning victims. There is no evidence that the municipal government effectively enforced either law. João do Rio, for instance, declared in 1903 that he knew of no establishment that fulfilled all the requirements of the 1896 law. Indeed, official inspections by the General Directorate of Hygiene and Public Assistance (the local board of health) to determine whether the casas de banhos were complying with the legislation seem to have been sporadic at best.[74]

Some of those establishments were quite large. For example, a bathing house that opened in the mid-1880s in Flamengo had 124 dressing rooms. An establishment built at Santa Luzia beach in the 1890s was of similar size; its blueprints show a two-story construction with a 32.4-meter façade and with 128 changerooms. In 1904, João do Rio reported that the seven bathing establishments at Boqueirão do Passeio beach had a total of more than 340 changerooms. The seven included the Boqueirão, founded by d'Ordan, which had begun with 50 rooms; by 1904, it had 100. The Fluminense, which had opened in late 1879 with 47 rooms and which claimed 120 rooms in 1904, was the largest establishment at that beach (figure 1.3).[75] João do Rio estimated that somewhere between five and six thousand bathers frequented every day (presumably in the summer) the establishments at Boqueirão do Passeio beach.[76] His estimate may be exaggerated. But, even if we were to cut it by as much as two-thirds, 1,650 to 1,980 bathers a day would still amount to a significant number in a city that, at the time, had fewer than 622,000 residents within its urban perimeter (table 1.1).

Moreover, João do Rio's estimate did not take into account the bathers who frequented the establishments in Flamengo or at the city's other beaches, or those who went bathing on their own. At the time, the casas de banhos by no means monopolized sea-bathing in Rio de Janeiro. On the contrary, in the

FIGURE 1.3. The Grande Estabelecimento de Banhos de Mar, 1905. By this time, the establishment had closed and work on the landfill that eliminated Boqueirão do Passeio beach was well underway (foreground). *RS* (26.2.1905), 2085.

second half of the nineteenth century and in the early years of the twentieth, just as in Schlichthorst's time, many residents of the city, including women, woke early and walked to the beach. João do Rio calculated in 1904 that every morning "more than a thousand" bathers, "coming from nearby streets," went bathing at Boqueirão do Passeio beach "for free." Still others took the tram to the beach. In 1879, for example, the *Gazeta de Noticias* published a request that a local tram company make available a four-thirty tram to take bathers to Lapa beach. A decade later, Christopher Columbus Andrews, who had served as US consul in the early 1880s, observed that "some ladies rise at four in the morning, ride in the street-car . . . , bathe in the salt water, and then go back home."[77]

Beyond any doubt, many Cariocas who went bathing on their own did so because they could not afford to rent a changeroom at one of the city's casas de banhos. Although information on the matter is scant, Rs.$200 seems to have been the common price charged by those establishments for a "single bath (*banho avulso*)" (i.e., the price of renting a changeroom) in the 1870s and 1880s. Customers who took out a "subscription for thirty baths" at Rs.5$000 received a discount; for those customers, each "bath" cost Rs.$167.[78] Both Rs.$200 and Rs.$167 were at the time small sums. They would, nevertheless, have weighed heavily in the pockets of poor free Cariocas, and a man like José Gonçalves Medeiros, a Portuguese-born clog-maker could scarcely have afforded the Rs.5$000 required for a subscription for thirty baths—a sum far beyond the means of a humble artisan.[79] Instead, Medeiros bathed for free at Boqueirão do Passeiro beach. When he died by drowning there in 1886, the authorities found a mere Rs.$320 in the pockets of his street clothes. The unfortunate clog-maker was certainly not the poorest free resident of Rio de Janeiro. For the many free Cariocas who survived on the meager incomes that they earned as casual laborers, washerwomen, beggars, street vendors, or stevedores, it was not a matter of choice: if they wished to go sea-bathing, they had to do so on their own. The same held true for the city's slave population.

Poverty alone does not explain why some bathers chose not to rent a changeroom at a casa de banhos but, instead, preferred to go bathing on their own. Those bathers, in fact, included men and women wealthy enough to have a slave or free servant pitch a small tent for undressing and dressing at the beach.[80] The less well-off and the poor, by contrast, did not bother with tents; they instead took advantage of the predawn darkness or the dim early morning light and any nearby rocks or vegetation to change more or less discreetly from their street clothes into bathing attire. Drowning reports, among other sources, sometimes allude to the practice of changing at the beach. For example, on a January morning in 1877, when Hilário Monteiro de Azevedo went bathing at Boqueirão do Passeio beach, "a few people saw him leave his clothes on the beach." He entered the water and shortly thereafter disappeared. Other bathers only realized that he was missing when they found his folded clothes still on the beach.[81] Other men who did the same lost their belongings, not their lives. This is what happened in 1876 to José Maria Pereira at Santa Luzia beach, where he left his clothing near a rock. While he was bathing, a thief "*cleaned* him of a silver watch" that he had left in the pocket of his waistcoat. Antônio Maria de Matos had a similar experience there. Before entering the water, he also left his clothes "next to a few rocks." But "when he returned to get dressed, he realized that he was completely *clean*"—cleaned out of the two documents, the Rs.7$000, and the silver watch and watch fob that he had left in his jacket and waistcoat. These men may not have been wealthy, but their ownership of silver watches indicates that they were hardly poor. Their experiences further show that, far from being a recent phenomenon, "beach rats [*ratos de praia*]"—as thieves who steal bathers' belongings have been known since at least the mid-twentieth century—have a long lineage.[82]

Still other bathers, including women sometimes accompanied by enslaved or free maids, left home "ready to enter the sea." Wearing a sheet or large towel over their bathing costumes, they walked to the beach to bathe and, then, "dripping through streets," walked back home. Among them was Michel Calógeras, whose father described his son's costume this way in 1865: "a knit jersey, trunks and a cap made of cotton, and all majestically covered with a cloth as though it were a royal cape." Some twenty years later, in the mid-1880s, Carpenter noted that, "at six o'clock the streets are full of ladies in dowdy dresses, with long rolls of moist hair down their back, going home from their matutinal plunge." Those "ladies," no doubt, shared the city's streets with an even larger number of "dripping" men who had also just finished bathing.[83] All indications are that more men than women went bathing—in 1896, for instance, *O Paiz* estimated that men occupied 60 percent of the changerooms at Boqueirão do Passeio beach.[84] Nevertheless, this meant that women (perhaps accompanied by male relatives) accounted for the other 40 percent of rooms. This estimate, along with the other sources cited in this chapter, indicates that women constituted a significant minority of bathers.

In the early nineteenth century, sea-bathing attracted a significant number of Cariocas to the city's bayshore, such as the "hundreds" of bathers that Brand saw in the waters just off the Largo do Paço in the late 1820s. In the following decades, sea-bathing became even more common and gave rise to a "bathing industry," consisting of the shops that sold bathing costumes and changing tents, the hotels that rented rooms to bathers, and, most notably, the casas de banhos located along Boqueirão do Passeio, Santa Luzia, and Flamengo beaches. The information about that "industry" together with the other evidence presented here indicates that sea-bathing had become a well-established practice in Rio de Janeiro by the late nineteenth century.

Cariocas of different classes and backgrounds engaged in that practice. They included the women and men who could afford to have an enslaved or free servant set up a tent on the sand or to rent a changeroom at a casa de banhos, as well as free workers of modest means, such as the Portuguese clog-maker José Gonçalves Medeiros and the Brazilian-born José Antônio de Oliveira, who worked at a bakery and who went bathing in Caju in 1870. They also included Henrique Fleiüss, a native of Cologne, Germany, who published the *Semana Illustrada*; Michel Calógeras, the son of a Greek immigrant who held a high-ranking position in the Brazilian Ministry of Foreign Affairs; and Antônio Maria de Matos, who, though he undressed and dressed at the beach, was well enough off to own a silver watch and fob. Sea-bathing, moreover, was not restricted to the free population; on the contrary, before 1888, they were joined by slaves such as those seen by Kidder and Fletcher in Flamengo in the 1850s and the African-born Manoel Cabinda who, in 1868, also plunged into the bay at the same beach.[85]

That sea-bathing had become a common practice and widespread habit among the city's residents was clear to João do Rio. In articles published at the start of the twentieth century, the chronicler described sea-bathing as "a Carioca custom." In his view, sea-bathing was a characteristic feature of everyday life in Rio de Janeiro that set the Brazilian capital apart from the world's other large cities.[86] Yet at least one major question remains: in a city that was plagued by repeated epidemics and poor sanitary conditions, what compelled most Cariocas to go bathing in the early morning hours? The next chapter answers that question.

2

Only on Doctors' Orders?

Sea-Bathing as Medical Treatment, Sport, and Recreation

IN 1938, LUIZ EDMUNDO (de Melo Pereira da Costa), a journalist and man of letters, published *O Rio de Janeiro do meu tempo* (Rio de Janeiro in My Time), in which he sought to paint a complete panorama of life in the city between 1901 and 1912. He dealt with a wide range of habits and customs, including sea-bathing, and described Boqueirão do Passeio beach as "a small hospital," explaining that, at the start of the twentieth century, sea-bathing was not yet a form of "recreation"; instead, it was a "medical prescription."[1] Nearly every author who has taken up the matter in recent decades has drawn directly or indirectly on Luiz Edmundo's memoirs to argue that, before the first years of the last century or even before the 1920s, sea-bathing in Rio was a strictly therapeutic activity—only for the sick and only when prescribed by a doctor. For example, Nicolau Sevcenko writes that, in Rio de Janeiro, "sea-bathing would become an elegant fashion only" sometime after 1902. Until then, Cariocas who entered the water were following recommendations made by physicians, who had incorporated saltwater immersions into their "therapeutic techniques" and who prescribed sea baths for "every sort of ailment." Roberto Kaz likewise contends that "going to the beach" in nineteenth-century Rio de Janeiro amounted to nothing more than "a simple therapeutic outing." Julia Galli O'Donnell also stresses the "therapeutic properties" assigned to sea baths in the nineteenth and early twentieth centuries and claims that, as late as the early 1910s, bathing in Copacabana was "never associated with leisure or sociability."[2]

The argument that sea-bathing in Rio de Janeiro in the nineteenth and early twentieth centuries was a strictly therapeutic practice has become part of what might be called the local common-sense understanding of the city's past. Carioca newspapers sometimes still reproduce the argument in articles on beach-going at the start of every summer. In January 2000, for instance,

O Globo published an article titled "Praia só com ordens médicas" (The Beach Only on Doctors' Orders) which informed readers that, until roughly 1910, "only the sick who were undergoing hydrotherapy went [sea-]bathing."[3]

This chapter begins by examining the medical use of sea-bathing in nineteenth- and early twentieth-century Rio de Janeiro. Doctors recommended it for a variety of ailments, while hygienists saw sea-bathing as a way to preserve and improve individual and collective health. Nevertheless, sea-bathing was far from a strictly therapeutic activity, for nineteenth-century Cariocas entered the water to bathe, to find relief from summer heat, and to engage in recreational and competitive sport. And they made sea-bathing into a recreational activity. Bathing establishments became places of elite and middle-class sociability, a regular part of many Cariocas' morning routine. In these ways, sea-bathing already displayed some of the features that would later be associated with beach-going in Rio de Janeiro. At the same time, sea-bathing raised moral questions and prompted social tensions, for men and women of all classes bathed together in states of partial (or even complete, in the case of some men) undress, and did so in the heart of Brazil's capital city. While sea-bathers developed codes of conduct that differed radically from those that governed the use of urban space, these were not accepted by all. Late-nineteenth-century newspapers regularly debated appropriate comportment and attire for bathers, while the police struggled to enforce vaguely defined norms of decency.

Therapeutic Bathing

In nineteenth- and early twentieth-century Rio de Janeiro, just as in Europe and the United States, sea baths were used for therapeutic purposes. Since the late seventeenth century, European physicians increasingly relied on saltwater immersions to deal with a wide range of diseases and medical conditions. As a result, according to some authors, sea-bathing in parts of Europe by the early nineteenth century had become a thoroughly medicalized practice, subject to rigid rules laid out by doctors. Jean-Didier Urbain, for example, states that, at the time, the practice in France stood at "the polar opposite of pleasure"; as a form of therapy, it had little or nothing to do with recreation. Physicians trained in Brazil after 1808, like their counterparts in Europe, continued to recommend sea baths as a treatment for various ailments and health complaints throughout the nineteenth century.[4]

Those who went bathing under doctors' orders included not only King

João VI (as we saw in chapter 1) but also his grandson's wife, Empress Teresa Cristina. In 1860, her doctors chose Russell beach as the ideal bathing locale for treating an unspecified medical condition. The palace, accordingly, requisitioned a large tent to be set up at the beach for the empress to change. Less than a month later, however, her doctors concluded that Russell beach was an "inappropriate" location for her sea baths, likely because it was situated in the crowded neighborhood of Glória and attracted other bathers. The empress, as a result, transferred her baths to Pombeba, a small island in the bay, which offered greater privacy and had the advantage of being much closer to the imperial palace in São Cristóvão. Later, in the 1870s, Teresa Cristina accompanied her husband when he went sea-bathing; Pedro II, who suffered from diabetes, bathed, like his grandfather, at Caju beach.[5]

The court's doctors were not the only physicians to recommend thalassotherapy, or therapeutic sea-bathing. An 1849 report to the Imperial Academy of Medicine, for instance, noted that a private hospital near the Saco do Alferes was ideally situated for such purposes. Starting in the 1860s, the hospital owned by Dr. Manoel Joaquim Fernandes Eiras in Botafogo also offered sea-bathing as a form of therapy. In the 1870s, still another private hospital, situated just off the Largo do Paço, informed prospective patients that it was just "two steps" away from the bay, making it easy for them to go bathing.[6] To be sure, these baths would have exposed patients to the port's already contaminated waters, but as we saw in chapter 1, pollution little worried bathers.

Aspiring doctors at Rio de Janeiro's medical school studied thalassotherapy. In 1845, José Ferraz de Oliveira Durão defended a thesis titled *Breves considerações acerca do emprego higiênico e terapêutico dos banhos de mar* (Brief Considerations on the Hygienic and Therapeutic Use of Sea Baths). Relying mainly on European authors, Durão prescribed sea-bathing for a range of diseases and ailments—everything from scrofula, chlorosis, chest problems, hypochondria, and somnambulism to rickets, spermatorrhoea, complications from surgery, rheumatism, and certain types of tuberculosis. Like earlier and later authors, he assigned considerable importance to the "reaction" once a bather left the water. The "reaction," he explained, consisted of a "kind of general effort by the [body's] economy to oppose the stupefying action, so to speak, of a sea bath and to reestablish the momentarily interrupted equilibrium of the [body's] functions." In other words, the "reaction" was nothing more than the body's warming-up after leaving the water. "To facilitate the reaction," Durão recommended a good rubdown and warm foot bath. In the

1870s, the sick and their physicians could consult not only local theses but also the translation of a French manual by one Dr. Claparède, on sale at the city's bookshops. Like Durão, Claparède recommended sea-bathing for a wide variety of medical conditions and also stressed the importance of the "reaction," but with a difference: for Claparède, the "reaction" that mattered came when bathers entered cold water and suffered thermal shock.[7]

The sea's therapeutic qualities, according to medical beliefs at the time, went beyond the shock caused by immersion in cold water. The "pure," "salty" air found along the shore, for example, supposedly brought health benefits. The action of the waves, so long as they were not too strong, could also be beneficial. Thus, according to Durão, the bather's muscles contracted in response to the waves' "percussions," resulting in "a true and fruitful form of gymnastics." Seawater's chemical composition was held to have curative properties, and some went so far as to recommend drinking it or using it in suppositories.[8]

References to bathing as a form of medical treatment also appear in contemporary fiction, such as the novels *Girândola de amores* (Love's Swirling Fireworks, 1882) and *Casa de Pensão* (The Boarding House, 1884), both by Aluísio Azevedo (1857–1913). In both novels, doctors prescribe sea baths for women suffering from nervous ailments, but one character refuses to follow the prescription, while forty baths have no effect on the other. Artur Azevedo (1855–1908), a playwright and poet and Aluísio's brother, also dealt with medical sea-bathing in a satirical poem set in the 1860s. In the poem, a young woman is forced by her parents to give up her young and handsome suitor and to marry a much older, wealthy merchant. The merchant, looking for a cure for his impotence, consults a physician, who recommends sea baths but with little faith in their efficacy. The newlyweds, accordingly, spend several weeks at a beach in Niterói, on the other side of the bay from Rio de Janeiro. Shortly thereafter, the young bride becomes pregnant and then gives birth to a baby boy. The merchant is overjoyed, and the doctor thoroughly surprised. Azevedo, however, makes it clear that sea-bathing did not cure the merchant's impotence; rather, the "cure" resulted from his bride's secret meetings in Niterói with her former suitor.[9]

Indications of skepticism about thalassotherapy's efficacy or doubts about doctors who prescribed it indiscriminately nevertheless demonstrate the prominence of medical sea-bathing. For example, in an 1872 cartoon in *A Vida Fluminense*, a rotund woman, to her surprise, encounters an acquaintance in the water. The acquaintance, an anemically thin woman, explains that, "on

FIGURE 2.1. Sea-Bathing as a Prescription for Different Medical Conditions, 1872. *VF* (24.2.1872), 896 (detail).

her doctor's orders," she has begun bathing to put on weight. The fat woman responds that her doctor has also recommended sea baths but as a way to lose weight. Both women then express doubts about the treatments that their doctors have prescribed (figure 2.1). Others touted the beneficial qualities of certain waters. In 1873, a property owner sought to auction off in lots his land in Caju. The lots, according to advertisements he placed in the local press, were located next to the neighborhood beach, where the sea baths, "thanks to their medicinal properties," were "regarded as providing the best results."[10] Regardless of whether the sales were successful, this advertisement, as well as the Azevedo brothers' skepticism and the cartoon characters' surprise, all underscore that many bathed in the sea for medicinal purposes.

Not Only On Doctors' Orders

Prior scholars have asserted that sea-bathing was a strictly therapeutic activity in Rio de Janeiro before 1910 or 1920. But, if this were the case, it would leave us with a "mystery" to explain: namely, the mysteriously rapid transformation of a "medical prescription" into a form of leisure by the 1920s.[11] Habits and customs can, of course, undergo radical changes in short spans of time. But such changes need to be explained; otherwise, they remain a "mystery." The secondary literature, however, offers no explanation for the rapid and radical transformation that sea-bathing supposedly underwent in Rio de Janeiro in the early twentieth century. Likewise, if correct, the argument would also present us with a hard-to-answer question. In Europe and the United States, sea-bathing—without ever losing its links with health concerns—became in the second half of the nineteenth century a leisure activity increasingly appreciated by not only the upper class but also the middle class. It was fashionable to spend time at a seaside resort. In parts of Europe and the United States, even better-off members of the working class began to make day trips and short holiday excursions to the seashore.[12] Bathing was then also becoming fashionable in Argentina, Chile, and Uruguay. For instance, by the mid-1890s, more than six thousand visitors regularly spent "the season" at Mar del Plata, Argentina's first major seaside resort. Across the River Plate, Montevideo already boasted beachside hotels and casinos in the first years of the twentieth century.[13] Wealthy and well-to-do Cariocas closely followed European trends and sometimes measured themselves against their River Plate neighbors. They adopted roller-skating, bicycling, rowing, and later, football (soccer). They also dressed according to the latest European fashions.[14] But the historiography on sea-bathing in Rio de Janeiro would lead us to believe that, though they had easy access to the sea, those wealthy and well-to-do Cariocas remained even as late as the early twentieth century unaware of the possibility of sea-bathing as a form of leisure. The existing literature provides no answers for Cariocas' alleged delay in adopting sea-bathing as recreation.

The delay, it bears noting, would not only relate to Europe, the United States, or the River Plate republics. By then, beaches in São Paulo had begun to attract holiday bathers. In 1882, the German governess Ina von Binzer accompanied a wealthy Paulista coffee planter and his family on vacation to a beach in Santos (São Paulo), where they went bathing. In the 1890s, Paulista investors transformed Guarujá (near Santos) into a luxury bathing resort, modeled in part on Newport, Rhode Island; theirs was a "real estate plan devoted to leisure." The 1890s also saw the opening of a large hotel at the Cassino beach in the city of Rio Grande, in the far southern state of Rio Grande do Sul. Inspired by similar hotels in Biarritz and Deauville, it had 150 rooms and offered its guests gaming salons, formal dances, concerts, and also, of course, the opportunity to go bathing.[15] Thus, the available literature would lead us to conclude that Paulistas and Gaúchos (residents of Rio Grande do Sul) discovered sea-bathing as a leisure activity before Cariocas. Such a conclusion would do more than harm the comfortable self-image that many Cariocas hold and have held of Rio de Janeiro as a cosmopolitan city that helped spread the latest international fashions and trends to other parts of Brazil—an image that scholarship has, by the way, borne out.[16] Far more important, the conclusion points to problems in the commonly accepted argument that sea-bathing was a strictly therapeutic activity in Rio de Janeiro in the nineteenth and early twentieth centuries.

To start, the argument does not take into account the fact that the link between sea-bathing and health concerns did not disappear after 1910 or 1920. On the contrary, doctors still heralded the medicinal benefits of saltwater immersions in the 1920s, 1930s, and 1940s. Thus, in 1938, Dr. Álvaro Caldeira, just as Durão had done almost ninety years before, recommended sea-bathing as a treatment for scrofula, rickets, and certain types of tuberculosis. Likewise, when the Hotel Balneário da Urca (Urca Bathing Hotel) first opened in 1925 at a bayside beach in Rio de Janeiro, it was linked to a "physiotherapeutic institute" supervised by a physician. The hotel provided its guests with various types of treatment, including sea baths, fresh- and saltwater showers, and sun baths. In the 1940s, the first bathers to arrive at the beach in Flamengo in the early morning had no "sporting inclinations"; they were instead following "medical prescriptions."[17] Indeed, even today, the beach in Rio de Janeiro continues to be associated with good health, or at least with healthy bodies.[18]

The argument also overlooks a seemingly obvious fact: it gets hot in Rio de Janeiro, and in the summer, it can get quite hot. One might object that, in the past, with greater forest cover, lower buildings, and a smaller paved area, the heat in Rio de Janeiro was less oppressive. Perhaps so, but much of the Tijuca Forest, covering one of the city's main mountain ranges, had been cleared by midcentury, which prompted in the 1860s a reforestation project by the imperial government concerned about water supplies and summer heat. According to an 1892 study of the city's climate, the highest temperature ever recorded in the city came on 8 December 1891, when the National Observatory recorded 39°C, while summer "highs generally [did] not surpass 37.5°." Located atop Morro do Castelo (Castle Hill), razed in the early 1920s, the observatory received cooling breezes from the bay. Today's meteorological service typically records the highest temperatures in low-lying neighborhoods like Bangu, Maracanã, or Mauá Square, the latter two at sea level.[19]

Although temperatures may have been milder in the past, it does not follow that the perceived discomfort caused by the summer's tropical heat was less intense. Rio de Janeiro's wealthy, in fact, found the season's temperatures so unbearable that, after the mid-nineteenth century, they sought to spend the better part of it in Petrópolis and in other towns in the mountains north of Rio de Janeiro. Situated at more than eight hundred meters above sea level, Petrópolis, where Pedro II had his summer palace and where, after 1889, presidents of the republic vacationed, became virtually a second national capital between January and March. The mountains, with their more temperate climate, also served as a refuge from repeated outbreaks of yellow fever, cholera, and other diseases that plagued city inhabitants, especially in the summer months, after the late 1840s.[20] Nevertheless, even the wealthy had to spend part of the summer in Rio de Janeiro to handle business matters or to fulfill other obligations. Members of the incipient middle class could barely hope to spend more than a few days in the mountains and, even then, only with considerable strain on the family budget.[21]

For the great majority of the city's residents—those with modest incomes, the free poor, and slaves—spending the "hot season" in the mountains was impossible. Summer after summer, they remained in Rio de Janeiro. They spent those summers in a city located in the humid tropics and without air-conditioning or even electric fans, which appear to have been rare in the city as late as the 1910s and 1920s.[22] Furthermore, many Cariocas slept all year round in bedrooms that were little more than "cubicles," often without windows and hence "without ventilation." On one night in January 1877, for instance, José Pinto, seeking relief from the heat, resorted in vain to "strolling in [the city's] landscaped squares . . . , [and relying on] fruit drinks, ice cream, and hand-held fans." Desperate and still unable to sleep, he stripped down completely and, "like our father Adam," stretched out on the roof of his house. Not even then was he able to get a good night's sleep, for the police arrested him.[23]

By day, the city's inhabitants, or at least those who aspired to a minimally "respectable" status, endured the type and quantity of clothing that fashion then demanded. Women—with their long dresses, layers of petticoats, corsets, and gloves—immediately come to mind, but men also suffered. In January 1868, *A Vida Fluminense* called attention to the incompatibility between "respectable" men's attire and the summer's heat. Wearing "tight trousers in a tropical country," the magazine commented, "is asinine, but it is the fashion in Paris." Men went through "ten shirts a day and [even so] always [remained] drenched" in sweat.[24] Men would continue to suffer for decades. In the 1910s and 1920s, when women could wear ever shorter sleeveless and pale-colored dresses made of light fabrics, decorum still required male office workers, liberal professionals, businessmen, and senior clerks at better stores to wear suits with waistcoats, ties, and long-sleeved shirts with stiff collars. Those norms also demanded that, while on the street, men keep their suit jackets on. Annie Peck, a US travel writer, warned her countrymen in 1916 that, "however hot the weather," they should never take off their jackets in public in Rio de Janeiro, lest they be confused with riffraff. "*Make note of this*," she wrote with emphasis, "even on the street a *gentleman* under no circumstances is expected to carry his coat over his arm." Peck reported that, "one American who did so was politely accosted by a Brazilian who said, 'Man, coat put on!' in the best English he could muster." Taking off one's jacket inside offices was also out of the question. For instance, during an unusually intense January 1917 heat wave, six employees of the National Treasury, all of whom wore jackets and ties, suffered heatstroke. The municipal government, therefore, allowed its office workers to take off their jackets but only if their supervisors agreed to this extraordinary—and temporary—concession.[25] Suits at the time were generally made of dark-colored wool or woolen broadcloth, which worsened the discomfort caused by the summer's heat. Senator Lopes Gonçalves caused a small scandal in late December 1924, when he appeared in congress wearing a light-colored jacket. Some journalists in the 1920s and 1930s went so far as to wage a press campaign to persuade men to adopt suits made of lightweight drill in light colors.[26]

It is not hard to locate complaints from the nineteenth and early twentieth centuries about the summer heat in Rio de Janeiro, sometimes described as African or Senegalese (*senegalesco*).[27] In that heat, a dip in the bay would be an easy way to cool off, and by the nineteenth century, Cariocas knew that. Although the secondary literature fails to mention that heat,[28] numerous sources make it clear that, at the time, just as today, the city's beaches attracted the greatest number of bathers during the "hot season [*estação calmosa*]," or the summer. Bathing at that time of the year served as a "cooling relief [*refrigério*]," a brief escape from the "rigors" of the "extreme heat [*canícula*]." Thus, in December 1875, Doutor Semana, the character that Henrique Fleiüss created to personify himself in his *Semana Illustrada*, declared: "In these hot times, I know of nothing that refreshes my spirit and body more than a [sea] bath and a good Havana" (figure 2.2). Emperor Pedro II took sea baths not only to treat his

FIGURE 2.2. Doutor Semana Refreshes Himself, 1875. *SI* (19.12.1875), 1.

diabetes but also to cool off. In December 1880, he noted that the heat in Rio de Janeiro was "horrible" and that he could not wait to leave for Petrópolis. In the meantime, he would continue to go bathing. Sixteen years later, in 1896, *O Paiz* pointed out that, while some residents of the city went sea-bathing for medical reasons, others did so with the goal of "refreshing themselves . . . on hot summer days."[29]

Still other Cariocas went sea-bathing quite literally to bathe; in other words, to wash themselves. For them, a plunge into the "salty element" took the place of a freshwater bath or shower.[30] Using the sea for washing would, no doubt, seem odd today; nowadays, most people do not feel clean with dried salt on their skin. However, as Georges Vigarello and other authors have shown, perceptions of bodily cleanliness have varied over time and across cultures. Furthermore, in nineteenth- and early twentieth-century Rio de Janeiro, many houses lacked access to running water, and bathrooms—that is, rooms with a tub or shower—were rare. A shower was, in fact, a special attraction worthy of note in rental advertisements.[31] Yet living in a house with running water did not always guarantee a daily or weekly bath or shower. Rio de Janeiro suffered from chronic water supply problems, which, for the most part, would be solved only in the 1960s. When supplies of fresh water ran short, many of the city's inhabitants had no choice: either they went for days without bathing or they plunged into the bay. In November 1883, during one more water shortage,

Angelo Agostini proclaimed in his *Revista Illustrada*: "The beaches are already becoming camping grounds. If we lack fresh water, fortunately we have salt water in abundance. Thank goodness!"[32]

Finally, the argument that sea-bathing in nineteenth- and early twentieth-century Rio de Janeiro was a strictly therapeutic activity rests on a false premise; namely, that activities regarded as healthy and healthful cannot also serve as a form of leisure or provide opportunities for sociability. An appropriate analogy would be with mineral spas in the nineteenth and early twentieth centuries. Many people did, of course, spend time at such spas hoping to cure real or imagined maladies. But "taking the waters" did not imply locking oneself up in a bare, antiseptically furnished hospital room. On the contrary, a water cure could be combined with the opportunities for amusement, sociability, and demonstrations of social status that spas such as Vichy, Baden-Baden, Saratoga Springs, Bath, and later, Poços de Caldas in Brazil offered: formal dances, carriage rides and strolls through landscaped parks, concerts, tea parties, and picnics, as well as horse races at the tracks and gambling at the casino. Novels such as Jane Austen's *Northanger Abbey* (1818) and Fyodor Dostoyevsky's *The Gambler* (1867) make it clear that mineral spas in nineteenth-century Europe were not just for the sickly. The healthy also spent time at spas, where, while amusing themselves, they "took the waters" to preserve their good health.[33]

A Hygienic Practice

Various sources, including Durão's 1845 thesis, describe sea-bathing as not only a form of therapy but also as a hygienic practice.[34] *Hygiene* at the time did not mean only or even primarily *cleanliness*. Rather, it referred to a branch of medicine concerned with the promotion and preservation of good health. It also encompassed activities that could supposedly prevent illnesses and debilitating conditions.[35] Sea-bathing as hygienic practice was therefore recommended for healthy individuals who wished to maintain their good health. Durão in fact encouraged the "vigorous" to go bathing and to practice swimming while in the water. He also prescribed sea baths for young children as part of their "physical education" to make them healthy and strong.[36]

Recognizing that sea-bathing was seen as a hygienic activity makes it possible to link its growing popularity in Rio de Janeiro to broader trends in Brazilian society. Since the early and mid-nineteenth century, physicians concerned with private and public hygiene had gained growing influence in Brazil; so, too, did hygienist ideology.[37] Proponents of hygiene recommended not only sea-bathing but also exposure to sunlight and fresh air. They further insisted on the need to promote the "physical education" of children and adolescents through "hygienic exercises" such as walks in the countryside, fencing, reading aloud, ball games, horse riding, gymnastics, and swimming. Hygiene also required, according to its proponents, that children and adolescents bathe regularly. For instance, an 1857 thesis on school hygiene recommended that children take daily "partial baths" and "full baths" at least twice a week. Summer bathing should preferably take place in the sea, in ponds, or in rivers because, there, they could practice swimming and because such baths could "calm the general heat, reduce perspiration . . . and tone the organs."[38]

The influence of hygienist ideology made itself felt in the curricula of several private boys' schools, which began requiring that their students take long walks, practice gymnastics, and learn to swim. For instance, in the late 1850s, the Colégio São Pedro de Alcântara had "a large swimming and bathing tank," measuring 96 by 46 palmos, or roughly 21 by 10 meters. At the Colégio São João Batista, in Niterói, across the bay from Rio de Janeiro, students bathed and swam not in a pool but, rather, in the sea at a nearby beach. In turn, the boys who studied at the Colégio Epifânio Reis, located near the beach in Flamengo, were required to have, among other pieces of clothing, two pairs of bathing trunks and large towels. References to swimming and other types of physical exercise are, perhaps not surprising, less common in the case of girls' schools. Nevertheless, even though Madame Geslin did not mention swimming in an 1838 advertisement that she placed for her girls' school in the neighborhood of Glória, she did note that the school's location made it convenient for sea-bathing. In the early 1860s, orphaned and abandoned girls entrusted to the Santa Casa de Misericórdia regularly took sea baths at Santa Luzia beach. The Colégio Santa Rita de Cássia would at the end of that decade include in its curriculum gymnastic classes.[39]

New ideas about the "hygienic body" and the importance of physical exercise also helped give rise to the "sporting fever" that took Rio de Janeiro by storm in the late nineteenth century and at the start of the twentieth. Sports not only promoted good health and served "to improve the race," but also marked "modernity" and "civilization."[40] Before football (soccer) came to dominate Carioca sporting passions, rowing was by far the most popular sport in Rio de Janeiro (alongside horse racing). As rowing gained popularity, it encouraged more and more Cariocas to look to the bay for recreational purposes.[41] The relationship, no doubt, also worked the other way round: for many young men used to taking "hygienic" baths in Guanabara Bay, it would have been an easy next step to adopt rowing as a "hygienic" form of exercise and as sport.

The histories of rowing and bathing share a common chronology. Apparently, the first regattas (rowing competitions) in Rio de Janeiro took place in the 1840s. But such competitions became common only in the 1870s and 1880s as the number of clubs devoted to the sport multiplied.[42] These years also saw the opening of commercial sea-bathing establishments in the city. Moreover, according to Brasil Gerson, it was at one of Flamengo's bathing houses that, in 1895, a group of "elegant young men," all of whom regularly went bathing at that beach, founded the Club de Regatas do Flamengo (Flamengo Rowing Club), which later also became one of the city's most popular football clubs. Other rowing clubs had their headquarters at Boqueirão de Passeio and Santa Luzia beaches, where the majority of the city's bathing establishments were located. The Club de Regatas Boqueirão do Passeio, founded in 1897, even had as its first treasurer Bernardo Eugênio de Oliveira Pinto, the owner of a nearby bathing house. One year before, some of "the most enthusiastic" young male bathers at that beach had organized the Club de Natação e Regatas (Swimming and Rowing Club).[43] Rowing craft manned by members of those clubs soon became a common sight at Rio de Janeiro's main bathing beaches.[44] The clubs also sponsored swimming races and, later, water polo competitions in the bay.

Some of the best-known rowers and swimmers in early twentieth-century Rio de Janeiro belonged to families that owned and operated casas de banhos (bathing houses) in the city. Between 1901 and 1916, for instance, Abraão Saliture, as a member first of the Club de Natação e Regatas and then of the Club de Regatas São Cristóvão, won thirteen national swimming championships, sponsored by the Brazilian Federation of Rowing Societies after 1913. Claudionor Provenzano, who belonged to the Club de Regatas Vasco da Gama, was part of the rowing team that Brazil sent to the 1932 Los Angeles Olympics. He later worked as a municipal lifeguard at a beach in the city's center, not far from where his father had owned a bathing establishment.[45]

It would not be surprising if these "sportsmen" internalized, with all sincerity, the language of hygienics and eugenics into their patterns of thought and speech and if they came to see rowing and swimming as hygienic exercises that could promote "the improvement of the race."[46] But, from there, it would be naïve to conclude that they rowed and swam only to comply with the recommendations of the medical community or to bring about "racial improvement." They surely enjoyed rowing and swimming, relished the applause that they received when they won competitions, and reveled in their sports' prestige. Likewise, influenced by medical discourse, many better-educated Cariocas probably came to regard sea-bathing as a hygienic activity—something that they should do for health reasons—even as they sought relief from the summer heat by wading or diving into the bay and amusing themselves while bathing. A medical discourse is, after all, a normative and prescriptive discourse, produced by intellectuals; however influential it may be, it may not reflect what people actually do when they engage in a particular activity. Nor does it necessarily capture the full range of motives for taking part in that activity.[47]

Moreover, we need to avoid exaggerating the influence of hygienists' discourse. Consider, for example, a group of "idle boys" who regularly gathered at Botafogo beach in the early 1860s. There, they climbed trees, gambled, and went bathing. When the boys entered the water, they were not following doctors' orders or concerned with hygiene; they were having fun or perhaps simply trying to cool off.[48] In all likelihood, they had no familiarity with the medical discourse that touted sea-bathing as a hygienic activity. Many of the city's adult residents, in turn, likely had little more than a vague and indirect familiarity with that discourse. The poverty that characterized the bulk of the population meant that most Cariocas could not afford to consult a formally trained physician. Equally important, even as late as 1906, fully one-third (33 percent) of Rio de Janeiro's inhabitants aged fifteen or older were illiterate.[49] Even if, by chance, a manual on the hygienic use of sea baths fell into their hands, they could not have read it.

Before 1888, the illiterate population included nearly all slaves who worked and lived in Rio de Janeiro and who accounted for nearly 40 percent of the city's population in 1849 and 16 percent in 1872.[50] Like Rio de Janeiro's free inhabitants, slaves also went bathing. It is not impossible that some slaves learned that bathing was supposedly good for their health. An enslaved maid who accompanied her mistress when she went to the beach to take "hygienic" baths might begin to imitate her mistress and comment with other slaves on the health benefits of sea-bathing.[51] However, the majority of all slaves in Rio de Janeiro in the mid-nineteenth century were Africans. Certainly, on at least some occasions when slaves and their children went bathing, cultural traditions originating in Africa (and having nothing to do with learned treatises defended at Rio de Janeiro's medical school) influenced their decision to enter the water. Yet the existing literature on nineteenth-century Afro-Carioca culture says nothing specifically about sea-bathing.[52]

Even when Africans and their descendants immersed themselves in the bay to deal with health problems, their decisions to do so may have been entirely unrelated to what was then regarded as formal medicine. Rio de Janeiro had no shortage of *curandeiros* (folk-healers), *feiticeiros* (spell-casters), and other practitioners of alternative medicines whose clients included not only slaves but patients of every social class. From the available sources, it is unclear whether any of those unofficial doctors prescribed sea-bathing. But, many years later, in the early 1930s, some of the bathers who frequented Virtudes beach (a prolongation of Santa Luzia beach) went there for reasons linked to Afro-Brazilian religion or because they were following recommendations made by curandeiros who prescribed early morning immersions to cure syphilis and gonorrhea.[53]

It is also necessary to take into account European cultural traditions. Although Alain Corbin stresses the strict medical regulation of sea-bathing in eighteenth- and early nineteenth-century Europe, he does note that, in several parts of that continent, from the Baltic to the Mediterranean, the practice retained its "playful" character long after physicians began prescribing saltwater immersions for therapeutic purposes.[54] Corbin does not mention Portugal, but in 1816, Louis-François de Tollenare observed that, in Lisbon, "the young and the old of both sexes surrender themselves to the pleasure of sea-bathing." "The most proper ladies," he added, "take part in that pleasure." Some sixty years later, "peasants" flocked to Figueira da Foz after the end of the harvest and after the end of the fashionable season at that Portuguese bathing resort. Known as *banhistas de alforje* (roughly, saddle-bag bathers), they stood out for their humble origins and also because they followed their own bathing habits. Even so, the days that they spent at the shore represented for them "some of the best moments . . . of their lives." About a fifth of Rio de Janeiro's population recorded in the 1872 and 1906 censuses had been born in Portugal, and these immigrants surely included at least some banhistas de alforje.[55] Finally, Indigenous influences, though undoubtedly diluted by time, may have also helped shape Carioca bathing habits. In the sixteenth century, Jean de Léry noted that the Indigenous peoples who lived near and around Guanabara Bay knew how to swim well and regularly entered the water.[56]

Recreation and Sociability

For all these reasons, it will not do to analyze sea-bathing in nineteenth- and early twentieth-century Rio de Janeiro relying only on the recommendations made by hygienists and other physicians. And, if we set those prescriptive texts aside, there is no shortage of sources to indicate that sea-bathing at the time was *not* merely a "medical prescription," only for the sick; for many Cariocas, it was already a form of "recreation" that provided opportunities for amusement and sociability. Those sources begin with one of the best-known novels in Brazilian literature: *Dom Casmurro* (1899) by Machado de Assis. In scenes set in 1871, the muscular and anything-but-sickly Escobar regularly goes bathing in Flamengo. In the 1860s and 1870s, Machado published short stories in which romance begins quite literally in the water. Thus, in the summer, Marcelina, the heroine of "A chave" (The Key, 1878–1879), goes early every morning with her father and a slave boy (*moleque*) to Flamengo. There, she changes in a tent and then dives into the water. Her father remains on the beach, sitting on a chair, reading a newspaper, and watching over her. The young, healthy, and attractive Marcelina is an accomplished and overly bold swimmer, which gets her into trouble when the bay suddenly becomes rough. She knows other bathers who regularly frequent Flamengo and speaks with them in the water. Likewise, it is in the water that she meets the story's male protagonist, who will become her suitor.[57]

Machado's descriptions of bathing in Flamengo match those of other nonfictional sources. For example, the British diplomat William Gore Ouseley, who was in Rio de Janeiro in the 1830s and again in the early 1840s, noted that "whole families" could be seen "in the hot season" "enjoying the invigorating and safe bathing afforded" by the sheltered cove in Botafogo. Kidder and Fletcher also used the verb *to enjoy* when, in 1857, they described bathing at the beach in Flamengo. "During the bathing season (from November to March)," they remarked, "a lively scene is witnessed each morning." Before dawn, a "stream of men, women, and children" arrived at that beach "to enjoy a bath in the clear salt water." Some women went alone, accompanied only by their slaves, who set up changing tents on the sand. In other cases, "men and women, hand in hand, enter[ed] the cool, sparkling element," while children ran along the beach, shouting in delight every time a larger wave broke on the shore.[58] The two North American missionaries thus stressed the pleasure of sea-bathing.

The *Revista Illustrada*, in turn, characterized bathing not as therapy but, rather, as a "fashion." *Crônicas* (periodic columns about society and culture) published in the magazine in the early 1880s noted that Flamengo's beach was a gathering spot for "the cream, the *gratin*," of Carioca society at the start of the summer. Without singling out any particular beach, the 1888 *Folhinha Laemmert* made similar observations. Sea-bathing, it remarked, had come to be regarded as reflective of "good taste in polite society [*de bom-tom*]," adding that "every morning," men and women crowded the bayshore "from Santa Luzia to the far end of Flamengo." Bathing was one of the "amusements" that Rio de Janeiro had to offer.[59]

The evidence about the city's bathing establishments points in the same direction. Beyond any doubt, some Cariocas frequented those establishments under doctors' orders to deal with health problems, and requests to open such establishments generally stressed the health benefits that they would bring to the city's population. But that does not mean that Rio de Janeiro's beaches were "little hospitals." In fact, sometimes, the requests put the emphasis on not therapeutic sea-bathing but, instead, recreation. For instance, in an 1888 request (which was denied), Francisco de Sales Torres Homem submitted a project to build a 111-meter-long pier with a pavilion in Botafogo Cove. The pier, which would have been used for bathing, would also offer various "amusements"; thus, it would hold concerts, rent recreational rowboats, sponsor rowing competitions, and house a café-restaurant. The project took its inspiration from the pleasure piers that had already become common at English seaside resorts.[60]

The possibility of attracting customers interested in amusement also occurred to the owners of a bathing barge that opened in 1873. Its large, covered men's pool was "furnished with every type of apparatus for gymnastics." There, according to the magazine *O Mosquito*, while swinging from trapezes and suspended rings, men amused themselves by engaging in "amphibicrobatic exercises [*exercícios anfibicrobáticos*]" (i.e., amphibious acrobatic exercises). After such exercises, they could join the female bathers and satisfy their hunger at the "splendidly served buffet" offered on the barge. On board, bathers could also enjoy "a large awning for strolling" and a "recreation room [*sala de recreio*]." The barge's name, in this context, is revealing: Grande Palácio Flutuante (Grand Floating Palace). That is not the name of a hospital or clinic.[61] Even more revealing is the name of one of the city's largest casas de banho, which opened in Flamengo in the mid-1880s: Ao High-Life (To the High Life). *High life* is an eighteenth- and nineteenth-century British expression referring to the "fast" living of upper-class sporting circles, hardly suitable for a hospital.[62]

Finally, we can turn to contemporary descriptions of bathing at the establishments at Boqueirão do Passeio and at other beaches, including those published in 1881 in the *Gazeta do Banho*.[63] The descriptions almost always mention sickly bathers, but they do not stress therapy; the emphasis falls instead on the pleasure of bathing as a social activity. Thus, according to the descriptions, the first bathers began arriving at four in the morning, when the establishments opened. Some arrived alone—not only men, but also "pale ladies wearing capes," who carried their bathing costumes in a basket. In other cases, they were groups of friends, couples, or "entire families" with children in tow who also took with them "sleepy" free or enslaved maids. On arriving, they had to pay the price of a "bath"; that is, the price of renting a changeroom. Bathers who had taken out a "subscription" for thirty baths could reserve one of the second-story rooms, which were apparently regarded as the best. Whatever the floor, the rooms, furnished with little more than a chair, a mirror, and a few hangers, were generally quite small. At one house built at Santa Luzia beach in the 1890s, they measured only 1.5 by 1.5 meters.[64] Once in the rooms, bathers changed into their costumes. If they did not own bathing attire, at some establishments they could rent it at an additional cost.[65]

Having changed, the bathers entered the water. Some establishments maintained for that purpose small docks, which allowed bathers to jump or dive directly into the sea and to avoid "gradually entering the water, which so many people find painful." Entering the water slowly was, the *Gazeta do Banho* noted in 1881, "a practice rightly condemned by most physicians concerned with hygiene," because when the chilly water reached "the upper parts of the body," the resulting "painful sensations" led some bathers to scream and even to return to the sand. They could not stand "the horrible spasms, the epigastric anxieties, [and] the breathing problems" that they experienced. Medical recommendations did not, however, always determine behavior. On the one hand, as the *Gazeta do Banho* also noted, many bathers preferred "gradual immersion" to allow their bodies to grow used to the water's cool temperature. On the other, photos from the 1910s caught bathers jumping and diving from a dock at Santa Luzia beach. Once in the sea—judging from cartoons published in illustrated magazines and from photos of Santa Luzia beach in the 1910s—some bathers swam, floated, or dove under the waves while others remained standing up or held onto the ropes attached to the diving docks. Those who could do so prolonged their bathing. Thus, "young men employed in commercial firms," "with one eye on the clock," sought "to spend more time in the water" and still "arrive early at work" (figures 2.3, 2.4, and 2.5.).[66]

FIGURE 2.3.
Divers at Santa Luzia Beach, 1914. *Careta* (11.4.1914), n.p.

FIGURE 2.4.
Male Bathers at Santa Luzia Beach, 1914. *Careta* (11.4.1914), n.p.

FIGURE 2.5.
Timid Female Bathers at Santa Luzia Beach, 1914. *Careta* (11.4.1914), n.p.

On getting out of the water, bathers returned to their rooms, where they dried off and changed. If they wished to pay more, at some establishments, they could take a freshwater "bath" (most likely in the form of a shower). But that does not seem to have been common, and not only because it entailed an additional cost. A sea bath, according to contemporary notions, cleaned the body; it would have made little sense then to take another bath to wash an already clean body. "No fresh water afterwards," declared Laura Oliveira Rodrigo Octavio, when, in her memoirs, she recalled her experiences at Boqueirão do Passeio beach at the start of the twentieth century: "nothing more than simply dusting off the sand." Dried salt on the skin, moreover, was believed to be good for the bather's health.[67]

Before returning home or going on to work, many bathers who frequented Boqueirão do Passeio stopped by the open-air bar (botequim) covered by a large awning, located next to that beach. There, they would drink "a small mug of café-au-lait," accompanied by a "brioche" and sometimes also by a shot of brandy. The establishments in Flamengo provided a wider range of food and drink options. Thus, Ao High-Life had a "restaurant," while another establishment at the same beach offered not only "coffee, cognac, and liqueurs" but also a "buffet."[68]

At these bathing establishments, people met friends and made new friendships on their way to the changerooms, while in the water, and over morning coffee. As the *Gazeta do Banho* observed, "numerous are the families who gather" at Boqueirão do Passeio, "establishing thereby new relationships" with other families. Thus, at the peak hours, the bathing houses at Boqueirão do Passeio saw, according to a 1904 article by João do Rio, "a feverish coming-and-going . . . , laughter, the shaking of hands, [and] cordiality of the type that results in long-lasting ties." The sea during those hours was "completely filled with bathers . . . a happy crowd, shouting" and exchanging "gossip" and "rumors." In another article, João do Rio referred to the "joyous multitude" that flocked to the city's beaches, where bathers spent their time "diving [under the water] with delight" and "breathing in voluptuously the salt air." "No degree of sadness," he added, could "resist the enchantment of [such] animated scenes."[69]

The animation, as an 1896 article in *O Paiz* noted, could take on an almost carnivalesque character. Once they had put on "that flannel jersey and pair of trunks," many men felt like "the most devilish boy." "There are gentlemen who go bathing at the Boqueirão beach just for the pleasure of making a ruckus [*matinada*] in public," a practice that "has altered the seriousness of our habits." Everywhere, in the changerooms, on the diving dock, and in the water, those "gentlemen" in their bathing costumes shouted, whistled, sang songs, told jokes, and reenacted scenes from plays. Some even "bark[ed] and bray[ed]," imitating dogs and donkeys. "Carnival," the article concluded, "is constant" at that beach.[70]

Bathing also offered opportunities for flirting and courtship. In an 1878 crônica, for instance, when a mother wakes her two daughters to go bathing at Boqueirão do Passeio beach at four in the morning, they leap enthusiastically from their beds. "Oh! Chiquinha! How wonderful!" says one of the girls; "I am going to see my Arturzinho." "And I," her sister responds, "my Carlinhos." Bathing, in fact, allowed for an unusual type of flirting disguised as a crab attack. When a young man spotted an attractive young woman or one in whom he was already interested, he would dive under the water and pinch her ankle. After jumping and screaming, the young woman would explain to her mother that a crab had bit her. Mothers, it seems, did not always find the explanation convincing. And, sometimes, according to the *Gazeta do Banho*, the young men missed their targets and ended up overturning the mothers in the water (figure 1.1 shows what may be a crab attack, though the submerged man appears to be kissing the woman's hand).[71]

Moral Ambiguities and Social Tensions

Men exchanging jokes, imitating donkeys and dogs, and flirting (disguised as crab attacks)—those are not hospital scenes. On the contrary, what we have here is a public space for a certain type of sociability and also one of the few activities that at the time allowed for an informal mixing of the sexes in public. That mixing, moreover, took place among partially undressed men and women. Here, it is important to point out that, until the mid- or late 1880s, men in Rio de Janeiro generally did not wear bathing costumes of the sort that most people today would associate with sea-bathing in the past: a pair of long trunks that might cover the knees and a jersey with or without sleeves. Instead, many men went bathing shirtless and wearing only drawers (trunks), which, judging from contemporary cartoons, were the size of a pair of boxer shorts and were often loose-fitting (see figures 1.1 and 2.7). An 1872 cartoon compared a pair of bathing drawers with the proverbial fig leaf and, in its caption, wondered which was "the more decent?" (figure 2.6, top center). Furthermore, as an anonymous observer pointed out in

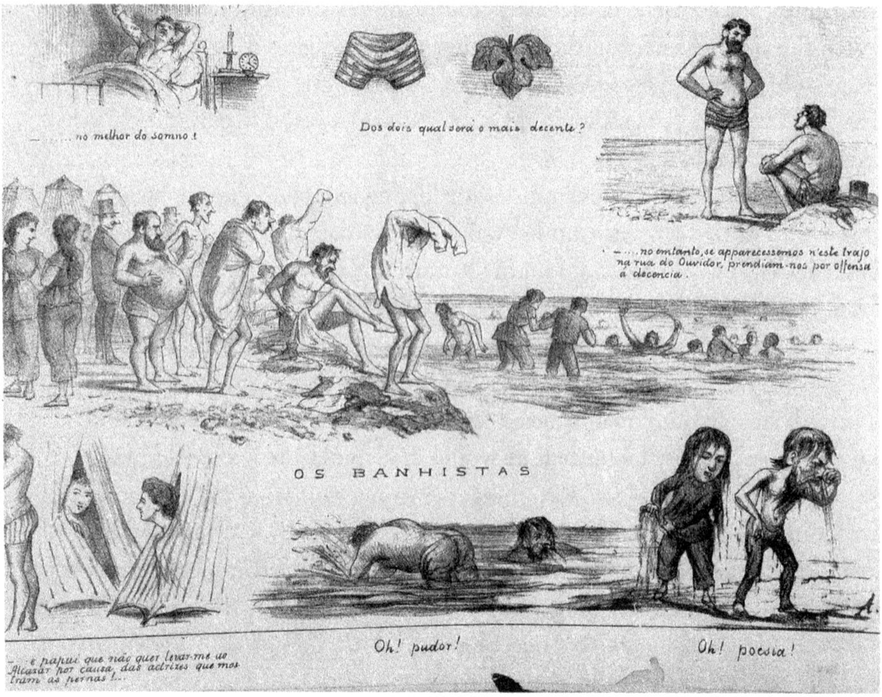

FIGURE 2.6. Debating Decency in Sea-Bathing Attire, 1872. *Mosquito* (9.3.1872), 8.

1878, those "short . . . tiny trunks [*calçõezinhos . . . curtinhos*]," often made of knit cotton, when wet, could easily become almost "transparent." Women, as would be expected, dressed far more modestly while bathing. In the 1870s, it was common for them to wear a costume that today would look like a pair of pajamas: a blouse that covered the hips, but with short sleeves, and loose pants that did not always hide the ankle; they might even show "a bit of leg" (figure 2.5).[72] Although bulky, that attire was not in any way comparable to what "respectable" women wore in other public settings. The same held true for men, whether they bathed in long trunks and a jersey or only in drawers.

Moreover, sea-bathing in nineteenth- and early twentieth-century Rio de Janeiro took place mainly at urban beaches, in a public space and in full view of passersby on adjacent streets, in what was not only the national capital but also Brazil's largest city, a major commercial center, and the chief port of entry for European travelers. Likewise, many bathers, wearing their costumes and wrapped in sheets, walked down some of the city's main streets on their way to and from the beach. Thus, since at least the mid-nineteenth century onward, sea-bathing had begun to alter the rules for the proper use of public space in Rio de Janeiro. Or, better, sea-bathing, as would later be the case with beach-going, generated its own rules for the use of urban public space—not only in the water and on the sand but also on nearby streets.

The 1872 cartoon drew attention to the differences between the rules that governed sea-bathing and those that applied to other public spaces in the city. In one scene in the cartoon, two shoeless and shirtless men who wear only short bathing trunks are talking. One of them remarks, "If we were to appear in this attire on Ouvidor Street [then the heart of most fashionable shopping district], we would be arrested for indecency." A second scene in the same cartoon shows two young women looking out from changing tents at a male bather dressed in nothing more than a pair of short drawers. One of the young women says to the other, "And father does not want to take me to the Alcazar [a theater known for its risqué shows] because of the actresses who show their legs" (figure 2.6, top right and bottom left).[73]

The second scene also deals indirectly with the presence of women in public spaces. Since Gilberto Freyre's *Sobrados e mucambos* (1936), the scholarly literature has recognized that, in nineteenth-century Brazil, the public space of "the street" was, for the most part, a masculine space, and that "respectable" women had only limited access to that space. To be sure, as Anton Rosenthal points out, it is easy to exaggerate the distinction between the public space of "the street" and the private space of "the house"; in practice, "house" and "street" "function[ed] as two points on a spectrum of behavior." More recent studies do indeed show that class differences shaped that distinction and that, in the nineteenth and early twentieth centuries, women gradually gained greater access to "the street." Those studies, nevertheless, also show that, even in the first decades of the twentieth century, gender-based rules continued to restrict women's access to public spaces.[74] By contrast, Schlichthorst in the 1820s and Kidder and Fletcher some thirty years later observed women who, accompanied only by a slave maid, left their homes before dawn or in the early morning to go bathing. Everything indicates that those women were white, "respectable," and not by any means poor; after all, they owned slaves. Kidder and Fletcher in fact called the women who went bathing alone in Flamengo "ladies."[75] Thus, like the 1872 cartoon, these travelers' observations suggest that, where bathing was concerned, different rules governed women's access to public space.

The moral ambiguities that surrounded sea-bathing derived in large measure from the fact that the practice allowed men and women to mix and interact in public in a state of relative undress. Partly for that reason, nineteenth-century European seaside resorts set aside some stretches of their beaches for men and reserved other stretches exclusively for women. Segregation by sex was enforced even as late as the 1910s at Montevideo beaches.[76] Rio de Janeiro's bathing barges also imposed rigid segregation by sex to preserve "decency" and "morality": men bathed on one side of the barge and women on the other. The regulations of the barge that operated in the 1850s, furthermore, prohibited a man from entering a woman's cabin "unless he first declares his address, making it possible to verify that he is her husband. Even then," the regulations stipulated, "that concession will be granted only in cases where ladies need their husband's aid."[77] By contrast, a lack of segregation by sex was the rule at the city's beaches: women and men bathed together.[78]

Moreover, since at least Schlichthorst's time, one enduring attraction that sea-bathing held for men was to watch women bathe. The city's beaches, by the late nineteenth century and probably before then as well, attracted "*mirones*"; that is, voyeuristic men who, fully clothed, went there only to ogle female bathers.[79] The bulky costumes made of serge, baize, and flannel that women wore at the time would seem extraordinarily modest today. But that did not deter the mirones from staring at female bathers. They knew that, once wet, those costumes clung to the body. As an 1882 crônica observed, "when a young woman leaves the water . . . therein lies the crux of the matter: the bathing costume adheres to the body"; as a result, "one can spot many finely shaped waists [and] many well-rounded breasts." "And then," the crônica added, "the wet locks, falling like a cascade over well-sculpted shoulders, recall our first mother . . . in Paradise . . . but dressed in a bathing costume." The same emphasis on the erotic appears in Machado de Assis's description of Marcelina, the main female character in "A chave": "Behold . . . the cut (*talhe*) [of her body], the loving curve of her hips, the bit of leg between her ankles and the cuff of her pants." Machado also called on his readers to imagine Marcelina in the water with "the flannel clinging to her bust."[80] Precisely because bathing costumes, whether wet or not, made it easier to evaluate accurately the "cut" of a woman's body, the *Revista Illustrada* recommended that men choose their brides at the city's beaches; there, they would not run "the risk of being fooled by cotton padding."[81]

At those beaches, some of the magazine's male readers might feel tempted to engage in crab-attack flirting: young men, wearing only short trunks and, thus, naked from the waist up, pinching the ankles of young partially undressed women—nothing could be further from the staid rules that governed respectable courtship in other contexts. Young men were not alone in taking advantage of the salt water. There were also, João do Rio noted, the "frightened ladies" who held on "as fast as nails" to the muscular arms of the banhistas nadadores (lifeguards) employed by Rio de Janeiro's bathing establishments. Not only were those "frightened ladies" latched onto a man other than their husband, but they were doing so in a state of partial undress in public and with a man who was also less than fully clothed.[82]

As the *Folhinha Laemmert* for 1888 pointed out, Rio de Janeiro's beaches often presented "gay and even quite risqué scenes in which our damsels learn to swim and learn many other things useful and necessary for domestic life." The *Folhinha* did not explain what those "other things" were, leaving the matter to the reader's imagination. Readers lacking in imagination could consult the city's illustrated magazines, which sometimes printed suggestive cartoons dealing with sea-bathing. Or they might buy a copy of *Rio Nú* (Naked Rio), a pornographic magazine that, between 1898 and 1915, published several short stories and cartoons that took sea-bathing as their theme. In the pages of *Rio Nú*, the city's beaches offered not only the possibility of seeing attractive partially undressed women but also opportunities for sex, including adulterous sex.[83] Likewise, in the early twentieth century, the bathing establishments at Boqueirão do Passeio and Santa Luzia beaches began to gain a dubious reputation. To watch women undress, men opened small holes in the thin walls that separated the changerooms. Then, on the beach or in the water, they would publicly comment on what they had seen.[84]

The moral ambiguities that characterized sea-bathing did not, however, stem only from what men saw or hoped to see at the city's bathing establishments and beaches. Women at the same beaches were exposed to male bathers who, as we have seen, wore little more than revealing trunks. It should, therefore, come as little surprise that the authorities more than once confronted the question of what constituted the acceptable, "moral," and "civilized" use of public space by bathers—not only in the water and on the sand but also on the streets. The question came up for the first time, it seems, in the late 1830s. Until then, as in eighteenth- and early nineteenth-century Europe, men in Rio de Janeiro generally bathed naked. The handsome and rakish Emperor Pedro I not only bathed in the buff but also stripped in public "in front of everyone." On one occasion, before entering the water in Flamengo, he made a point of showing his "completely nude" body to a group of women who were looking out of a window in the Prussian consul's house. Although more discreet than the emperor, Schlichthorst also bathed in the nude. "I undress under the flowering orange trees," he wrote in describing his morning sea baths in Flamengo; "then, without anyone noticing, I drop my last piece of clothing and, with a leap, throw myself into the water."[85] When the municipal council revised the city's code of ordinances in 1838, it prohibited nude sea-bathing during daytime hours. The new ordinances required that all bathers—men and women, free and enslaved—dress "so as not to offend morality."[86]

Notwithstanding this bylaw, many poor free men and male slaves continued, even in the second half of the nineteenth century, to strip down completely and then plunge into the bay at all hours of the day. Although not always with the same intensity, the police waged a long-term campaign against that practice by taking into custody naked bathers. To cite only a few examples: In January 1857, they arrested a slave named Manoel who was bathing in the nude at Lapa beach. Less than a month later, a block inspector (a local civilian police official) became "indignant" when he saw twenty-odd naked men and boys bathing at Boqueirão do Passeio beach at four o'clock in the afternoon. He summoned the police, who caught five of them; the others managed to escape. The authorities had greater success in January 1864, when they arrested, on a single occasion, two male slaves and ten free men who were "cooling off" "by bathing in mythological [i.e., non-existent] clothes" at another beach. In 1885, the slave Dionísio likewise found himself under arrest when the police caught him bathing naked in Flamengo.[87]

Reports about men arrested for bathing with nothing on also appear in newspapers from the 1910s and 1920s, an indication that, even in those decades, some lower-class Carioca men saw nothing wrong in going bathing naked in public. Or perhaps they did see something wrong but simply could not afford a bathing suit. Even Harry Franck, an American who worked as a secret inspector for a tramway company in the mid-1910s, preferred to bathe in the nude for reasons of cost. The line to Ipanema, at the time a distant and almost deserted beach, was "particularly attractive" for Franck, because there he "could take a dip in the sea between inspecting trips without going to the expense of acquiring a bathing-suit."[88]

The repression of nude bathing was part of a more general effort by the police and other authorities to control and regulate the behavior of lower-class

Cariocas, including, before 1888, slaves. It also fit into a broader project to "civilize" and to "Europeanize" Rio de Janeiro that dates back at least to the arrival of the Portuguese Court in 1808. Indeed, one of the first measures taken after João and the court took up residence in the city was to prohibit recently imported, shackled African slaves from trudging naked through the streets, from the quays where they were unloaded to the warehouses where they would be put up for sale.[89] However, as noted in chapter 1, efforts to "Europeanize" and "civilize" the city were slow-moving; they would not gain momentum until the first years of the twentieth century.

Police repression at the city's beaches that fit into that "civilizing" project did not only target nude bathing. In the late nineteenth century, the police also arrested "indecently" dressed bathers. Santiago Stephane, for instance, found himself in jail in January 1877 after a policeman caught him bathing "in indecent attire" at Boqueirão do Passeio beach. One year later, the police chief went bathing at the same beach, where he became "truly indignant on seeing some men dressed like Father Adam just before the fall from grace." Therefore, "taking into account" the presence of "families" at that beach, and more generally, "concerns about moral propriety [*pudor*]," he issued orders requiring male bathers to be "decently dressed." The orders provoked a protest of sorts by a man who showed up at the same beach in short trunks and without a shirt, but wearing a frock coat, a tie, gloves, a top hat, and shoes. Although, obviously, the police chief was not proposing that men wear formal dress while bathing, it is unclear what he considered "decently dressed." Cartoons published between 1880 and 1887 do not clarify the matter; they continue to show men who bathed at the city's beaches wearing nothing more than a pair of short trunks (see figure 2.7).[90]

While little ambiguity obtained when it came to arresting nude bathers, matters were far less clear when it came to determining whether a bather was dressed "so as not to offend morality." Even the police chief recognized in 1880 that the 1838 ordinances failed to specify what did and did not constitute "decent" bathing attire. The police, it is true, could invoke national legislation in arresting nude or scantily dressed bathers. The 1830 Criminal Code and the 1890 Penal Code classified as a crime any act practiced in public that "offends morality and propriety [*bons costumes*]" and "obscene exhibitions, acts, and gestures . . . in a public place or a place frequented by the public that . . . outrage and scandalize society." But the two codes did not spell out in detail which acts should be regarded as crimes against public morality.[91] Thus, neither the authorities nor bathers could know for certain what sort of costume would "offend . . . propriety" or "scandalize society."

The issue was even more complex because, as drowning reports and other sources make clear, a lack of social segregation characterized Rio de Janeiro's beaches at the time. "Family" bathers, members of "good society" who saw themselves as worthy of respect and who demanded recognition of their real or imagined higher social rank, shared the city's main bathing beaches with poor free workers, with prostitutes (*mulheres de vida irregular*), and before 1888, with slaves. As Artur Azevedo observed in the mid-1880s, "serious folks," "rude adolescent boys," "married ladies," and "young damsels" all bathed at Boqueirão do Passeio beach at the same early morning hour. So, too, did "ulcerous mulattas" from Senhor dos Passos Street, where low-end prostitutes lived and worked. They walked to the beach, according to Azevedo, dressed in "white-trimmed blue sacks made of thin wool," "with their hips swaying." The "rude adolescent boys" who frequented Boqueirão do Passeio beach aimed their jokes indiscriminately at both the mulatta prostitutes and the "honest ladies" who went bathing there. In the same decade, according to the *Revista Illustrada*, "the cream" of Carioca society bathed at Flamengo's beach. But that did not prevent slaves and the free poor from also entering the water there.[92]

The lack of segregation in bathing did not momentarily erase social distinctions, nor did it make Rio de Janeiro's beaches into spaces for a harmonious mixing between bathers of different classes. On the contrary, it generated tensions that led to complaints made by "families," who, through the press, repeatedly demanded that the authorities "police" and "moralize" bathing in the city. In some cases, they complained about the "abuses" practiced by other bathers: the "scenes lacking in decorum" that those bathers staged on the sand and in the water, the "obscene" language that they used, and the "insults" with which they provoked "families." The *Jornal do Commercio* warned in 1873 that, if the police did not put an end to such "abuses," a "serious conflict" could easily result.[93]

Above all, the complaints targeted the men, both free and enslaved, who bathed in the nude or in "indecent" suits. On at least thirteen occasions between 1853 and 1862, the *Correio Mercantil* called the authorities' attention to the "scandal" seen at Rio de Janeiro's beaches: men of "all colors," according to the paper, went bathing "without wearing so much as a loincloth." The *Correio* was not the only newspaper to pass on such complaints. Thus, in 1861, the *Jornal do*

Commercio "once again" requested that the police "put a halt to the scandalous practice of bathing at all times of the day in a highly indecent state." The newspaper reported that, at Saúde beach, "an entire family" had recently been "insulted by a group of slaves" after the head of the family "had warned them about the indecency of their nudity and the looseness [*desenvoltura*] of their language and gestures." A decade later, in a letter sent to the weekly *Comédia Social*, a group of "family fathers" denounced the "mature boys [*rapagões*], aged sixteen to eighteen," who went bathing naked at the same beach. They also complained about the men who frequented that beach wearing only "short" "underwear [*cuecas*] . . . that barely cover[ed] their hips." According to the letter, which requested police intervention, one of those men a few days before had dared to compliment a "family"; in exchange, he received from the head of the "family" "two good blows with a cane" to his back. Seven years later, *O Cruzeiro*, having received complaints from residents of Flamengo, drew the authorities' attention to the bathers who, at that neighborhood's beach, wore "inappropriate and indecent attire," "offending the moral propriety [*pudor*]" of respectable "families."[94]

Yet, the same "family" bathers who made those complaints engaged in a morally ambiguous activity that attracted "rowdy young men [*gaiatos*]," poor free workers, "carousing revellers [*pândegos*]," slaves, and prostitutes, as well as voyeuristic mirones. It was, of course, one thing to arrest a slave or a poor free worker for bathing in the nude or in "indecent" attire and quite another thing to arrest a "family" bather for not being dressed "so as not to offend morality." But the lack of segregation at Rio de Janeiro's beaches meant that the authorities could not always readily discern a bather's social standing. Moreover, the "ulcerous mulattas" from Senhor dos Passos Street were not alone in occupying the public space of the city's streets in a state of partial undress as they walked to and from the beach; some bathers belonging to "good society" did the same.

As a result, "family" bathers who claimed to be members of "good society" could easily find themselves at odds with the police. This is clear from an 1885 incident at Boqueirão do Passeio beach that involved "distinguished merchants," "totally respectable ladies," and even a priest, which resulted in a controversy that would occupy the city's press for several days (figure 2.7).[95] In the incident, a *subdelegado* (an assistant supervising officer in charge of a police precinct) accused more than twenty men and women of undressing and dressing at that beach and of drying themselves "in a way that offend[ed]

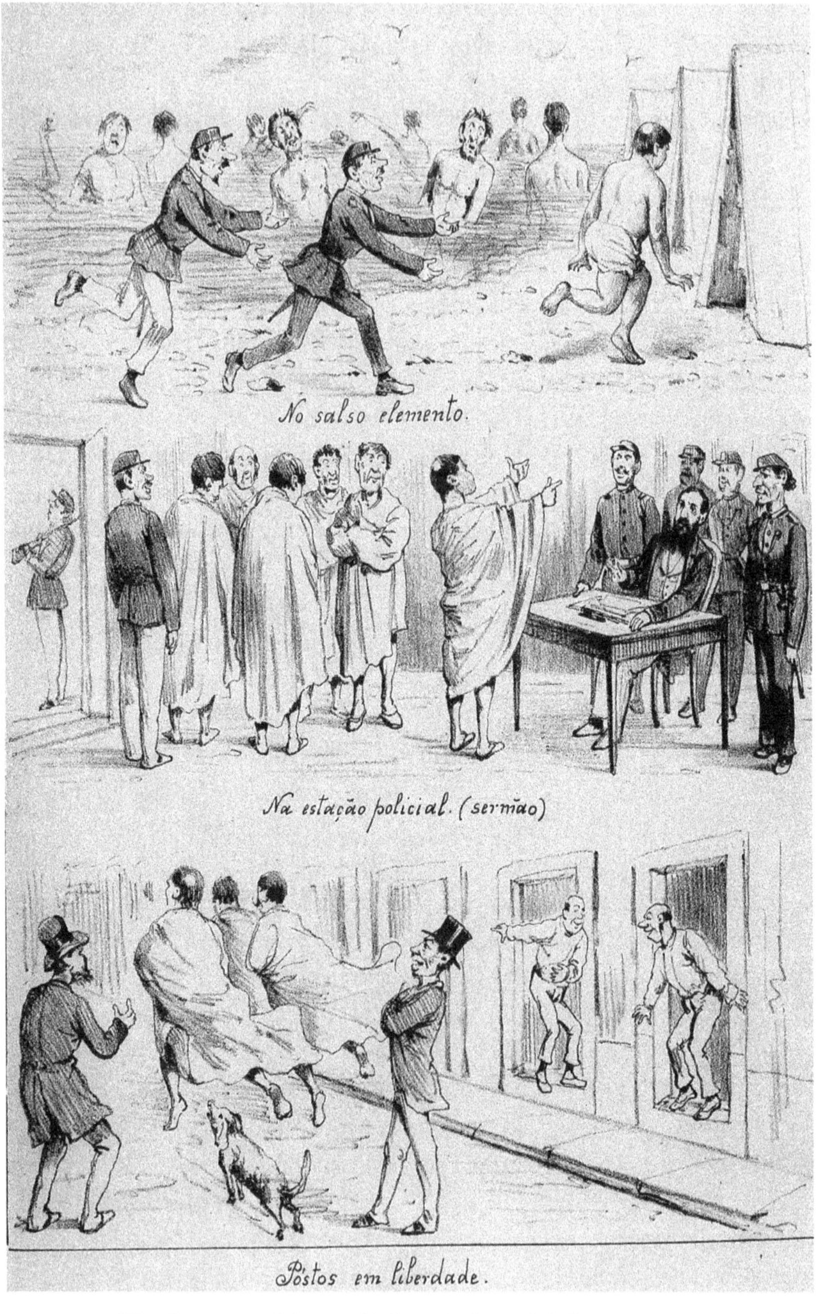
No salso elemento.
Na estação policial. (sermão)
Postos em liberdade.

FIGURE 2.7. The Controversial Arrest of Indecently Dressed Bathers, 1885. *Mequetrefe* (20.11.1885), 8.

public morality." He therefore required them, despite their protests, to walk several blocks in their bathing costumes to the central police station; there, he gave them a severe scolding and then sent them on their way.

Some of the bathers scolded by the subdelegado resided on or near the Cais da Glória (Glória Quay), regarded at the time as a fashionable address, and classified themselves as "distinguished gentlemen and respectable ladies." Rather than dropping the matter, they reacted to the incident through a series of articles, some paid, in the press. Although they acknowledged that the police were charged with "not allowing bathers to engage in improper behavior or to go bathing in inadequate attire," they insisted that they had not changed on the beach. On the contrary, living in the nearby neighborhood of Glória, they had no need to undress or dress on the sand. They instead put on their bathing costumes at home and then walked to the Boqueirão do Passeio wearing "sheets" over their costumes while on the street. Going to the beach "ready to enter the sea" was, they claimed, a "customary right" that they had long exercised and that no authority before had questioned. The subdelegado had indeed questioned that "right" because, in his view, walking through the streets in bathing attire "was an offense against morality."[96] The bathers further accused the subdelegado of "excessive zeal" and characterized his actions as "scandalous," "violent," "revolting," and "arbitrary." The subdelegado denied the accusations and tried to disqualify his accusers. He pointed out that the bathers required to go to the central police station included "three women (of black color) [*três mulheres (de cor preta)*] who live[d] on Senhor dos Passos Street and who [had] also undressed and dressed behind a sheet at the beach." The subdelegado thus insinuated that the bathers who complained about his actions had been consorting with Afro-Brazilian prostitutes. The three Black women present that morning perhaps did earn their living from prostitution; that would not be impossible. Nevertheless, the "respectable" status of the bathers who made the complaints is strongly suggested not only by the references to a priest, to "distinguished merchants," to "ladies," and to "families," but also by the simple fact that those bathers were able to have their complaints against the subdelegado repeatedly published in some of Rio de Janeiro's major newspapers for nearly a week.

C. C. Andrews, who had served as US consul in Rio de Janeiro in the early 1880s, observed in 1889 that "sea-bathing [was] very popular in Rio de Janeiro."[97] Indeed, bathing's popularity attracted to the same beaches and often at the same time of the day men and women of all colors and of different classes, which resulted in a close social mixing in the water and on the sand. That mixing did not, however, eliminate class distinctions even for a few predawn or early morning hours; nor did it transform those beaches into "democratic spaces." Very much to the contrary, the mixing gave rise to tensions. Evidence of those tensions comes from the repeated complaints by "family" bathers, who called on the authorities to "police" and "moralize" bathing. The police, in turn, did arrest naked and scantily dressed male bathers as part of a broader project to discipline Rio de Janeiro's lower class and to "civilize" the city. But they failed to put a complete halt to the practice of bathing in "mythological clothes." Even in the 1910s and 1920s, some men persisted in entering the water wearing nothing at all. Other men would, well into the twentieth century, continue to bathe in what the authorities regarded as "indecent" and "immoral" attire.

Yet, perhaps more important, sea-bathing in nineteenth- and early twentieth-century Rio de Janeiro already displayed some of the features that would later characterize beach-going. For example, sea-bathing, far from being merely a therapeutic activity, offered ample opportunities for sociability; it often served as a form of recreation and as a means of momentarily escaping the summer's heat; and it allowed for the public exhibition of partially undressed bodies, which resulted both in a more or less explicit emphasis on the sensual and the erotic and in moral ambiguities. Sea-bathing, furthermore, generated, but not without conflicts, its own code for the use of urban public space—in the water, on the sand, and on nearby streets. Thus, if a "vocation for the beach," since the mid-twentieth century, has come to hold a special place in Rio de Janeiro's identity as a city, that "vocation" was built on a long prior history of sea-bathing within an urban context.

It should therefore come as no surprise that João do Rio tellingly described Boqueirão do Passeio beach in the late nineteenth century and at the start of the twentieth not as a "small hospital" but rather as "an open-air party." "A party"—the same expression appears in descriptions of the beach in Copacabana on sunny summer mornings in the late 1920s and early 1930s.[98] Nevertheless, major differences separated sea-bathing in the nineteenth and early twentieth centuries from the practice of beach-going that would develop in Rio de Janeiro in the 1920s. Neither Boqueirão do Passeio nor Flamengo in the 1880s or even in 1903 came close to simply representing an early version of Copacabana in 1928 or 1934, or Ipanema in the 1960s and 1970s. Still lacking at the time were the sun and a reasonably broad stretch of sand. The path that led some segments of Carioca society to discover sand and sun on the shores of the South Atlantic was not, however, a straight one. The next chapter, among other things, explores some of the twists and turns that that path took in the first decades of the twentieth century.

3

Dreaming of a Brazilian Biarritz

Social Geography and the Beaches

IN 1911, JOÃO DO RIO feared that residents of Rio de Janeiro were giving up the habit of sea-bathing. If that "Carioca custom" disappeared, the Brazilian capital, he believed, would be no different from any other large city in the world. His fears, however, proved unfounded. Five years later, in March 1916, he observed that Cariocas had a "passion for the sea" and that bathers crowded the city's beaches during the summer months. The following year, he published an article praising the beauty of Ipanema's beach. Shortly thereafter, he moved to Ipanema, at the time a new and still sparsely populated neighborhood on the city's southern edge.[1] João do Rio (1881–1921) did not live long enough to witness the shift from sea-bathing to beach-going, but in his lifetime, he did see some of the major changes that transformed Rio de Janeiro after the late nineteenth century. These changes unleashed trends that accelerated after his death and that directly and indirectly paved the way for the development of a recognizably modern form of beach-going in Copacabana and Ipanema in the mid- and late 1920s.

The following pages sketch out those changes and trends and show that they entrenched lasting divisions within Rio de Janeiro's social geography. They also gave rise, in the 1910s, to new social distinctions in sea-bathing, which, in Flamengo, became a prestigious activity. They also brought in their wake proposals to develop a European- or American-style seaside resort at Rio de Janeiro's oceanfront beaches that would cater to tourists and wealthy Cariocas. This chapter analyzes these proposals, however, to demonstrate that tourism had little influence in shaping the history of beach-going in twentieth-century Rio de Janeiro. Despite hopes at the time, neither Copacabana nor Ipanema ever became a Brazilian version of Biarritz, Ostend, Miami, or Deauville. Instead, the social distinctions in sea-bathing that emerged in tandem with the urban reforms undertaken by Mayor Francisco Pereira Passos, which made

Flamengo the chic beach of the 1910s, laid the groundwork for the development of beach-going in Copacabana in the 1920s.

A Changing Rio de Janeiro

On 13 May 1888, Princess Isabel, acting as regent for her father, Emperor Pedro II, who was overseas, signed the law that finally abolished slavery in Brazil. The law freed the fewer than 725,000 men and women who still remained in bondage throughout the country and ended an institution and a labor regime that had molded Brazilian society and sustained the country's economy for more than three centuries. Rio de Janeiro erupted into eight days of joyous celebration, "the greatest festival" that the Brazilian capital had ever seen, as Eduardo Silva puts it.[2] Eighteen months later, on 15 November 1889, with no upheaval and no popular participation (and no subsequent celebration), the military overthrew the monarchy in a bloodless coup, sending the sixty-four-year-old emperor and his family into exile and establishing a republican regime. That regime, commonly known today as the Old Republic, would last until 1930. While continuing to serve as the national capital, Rio de Janeiro ceased to be the Municipality of the Court; it became officially the Federal District.

TABLE 3.1. *Population of Rio de Janeiro, 1906–1960*

Year	*Urban Districts All Districts, and (after 1940)*	*Suburban Districts Including Rural Districts*
1906	621,933	805,335
1920	790,823	1,147,599
1940	1,597,956	1,764,141
1950	2,118,569	2,377,451
1960	3,198,591	3,281,908

No national census was carried out in 1930. The distinction between urban-suburban districts and rural districts follows Abreu, *Evolução*, 109. Sources: Brazil, *Recenseamento* (1906), 22, 27; Brazil, *Recenseamento* (1920), vol. 4, pt. 1, pp. 6–7; Brazil, *Recenseamento* (1940), série regional, pt. 16, p. 51; Brazil, *Recenseamento* (1950), série regional, vol. 25, t. 1, p. 64; Brazil, *Recenseamento* (1960), série regional, vol. 1, t. 12, pt. 1, p. 68–70.

By this time, Rio de Janeiro's population was growing rapidly (table 3.1). The population of the city's urban districts, which had stood at less than 230,000 in 1872, had surpassed 422,000 by 1890. Thirty years later, in 1920, the city boasted more than 790,000 inhabitants, by which time Rio de Janeiro was no longer simply a large city; it had begun to take on the proportions and features of a modern metropolis. Indeed, the 1920s saw the construction of the city's first skyscrapers, such as the 103-meter high Edifício A Noite, opened in 1929.[3] The number of skyscrapers in the city grew in later decades as the population of the Federal District's urban and suburban areas increased to just over 1.6 million inhabitants in 1940. Twenty years later, when the population in those areas had reached nearly 3.2 million, Rio de Janeiro was roughly four times larger than it had been in 1920.

The city's growth resulted in no small measure from migration. After abolition, numerous former slaves and poor men and women who had been free before 1888 moved to the city from the declining coffee-producing areas in the Paraíba Valley. After 1940, those fleeing extreme poverty in northeastern Brazil began to make their way to the city in large numbers. Immigration from overseas further contributed to Rio de Janeiro's growth, especially in the late nineteenth and early twentieth centuries. The foreign-born, numbering just over 111,900, accounted for 26 percent of all inhabitants in 1890. Although the Portuguese made up by far the single largest immigrant group, followed by Italians and Spaniards, immigrants also came from nearly every part of Europe as well as from the Middle East. The proportion of foreign-born among the Federal District's inhabitants declined to just under 14 percent by 1940, but their absolute number had increased to more than 217,000.[4]

The Brazilian capital attracted internal migrants and immigrants from overseas because, despite occasional downturns, its economy experienced long-term growth in the first half of the twentieth century. The expansion of government played a role in that growth. The number of civil servants employed by the national government underwent a fourfold increase after 1872 to reach about 40,000 in 1920. Of that total, 40 percent, or roughly 16,000, lived and worked in Rio de Janeiro. The size of the bureaucracy continued to increase in later years. Setting aside members of the military and the police forces, more than 61,000 Cariocas were employed in one capacity or another in public service at the national and local levels in 1960.[5]

Rio de Janeiro remained a major entrepôt for international trade. To be sure, coffee exports slumped in the 1880s and Santos, in the state of São Paulo, overtook Rio de Janeiro as the country's main port for the coffee trade in the 1890s, as production declined in the western Paraíba Valley. Increased coffee production in Minas Gerais and Espírito Santo, as well as in northern areas of Rio de Janeiro state allowed coffee exports through the city to rebound by the 1920s to nearly the peak levels of forty years earlier. A large share of everything that Brazil imported (39 percent in both 1905–1909 and 1925–1929), moreover, continued to pass through the city's harbor. The city also remained an important financial center. The Banco do Brasil, the country's largest bank, and several other major banks had their headquarters in Rio de Janeiro, which could, in addition, claim what was for many years Brazil's main stock exchange.[6]

The development of industry further contributed to the city's economic growth. A 1907 survey revealed that the Federal District ranked as Brazil's most important manufacturing center. The city in that year had more than 660 "industrial establishments," employing nearly 35,000 workers. Although some of these establishments were little more than workshops with only a handful of employees, their numbers also included several large factories, among them six textile mills, each with more than 750 workers; the largest mill employed 1,800 men and women. By 1920, the state of São Paulo had replaced the Federal District as the country's industrial center, but Rio de Janeiro still accounted for more than one-fifth (22 percent) of Brazil's industrial output in that year. The Federal District's factories by then had more than 56,000 workers on their payrolls.[7]

The worldwide economic crisis of 1929–1930 dealt a severe blow to Brazil's export-based economy. International prices for coffee and the country's other main export commodities plummeted and exports fell to less than 40 percent of their 1928 value by 1932. The ensuing economic crisis helped bring about the Revolution of 1930, which overthrew Brazil's oligarchic Old Republic (1889–1930) and brought to power Getúlio Vargas, who would head the national government until 1945. Although exports increased after 1933, the recovery in the 1930s was only partial; as late as 1939, exports still had not returned to their 1928 level. The 1930s, nevertheless, were not a decade of economic depression in Brazil. After contracting in 1931 and 1932, the country's gross domestic product grew rapidly during the rest of the decade. By 1939, it was 52 percent larger than in 1930. Industry registered even faster growth. Total industrial output increased by 86 percent over the course of the decade. Output continued to expand in later decades as Brazil underwent a full-fledged process of import-substitution industrialization.[8]

Part of that expansion took place in Rio de Janeiro. The 1940 national census found more than 4,160 industrial firms, employing 123,459 workers, in the Federal District. By 1950, Rio de Janeiro could claim 5,693 industrial firms with a labor force of more than 171,000 workers. Manufacturing at the time employed 24 percent of the city's economically active population, a larger share than either government or commerce. "Modern sectors" producing machinery, chemicals, plastics, pharmaceuticals, and electrical and metallurgical materials led this growth after 1940.[9] Nevertheless, Rio de Janeiro's share of Brazil's total industrial output declined from 22 percent in 1940 to 9 percent by 1970, reflecting the even more rapid development of industry in other areas of the country and especially in the state of São Paulo, which accounted for 56 percent of Brazil's industrial output by 1970. By then, too, São Paulo was the country's most important financial center.[10]

The rise of manufacturing in Rio de Janeiro in the first half of the twentieth century resulted in a growing and more diverse urban working class that now included both skilled and unskilled factory workers as well as stevedores, domestic servants, tram conductors, janitors, railway engineers, bricklayers, telephone operators, bus drivers, and trash collectors. Industrialization also fostered the expansion of the city's white-collar middle class as more and more managerial and technical positions and office jobs opened up in manufacturing and in firms tied to manufacturing. The ranks of the liberal professions expanded, and the growth of government created further opportunities for white-collar employment. Yet, the city's middle class, like its working class, did not form a homogeneous group. Although elements of the urban middle class were predominantly white, and although nearly all male members of that class wore a jacket and tie or at least a tie while at work, they did not all enjoy the same levels of income.[11]

Economic growth and development also resulted in the expansion of the city's upper class, which constituted only a small portion of the total population. A growing number of industrialists, executives in manufacturing firms, and owners of firms tied to industry joined an upper class previously defined by bankers and owners and directors of major commercial and construction firms. The result was a larger and more diverse upper class. Although some members of that upper class may have descended from the great planter families of the colonial period and the nineteenth century, their fortunes increasingly depended not so much on agriculture as on a varied array of urban activities in a rapidly industrializing Brazil. In Rio de Janeiro, upper-class social circles further included politicians holding high elected or appointed positions in the government, often from elsewhere in Brazil, such as senators, federal deputies, and cabinet ministers. Local directors of foreign firms with investments in Brazil in some cases also moved in those social circles. The same was true of some foreign diplomats and of some higher-ranking military officers.[12]

Finally, despite long-term economic growth and development, the majority of Rio de Janeiro's inhabitants remained poor and often even wretchedly poor. Evidence, in some cases highly visible evidence, of their poverty came from the favelas, which multiplied in number and grew in size. Favela life was characterized by legal and economic insecurity, with residents often renting lots from local strongmen in an informal real estate market or occupying areas nominally in the domain of local employers, such as factories. And residents often held informal employment as cooks, handymen, and maids. Both residential and employment patterns were often precarious, subject to sudden disruption by authorities. This precariousness was mirrored in favela housing, usually self-built and often lacking running water, sewage service, and electricity.[13]

A "Civilized" Rio de Janeiro and the City's Social Geography

The city of Rio de Janeiro itself underwent profound transformations in the early twentieth century. Perhaps the most striking of those transformations came between 1902 and 1906, when Francisco Pereira Passos served as the appointed mayor of the Federal District. His administration launched sweeping reforms, which went forward along three main fronts.[14] The first was the construction of a sorely needed, entirely new, modern port, completed in 1911. The lack of adequate docking facilities obviously represented a major shortcoming in a city whose economy depended heavily on international trade.

The second main front also met a pressing need. Since the mid-nineteenth century, repeated outbreaks of yellow fever, cholera, and other diseases such as smallpox and the plague had sent thousands of Cariocas to their graves. They had also given Rio de Janeiro an international reputation as a tropical pesthole. So long as the Brazilian capital retained that reputation, it could not attract increased attention from foreign investors or a greater flow of European immigrants both to meet labor needs and to "whiten" the population. Therefore, the national government launched a large-scale public health campaign in the Federal District. Under the direction of a young physician, Oswaldo Cruz, teams of health inspectors worked their way through the city, entering public

FIGURE 3.1. Avenida Central, ca. 1913. Central Ave., "The 11,000,000 Boulevard," North to Bay, Rio de Janeiro, S.A., Library of Congress.

buildings and private residences, where they sprayed disinfectants, killed rats, and ordered the drainage of stagnant pools of water in which mosquitoes could breed. They further ordered the demolition of housing deemed unsanitary. The public health campaign also included a program of compulsory vaccination against smallpox. Although well intentioned and on the whole successful, the campaign was carried out in a high-handed and, indeed, authoritarian fashion. In the name of sanitation, "civilization," and hygiene, Pereira Passos prohibited such practices as spitting on the floors of tramway cars, the sale of various food products by street vendors, and begging. He also ordered the removal from the city's streets of all kiosks; that is, the corner stands that sold coffee, cheap alcohol, snacks, tobacco, and newspapers.

The third reform front aimed at remaking the Brazilian capital into a "Paris in the tropics" by widening streets and opening entirely new avenues in the city's center. The most important of these was the Avenida Central (later renamed the Avenida Rio Branco), which cut a wide straight swath, nearly two kilometers in length, running roughly north to south, through the heart of the city (map 3.1). The new buildings lining the avenue, which had to have their designs approved by a specially appointed committee and which generally followed the Beaux-Arts and Eclectic architectural styles then in favor in

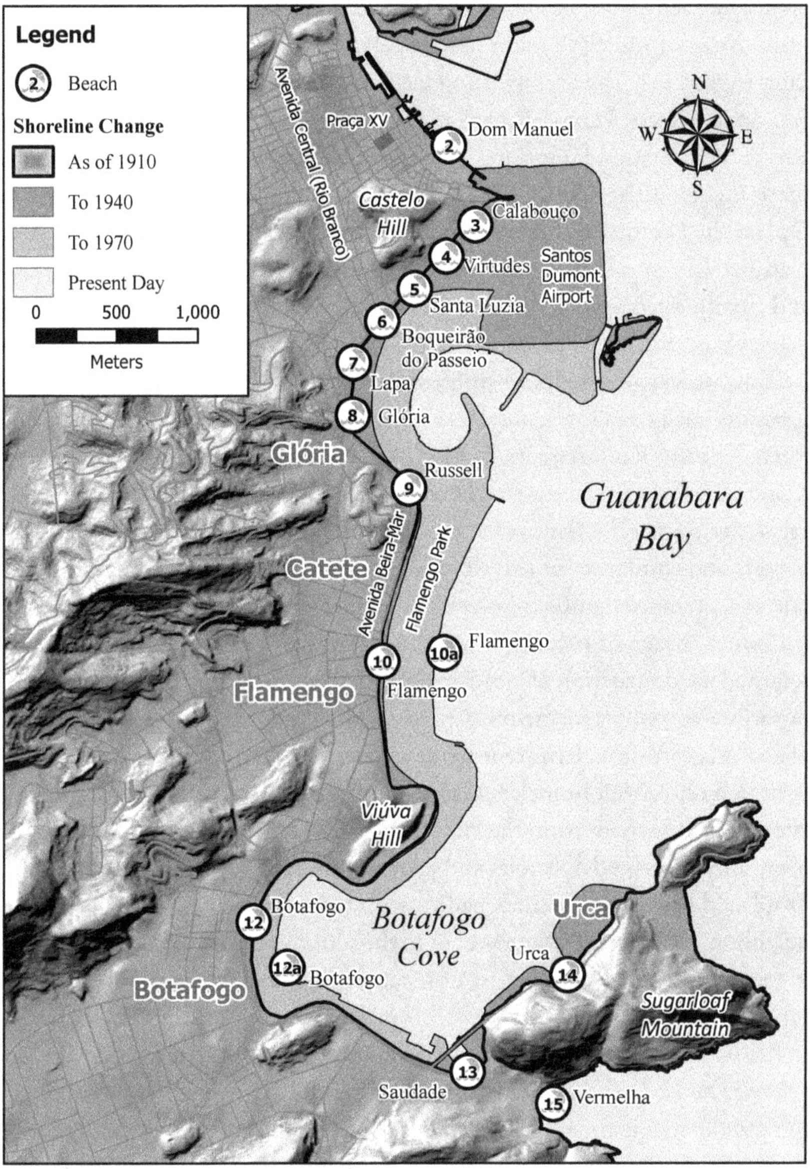

MAP 3.1. Rio de Janeiro in the Early Twentieth Century. Extensions of the 1910 street grid, and new streets in the landfilled areas not shown. 10a and 12a indicate the relocated Flamengo and Botafogo beaches.

France, housed banks, the offices of major commercial, shipping, and industrial firms, some of the city's main newspapers, as well as fashionable shops and cafés (figure 3.1). The avenue culminated at its southern end, where the new Rio de Janeiro of Pereira Passos was perhaps more Parisian than anywhere else. A set of new and imposing buildings dominated that end of the avenue; these included the Municipal Theater, with a design inspired by the Paris Opéra; the National Museum of Fine Arts; the naval and military clubs; the National Library; the socially prestigious Jockey Club; the Supreme Court; and finally, overlooking the bay, the domed Monroe Palace, where, during many years, the Senate met.[15]

Thus, at least in the more visible quarters of the city's center, upper-class Cariocas finally had for themselves a "civilized," "European" capital to show to foreign visitors and investors. Remodeling Rio de Janeiro, however, came at a tremendous cost that went well beyond the need to repay the loans taken out for the purpose. The removal of kiosks from the city's streets deprived their owners and employees of a livelihood. Likewise, the prohibition against the sale of certain foodstuffs by street vendors left many poor women and men without a source of income. The opening of the new avenues, in turn, had required the destruction of hundreds of buildings, including many of the city's notorious cortiços (tenements). Others were torn down under the provisions of a 1903 law. Although the tenements were often overcrowded and unhealthy, their demolition left homeless a large number of lower-class Cariocas and, in effect, expelled them from the city's center. The cortiços' destruction, moreover, only worsened a serious and growing shortage of affordable housing. Displaced tenement-dwellers had to seek what housing they could find in neighborhoods outside the center or in the suburbs. Others resorted to building makeshift shacks in favelas. Ironically, some of those early favelas arose on hills in the city's center.[16] The reforms also faced opposition, most notably in the much-studied November 1904 uprising known as the Vaccine Revolt (*Revolta da Vacina*), in which "a cross section of Rio's inner-city population" took to the streets for a week of violent protests. The government prevailed.[17]

The Pereira Passos reforms reinforced the marked divisions within Rio de Janeiro's social geography that had already begun to take shape before 1900 and that, though modified by the city's expansion, persist in large measure even today.[18] At the core of that geography is the center, which corresponds roughly to the urban parishes of colonial Rio de Janeiro and which Cariocas often call simply "the city." As the center became a predominantly business and commercial district, its residential population suffered a long-term decline. Thus, whereas, in 1890, nearly 228,000 people, or 54 percent of Rio de Janeiro's total population, resided there, by 1960, the center had fewer than 60,000 residents, less than 2 percent of Cariocas.[19]

To the west and northwest of the center is the Zona Norte (North Zone), so called because it lies north of the Carioca and Tijuca Mountain Ranges that, running roughly east to west, create a north-south divide within the city.[20] The Zona Norte consists of neighborhoods developed in the nineteenth century that, with a few exceptions, became predominantly working-, lower middle-, and middle-class residential districts and that also came to house numerous industries. Vila Isabel, Grajaú, Andaraí, and especially Tijuca, which have historically had substantial middle- and upper middle-class populations, stand out as the chief exceptions. Indeed, even in the late twentieth century, some wealthy families continued to live in Tijuca.[21]

Stretching beyond the Zona Norte are the suburbs: a seemingly endless series of mainly working-, lower middle-, and middle-class neighborhoods and industrial districts that sprang up along the Central do Brasil and Leopoldina Railways and their feeder lines starting in the 1880s and 1890s. In the mid-twentieth century, the suburbs' population increased from less than 771,000 in 1940 to more than 1.6 million two decades later, but the provision of basic urban services, such as running water, sewers, and paved streets, often lagged woefully far behind that growth.[22] By 1950, moreover, metropolitan Rio de Janeiro had already spread beyond the suburbs and, indeed, beyond the boundaries of the Federal District and had come to include the Baixada Fluminense (Fluminense Lowlands), often simply known as the Baixada, in the state of Rio de Janeiro. The population of the Baixada municipalities more than doubled between 1940 and 1950, growing from just over 140,600 to nearly 361,000, and it did so again by 1960, reaching 883,300. Their poor, working- and lower middle-class neighborhoods then mostly lacked access to running water and other basic urban services.[23]

In the opposite direction from the railway lines that led north and west from city's center toward the suburbs and the Baixada lies the Zona Sul (South Zone): a sequence of neighborhoods, including Flamengo, Laranjeiras, and Botafogo, located along or near the southern shore of Guanabara Bay that, by the late nineteenth century, had already emerged as a preferred place of residence for the well-to-do. After 1905, the Zona Sul expanded to encompass what were at the time the new upper- and upper middle-class oceanfront neighborhoods of Copacabana and Ipanema and, later, Leblon. The Zona Sul eventually came to include the affluent nonoceanfront neighborhoods of Humaitá, Jardim Botânico, Lagoa, and Gávea.[24]

A pronounced pattern of residential segregation by class came to mark the Rio de Janeiro that resulted from the Pereira Passos reforms, and the distribution of income across neighborhoods would, in fact, remain highly unequal in the city in the late twentieth and early twenty-first centuries. The disparities were in some cases enormous. In 2010, for example, mean monthly income for individuals aged 10 or older stood at just under R$5,045.00 (US $2,866) in the upper- and upper middle-class beachfront neighborhood of Leblon, in the Zona Sul, but at a mere R$73.73 (US $41.89) in Gerocinó, located in the city's western suburbs. Average income in Leblon, thus, was sixty-eight times greater than in Gerocinó. The disparities across neighborhoods went beyond differences in income; at the time, as in earlier years, they also extended to rates of literacy and infant mortality and to access to running water, medical care, the sewer system, and regular trash collection.[25]

Given that, historically, color, or race, has in part overlapped with class in Brazil, it will come as no surprise that the social geography of Rio de Janeiro has tended to reflect that overlap. The 1940 national census, for instance, classified as Black (*preto*) or brown (*pardo*) 29 percent of the city's population. Fully 54 percent of all Afro-Brazilians in Rio de Janeiro at the time lived in the suburbs. In some suburbs, such as Madureira, Pavuna, and Anchieta, Blacks and pardos made up more than 40 percent of the population. By contrast, less than one-tenth of all Cariocas of color made their homes in the Zona Sul, where 77 percent of all residents were white.[26]

Rio de Janeiro's social geography was, however, more complex than it might seem at first view. In the first decades of the 1900s, several large textile factories, with company housing for workers, operated in the Zona Sul. They closed only in the 1930s and later, with the land that they occupied being subdivided for residential purposes. Perhaps more important, in the middle of the twentieth century, the Zona Sul's affluent neighborhoods were not the city's "whitest." Blacks and pardos, in fact, accounted for 23 percent of all the Zona Sul's inhabitants in 1940. In Copacabana, which by then already ranked as one of Rio de Janeiro's most fashionable neighborhoods, they made up more than one-fifth (21 percent) of the population. As Luiz de Aguiar Costa Pinto noted in his pioneering 1953 sociological study of "race relations" in Rio de Janeiro, the very affluence of Copacabana and other Zona Sul neighborhoods explains why they had sizeable populations of color. The wealthy households in those neighborhoods maintained a large number of domestic servants, mostly Afro-Brazilian women, who often had as their sole place of residence the households in which they worked.[27]

Favelas, as Costa Pinto also pointed out in 1953, further complicated the city's social geography. They could be found in all parts of the city, including the Zona Sul, though some would be razed and their residents forcibly relocated in the 1960s and early 1970s. Nevertheless, Rio de Janeiro's favelas, with populations that have historically been disproportionately Afro-Brazilian, have grown in size and number. Thus, just as in the mid-twentieth century, pockets of poverty, some very sizeable, continue to exist even in the city's wealthiest districts. Costa Pinto observed that "distance in physical space clearly reflects distance in social space." The physical distance could be measured in the kilometers that separated the suburbs from the Zona Sul and the oceanfront beaches. Or it could be measured "on the vertical plane," in the meters that separated the street level from "the hilltops, . . . the favelas," where the city's poorest residents at the time lived.[28] Not all favelas in the city were, or are, located on hillsides. Even so, had Costa Pinto published his study in the late twentieth or early twenty-first century, he might very well have made the same point by resorting to the distinction now widely used in Rio de Janeiro between *morro* and *asfalto*; that is, between *hill*, meaning favela, and *asphalt*, in other words, the adjacent neighborhoods with their paved streets and other urban services.[29]

"All the Population is Beginning to Worry"

Today, when the Pereira Passos reforms are recalled, authors always mention the Avenida Rio Branco, originally known as the Avenida Central. They are less likely to mention the Avenida Beira-Mar (Sea-Shore Avenue), built at the same time; despite its name, it bordered not the sea, but rather Guanabara Bay. Thirty-three meters wide and adorned with landscaped gardens, it followed the bay's curving shore for more than five kilometers from the southern end of the Avenida Rio Branco to the far end of Botafogo. In a 1930 *National Geographic* article, Frederick Simpich noted that it was "often styled the finest ocean boulevard in the Western Hemisphere." That same year, Agnes Rotherby, an American traveler, wrote that the avenue "surpasses the most perfect praise" (figure 3.2).[30] Avenida Beira-Mar eliminated Boqueirão do Passeio, until then

FIGURE 3.2. Avenida Beira-Mar, 1906. Arquivo Images2You.

FIGURE 3.3. Santa Luzia Beach, 1920. *Careta* (17.1.1920), n.p.

the city's main bathing beach. The bathing establishments that had long operated there had to close and were demolished. They gave way to the Monroe Palace, and authorities prohibited bathing in front of the palace. Even before the new avenue was inaugurated, the *Jornal do Commercio* noted that "all the population is beginning to worry, seeing that, to date, no provisions have been made so as not to deprive it entirely of [the opportunity to go] sea-bathing." The newspaper went on to ask where all the bathers who frequented Boqueirão do Passeio would find another conveniently located beach.[31]

Although those bathers may have been genuinely worried, they ran no risk of having to give up sea-bathing. Flamengo would for decades continue to attract bathers even though the construction of the Avenida Beira-Mar had reduced the width of the beach there and, for a time, as we shall see, it became the city's chic beach.[32] Of course, for residents of the center, where, as late as 1906, 42 percent of Rio de Janeiro's population lived, Flamengo was not nearly so convenient as Boqueirão do Passeio beach had been. But they did not need to go to Flamengo; they could still bathe at Lapa and Russell beaches (map 3.1). For example, a young Carmen Miranda, whose family lived in Rio de Janeiro's center, learned to swim at the beach in Lapa in the 1910s. The center's residents might also choose Santa Luzia beach (figure 3.3), where two large casas de banhos still served numerous bathers. Indeed, everything indicates that Santa Luzia, which had little or no sand, became the main bathing beach for working-, middle-, and lower middle-class Cariocas who lived in the city's central districts after 1906.[33]

Santa Luzia beach all but disappeared in the early 1920s with the landfill that resulted from the razing of the Morro do Castelo (Castle Hill), but this project created two new beaches in the city's center: Virtudes, a prolongation of Santa Luzia, and Calabouço, which was, in turn, a prolongation of Virtudes. Both would later disappear as a result of subsequent landfills. The two had very little sand, and in 1920, Virtudes amounted to a rocky embankment with no sand at all (figure 3.4). But, as noted in chapter 1, the absence of sand did not prevent sea-bathing. At both beaches, bathers could in the 1920s and 1930s rent makeshift cabanas to change from their street clothes. Large numbers of working- and lower middle-class Cariocas well into the twentieth century bathed at Virtudes and Calabouço.[34] And, just as in the nineteenth century, some of the city's residents continued to go bathing in the waters near the Praça XV, known before 1889 as the Largo do Paço (Palace Square), and in front of the city's main market. They included Samuel Malamud, who arrived in Rio

FIGURE 3.4. Virtudes Beach, 1930. *Careta* (18.1.1930), 3.

de Janeiro with his parents in 1923 from the Ukraine at the age of sixteen and who lived in the Praça XI neighborhood, just west of central Rio de Janeiro, where many Eastern European Jewish immigrants settled. In his memoirs, he recalled bathing in those waters amid "all sorts of rotten fruit and vegetables" that the market vendors had discarded. Malamud also remembered that, following the example of their non-Jewish neighbors, his family and other Jewish residents of the neighborhood made summer weekend outings to the beach in Caju, which then attracted mainly working- and lower middle-class bathers.[35]

If Malamud's family had wished to travel a bit further, they might have gone bathing at a bayshore beach in one of Rio de Janeiro's northern suburbs, where a growing share of the city's population lived in the early twentieth century. From at least the 1920s on, working-, middle-, and lower middle-class bathers plunged into the water at beaches such as Porto de Inhaúma, Penha, and especially Ramos (also known as Maria Angu), all located in the suburbs served by the Leopoldina Railway. At Ramos, the municipal government opened a large bathing house in 1948.[36]

Nonetheless, the concerns of "all the population" raised by the *Jornal do Commercio* did reach Rio de Janeiro's municipal council, where Campos

Sobrinho took up the matter in early 1905. Claiming that the construction of the Avenida Beira-Mar would "deprive" the population of the city's central districts of easy access to sea-bathing, he proposed a law that would provide incentives to encourage the construction of bathing establishments, approved with only slight modifications in September 1906. But the legislation actually offered few incentives. It authorized the Federal District's government to take bids for concessions to build and operate bathing establishments on the city's shoreline. Municipal authorities would, however, draw up the plans for the establishments and determine their locations. At those locations, the concession-holders were forbidden to hinder the free use of the beach or the water for fishing or rowing or for "maritime festivals" sponsored by the municipal or national government. The law further required concession-holders to maintain lifesaving services at their establishments. Finally, the concessions would last only fifteen years. At the end of that period, ownership of the establishments would revert to the municipality, and "under no hypothesis" would concession-holders receive any compensation.[37]

Five years later, Mayor Bento Ribeiro recognized the law's "inefficacy" and the city council began working on a new law to promote the construction of bathing establishments, finally approved in September 1912. It offered a few more incentives than the 1906 legislation did. Concessions could be granted for up to fifty years, and, during that time, the establishments would be exempt from municipal taxes. But concession-holders would not enjoy a monopoly at any particular beach; their area of exclusivity would be no more than a "radius" of 500 meters. The establishments were also prohibited from restricting "free circulation" along the beaches where they operated; in other words, they could not prevent anyone from bathing there for free. The municipal government would, moreover, determine the fees charged by the establishments; if their profits exceeded 12 percent a year, the authorities would lower the fees. Those restrictions, no doubt, explain why the law proved a failure; it did not lead to the construction of a single new bathing establishment. In his 1913 address to the municipal council, Mayor Bento Ribeiro lamented the law's "lack of success."[38] Although they failed to yield results, the 1906 and 1912 laws indicate that municipal authorities recognized the importance that sea-bathing held in the city's life. And, despite the limited incentives offered by the two laws, the Federal District's government received at least a dozen proposals to build bathing establishments between 1906 and 1920.[39]

A Brazilian Biarritz, Ostend, or Miami?

In the debates that led to the passage of the 1912 law and in the proposals to build new bathing establishments, Copacabana and the city's other oceanfront beaches emerged more than ever before as a focus of attention. In 1915, Mayor Rivadávia da Cunha Correia suggested to the council that, if it granted "favors and advantages," a firm might be willing to build in Copacabana, Ipanema, or Leblon a large bathing establishment "worthy" of Brazil's national capital, which would include "a large hotel surrounded by gardens" and also "all the conveniences and amusements" found at seaside resorts elsewhere in the world.[40] It is not hard to explain burgeoning interest in those beaches. But any explanation, it must be stressed, should have nothing to do with Sarah Bernhardt (1844–1923), the world-renowned French actor. Some authors argue that, while on tour in Rio de Janeiro in 1886, she revealed the possibilities of sea-bathing in Copacabana. Ricardo Boechat goes so far as to call her Copacabana's "first bather." Supposedly, the French actor shocked Carioca society by remaining at the beach after seven in the morning and, in that way, helped transform local bathing habits and attitudes toward the sea and the sun. Bernhardt may very well have gone bathing in Copacabana, but if so, someone must have taken her there. Likewise, if she did remain "scandalously" on the beach after seven, the scandal did not find its way into the pages of some of Rio de Janeiro's main papers—not even *O Paiz*, which had assigned a special reporter to follow her steps.[41]

If she did in fact wade into Copacabana's waves, Bernhardt would not have been that beach's "first bather." Nor would she have been the first foreigner to appreciate its beauty. Jean-Baptiste Debret, Maria Graham, Carl Schlichthorst, Charles Landseer, Johann Moritz von Rugendas, and Daniel P. Kidder all made excursions to Copacabana in the first half of the nineteenth century. For his part, Schlichthorst did more than visit that beach; he went bathing there in the early 1820s. A property owner announced some thirty years later that he had "houses for recreation, bathing, and [taking in the] sea air" to rent in Copacabana.[42] And, in 1878, six years before Bernhardt gave her first performances in Rio de Janeiro, Dr. Francisco Bento Alexandre de Figueiredo Magalhães [*sic*] opened the Grande Hotel de Copacabana. According to an advertisement for the hotel, Copacabana stood out for its "beauty" and as the "only" beach on Rio de Janeiro's "outskirts" that afforded "true sea baths." Yet, to attract guests to his establishment, Figueiredo Magalhães had to provide them with a special carriage service. The carriages that transported those guests departed from Botafogo and followed the narrow road that twisted its way up and down the steep hills that isolated the beach from the rest of the city.[43] In opening his hotel, Figueiredo Magalhães may very well have been counting on the plans of a local firm that, in 1878, began work on a tramway line to Copacabana. The same firm also planned to build a bathing establishment there, but judicial disputes over concession rights halted construction. Other efforts in the 1880s to extend tram service to Copacabana also failed.[44]

In 1890, however, when the foreign-owned Companhia Ferro-Carril do Jardim Botânico (originally called the Botanical Gardens Railway Company) negotiated a renewal of its tramway concession, the new agreement required the company to build a line to Copacabana. Almost immediately, it began to bore a tunnel to link that beach with the rest of the city. The company completed the tunnel, now commonly called the Túnel Velho (Old Tunnel), in 1892 and inaugurated tram service to Copacabana that same year. The new line's original last stop was located in what is now Serzedelo Correia Square, a block back from the halfway point between the two the extremes of Copacabana's beach. From that stop, the company soon thereafter extended its lines eastward to Leme and, then, westward to Ipanema. In 1904, through the same chain of low but steep hills, it opened a second tunnel, which even today, more than a century later, is still known as the Túnel Novo (New Tunnel) and which further facilitated access to the city's oceanfront beaches (see map 4.1).[45]

With the problems of access largely resolved, it is not at all surprising that proposals to build new bathing establishments would increasingly focus on Copacabana and the other oceanfront beaches. The most ambitious of those proposals, in fact, date from 1891, shortly after work on the Old Tunnel began. In that year, a firm headed by Ricardo Domingues proposed a real estate development that would "endow Rio de Janeiro with a splendid [new] neighborhood" and transform Copacabana into "a Brazilian Biarritz"; that is, a local equivalent of the famous seaside resort on France's Basque coast. Crisscrossed by newly opened streets, the Brazilian Biarritz, according to Domingues's plans, would have a hotel, a bathing establishment, and a theater. That same year, the Companhia da Cidade da Gávea (City of Gávea Company) released an even more ambitious project. It entailed a real estate development to create a "bathing city [*cidade balneária*]" that would extend more than eleven kilometers along the city's Atlantic shoreline, from Leme to São Conrado. The result would be "a most pleasant point of residence, rivaling the aristocratic bathing cities in Europe." The project also included the construction of a hotel and of saltwater pools at those stretches of the beach where the currents made bathing dangerous.[46]

Later proposals, though less ambitious, also aimed at constructing a luxury bathing resort on Rio de Janeiro's Atlantic shoreline. Among those proposals, one that drew considerable attention had its origins in articles published in 1914 by Iracema, author of the women's column for the *Revista da Semana*. She noted that Carioca bathers, after a dip in the sea, spent little or no time on the sand. As a result, in her view, the city's beaches lacked "life." She, therefore, called for the transformation of Copacabana into an "elegant beach," where the city's "smart set"—she used the English expression—could gather. She envisioned a Copacabana where Carioca women could not only go sea-bathing but also display themselves dressed in the latest Parisian fashions on the sand and at "paradise-hotels [*hotéis-paraíso*]," fine restaurants with itinerant orchestras, and casinos. The columnist urged the "ladies" of Copacabana, which, by 1914, had a rapidly growing population, to take the first small steps in that direction. When her readers asked what they should do at the beach, Iracema responded by giving them a lesson based, she claimed, on her own experiences at Ostend, Belgium's most famous seaside resort, and at French resorts such as Trouville and Biarritz. They should, on summer mornings, have their servants set up on the beach large, colorful, pavilion-style tents, where they could change in and out of their bathing attire. But, more than that, the tents, with wicker furniture inside, would allow them, shaded from the sun, to spend their mornings relaxing, watching their children play, and entertaining friends over tea and hot chocolate. Yes, hot beverages on a tropical beach in the summer![47]

Iracema's call for the transformation of Copacabana into an "elegant" beach gained the endorsement of Binóculo, the influential *Gazeta de Notícias* social columnist, who took his cue from Iracema and insisted on the need to "ostendize" Copacabana; in other words, to make it into a Brazilian version of the Belgian resort. Her call also won the support of the then-socially prestigious Automobile Club of Brazil, which, in 1915, submitted to Rio de Janeiro's municipal government a proposal to build a large luxury bathing establishment in Copacabana. The club attached to its proposal a magazine clipping describing the Hotel Excelsior, located at Venice's Lido beach, then a major bathing resort for Europe's wealthy. The clipping pointed out that the Excelsior had four hundred guest rooms, three hundred cabanas for bathers, golf links, and a roller-skating rink.[48]

By the time that the Automobile Club put forth its proposal, two engineers, Otávio Ribeiro da Cunha and Vicente Licínio Cardoso, had already begun to draw up their own project for a bathing resort in Ipanema. Their project included the construction of "a modern hotel," designed to attract "foreigners . . . in transit" and especially those Argentines and Uruguayans "who flee the winter cold" in their home countries. For Cariocas, the two engineers argued, it would serve as a summer retreat. The hotel would provide its guests various types of water and sun therapy and would also have a restaurant, bar, theater, cinema, gaming salon, and skating rink, as well as cabanas where bathers could undress and dress. The Automobile Club and the two engineers had a competitor in Samuel Pelitzer, who sought permission in 1915 to build at Rio de Janeiro's oceanfront beaches "bathing resort hotels [*hotéis balneários*]" comparable to those in Ostend, Biarritz, and Atlantic City. The first of those hotels, according to his plans, would be located in Copacabana.[49] Pelitzer's proposal, like those submitted by the Automobile Club and by Cunha and Cardoso, fit into what were, in the 1910s, ongoing discussions in the press and among authorities about the future of sea-bathing in the city and about the possibility of developing Rio de Janeiro's oceanfront into a beach resort comparable to famous European seaside resorts or, at the very least, to Montevideo's Ramírez and Pocitos beaches.[50]

The proposals to build luxury bathing establishments in Copacabana or at one of the city's other Atlantic beaches had two main goals. One was to provide wealthy Cariocas with a "civilized," European-style resort, where they could go sea-bathing without mixing with lower-class residents of the city. In that regard, the proposals fell in line with Pereira Passos's efforts to make Rio de Janeiro into a "civilized" "European" capital in the tropics, with the increased social segregation that resulted from his remodeling of the city. The other main goal was to attract a flow of tourists to Rio de Janeiro's oceanfront beaches. Indeed, in 1905, Pereira Passos, whose tenure as mayor saw the start of the construction of the Avenida Atlântica, Copacabana's beachside avenue, argued that, "with its incomparable beauty," the new neighborhood could become "the Nice of Atlantic beaches."[51]

The projects to transform Rio de Janeiro's oceanfront beaches into a European- or American-style seaside resort even inspired a novel: *Praia de Ipanema* (Ipanema Beach), by Théo-Filho (Manoel Theotonio de Lacerda Freire Filho); published in 1927, it was a bestseller by the standards of the day. The novel's protagonist, Otto O'Kennutchy Guimarães, bears a name that is a direct allusion to Raul Kennedy Lemos, a real estate speculator who developed much of Ipanema in the early twentieth century. Otto, a young engineer, dreams of making Ipanema into a Brazilian equivalent of Palm Beach, Miami, or Atlantic City, with "sumptuous hotels," occupying "skyscrapers," which would have a total of six thousand guest rooms, "luxurious casinos," a "one-hundred-meter pier," and a "floating dock" for yachts, motor launches, and sailboats. Ipanema, in short, would become "a city of pleasure and sporting amusements," "a South American Newport." To realize his dream, he founds a firm that initially receives support from Rio de Janeiro's lords of finance. Other characters include Aglaé Lacerda, a naïve blonde, with whom Otto falls in love; Hong-Láo-Tcháo, the "sinister" owner of an opium den in Ipanema; Sílvia Martins, a Charleston-dancing brunette who tries to break up Otto and Aglaé's romance; and Clarindo, Otto's faithful bookkeeper and secretary, who detests having to ride the trams four or five times a day. There is also Mr. Tom Johnson, a Wall Street financier with ties to international banks and to the Anglo-Canadian Rio de Janeiro Tramway, Light & Power Company, Ltd. In the unfolding of the novel's wild plot, Mr. Johnson successfully undermines Otto's plans. On learning that, as a result, his employer faces financial ruin, Clarindo, rather than live out the rest of his life riding the trams, throws himself off a cliff into the sea. Otto, at the novel's conclusion, does manage to save his honor and to retain Aglaé's love, but with his fortune lost, his dream is still only a dream.[52]

Praia de Ipanema's ending gains, in retrospect, a significance that its author could not have foreseen in 1927. Like Otto's dream, none of the proposals to develop one of Rio de Janeiro's oceanfront beaches into a luxury resort comparable to Biarritz, Ostend, Deauville, Miami, or even Mar del Plata ever materialized. It is true that the Hotel Balneário da Urca (Urca Bathing Hotel) opened in 1925 at the small bayshore beach of Urca. It boasted a restaurant, a bar with live music, water chutes, and by 1934, 120 changerooms for bathers. Bathing there was briefly fashionable among wealthy Cariocas in the 1920s. The hotel itself, however, was quite small; it had a mere thirty-four guest rooms. Moreover, it closed in the 1930s, and the building was converted into a casino that became famous for its floor shows.[53] It is also true that, in 1922, Rio de Janeiro's municipal government opened in a small square facing Copacabana's beach, the Praça do Lido, a "bathing park [*parque balneário*]" with a restaurant, a skating rink, and changing cabanas. Although the restaurant would continue to operate for years, the cabanas, numbering only thirty-six, had disappeared by the early 1930s.[54]

FIGURE 3.5. Copacabana Palace Hotel, 1920s. Arquivo Images2You.

The closest that Rio de Janeiro ever came to the dream of transforming its Atlantic shoreline into a Brazilian version of Biarritz, Deauville, or Ostend was the construction of the beachfront Copacabana Palace Hotel. With a design inspired by the Hotel Negresco in Nice and by the Carlton Hotel in Cannes, it opened in 1923 with 250 guest rooms and would later also have a casino (figure 3.5). The Copacabana Palace was and is a first-class hotel, whose guests have included presidents, prime ministers, European royalty, and numerous international celebrities.[55] But it was just one large luxury hotel.

It was also the only hotel located in Rio de Janeiro's oceanfront neighborhoods that the *South American Handbook* recommended in its editions for the years 1925 to 1938. Even in 1941, the *Handbook* recommended only three hotels in Copacabana, all overlooking the beach: the Copacabana Palace, the Luxor, and the Riviera, which had a combined total of 420 beds. The *Handbook*'s recommendations excluded second- or third-rate hotels and small establishments, such as "pensions," which offered fixed rates and board. A locally produced guidebook mentioned a few more Copacabana hotels in 1939. The

Handbook's recommendations can, nevertheless, serve as a point of comparison between Rio de Janeiro and Santos, São Paulo's main bathing resort at the time, and which since the late nineteenth century had attracted visitors from that state's capital and its other inland cities. Already in its 1933 edition, the guide strongly recommended seven beachfront hotels, with a total of more than nine hundred beds, in Santos, as well as the seaside Grande Hotel (with three hundred beds) in nearby Guarujá.[56] Thus, far from being transformed into a Brazilian Ostend, Deauville, Biarritz, or Miami Beach, Copacabana by the end of the 1930s had not even become a Carioca version of Santos.

What was lacking was a market that could justify the investments needed to develop the city's oceanfront beaches into a large-scale European- or American-style bathing resort for wealthy Cariocas and for tourists. Rio de Janeiro's well-to-do did not need such a resort to go sea-bathing. As chapter 4 will show, after 1905, more and more upper- and upper middle-class Cariocas would move to Copacabana, either permanently or just for the summers. Once they moved there, they had no need for hotels or for *balneários* (establishments with changing facilities), whether luxurious or not. They could change at home and walk to the beach. Furthermore, in the first years of the twentieth century, Copacabana, despite the opening of the tunnels, remained a distant neighborhood on Rio de Janeiro's far southern outskirts. Wealthy Cariocas living in Flamengo, Laranjeiras, and Botafogo, the city's most "aristocratic" neighborhoods at the time, had much closer at hand the beach in Flamengo. They could don their bathing costumes at home and easily walk to that beach just as many of their parents and grandparents had done in the previous century.[57]

Moreover, the number of tourists visiting the city was quite small in the first half of the twentieth century. The arrival of foreign tourists in the city was, in fact, still newsworthy even in the late 1920s and early 1930s. In November 1928, for example, the *Jornal do Brasil* informed its readers that 250 American tourists on a South American cruise would spend three days in Rio de Janeiro. Another daily observed two years later that, despite all its fame, Copacabana lacked installations comparable to those found at "the world's most celebrated beaches," where a "multitude" of holiday excursioners made up the majority of all bathers. The paper went on to explain the lack of such installations by noting that "we are still not a country of tourism."[58] Perhaps the only major exception were Argentine tourists, but their numbers do not seem to have been large.[59]

The available statistical information, though woefully scant for years before the 1960s, tends to confirm *O Jornal*'s observations. For instance, in the months of January, February, and March 1938, nine cruise ships, with a total of 4,402 tourists aboard, docked in Rio de Janeiro. We can take that total and multiply it by four to reach an estimate, undoubtedly exaggerated, of the number of foreign tourists who visited Rio de Janeiro in 1938. The result is 17,608. By contrast, Blackpool, one of Britain's most important seaside resorts welcomed four million visitors in 1913 and seven million in 1931. Even Weymouth, a far more exclusive beach resort than Blackpool and more distant from major urban centers, received some 400,000 visitors in 1932.[60] By then, passenger air service was available to Rio de Janeiro from the United States (and, briefly, from Germany on the Zeppelin), but none of these aircraft carried many passengers and fares were costly.[61] Most foreigners who visited Rio de Janeiro in the first half of the twentieth century arrived by ship.

Cruise ship passengers needed no hotel rooms; moreover, their stay in the city might be quite brief. Of the 4,402 tourists on the nine cruise ships that docked in Rio de Janeiro in the first three months of 1938, three-fifths (60.5 percent) spent fewer than five days in the city; 42 percent stayed just three days. Other tourists spent even less time in the Brazilian capital. The British cruise ship *Viceroy of India* gave its 233 passengers only a single day in the city in 1934. The Touring Club of Brazil, accordingly, laid out sightseeing tours for travelers—based on its 1938 *Rio de Janeiro in a Few Hours: A Guide Book for Tourists* (published in English)—with anywhere from two to forty-eight allotted hours in the city as well as tours for those "without [a] set time limit." Although the Touring Club recommended a drive along the city's oceanfront beaches in all its tours, it did not suggest that the travelers sun themselves or take a dip at those beaches.[62]

That may come as a surprise given that, since at least the 1960s, travel guides and similar publications have stressed lounging on the beach as a central part of both the tourist experience in Rio de Janeiro and the Carioca lifestyle.[63] A few such publications began to do the same in the 1930s, especially in the second half of that decade.[64] Nevertheless, the Touring Club's guide did not differ from most other guides published before 1940. In those guides, as Celso Castro and Isabella Perrotta have shown, the emphasis fell not on beach-going at Copacabana or Ipanema, but, rather, attractions that, for the most part, today would probably not rank high on a list of the city's sights, such as downtown public buildings and monuments. The guidebooks also stressed the natural beauty of Rio de Janeiro's setting: Guanabara Bay and the hills and mountains that rise up in the middle of the city, some of which afford spectacular views of the bay and the city. Tourist maps at the time focused the viewer's attention not on the city's oceanfront beaches and the Zona Sul, but, instead, on Rio de Janeiro's center, where what were regarded at the time as the main sightseeing attractions were located.[65] The Federal District's government, as part of its fledgling efforts to attract foreign visitors, established in 1931 an "official tourist season," divided into "two phases" that excluded December and most of the other summer months, apparently assuming that tourists wanted to avoid the hottest months of the year.[66]

It is hard to escape the conclusion that, though authorities and upper-class Cariocas may have hoped to see Copacabana or Ipanema become a South American Biarritz, Miami, or Deauville that could attract tourists, they did not want foreigners to regard their city as primarily a beach resort. In their view, Rio de Janeiro was first and foremost Brazil's national capital, a "civilized" and "modern" metropolis on par with the world's other great cities but also with a key difference: the extraordinary beauty of its natural setting. *Travel in Brazil*, a 1939 government publication in English, made up mainly of photos, exemplifies that view. In its section on Rio de Janeiro, it does not contain a single photo of any of the city's oceanfront beaches. It does, however, include photos of such sights as the Municipal Theater, the monument to Emperor Pedro I, the presidential palace, the Gávea Golf Club, the formal gardens of the large Praça Paris, and even the Institute of Education. Other photos show the soaring 780-meter Corcovado Mountain with the giant statue of Christ on its peak, a ship entering Guanabara Bay and sailing past the conical bare granite Sugar Loaf Mountain at the bay's mouth, and a view of Rio de Janeiro and the bay taken from the Tijuca Mountains.[67] Some foreign travelers seem to have shared a similar sentiment. In a forty-seven-page article published in 1930 in *National Geographic*, Frederick Simpich devoted exactly four words to sea-bathing in Rio de Janeiro. The article begins with a photograph of the Botanical Gardens and includes another twenty-two photos showing sights like those featured in *Travel in Brazil*. None of the photos shows bathers at any of Rio de Janeiro's beaches. In a 1939 article on the city, also written for *National Geographic*, W. Robert Moore paid more attention to beach-going but not much more: only five short paragraphs and two photos of bathers resting on the sand in Copacabana in a forty-two-page article with forty-five paragraphs.[68]

A similar lack of emphasis on beach-going also shows up in the two most important Hollywood movies set in the city from the first half of twentieth century: *Flying Down to Rio* (1933), with a cast that includes Dolores del Río, Gene Raymond, Raul Roulien, Fred Astaire, and Ginger Rogers; and Alfred Hitchcock's 1946 *Notorious*, starring Cary Grant, Ingrid Bergman, and Claude Rains. The two films, much like the 1930 and 1939 *National Geographic* articles, portray Rio de Janeiro as a modern and glamorous city, not as a beach resort. Both, it is true, do include scenes of Copacabana's beach. Under a fictional name, the Copacabana Palace Hotel, in fact, figures prominently in *Flying Down to Rio*. Likewise, Bergman's character in *Notorious* takes an apartment in Copacabana with a view of the beach. But the beach as seen from the balcony of her apartment in the film is completely empty of bathers. Just as important, in neither film do any of the characters spend time on the sand or diving into the waves in Copacabana. The closest that viewers come to seeing a character on the beach in the two movies is a less-than-two-minute-long scene in *Flying Down to Rio* in which, without any explanation, Belinha, played by Dolores del Río, suddenly appears on the Copacabana Palace Hotel terrace in a bathing suit. All the other characters in the scene are fully clothed.[69]

As I have shown elsewhere, the later era of mass international air travel also did not turn Rio de Janeiro into a major destination for beach-going tourists. The city was too far from North America and northern Europe, whose middle classes had much more accessible beaches at hand in, respectively, the Caribbean and the Mediterranean. Low incomes and the availability of beaches much closer to other Brazilian population centers impeded the development of domestic tourism.[70] To be sure, Copacabana's fame spread throughout Brazil via the illustrated magazines that circulated nationally, but this did not mean that many Brazilians could visit it. In 1949, *O Cruzeiro*, in one more article celebrating the beach neighborhood, described Copacabana as a "collective dream among Brazilians." It added that, when "a lucky fellow from, say, Maranhão" (a state in far Northeastern Brazil) who had managed to spend his vacation in Rio de Janeiro returned home, the first question his friends asked him was, "And how was Copacabana?"[71]

Unlike what took place in many other cities that have become famous for their beaches, tourism did not play a significant role in shaping the history of beach-going in Rio de Janeiro. The city was, indeed, slow in developing the infrastructure needed to handle any large flow of tourists. In 1956, the *New York Times* observed that "sight-seeing" in Rio de Janeiro was "still on a do-it-yourself basis." The paper pointed out, among other deficiencies, an insufficient number of hotel rooms. Twelve years later, the *Jornal do Brasil*, listing a series of problems, noted that Rio de Janeiro was not prepared to receive large numbers of tourists. It also calculated that the city's forty-six first-, second-, and third-class hotels, twenty-three of which were located in Copacabana and Ipanema, could accommodate at most 15,000 guests. Rio de Janeiro's tourist infrastructure did undergo significant improvements in the last decades of the twentieth century. Nevertheless, as late as 2010, only twenty-seven hotels overlooked the 8.2 kilometers of beach in Copacabana, Leme, Arpoador, Ipanema, and Leblon (by no means were all of the twenty-seven large).[72] The dream of creating a Brazilian Biarritz remained exactly that—a dream.

Flamengo in the 1910s and early 1920s

The dream of an "elegant" beach, nevertheless, persisted among well-off Cariocas and would influence the social geography of sea-bathing, and later, beach-going in Rio de Janeiro. In the nineteenth century, bathers of all classes had shared the city's main beaches. That began to change in the first decades of the twentieth century. By the late 1920s, Copacabana would come to hold an unrivaled position as Rio de Janeiro's "most elegant" beach, as we shall see in chapter 4. Before then, however, the city's wealthy and well-to-do abandoned the beaches located in the center, leaving them to working-, middle- and lower middle-class bathers. They did not give up bathing, and instead, made Flamengo, with its narrow and small stretch of sand, their preferred beach for a morning dip.

Flamengo, to be sure, had long attracted some wealthy bathers (chapter 1). It was conveniently located in the mainly upper-class neighborhood of the same name and within walking distance of Botafogo and Laranjeiras, where many of Rio de Janeiro's wealthy lived. Now, however, bathing at that beach became itself a socially prestigious activity. Evidence of Flamengo's prestige in the 1910s and early 1920s comes from what was then a new type of publication made possible by advances in printing technology: weekly magazines illustrated, sometimes lavishly so, with photographs.[73] These photographs documented the Rio de Janeiro that had emerged from the Pereira Passos reforms and from later changes aimed at further modernizing the city. The magazines also routinely included photos of elite social gatherings and "*instantâneos* [snapshots]" of smartly dressed women, in skirts that grew noticeably shorter in the 1910s and the 1920s, and who, unaccompanied by men, strolled along the Avenida

Rio Branco or in the Largo do Machado, a landscaped square in Laranjeiras. The magazines' photographers also aimed their lenses at the afternoon *footing* (promenade) along the Avenida Beira-Mar in Flamengo, where, especially on Sundays, wealthy Cariocas went to see and be seen, to exchange greetings and compliments, and to flirt in a ritual typical of bourgeois sociability at the time. The new photo-illustrated magazines helped to define, in Ana Maria Mauad's words, "the geography of being modern" in Rio de Janeiro in the early twentieth century.[74] They also helped to define the geography of a new, "civilized" Rio de Janeiro and a geography of upper-class behavior.

Bathing in Flamengo figured in those overlapping geographies. After about 1914, some of Rio de Janeiro's most important illustrated magazines, such as *Careta* and the *Revista da Semana*, began publishing frequent photo spreads of Flamengo beach during the "hot season" (November–March). *Careta*, for instance, printed more than fifty such spreads between January 1914 and the end of December 1920. In both magazines, some of the photos, taken from the seawall that separated the Avenida Beira-Mar from the beach, show numerous bathers in the water or standing on the narrow strip of sand. Others focus on small groups of bathers or on one or more female bathers, who often appear to be posing for the camera. In still other cases, they show men and women in bathing attire walking along the Avenida Beira-Mar on their way to or from the beach (figures 3.6 and 3.7).[75] Such photo spreads did more than simply inform readers that a sizeable number of bathers frequented Flamengo during the summer months. They sent the message that bathing at that beach between six and eight in the morning constituted a "civilized," "modern," upper-class activity. Here, the photos of female bathers, like those of unaccompanied women strolling along the Avenida Rio Branco or in the Largo do Machado, hold additional significance. They conveyed the message that the increasingly visible presence of well-to-do and wealthy women in public was and should be, at least in certain contexts and spaces, an integral part of life in a "modern," "civilized" Rio de Janeiro.

Newspaper and magazine articles complemented the visual messages contained in the photographs. For instance, though she sought the transformation of Copacabana into a Brazilian Ostend, Iracema acknowledged in 1917 that, for the time being, Flamengo was "the most elegant . . . of Rio de Janeiro's beaches." What she called "the flowers of Botafogo"—that is, young women from wealthy families who lived in that "aristocratic" neighborhood—went sea-bathing there. Binóculo, the *Gazeta de Notícias*'s social columnist, for his

FIGURE 3.6. Bathers on Flamengo Streets, 1912. *Careta* (16.11.1912), 17.

FIGURE 3.7. Bathers on Flamengo Beach, 1910. *Careta* (22.1.1910), 25.

part, described Flamengo in 1920 as Rio de Janeiro's "chic beach par excellence." He noted three years later that, during the summer months, there were two main places to see "the most enchanting female figures that our high society possesses": the Largo Dom Afonso, a large landscaped square in Petrópolis, and the beach in Flamengo, where, if they were in Rio de Janeiro, they bathed in the bay's salty water. Binóculo, like other social columnists at the time, frequently published the names of women who attended society balls and receptions or whom he had spotted "doing the Avenue [*fazendo a Avenida*]"—that is, strolling down the Avenida Rio Branco—or taking part in the promenade along the Avenida Beira-Mar. Starting in 1917, he also began citing the names of "enchanting female figures" seen bathing in Flamengo.[76] Bathing in Flamengo, as a 1915 article in *Careta* noted, had, in many ways, become the morning counterpart to the afternoon elite promenade along the avenue lining that beach. The *Revista da Semana* equated the two in 1918 through a full-page photo spread. A panoramic photo of the beach in Flamengo crowded with bathers "in the morning . . . at bathing time" occupies the top half of the page. The bottom half is given over to a photograph of the afternoon promenade (figure 3.8).[77] Sea-bathing in Flamengo in the 1910s and early 1920s constituted, in short, far more than simply a means to cool off in the summer or a chance to meet acquaintances and make new friends. At least for younger members of a rising bourgeoisie, both men and women, it amounted to an opportunity to demonstrate social status.

While Flamengo's reputation as a fashionable destination for sea-bathing flourished, bathing attire changed, reviving anxieties about the delicate balance between fashion, utility, and propriety. In 1916, the *Revista da Semana* claimed that morning bathing there amounted to a "gallery of nudes," incompatible with a city that "was becoming civilized." To be sure, on Flamengo beach, Cariocas had first seen the women's maillot, worn by Carmen Lydia, a young woman well known for her performances at "*bailados artísticos*." Her fame increased in 1915 and 1916 when, dressed in a maillot, she demonstrated her swimming skills and did "artistic" leaps on Flamengo and Botafogo beaches. The press dubbed her the "Brazilian Kellerman," an allusion to the great Australian swimmer, Annette Kellerman, who had gained international fame when she first wore a maillot to swim in public in 1907.[78] Nevertheless, to judge by photographs published in illustrated magazines, few of those who frequented Flamengo beach followed young Carmen Lydia's example. They preferred to wear longer bathing dress (see figure 3.6). But, at that time, many bathers

FIGURE 3.8.
Morning Sea-Bathing and Afternoon *Footing*, Flamengo, 1918. *RS* (5.1.1918), n.p.

abandoned early-twentieth-century styles, which generally included a long shirt and long pants, which covered the entire leg, sometimes even including the ankles. The new styles frequently consisted of a shirt and trunks [known by the French term, *caleçon*], or in some cases, a sort of tunic, underneath which they wore a caleçon. Ever shorter and gradually reaching the level of the knees, these outfits left much of the leg visible.

The greatest problem, however, was not in the water nor even on the narrow strip of sand between the bay and the seawall. Rather, it was on the neighboring streets, and took the form of wet bodies with bare knees. From the middle of the 1910s, newspaper articles regularly denounced the "uncivilized" and "indecorous" morning spectacle as young and well-off Flamengo bathers went on foot to the beach and returned home dripping wet, "almost in Adam's state [*estado quase adâmico*]." According to the articles, this would never have been permitted at the "civilized" bathing stations of Europe. And what would European visitors think should they see this spectacle? wondered many a journalist.[79]

What is perhaps surprising is that men, as much as women, were the critics' principal target. When women went to bathe and returned from the water, they generally wore a sort of bathrobe with a hood, or wrapped themselves in a large sheet. Male bathers, by contrast, generally wore a simple jacket over their bathing dress. The jacket did not cover the naked knees; worse yet, some did not button it, which indiscreetly left their bathing trunks visible at the level of the crotch. Worst of all, some did not bother to wear a jacket; they went to the beach and returned home wearing only trunks and a bathing shirt (see figure 3.6).[80]

In March 1917, the police announced that they would take measures to "repress the old habits" of those bathers who went to the beach "in skimpy attire [*trajes ligeiros*]" that the police judged indecent, about which the press had long complained (including white shorts, presumably because they became almost transparent when wet). Orders to that effect were issued by the

FIGURE 3.9. Mocking the Police Requirement for Men to Wear Jackets over Bathing Dress, 1917. *Careta* (28.4.1917), 11.

delegates responsible for Flamengo, Santa Luzia, and Copacabana beaches. The moralizing campaign, however, did not last long, for the delegates did not issue similar orders in the summers of 1917–1918 and 1918–1919, perhaps because of the disruptions caused by the Spanish flu in the latter summer, which likely reduced the number of bathers.[81] That some greeted the campaign with derision may also have contributed to its short duration. One man mocked the police by posing with a tuxedo jacket over his bathing attire, waving a top hat, a sort of living satirical statue (figure 3.9).

The press complaints that, at least in part, motivated the 1917 police measures did more than just attack the "indecency" of bathers' dress. They also raised the question of whether sea-bathing was compatible with an urban context and with Rio de Janeiro's status as a "civilized" city. The complaints, it should be noted, did not principally target the poor, whose activities were routinely subject to police repression. Rather, the press focused on bathing in Flamengo. This beach attracted prosperous bathers as well as the poor, but it was the period's "chic beach," where the Carioca "elegant set" met during the summer.[82] Thus, in criticizing those who frequented Flamengo beach, the press implicitly questioned the morality and level of civilization of an activity that, besides being socially prestigious, was a major leisure activity for well-off and even elite Cariocas—in other words, the very people whom the press itself judged the most "civilized" and who saw themselves as "civilized." These issues would again be extensively debated from the 1920s to the 1940s in Copacabana, a topic taken up in chapter 5.

From the late nineteenth century to the first decades of the twentieth, Rio de Janeiro underwent rapid changes, as the city became an ever-larger metropolis; slavery ended and industrialization accelerated. The Pereira Passos reforms radically altered the appearance of parts of central Rio de Janeiro and reinforced divisions in the city's social geography. The city that Ulick Ralph Burke had described as "an enormously straggling town" in 1882 became ever more "straggling."[83] Suburbs, housing a growing working class and middle and lower middle class, stretched for kilometers and kilometers along the railway lines to the north and the west of the city's center. By then, the city's wealthy and well-to-do, for the most part, resided in the Zona Sul, which expanded to include the new oceanfront beach neighborhoods of Copacabana and Ipanema, and later, Leblon.

These changes would over the long run influence the history of beach-going in Rio de Janeiro from the 1920s onward. In the short run, they resulted in proposals to transform Copacabana or one of the city's other oceanfront beaches into a luxury resort similar to Ostend, Biarritz, Deauville, or Miami. There, without mixing with the city's lower class, Rio de Janeiro's wealthy, its "smart set," would be able to go sea-bathing at a "civilized," "elegant beach," compatible with the "civilized" Rio de Janeiro that had resulted from the Pereira Passos reforms. The same proposals aimed at attracting tourists. Distance and cost, however, discouraged any significant flow of tourists to the city from North America and Europe during much of the twentieth century, while Brazil's highly unequal distribution of wealth and income, among other factors, prevented Rio de Janeiro's beaches from becoming a destination for large-scale internal tourism comparable to, say, Blackpool or Atlantic City. Tourism, consequently, did not play a major role in shaping the history of the beach in the city in the twentieth century. In that regard, Rio de Janeiro stands apart from many other cities that are famous for their beaches. The lack of any large-scale flow of tourists explains why the Copacabana Palace Hotel, which opened in 1923, long remained the sole large luxury hotel overlooking the city's Atlantic shore.

In the Pereira Passos reforms' aftermath, the city's wealthy abandoned the beaches in the city's center to middle-, lower middle-, and working-class bathers and turned Flamengo into Rio de Janeiro's "elegant beach," a place to see and be seen for younger members of a rising bourgeoisie. Bathing there in the morning, like taking part in the afternoon promenade along that beach, ranked as a socially prestigious activity and afforded opportunities to demonstrate status. Flamengo, however, presented certain disadvantages. Its small and narrow stretch of sand could scarcely accommodate all of Rio de Janeiro's wealthy and well-to-do bathers, whose numbers grew as the city's economy expanded. Perhaps more important, its location made it readily accessible to bathers of diverse classes. Cariocas who lived in mansions in Laranjeiras, Botafogo, and Flamengo could easily walk there for a morning sea bath, but so, too, could lower-class residents of parts of central Rio de Janeiro as well as the more than 1,500 workers and their families who lived in company housing at a large textile mill located in Laranjeiras. Furthermore, the district of Glória, made up mainly of the "aristocratic" neighborhoods of Laranjeiras and Flamengo, had its share of cheap rooming houses, tenements, and other types of lower-class housing. The same was true of the adjacent and equally "aristocratic" neighborhood of Botafogo. It should therefore come as no surprise that, despite all its cachet, Flamengo in the 1910s and early 1920s was far from being an exclusively upper-class beach. Binóculo was undoubtedly correct in proclaiming Flamengo to be Rio de Janeiro's "chic beach par excellence" in 1920 and in pointing out three years later that, in the summer, bathing there attracted some of "the most enchanting female figures that our high society possesses." Yet, as he also acknowledged in late January 1922, bathers of "all social conditions" gathered at that beach, "squeezing themselves together and running into each other on a half-dozen square meters" of sand. Here, he wrote less than two weeks later, is the "paradox": "Our beach regarded as chic is [also] the paradise of the unemployed and of idlers (*vadios*) who, given the ease of access and the nearness to their residences, infest it."[84] To find a more socially exclusive and also, for that matter, more spacious beach, Rio de Janeiro's wealthy and well-to-do needed to traverse the Old and New Tunnels, which they would do in larger and larger numbers in the first decades of the twentieth century. On the other side of the tunnels, as the next chapter will show, they would begin to invent the current practice of beach-going.

4

From Albert I to Prince George

The Rise of Beach-Going

IN SEPTEMBER 1920, Albert I, King of the Belgians, arrived in Rio de Janeiro on an official visit. Setting aside the deranged Queen Maria, who, with her son, João, fled Napoleon's troops for what was then colonial Portuguese America in 1807, it was the first time that a ruling European monarch had set foot on Brazilian soil. He spent more than three weeks in the Brazilian capital, where authorities carried out a series of celebratory events. The king, then forty-three years old, was regarded as a hero for his efforts to defend Belgium against Germany during the First World War. He also had a reputation for being athletic, so much so that the Brazilian press called him the "sportsman king." The authorities, nevertheless, did not anticipate that, while in Rio de Janeiro, he might want to engage in any sort of physical activity in the water. But, within hours of arriving, the king made it known that he wished to go sea-bathing. Early the next morning, an official car took him from Guanabara Palace, in Laranjeiras, to the far end of Copacabana. It was barely seven when the car reached the beachfront mansion owned by Alexander MacKenzie, local director of the Anglo-Canadian Rio de Janeiro Tramway, Light & Power Company, Ltd. At the mansion, he changed and proceeded to the beach, where he threw himself into the water and demonstrated his skills as an "excellent swimmer." He subsequently returned to Copacabana for an early morning sea bath throughout his stay in Rio de Janeiro, always accompanied by municipal lifeguards. After his swims, which generally lasted about a half hour, the king put on a robe and took a vigorous walk along the Avenida Atlântica, the avenue bordering Copacabana's broad, sandy beach. The press gave the monarch's bathing excursions considerable coverage, and crowds gathered to see him in the water.[1] Yet, despite all the attention that his daily excursions to Copacabana received, the Belgian monarch did nothing new: he went sea-bathing just as thousands of Cariocas had done since at least the early nineteenth century.

Eleven years later, Rio de Janeiro received another official visit by European royalty. This time it was Edward, Prince of Wales, who would briefly rule Great Britain as Edward VIII. Accompanying him was Prince George, his younger brother and the future George VI. On 8 April 1931, the thirty-five-year-old Prince George, like his cousin, Albert I, took advantage of his stay in Rio de Janeiro to dive into the waves in Copacabana, which, by then, ranked as the city's most "aristocratic" and "elegant" beach. Unlike the Belgian king, however, the prince, who at the time was staying at the Copacabana Palace, arrived not early in the morning, but shortly before eleven. Just as important, the prince did not, after his quick swim, take a walk along the Avenida Atlântica. Instead, he returned to the sand and remained there, with two members of his entourage, sunning himself for an hour or so.[2] Whereas King Albert had gone sea-bathing, Prince George engaged in beach-going. And, like the prince, many of the Cariocas at the beach in Copacabana on that sunny autumn day in April 1931 spent much of their time on the sand and not in the surf. The eleven years that separated the two royal visits saw the shift from the nineteenth-century practice of sea-bathing to a recognizably modern form of beach-going in Copacabana and Ipanema. A mix of technological changes; patterns of urbanization; the influence of medicine, eugenics, foreign fashion, and real estate speculation; the expansion of Rio de Janeiro's upper and upper middle classes as well as investment by government and privately owned utility companies, in different ways, all combined to bring about the shift. That mix can, however, be distilled to four main factors: Copacabana's development as a fashionable, elite residential neighborhood; the growth in automobile ownership; the establishment of an effective lifeguard service in the 1910s; and perhaps most important, the rise of tanning as a fashionable custom. Together, these factors promoted beach-going as a fashionable leisure activity in Rio de Janeiro and helped make Copacabana and Ipanema the city's "elegant" and "aristocratic" beaches, as the press regularly called them. Rio de Janeiro's oceanfront beach neighborhoods did not develop into the "Brazilian Biarritz" envisioned by some locals in the early twentieth century (chapter 3). Instead, they developed into posh residential neighborhoods for the city's upper and upper-middle classes, with the beaches themselves becoming the preferred playground for those Cariocas.

FIGURE 4.1. Copacabana in the 1890s. Arquivo Images2You.

"An Immense Expanse of Sand" Transformed into "the Most Aristocratic Neighborhood"

When the Companhia Ferro-Carril do Jardim Botânico opened the Old Tunnel and extended tram service to Copacabana in 1892, residents of Rio de Janeiro finally gained relatively easy access to the city's Atlantic shoreline. Cariocas who took the tram through the tunnel found in Copacabana a broad, sandy beach quite unlike the bayshore's narrow beaches.[3] Initially, however, Rio de Janeiro's residents had few reasons to take the new tramline. Copacabana at the time amounted to little more than "an immense expanse of sand," bordered by low, brambly vegetation and numerous *pitangueiras* (Cayenne-cherry trees) and *cajueiros* (cashew trees). Here and there among the trees stood the small houses of an unknown number of fishing families and a few other modest dwellings, barely visible in a photo of Copacabana taken in the mid-1890s by Marc Ferrez (figure 4.1). Entirely missing from the photograph are the streets that local landowners had received permission to open since the 1870s, for most of them existed only on paper. Those landowners proposed opening other streets in the hopes of dividing their properties into residential lots for sale, but it proved difficult to find buyers. Copacabana, located on what was then

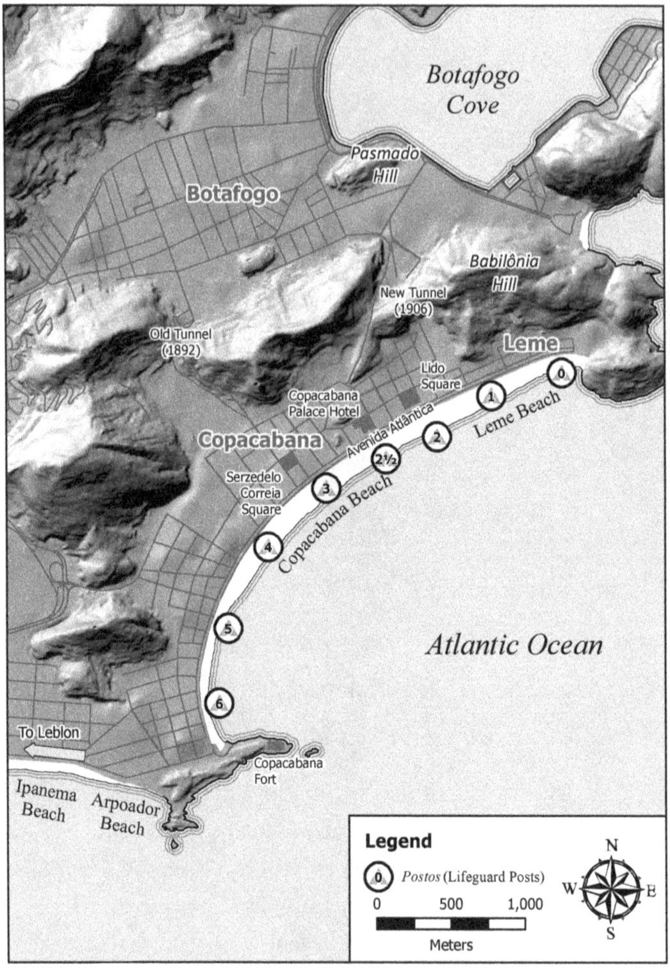

MAP 4.1. Copacabana in the First Half of the Twentieth Century. *Posto* locations approximate; map shows 1940 street grid.

the far southern edge of Rio de Janeiro, lacked even a minimum of basic urban infrastructure. Moreover, until 1900, the Companhia Ferro-Carril do Jardim Botânico barred private traffic through the Old Tunnel; only the company's trams could use it (map 4.1).[4]

To increase traffic, the Companhia Ferro-Carril do Jardim Botânico began printing on its ticket stubs short rhyming verses that encouraged passengers to visit Copacabana. Copacabana, according to the verses, was an ideal location for "fashionable young men" to take "graceful young ladies" for a picnic; it offered easy profits for "capitalists" interested in investing in real estate; and it was a "powerful sanatorium" for those suffering illnesses of "the body or the soul." Another verse claimed that promising a bride to build a house in Copacabana would ensure marital happiness.[5] To attract even more passengers, in 1905 the company opened a large bar on the beach in Leme, which it shortly thereafter leased to the Brahma Brewery; the bar offered drink, food, and amusements such as obstacle races and fireworks. By then, another nighttime establishment was already operating at the opposite end of the beach: the restaurant and cabaret known as Mère Louise. Owned by the French-born Madame Chabas, it also let out "furnished rooms" for bathers to change. After 1907, bathers had other options, especially if they planned to spend more than a day at the beach. They could take a room at the large Pensão Oceânica or at one of the smaller pensions in the neighborhood.[6] Nevertheless, many visitors to Copacabana in the first two decades of the twentieth century had no intention of entering the water. Instead, they went there in the late afternoon or the evening on hot summer days. Fully clothed, they sat at the open-air tables at the Brahma Brewery's bar or directly on the sand; joined by local residents, also fully clothed, they took in the cooling ocean breezes.[7] Other nighttime visitors had less innocent purposes. Unmarried couples sought out the shadowy rocks beyond the Brahma Brewery's bar or rented one of Madame Chabas' "furnished rooms" for discreet amorous encounters.[8]

Whatever their purpose, visitors to Copacabana in the middle years of the first decade of the last century found a neighborhood that was finally beginning to show signs of significant growth. A municipal sanitation inspector reported in 1905 that, setting aside shacks and huts, Copacabana, Leme, and Ipanema together had 483 buildings, most of which were houses, and another 65 under construction. He also estimated that the neighborhoods had a combined population of some 3,000 inhabitants. The majority of those inhabitants, in all likelihood, lived in Copacabana or Leme, given that the tramway did not reach most of Ipanema until 1902.[9]

Nothing guaranteed that Copacabana and Ipanema would become preferred places of residence for Rio de Janeiro's upper and upper middle classes. Their natural beauty was undeniable, but Rio de Janeiro had no shortage of areas that stood out for their natural beauty. Some of those areas, already endowed with tram service and a basic infrastructure, were even regarded as fashionable at the time. But, in most cases, they were transformed after 1910 into working-, middle-, and lower middle-class neighborhoods and industrial districts.[10] Copacabana and Ipanema might easily have met the same fate.

Indeed, in 1894, city councilor Alfredo Barcelos argued that, given the lack of basic infrastructure, no one would build palatial mansions on the barren, windswept sands of Copacabana and Ipanema. "Let us be logical," he stated, and "allow the proletariat and individuals of modest means to erect their shacks [*choupanas*] and . . . small houses" without having to meet the building requirements that applied to the city's central areas and its other already urbanized districts. In his view, only after lower-class "settlers [*povoadores*]" had "cleared [*desbravado*]" "the terrain" should the authorities enforce the requirements. His arguments ended up carrying influence at least in the short run. In 1898, the municipal council granted builders in Ipanema "freedom of construction [*liberdade de construção*]" for five years; in other words, they were exempted from having to follow the building code. In 1902, councilors passed a new law exempting builders in both Ipanema and Copacabana from meeting the building code's requirements for ten years.[11] Regardless of the legislation, the municipal government seems to have paid little attention to the new buildings being constructed in the neighborhood in its early years or to the state of existing buildings there. The sanitation inspector who surveyed Copacabana in 1905 reported having found numerous "shacks," which he did not bother to count. Some of them, no doubt, belonged to people who lived from fishing or were located on the hills overlooking Copacabana, where favelas, which would later expand rapidly, were already springing up. Other shacks, in all likelihood, lined the neighborhood's still unpaved back and side streets. Moreover, as *O Paiz* reported in April 1905, cortiços (tenements)—a type of construction that the authorities were busy demolishing in the city's center—had begun to proliferate in Copacabana.[12]

A few months later, at the urging of Mayor Pereira Passos, the municipal council revoked the 1898 and 1902 exemptions from the building code. The Federal District's government, still headed by Pereira Passos, began work on the construction of the Avenida Atlântica, a paved avenue with electric lighting along nearly the full length of the graceful curve of Copacabana's 4.15-kilometer beach. The mosaic sidewalk on the beach side of the avenue displayed a pattern of alternating white and black "waves." Although the avenue has since been rebuilt and widened more than once, the sidewalk next to the sand still displays the same pattern, which has become one of the best-known symbols of Copacabana.[13]

In 1907, one year before the new avenue was completed, Copacabana had a population large enough to sustain its own newspaper, *O Copacabana*, which came out, often with photographs, every fortnight and which ceased publication only in 1919. Like its longer-lasting and much more ambitious successor, *Beira-Mar*, published regularly between 1922 and 1944, the newspaper reported on the social activities of Copacabana's residents and on topics of local interest. Both periodicals also routinely called on municipal authorities to improve the neighborhood's infrastructure.[14] Precise information about who lived in Copacabana during the years that *O Copacabana* circulated is scarce. There were, of course, the fishers, their families, and the inhabitants of the cortiços and of the hillside shacks, all of whom, it is safe to assume, seldom read the newspaper. The neighborhood, however, had also begun to attract wealthier residents. As early as 1908, *O Copacabana*, which was sold only in the beachside neighborhood, featured advertisements for Patek Philippe luxury watches.[15]

By 1914, the "immense expanse of sand" of the 1890s was giving way to a fast-growing neighborhood of neatly laid-out streets lined by spacious, detached single-family houses.[16] The neighborhood's growth led the municipal council in 1914 to detach Copacabana from the district of Lagoa and to create the new district of Copacabana, which encompassed not only Copacabana and Leme, but also Ipanema. Six years later, the 1920 national census counted 22,761 permanent residents in the district—more than a sevenfold increase in fifteen years.[17] That rapid growth continued, and by 1940, the Copacabana district had 74,133 residents.[18]

Numerous complaints about inadequate or faulty urban services and infrastructure (routinely published in *O Copacabana* and *Beira-Mar*) give the impression that the fast-growing beach neighborhoods of Copacabana and Ipanema suffered from municipal neglect. There was, most certainly, room for improvement, especially in the early decades of the twentieth century: some side streets remained unpaved, potholes were common, and wild vegetation threatened to take over parts of Ipanema beach. And, just as today, heavy rains produced *línguas negras* (black tongues), narrow rivulets of fetid black water that slowly made their way through the beaches to the sea, for some areas still lacked connections to the underground sewer system.[19]

Such challenges notwithstanding, the two fast-growing beach neighborhoods actually benefited from disproportionately generous investments by the municipal government and by the foreign-owned utility companies; both favored Copacabana and Ipanema over the suburbs. This favoritism began during the Pereira Passos administration with the construction of the Avenida Atlântica and was extended to Ipanema and Leblon under later administrations. In 1917, the authorities inaugurated the Avenida Vieira Souto, Ipanema's equivalent of the Avenida Atlântica: a paved beachfront avenue with electric lighting. Two years later, they opened the Avenida Delfim Moreira, another paved avenue with electric lighting, lining the 1.25 kilometers of beach in Leblon. There would, at first view, be nothing especially noteworthy in the opening of that avenue except that, unlike Copacabana and Ipanema, Leblon at the time was a sparsely inhabited neighborhood, little more than "an immense expanse of sand," as Copacabana had been in the 1890s.[20] The construction of the Avenida Delfim Moreira, in effect, paved the way for Leblon to take its place, alongside Copacabana and Ipanema, as a mainly upper- and upper middle-class beach neighborhood after 1930. By 1933, the great majority of the streets in the district of Copacabana were paved; and most had electric lighting. Nearly three-fourths had sewer lines, more than 93 percent had access to running water, and the district was well served by streetcars.[21]

In the suburbs, by contrast, unpaved streets predominated, often by a wide margin, and electric lighting was the exception. Likewise, in five suburban districts, not a single street had connections to the sewer system; in a sixth district, Irajá, one of the fastest growing suburbs, sewer lines ran along only 0.8 percent of all streets. Residents of the sprawling suburbs also had less access to tramways and bus lines than their counterparts in Copacabana. In all but two suburban districts, wood houses, shacks, huts, and sheds (*casas de madeira*, *casebres*, *barracões*, and *galpões*) accounted for at least one-fifth of all built structures; in Anchieta, the proportion surpassed 40 percent. But, in Copacabana, more than 92 percent of all houses and other structures were built of brick and mortar or reinforced concrete.[22]

Photographs taken by Augusto Malta in the 1920s and 1930s provide visual corroboration of Copacabana's development.[23] They show streets lined by well-built and spacious detached houses known at the time as bungalows (*bangalôs*) or chalets (*chalés*); they had two to three stories, front gardens, separated from the street by a wall, which was generally low, and backyards (figure 4.2). Purchasing such a house or having one built would have almost certainly required at least an upper middle-class income. In one of Copacabana's numerous bungalows, the journalist and humorist Sérgio Porto (1923–1968), who also wrote under the pseudonym Stanislaw Ponte Preta, spent his childhood

FIGURE 4.2. Copacabana in 1907. Arquivo Images2You.

and adolescence. His family at the time lived on the Rua Leopoldo Miguez, three blocks back from the beach, and serves as an example of the many upper middle-class families that took up residence in Copacabana from the late 1910s onward. His maternal grandfather and great grandfather were prominent civil engineers. His father, who belonged to a family of rural landowners, worked for the Banco do Brasil, the country's largest bank. Many (male) members and would-be members of the middle and upper middle classes, at the time, coveted white-collar positions at the Banco do Brasil because they brought status and came with attractive salaries, job security, generous pensions, and other benefits. Given his family's economic situation, Sérgio, not surprisingly, studied at private schools, including, for a while, a boarding school. Except for the period at the boarding school, he grew up going to the beach almost daily. And, in passing, it is worth noting that he married a young woman, who also grew up in Copacabana and who frequented the same stretch of the beach that he did.[24]

In the photos that he took of Copacabana in the late 1920s and early 1930s, Augusto Malta caught in his lens not only chalets and bungalows but also much larger houses, some of which contemporaries would have classified as *palacetes* (palatial mansions) (figure 4.3). Owners of such residences included the Guinle family, whose members controlled the Companhia Docas de Santos, which held a ninety-year monopoly concession to operate the docks in Santos, Brazil's busiest port. One member of the family, Otávio Guinle, built the Copacabana Palace Hotel.[25]

A photograph of Copacabana taken in 1936 by German photographer Peter Fuss shows a thoroughly urbanized neighborhood that had benefited from the generous investments made by the municipal government and by the utility companies during the previous quarter century (figure 4.4). Over time, the well-to-do residents of the oceanfront beach neighborhoods, unlike the working-, middle-, and lower middle-class inhabitants of the suburbs, had sufficient political influence to obtain from the authorities further improvements in urban infrastructure.

To be sure, not all residents of the beachfront neighborhoods were affluent. Copacabana counted among its inhabitants a large contingent of maids, cooks, nannies, and other live-in servants.[26] The district's population also included numerous, generally poorly paid service workers such as doormen, delivery boys, women who took in washing, janitors, gardeners, and chauffeurs, as well as salesclerks employed by neighborhoods shops. To that list—and not counting fishers and their families—it is necessary to add restaurant cooks, the waiters, and bartenders who worked at restaurants, cafés, bars, and taverns (*botequins*) in the beachfront neighborhoods, hotel employees, and bakers' assistants, who, at local bakeries, turned out dozens and dozens of loaves of fresh French bread (*pão francês*) every morning.[27] Some of those workers lived on the premises where they were employed. But most had to find their own lodgings at a convenient distance from their place of work. That might mean living in a shack in one of the district's hillside favelas, which continued to grow in the first decades of the twentieth century.[28] Shacks were not, however, confined to the favelas, and remained common on the district's back and side streets in the 1930s. In 1933, the district had 819 houses located in what were at the time misleadingly called *avenidas* (avenues), which today are more often known as *vilas*. In the past, just as today, an avenida, or vila, consisted of a narrow and often gated cul-de-sac lined on both sides by small row houses of the sort that a better-off working-class or lower middle-class family could afford to rent.[29]

Copacabana housed a small army of service workers precisely because it had become one of the preferred places of residence for Rio de Janeiro's expanding

FIGURE 4.3. *Palacetes* in Copacabana, ca. 1920. Arquivo Images2You.

FIGURE 4.4. Copacabana in the Mid-1930s. Fuss, *Brasilien*, plate 74. Arquivo Images2You.

upper and upper middle classes. Thus, the existence of favelas and avenidas, as well as shacks and huts on back and side streets, paradoxically attests not to the district's poverty but, rather, to its wealth. As early as 1925, the *Revista da Semana* noted that Copacabana and Leme had come to rival Botafogo as the city's most "elegant" neighborhood. Twenty years later, *O Cruzeiro* described Copacabana as "the most aristocratic neighborhood" in Rio de Janeiro. By 1946, over 300 of 1,000 individuals listed in *Nossa Sociedade*, the city's prestigious social register, lived in Copacabana and Leme. Another 100 lived in Ipanema and Leblon. These four neighborhoods had supplanted Botafogo and Flamengo as the home of the city's elite.[30]

The registry also reveals that, of the 306 residents of Copacabana whose names appear in its pages, at least 70 lived in apartments. Some of them may have resided in the high-rise apartment buildings shown in Fuss's panoramic photo taken about a decade before the registry was compiled (figure 4.4). Construction of apartment buildings was key to Copacabana's growth. The first apartment building in Copacabana, with a mere four stories, went up in 1923; it stood out in a neighborhood where single-family dwellings predominated. In the next decades, as local construction firms began routinely building with reinforced concrete, the number of apartment houses multiplied. The 1928 Condominium Law facilitated the spread of apartments by clarifying the relationship between apartment owners and the building.[31] They soon became a characteristic feature of the neighborhood's landscape, displacing single-family dwellings. Already in 1933, the district of Copacabana boasted forty-two buildings with at least five stories.[32] Five years later, the *Correio da Manhã* reported that Copacabana led the way in the construction of "skyscrapers," which the paper defined as buildings with at least six stories. Forty such buildings, seventeen of them with nine or more stories, were inaugurated in 1934 alone. The first six months of 1936, in turn, saw the construction of fourteen "skyscrapers" in Copacabana, eight of which had ten or more stories; the tallest had fourteen. The paper dubbed Copacabana "the neighborhood of reinforced concrete."[33]

Many of these apartment buildings had ornately appointed foyers and impressive main doorways that publicly declared their residents' wealth and status, as well as and large apartments destined for upper- and upper middle-class families, accessed by elevators. For instance, in the Edifício Guidamar, built in 1944, each apartment occupied an entire floor and had four bedrooms, a foyer, living room, formal dining room, music room, sewing room, lunchroom, one half-bath and two full bathrooms, a kitchen, a breakfast room, and two balconies, one of them glass-enclosed (a *jardim de inverno*). The apartments also came with living quarters for servants, a servants' bathroom, and a "service area [*área de serviço*]" for washing clothes and the like.[34]

As the Guidamar's 1944 inauguration suggests, the Second World War did not put a stop to Copacabana's expansion, not even after Brazil entered the conflict on the side of the Allies in August 1942. A significant number of well-to-do European refugees took up residence in Copacabana. Harry Franck, who visited Rio de Janeiro in mid-1941, noted that "Copacabana was [already] so crowded with refugees, many of them act[ing] as they were there to stay," that it was difficult to book a hotel room on short notice. While many Europeans at least initially stayed in hotels, others preferred rented apartments. Refugees, moreover, often brought with them their life's savings, part of which some invested in new apartment buildings. Doing so provided them with not only a fairly safe haven for their savings (with the possibility of a good return) but also a place to live that they could call their own, and in a building that they had helped construct.[35] Furthermore, a combination of inflation and wartime profits from industry, trade, and export production encouraged real estate speculation, which in Copacabana meant raising new apartment buildings.[36] The war did bring about a short-lived novelty: some of the new buildings put on the market at the time came with underground air-raid shelters.[37]

The contrast between two photographs of Copacabana's Avenida Atlântica, one from the mid- or late 1920s and the other from the early 1940s, makes clear the changes brought about by reinforced concrete and real estate speculation (figures 4.5 and 4.6). The first photo shows an avenue lined with large houses, mansions, palacetes, and what appear to be a few small apartment buildings. In the second, many of those houses, mansions, and palacetes have given way to a wall, albeit interrupted, of ten-to-twelve-story apartment buildings overlooking the beach.[38]

Not all the apartment buildings constructed between the late 1920s and the early 1940s still stand today; newer buildings have long since replaced many of them. Some of those that have survived have left Copacabana with a legacy of superb art deco architecture. Far more important, the construction of numerous apartment buildings in Copacabana and in Ipanema allowed a growing number of families from Rio de Janeiro's expanding upper and upper middle classes to move to the two oceanfront neighborhoods. As a result, Copacabana's population density more than tripled from 2,816.5 inhabitants

FIGURE 4.5. Avenida Atlântica, 1920s.
Arquivo Images2You.

per square kilometer to 9,173.4 between 1920 and 1940.[39] Living there, members of those well-off families had only to cross the street or walk a few blocks to reach the broad, sandy beaches of Copacabana and Ipanema, where they helped invent a recognizably modern form of beach-going as an upper- and upper middle-class leisure activity from the mid-1920s onward.

Participating in that process did not, however, require moving permanently to one of the neighborhoods along Rio de Janeiro's Atlantic shoreline. Wealthy Cariocas from other neighborhoods could spend their summer mornings at the beach in Copacabana by taking up temporary residence at the Copacabana Palace Hotel or at one of the neighborhood's other hotels. In a crônica published in the *Ilustração Brasileira* in February 1925, the narrator encounters, almost by chance, at the beach in Copacabana her friend Marina, whom she has not seen in several days. "I have been staying, like most of our select set [*escol*]," Marina explains, "at the Copacabana Palace." Staying there, she adds, allows her to go to the beach every morning and afternoon.[40] Other wealthy and upper middle-class Cariocas could do the same by renting a house or apartment in Copacabana or Ipanema during the "bathing season." The classified sections of Rio de Janeiro's papers routinely carried, from the mid-1910s, ads offering for rent furnished flats and houses in Copacabana and Ipanema and, later, Leblon during the "bathing season." They also published ads placed by those

FIGURE 4.6. Avenida Atlântica, 1941. Photograph by Geneviève Naylor. Arquivo Images2You.

seeking to lease a summer residence near the beach in one of those neighborhoods.[41] A summer spent in Copacabana serves, in fact, as the backdrop for a 1938 children's book by the poet and journalist Cecília Meireles (1901–1964). In it, a well-off family from Tijuca, along with their cook and maid, move to the beachside neighborhood for the summer.[42] Whether they stayed at the Copacabana Palace, as Marina and her "set" did in the 1925 crônica or at another hotel or at a rented house or apartment for the season, upper- and upper middle-class Cariocas who lived elsewhere in the city, like their counterparts who resided permanently in the oceanfront neighborhoods, played a role in transforming Copacabana and Ipanema into "elegant" and "aristocratic" beaches. Thus, while Copacabana did not become a Brazilian Biarritz for international tourists (chapter 3), it offered a posh lifestyle to members of the local upper class and aspiring upper-middle class.

"A Long Line of Polished . . . Luxury Automobiles Sparkling by the Sea"

Well-heeled residents of neighborhoods like Flamengo, Laranjeiras, Botafogo, or Tijuca also sought a means to visit the beaches of Copacabana and Ipanema for the day. They could not simply take a bus, because buses barred passengers in bathing attire. The trams also imposed severe restrictions on such passengers.[43] The solution to this problem came on four wheels with the technology of the internal combustion engine; in other words, with the automobile.

Although the first cars appeared on Rio de Janeiro's streets in the late 1890s, there were a mere sixty-six in the city by 1906. Even as late as 1909 to 1913, the average number of passenger cars registered annually with the Federal District's government was only 349.[44] The real leap in car ownership came after the end of the First World War, in the years that saw Copacabana emerge as Rio de Janeiro's most fashionable beach. In 1919, Ford began producing finished automobiles at a plant in São Paulo, using what were known as complete knock-down kits. Workers at the plant assembled vehicles from imported parts in the kits. Ford later opened similar plants elsewhere in Brazil, including one in Rio de Janeiro in 1927. General Motors, by then, was also assembling finished vehicles from knock-down kits at a plant in São Paulo. The establishment of those plants did not make passenger cars inexpensive in Brazil; on the contrary, for decades, they would remain almost a luxury item. But local production did make cars far more readily available. Official records reflect that greater availability. By the early 1930s, owners were registering thousands of new cars in Rio de Janeiro each year. In 1940, the Federal District licensed 19,961 such cars (or eleven per thousand inhabitants).[45] That number, though extremely low by current standards, indicates a substantial increase in car ownership among Rio de Janeiro's well-to-do. Owning a car made it easy for them to reach one of the oceanfront beaches regardless of where they lived in the city. As early as 1916, João do Rio had noted in an article that "the rich," already dressed in bathing attire, went to the beach by car.[46]

Car ownership alone did not initially solve all the problems of motorists who wished to spend a morning or afternoon in the water and on the sand in Copacabana. A 1915 municipal law required that all drivers wear a shirt and jacket. That posed no difficulty for the many car owners who at the time employed chauffeurs. Indeed, a photo accompanying João do Rio's 1916 article shows a woman in a bathing costume stepping out of a chauffeur-driven motorcar. The 1915 law did, however, represent an inconvenience for those motorists who wanted to go bathing and who did not have a chauffeur. The inconvenience did not last long; enforcement of the dress code, at least when it came to motorists driving their own cars, soon fell by the wayside. Even so, in 1927, the Federal District's Inspectorate of Vehicles issued new orders prohibiting motorists from driving in bathing attire. Álvaro de Penalva, a columnist for the *Gazeta de Notícias*, complained that, as a result, he found himself in a predicament. Penalva, who lived far from the shore, wanted to go bathing. Although he did own a car, he could not afford to hire a chauffeur to drive him to the beach in his suit. "Why," he asked, was "bathing attire incompatible with the steering wheel?" The Inspectorate apparently came to agree with Penalva and ceased enforcing the prohibition.[47] Nevertheless, for decades, the authorities would continue to try to regulate what beach-going drivers did and did not wear. Thus, (male) drivers in trunks had to wear a sport coat or, later, at the very least a shirt while at the wheel.[48] But the ban on shirtless driving scarcely amounted to an obstacle so great as to prevent men from using their cars to take family or friends to the beach or to go alone.

By the late 1920s, it had become common for affluent Cariocas to drive to the beach in Copacabana, and later, to Ipanema. *O Cruzeiro* published in 1928 a serialized short story in which Jorge, a well-heeled young man, picks up his girlfriend, already wearing her bathing suit, and then speeds off in his motorcar to Copacabana, where the couple spend the morning at the beach. One year later, *Beira-Mar* called attention to the rows of automobiles parked along the Avenida Atlântica on one Sunday when the beach was crowded. The German novelist Kasimir Edschmid shortly thereafter visited Rio de Janeiro, where he witnessed numerous cars pull up and park along the same avenue. Out of the cars spilled "men and women in bathing dress." In turn, the *Jornal do Brasil* in 1932 noted "the expensive [parked] cars" lined up in front of one stretch of Copacabana's beach "in a display of elegance and wealth"; they were awaiting their owners, who were on the sand or in the water. Three years later, an article in *Careta* observed that, "on sunny Sundays, a long line of polished . . . luxury automobiles sparkling by the sea" regularly stood parked along Arpoador, the portion of beach in Ipanema nearest to Copacabana. Although most of those cars were driven by men, who might in some cases have been chauffeurs, women also drove to the beach. In the late 1930s, the German traveler Wolfgang Hoffmann-Harnisch saw "luxury cars," with "ladies in maillots" behind the wheel, arrive in Copacabana.[49]

Beach-goers could also take a taxi. The number of taxis, like the number of passenger cars, grew rapidly in Rio de Janeiro after the First World War. Some taxi drivers apparently refused to accept beach-going passengers in bathing attire, especially those returning home after a morning or afternoon on the sand and in the water, for understandable reasons: if their suits had not yet dried and they were not wearing a robe, they would leave the taxi's back seat unpleasantly wet for the next passengers, and the sand inevitably still clinging to their bodies would also rub off on the back seat. Nevertheless, other taxi drivers did accept beach-going passengers in their suits, who, of course, needed to be well enough off to afford the fares to and from the beach.[50]

The use of private cars fell dramatically during the Second World War, particularly for luxury purposes, due to strict rationing of gasoline and to declining availability of European and American imported cars and auto parts.[51] With peace, however, the government ended gasoline rationing, new imported passenger automobiles again became readily available for purchase, and the flow of affluent bathers driving to the oceanfront beaches grew dramatically. The Federal District issued licenses to 37,481 privately owned passenger cars in 1949, or just under sixteen passenger automobiles per thousand residents. Clearly, car ownership in the immediate postwar years remained by and large a privilege of the upper and upper middle classes. The number of vehicles registered in 1949 nevertheless represented an 88 percent increase over 1940.[52]

With the rapid expansion of car ownership after the First World War, Rio de Janeiro's wealthy and well-to-do could continue to live in Flamengo,

Botafogo, Laranjeiras, or even Tijuca (in the Zona Norte), and drive in their own cars to Copacabana and Ipanema for a morning on the sand and in the surf. At those beaches, together with the ever-growing number of upper- and upper middle-class Cariocas who did live in Copacabana and Ipanema, they took part in developing the new practice of beach-going.

Overcoming "a Macabre Tradition"

The transformation of Copacabana and Ipanema into "aristocratic" beaches also required public investments to ensure bathers' safety. Copacabana and Ipanema are open oceanfront beaches. Not only do the waves break there with greater force than they do along the bayshore, but riptides and undertows make bathing in Copacabana and Ipanema far more dangerous than at beaches located within the bay. In Copacabana, the tides form ever shifting "valleys" (*valas* and *valões*) below the surface, where currents rush out into the open ocean, easily carrying unsuspecting bathers with them. The dangers have not disappeared in recent decades. On some days, unwary bathers who enter the water at Rio de Janeiro's Atlantic beaches find themselves caught in a quick-moving undertow or repeatedly pushed down by the pounding surf.[53]

Those dangers, as the *Revista da Semana* noted in 1916, help explain why so many bathers continued to prefer Flamengo. Copacabana had, in the words of the magazine, "a macabre tradition" of fatal drownings. Some of Copacabana's early bathers recognized the need for a lifesaving service and they founded in 1900 the Sociedade de Socorros Balneários (roughly, the Bathers' Aid Society), a private club that provided fee-paying members with the services of a banhista nadador comparable to those employed at the city's bayshore bathing establishments. The society, which failed to obtain official support from the municipal government, functioned until 1908. Three years later, some of the same bathers established a similar organization, the short-lived Sociedade de Sauvetage de Copacabana (Copacabana Lifesaving Society). Bathers who did not belong to one of the two societies would presumably have been forced to rely, if they found themselves in trouble, on the aid of local fishermen.[54]

Neither the two societies nor the efforts of local fishermen put an end to the cases of fatal drownings in Copacabana, some of which can only be described as calamitous. For instance, in late March 1911, Lieutenant Frederico Borges, the son of a federal deputy representing the state of Ceará, his wife, Guiomar, and Maria da Glória, his fourteen-year-old sister-in-law, gathered at the beach for their regular morning sea bath. They were joined by Mário Miranda, employed by the Customs Department, Carolina, Miranda's wife, and the couple's son, Sílvio, aged twelve. The two families, which both lived in Copacabana and which were neighbors, entered the water together. The sea was apparently rough that morning. Within minutes, other bathers on the sand heard their cries for help. So, too, did José de Castro, a local fisherman, who happened to be passing by and who had saved several other bathers in the past. Without hesitating, Castro threw himself into the water and managed to rescue the young Sílvio, whom he left safe on the beach. The fisherman then dove back into the water, hoping to rescue the others. Sílvio, seeing his mother still struggling with the waves, followed Castro; engulfed by the sea, the boy, who did not know how to swim, drowned. In the end, five of the original party of six had perished; only Carolina survived. *O Copacabana*'s reporting on the tragedy emphasized the urgent need for a lifesaving service in Copacabana.[55]

Two years later, in 1913, Rio de Janeiro's municipal council finally approved a law authorizing the Federal District's government to organize such a service. The first timid step in that direction came shortly thereafter: an ambulance, with a doctor from the city's General Directorate of Hygiene and Public Assistance, parked every morning on the Avenida Atlântica at about the mid-point of Copacabana's beach. Mayor Bento Rivadávia expanded the service in 1916 when he inaugurated at the far end of Copacabana (near what is now Post 6) a "provisional lifesaving post," staffed by a physician and "swimmers [*nadadores*]"—that is, lifeguards—"supplied . . . with medications and equipment to aid the asphyxiated" as well as lifesaving boats. Apparently, the original plans called for the establishment of two other such posts, one in Leme, at the opposite end of the beach, and the other at its mid-point.[56] Even three lifesaving posts could not possibly have offered adequate protection for bathers at a beach more than four kilometers in length (not counting the nearly three kilometers of beach in Ipanema). Cases of fatal and near fatal drownings, not surprisingly, continued to occur after 1913, keeping alive Copacabana's "macabre tradition" and prompting the press to demand improvements in the lifesaving service.[57]

It took the drowning death of Maurício França for authorities to make those improvements. França, an accomplished young doctor who lived in Copacabana, regularly went bathing there and knew how to swim. Nevertheless, on a March morning in 1917, he got trapped in a whirlpool. Other bathers unsuccessfully tried to rescue him. One of them then rushed to his car and drove to the recently established lifesaving post at the far end of Copacabana, less than a kilometer and a half away, to seek help. But it was too late. The press reported extensively on França's death and used it to point out the lack of an adequate lifesaving service.[58]

In May 1917, Mayor Amaro Cavalcânti issued a decree that laid the foundations of Rio de Janeiro's current lifesaving service. The authorities divided the beach into six numbered "bathing posts [*postos de banhos*]," also known as "lifesaving posts [*postos de salvamento*]," roughly 660 meters from one another, with Post 1 located in Leme and Post 6 at the far end of Copacabana. Each of the six posts had a fifteen-meter-high masthead-like observation tower (figure 4.7 and map 4.1). Atop the tower sat a member of the lifesaving service under an umbrella, keeping watch over bathers in the water. The umbrella not only sheltered him from the sun but also served to signal the sea's condition. When bathing was safe, the observer raised a white umbrella; a red umbrella meant that the sea was dangerously rough, and that bathing was prohibited. White and red flags flying from small poles on the beach itself would, in later years, serve the same purpose. Each post also had two "swimmers" as well as a lifesaving boat manned by two oarsmen and a coxswain. In their rescue operations, the lifeguards could also use a two-hundred-meter rope to tug bathers into shore. An electric signal system (later replaced by telephones) connected the posts to a central lifesaving station, which had an ambulance; the station, staffed by a physician and other members of the city's General Directorate of Hygiene and Public Assistance, was originally located at about the beach's mid-point and then transferred in 1922 to the Praça do Lido (Post 2). Using the electric signals or, later, the telephone, a post could, when necessary, request an ambulance to take rescued drowning victims to the station. There, its staff would try to revive them and provide other needed medical care.[59]

The number of posts would gradually increase in the 1920s and 1930s as the authorities extended the lifesaving service to Ipanema (Posts 7 through 10) and later to Leblon (Posts 11 and 12). They also established two new posts in Copacabana: Post 0 at far end of Leme and Post 2½ in front of the Copacabana Palace Hotel (neither of which exists today), as well as posts at the bayshore beaches of Flamengo, Virtudes, and Ramos.[60] Not only did the number of posts increase over time, but at least at the city's oceanfront beaches, the posts themselves underwent transformations. The original wooden mastheads gave way in the mid- and late 1920s to structures built of reinforced concrete. Then, beginning in 1935, the reinforced concrete structures were slowly replaced by new three-story observation towers with an art deco design intended to

FIGURE 4.7. Lifesaving Post, ca. 1920. Arquivo Images2You.

resemble "a ship's command bridge"; the design reportedly won praise from Le Corbusier, the influential French modernist architect (figure 4.8). Those towers were, for the most part, demolished in the early 1960s. The construction of new towers, with public washrooms and showers, which bathers could use for a modest fee, began only in the late 1970s. In the meantime, the lifeguards watched bathers directly from the sand and took shelter under small tents pitched on the beach, just as most of them do today.[61]

The numbered lifeguard posts still exist, as anyone familiar with Rio de Janeiro's beaches can attest. Today, most inhabitants of Rio de Janeiro, or at least most who live in the Zona Sul, also know that, with the exception of Post 1 (Leme), the original six posts, in time, christened areas within Copacabana as a neighborhood. When asked where they live in Copacabana, residents often answer, "In Post 6," or "In Post 3," as the case might be. The actual address could be on the oceanfront Avenida Atlântica and within or almost within sight of the lifesaving post; yet, it is just as likely that a reference to Post 3 indicates an address on a back or side street near that post, but two or three blocks from the beach.[62] Although the numbered lifeguard posts remain today a prominent feature of Rio de Janeiro's beach landscape, few current beach-goers or other Cariocas will know that, for decades, the posts were not simply the locations of lifeguard observation towers as they are today. The "instructions" issued in 1917 by then–Director of Hygiene and Public Assistance Paulino Werneck, which expanded on the May 1917 municipal decree that reorganized the municipal lifesaving service, make clear that they were, instead, 260-meter stretches of the beach, set off by small flags on poles; there, supervised by lifeguards, bathers were allowed to enter the water.

Werneck's instructions, like the May 1917 decree, imposed a number of other restrictions and requirements. They required that bathers present themselves in "appropriate and decent attire." That meant, in the case of men, not wearing "short trunks" that did not cover their knees or trunks made of "cotton knit [*de meia*]." Not only was bathing "expressly forbidden" outside the limits

FIGURE 4.8. Lifesaving Post, Mid-1930s. Fuss, *Brasilien*, plate 76. Arquivo Images2You.

of the post, but, within those limits, bathers were prohibited from venturing beyond the "breakers." Failure to comply with the instructions would result in a fine of Rs.20$000 (roughly US $5.00 at the time) or five days' imprisonment. Werneck's instructions ended by warning that the sea in Copacabana did not lend itself to swimming and that bathers should therefore avoid the practice.[63]

The restrictions and requirements included in the instructions would, over time, lapse. But, early on, the lifeguards did their best to enforce them rigorously. The English traveler W. H. Kobel, who visited Rio de Janeiro shortly after the inauguration of the lifesaving posts, noted that "bathing at Copacabana is by no means that free and easy proceeding . . . usually associated with tropical beaches [and] Blue Lagoons." He went on to note that "there are high and stern authorities who lay down the law as to where the cosmopolitan inhabitants . . . shall bathe, and how they shall do it."[64]

Kobel might have added that those "high and stern authorities" also sought to determine when bathers entered the water. The May 1917 decree and Werneck's instructions established official bathing hours, during which the lifeguards would be on duty. Between 1 December and 31 March, those hours went from five to eight in the morning and from five to seven in the evening. The hours for the rest of year were from six to nine in the morning and from four to six in the afternoon. On Sundays and holidays, bathers were allowed an additional morning hour to enjoy the sea. The instructions prohibited bathing at all other times of the day.

The existence of official hours did not deter some bathers from diving or wading into the sea at other times of the day. As early as September 1917, Paulino Werneck noted that "a large number of people," "especially on Sundays and holidays," went bathing outside the official hours. He therefore requested that the police assign three patrolmen on bicycles to put a halt to the prohibited practice. A 1921 law altered Werneck's instructions by allowing bathing outside the official hours and outside the posts. The law, however, warned that bathers did so entirely at their own risk. Despite the law, authorities would sometimes forbid all bathing except during the officially established hours and within the limits of a post. In 1926, for example, Joaquim Pinto de Carvalho and Antenor Almeida went bathing outside those hours and ventured beyond the surf. They ended up at the local police station, where they each had to pay the Rs.20$000 fine. One year later city councilor João Clapp Filho unsuccessfully proposed a "permanent" lifesaving service in Copacabana; that is, guards would be on duty from early morning until early evening, with no midday break.[65]

Over time, however, the authorities did expand the official bathing hours and shifted them, in the case of the morning hours, toward later in the day. By summer 1949–1950, lifeguards were on duty without a midday break at Posts 2, 2 ½, and 4 in Copacabana. Bathing at those posts and also in Flamengo was allowed from seven in the morning to seven in the evening. The following summer, the lifesaving service finally began operating at all of Copacabana's posts from half past six in the morning until half past seven in the evening with no interruption in the middle of the day.[66]

Nevertheless, lifeguards were not infallible. Some bathers caught up in an undertow or a whirlpool had already taken in too much water by the time the guards reached them. Yet, in a city and also, for that matter, a country where citizens could rightly complain about the inefficiency of many government agencies and the poor quality of the services they offered, Rio de Janeiro's lifesaving service stood out as an exception; it won the admiration and respect of beach-goers and repeated praise from the press. Even the *New York Times* reported favorably on the service in 1958.[67]

The service owed the respect that it enjoyed in no small measure to the often-selfless efforts of the poorly paid lifeguards who manned the posts at Rio de Janeiro's Zona Sul beaches and who were generally known as banhistas (bathers). *Beira-Mar* in 1936 called them "everyday heroes." Information about them and their background is scant. Most were dark-skinned Afro-Brazilians, a fact emphasized and even exaggerated in travelers' accounts from the 1930s. In 1931, for example, Kasimir Edschmid classified them as "all . . . regular Negroes." W. K. von Nohara, a few years later, described them as "Herculean blacks." In truth, though the service was mostly Afro-Brazilian, photographs reveal a mixed population.[68] Many of the first lifeguards in Copacabana were recruited from among local fishermen. But at least one of those fishermen, Elviro José Leite, nicknamed China, was not a native Carioca. In a 1976 interview, the then–elderly China recounted that he was Indigenous, originally named Guaraciaba, from the Northern state of Amazonas, taken as a young boy to Rio de Janeiro. He did not explain how or why. He did, however, tell his interviewer that he worked as a fisherman and then joined the lifesaving service in 1917. He was, in fact, one of the three lifeguards who accompanied King Albert in 1920 when the Belgian monarch went for his early morning swims in Copacabana. China, who held the record for the number of successful rescues by 1936, still worked for the lifesaving service as late as 1939. Other lifeguards who became well-known figures among beach-goers in Copacabana and Ipanema in the late 1920s and the 1930s include Carlos Correia de Sá, João da Silva, Isidro Pacheco Soares, and Manoel Francisco Borges. Isidro and Manoel Francisco won in 1930 municipal gold medals for having, "with risk to their own lives," rescued two bathers. Isidro, like China, had a long career; by 1954, he had saved some nine hundred lives. Carlos Correia de Sá and João da Silva, for their part, received in 1937 presidential silver medals for having rescued, while off duty, an American tourist.[69]

The admiration in which beach-going residents of Copacabana and Ipanema held the lifeguards resulted in an annual commemoration, the Dia do Banhista (literally, the Day of the Bather, but better translated as Lifeguards' Day), celebrated on 28 December and starting in the early 1930s. On that date, lifeguards had the day off from their normal duties, allowing them to take part in various festivities, swimming races, and other competitions, attended by residents of the oceanfront neighborhoods and by municipal dignitaries.[70]

The relationship between beach-goers and lifeguards often went beyond one of admiration. Bathers who frequented a particular post in the Zona Sul in the 1950s and 1960s came to know well the guards who worked at that post. In some cases, the acquaintance began when the bathers were children; the guards would carry those young bathers on their shoulders, play with them, tell them stories, and give them advice on learning how to swim. The relationship would continue and evolve as the lifeguards saw them grow up. Because the posts had telephones until the mid-1960s, bathers, before leaving home, could call the lifeguards to find out which of their friends had already arrived at the beach. Some might even bring sandwiches from home for the lifeguards. Occasionally, the guards received an invitation to have lunch with a family that regularly went to the beach at their post in the family's apartment. It should come as little surprise, then, that *O Cruzeiro* in 1961 described lifeguards as forming, along with bathers, "the beach's extended family." Lifeguards and beach-goers, the magazine observed, often shared a genuinely friendly relationship.[71]

But that relationship, as friendly as it may have been, was not a relationship between social equals. The lifeguards who manned the posts at the beaches in the affluent oceanfront Zona Sul neighborhoods were poorly paid working-class men. The earliest information on their pay dates from 1959, when their starting monthly salary was Cr$8,400; guards with twenty years of experience earned Cr$12,680 a month. Those sums amounted, respectively, to US $55.66 and US $85.21 at the time, or to only 1.4 and 2.1 times the monthly minimum wage in the Federal District. Despite their low wages, the guards could at any moment be called on to risk their own lives to save well-to-do bathers caught in a dangerously swift undertow even when, ignoring the red flags, the imperiled bathers had got into trouble because of their own foolhardiness. Lifeguards who worked the morning shift and who lived far from the Zona Sul, moreover, might have to wake up at four in the morning and take two or more buses to arrive at their posts on time. By contrast, provided that they had no other obligations, upper- and upper middle-class beach-going residents of Copacabana, Ipanema, and Leblon could sleep in and then simply cross the street or walk a few blocks for a morning or afternoon on the sand and in the water.[72] Those residents, while at the beach, were spending part of their leisure time; the lifeguards at the same stretch of beach were at work.

Beneath the "Blazing Sun"

The transformation of sea-bathing into the practice of beach-going also entailed a changing relationship to the sun and changing attitudes regarding tanning.[73] In the early days of the lifeguarding service, a fair complexion remained the aesthetic ideal; white bathers and those of mixed ancestry, therefore, continued to avoid prolonged exposure to the sun, especially in the middle of the day. *O Paiz* reported in March 1917 that the authorities would take into account the desirability of avoiding the "blazing sun"—hence the initial restrictions of bathing hours to the early morning and the early evening, the times of the day when the sun's rays were at their weakest.[74]

Even in the early 1920s, when some bathers had begun to spend a good deal of their summer mornings at the beach in Copacabana, they still sought to avoid the sun by sheltering under beach umbrellas or small tents. Or, as a 1924 crônica by Maria Eugênia Celso reveals, they tried to minimize and disguise the effects of the sun. In the crônica, "Senhorita" goes every morning to the beach in Copacabana in December and early January. But she takes a few precautions: she applies a bit of makeup and wears a hat. The precautions, however, prove insufficient. After a few weeks, "not even the memory of her milky whiteness remains; her legs, arms, neck, and face are thoroughly toasted." She concludes that she looks like "a piece of bacon [*um torresmo*]." Therefore, when she goes out to stroll along the Avenida Rio Branco in the center of Rio de Janeiro in the afternoon, she puts on "long white silk gloves to hide the *damage* from the sun on her arms." Presumably, her stockings hide "the *damage*" on her legs. Her face, covered by a heavy dose of makeup, takes on the "tones of Sèvres porcelain." And, seeing "that marvelous transformation," one has to ask, "Where is this morning's little piece of bacon?"[75]

Yet, when Maria Eugênia Celso published her crônica, aesthetic ideals were about to undergo a radical change. Starting in the mid-1920s, more bathers in Copacabana began to expose themselves to the sun with the goal of darkening their skin. The fashion of tanning, which arose in Europe and the United States in the early 1920s, did not take long to reach Rio de Janeiro.[76] In December of 1925, the magazine *Para Todos* proclaimed "tan [*a cor morena*] is the fashionable color," explaining that bathers acquired that color by spending their mornings at the beach in Copacabana. A few weeks later, the writer Clara Lúcia observed in the *Revista da Semana* that "the pure, unmistakable tone somewhere between the color of old gold and the color of a cigar . . . today constitutes the ideal complexion." That tone, she added, could be "obtained only with a good hour of sun at the beach."[77] Tanning took hold so rapidly at Rio de Janeiro's oceanfront beaches that, by 1930, "the sun-bathing craze" alarmed some doctors. They warned that spending long hours under the sun, as beach-goers did in Copacabana, could result in serious health problems, including skin cancer.[78] Their warnings, however, had little effect. In 1933, the *Jornal do Brasil* pointed out that a "tanned color [cor morena] wields so much fascination among young people that not even medical advice or the most basic common sense will steer them away from the wrong path." "At the beach," the newspaper added, "they think only about toasting themselves dark brown."[79]

Special products for tanning began to appear on store shelves. Luba was one of the first: an oil for "sun-bathing," it promised, according to a 1934 advertisement, to preserve a "tan color [cor morena]" and prevent sunburns. Two years later, a similar product, Dagelle, was being sold. Luba and Dagelle would soon have to compete with Delial and, later, with tanning lotions made by Elizabeth Arden.[80]

The "sun-bathing craze" did more than encourage the sale of tanning lotions; it also helped change the time of day when people went to the beach. If the goal was to darken the skin, it made little sense to go the beach before dawn or even between five and seven in the morning, when the sun's rays were still weak. Binóculo, the social columnist for the *Gazeta de Notícias*, noted in 1927 that, "in the past, it was fashionable to be at the beaches very early so as to witness the sun rise." But, as soon as the sun "began to heat up, all the bathers deserted" the shore. That, however, had changed. Now, the columnist wrote, "it is fashionable to leave home at nine. By ten in the morning, all the bathers are on the sand, [roasting] like pieces of meat in ovens." A few years later, in 1931, *Beira-Mar* observed that, on Sundays, many bathers arrived at the beach in Copacabana only at eleven.[81]

Exposing oneself to the sun was possible at any of Rio de Janeiro's beaches, even at Virtudes, which consisted of little more than a rocky embankment and which attracted large numbers of working- and lower middle-class bathers in the 1920s and 1930s. But contemporary sources associate tanning with the oceanfront beaches, and most often, with Copacabana. In 1928, for example, *O Cruzeiro* described the narrow beach in Flamengo as "the Copacabana of the urban center," but with a major difference: at the bayshore beach, it remarked, "there is no sun-bathing; sea-bathing is the reality." Given the narrowness of Flamengo's beach, bathers found almost no room to lie on the sand or even just to sit down on a crowded Sunday; most had to stand around or "squat." The article noted that in Copacabana, with its broad stretch of sand, "what people do least is go sea-bathing." "All those elegant, cultured folks believe that the best bathing is on the sand, under a burning sun, or in pleasant breezes [enjoyed] under . . . beach umbrellas."[82]

That tanning had become fashionable in Europe and the United States explains in part the rapid adoption of the practice at Rio de Janeiro's oceanfront beaches after the mid-1920s. Wealthy and well-to-do Cariocas had long followed the latest European fashions and did the same when it came to darkening the skin through exposure to sun. "If Parisian women have decreed . . . [tanning] to be the fashion," then Brazilian women, the *Ilustração Brasileira* declared in 1926, would follow their lead and could do so "with greater ease" than their French counterparts.[83] It was not, however, just women; men, especially younger men, who went to the beach in Copacabana and Ipanema also quickly took up the new practice.[84]

Rising enthusiasm for heliotherapy, the use of exposure to sunlight for therapeutic purposes, also shaped beach-going. Research in the late nineteenth and early twentieth centuries demonstrated that sunlight could be useful in treating tuberculosis, lupus, rickets, anemia, gout, bronchitis, syphilis, and rheumatism.[85] The celebrated Carioca physician Dr. Artur Moncorvo Filho published three books on sun cures between 1917 and 1924.[86]

Further reinforcement of belief in the health benefits of sunshine came from eugenics. The 1920s and 1930s—the decades in which tanning took hold at Rio de Janeiro's oceanfront beaches—stand out as the years in which eugenic thinking and ideas, generally in a neo-Lamarckian version, held their greatest sway among Brazilian intellectuals. The foremost advocate of eugenics in Brazil was Renato Kehl, author of numerous books and articles on the topic. Kehl argued that exposure of minimally dressed men and women to sunlight would "improve the race." He called the sun "remedy number one" ("remedy number two" was fresh air).[87] Such ideas appeared implicitly, and often explicitly, in contemporary discussions of sunbathing and tanning at Rio de Janeiro's beaches.[88]

Whether influenced by eugenics, heliotherapy, or French fashion, or some combination of all three, a growing number of well-to-do men and women who went to the beach in Copacabana sought, from the mid-1920s onward, to darken their skin through exposure to sunlight.[89] And, in Rio de Janeiro, just as in Europe and the United States, a tanned complexion could indirectly signal social class, insofar as obtaining a tan required the luxury of spending hours beneath the sun without engaging in any paid or productive activity. Thus, the new fashion radically inverted a traditional sign of social hierarchy, namely, the long-standing association of sun-darkened skin with manual laborers who worked outdoors.[90]

The introduction of tanning as a fashion at Rio de Janeiro's oceanfront beaches also involved complex implications for notions of color and race. Tanning had potential meanings in Brazil that the practice did not have in Europe and the United States. Here, consider the distinction between the color of a tanned white body and that of someone of mixed African and European ancestry, which, today, might seem naturally obvious. Perceiving the difference would seem to require little more than a bit of "visual 'common sense.'" But, as Ann Stoler reminds us, "visual 'common sense' is not a historical constant"; it varies over time and from one society and culture to the next.[91] After all, race is—to use a now tired but still valid expression—a socially constructed category. Sara Ahmed, in turn, persuasively argues that "the meanings of tanned skin are not always assured"; that is, they are not fixed. On the contrary, "the relationship between 'racial colour' and 'tanned colour' is open to confusion" and "is not guaranteed in the form of a linear narrative: being white and *becoming* brown" through sunbathing.[92] The possibility of "confusion between 'racial colour' and 'tanned colour'" was all the greater in Brazil because, in daily life, the language used by Brazilians, both in the past and the present, to classify themselves and other individuals by color explicitly recognizes multiple intermediate categories in a continuum between *preto* (black) and *branco* (white).[93] As a rule, Brazilian censuses and official surveys limit to four, and now five, possible answers to the question, "What is your color?": *branco* (white), *preto* (black), *pardo* (brown, but generally understood to indicate mixed ancestry, and also until 1991, encompassing Indigenous people), *amarelo* (yellow; that is, of East Asian ancestry), and since 1991, *indígena* (Indigenous). But, in 1976, an official survey gave respondents total freedom when it came to answering the question about their "color." The survey yielded no fewer than 135 different answers. Most of the 135 "colors," it is true, appeared in only a handful of responses, and seven "colors" accounted for "approximately 95 percent" of all responses. Those seven "colors" do, nevertheless, form a continuum with *preto* at one extreme and *branco* at the other.[94] Furthermore, in classifying themselves and others by "color," Brazilians have traditionally taken into account not only skin pigmentation (however perceived) but also facial features, eye color, and type and color of hair.[95]

In any event, for more than one observer of Rio de Janeiro's Atlantic beaches in the 1920s and 1930s, the distinction between the color of a tanned white body and that of a *mestiço* (meaning in this context, an *afro-mestiço*, or someone of mixed European and African ancestry) was anything but obvious or clear-cut.[96] On the contrary, in their view, the two colors closely resembled each other. Here, a few examples will suffice. The first example comes from a 1927 article in *Para Todos*, which noted that the ocean in Copacabana did not lend itself to adventurous swimming. Nevertheless, female bathers at that beach were content so long as they could stretch out on the sand, "burning their skin in the sun's golden rays." That was, according to the article, "the most inoffensive way of keeping up with fashion; that is, [becoming] tan [*morenas*]. . . . It is fashion hand in hand with hygiene. . . . Ah!" the article added, "to be *acajou* [cashew-colored] like Josephine Baker." Three years later, the Rio de Janeiro correspondent of a newspaper in southern Brazil pointed out that, with "the craze for sun-bathing," many members of "Carioca high society" spent hours at the beach in Copacabana "under the blazing sun" with the goal of "acquiring the color of Josephine Baker." The two articles thus liken the color of a suntan to that of the legendary African American dancer and singer, who took Paris by storm in the interwar years and whose international fame in part rested on the fact that she was an African American of mixed descent.[97]

Chermont de Brito, the *Jornal do Brasil*'s social columnist, took up the matter on two occasions in the 1930s. The first was in a 1934 article in which he described his friend "I.," who "was white and is now tan [*morena*], almost black tan [*morena quase preta*]. Copacabana's sun," he added, "has left her in this enchanting state. It is elegant nowadays to be a mulatta, and madame obeys the demands of fashion." Chermont de Brito went on to note that, when she passed by a beachfront bar in Copacabana, an admirer "murmured: 'Darker [*mais morena*] and more beautiful than the Queen of Sheba!' Needless to say, the compliment pleased madame." It matters little whether "I." really existed or was an invention of the columnist. What matters is the apparently radical transformation he described: after so much time under the sun, a woman who "was white" now looked "almost Black."[98] Few women who saw themselves as white would have taken the comparison to the African queen's color as a compliment.[99] In this light, Chermont de Brito's article may contain a sarcastic, veiled warning to white women with naturally darker-hued complexions: they needed to take care in sunbathing to avoid going beyond a poorly defined and shifting line that separated a tan from the color of an Afro-Brazilian of mixed ancestry.

Chermont de Brito returned to the matter in a 1938 article. In it, he described "Madame Z.," a "famous blonde" with "blue eyes." He had last seen her at New Year's, when she was "whiter than a lily." But now, after spending an entire month sunbathing at the beach in Copacabana, she was "so burnt, so tanned [*amorenada*] that she more precisely looked like a delicious mulatta." Once again, the columnist saw a close resemblance between the color of a deep tan and that of someone of mixed African and European ancestry. But there is a crucial difference between "I." and "Madame Z."; namely, the color of "Madame Z.['s]" eyes and hair.[100]

The issue of hair color came up again in an unsigned 1939 article in the *Correio da Manhã*. The writer begins by observing that, at Copacabana's beach, the sun "tans [*pinta de bronze*], during hours, almost naked men and women." Among those men and women, "the blonds can still maintain the proof of their *race* [*prova racial*] in their hair." That, however, was not the case with the "morenos," which, in the context at hand, meant white individuals with dark hair and, in all likelihood, also a naturally darker-toned but still white complexion. "The morenos," the author's article wrote, "will pass for mestiços"; that is, "if they do not lift up their trunks to show the epidermal certificate of their *whiteness* [*o princípio* branco *do atestado epidérmico*]."[101]

Yet, here, a question arises: How did the author know that the morenos were not mestiços if, in his or her view, they could pass for mestiços? Presumably, the author did not walk up and down the beach, requesting bathers to lift up their trunks. (In passing, it should be noted that, at the time, women's maillots often consisted of a top and a pair of trunks, or bottoms, but with no bared midriff.) But there would have been no need to make that request. Brazilians at the time, just as in earlier and later years, were used to relying on a range of criteria to decide who, in their view, was or was not white. Those criteria included facial features, hair color, and the type of hair. It is even possible that, at the beach, those criteria carried greater weight than elsewhere. Occupation and social class may have come into play in some cases. Here, to cite merely a few examples, we might think of a walking ice cream vendor, a lifeguard, or a nanny who watched the children of an upper- or upper middle-class family at the beach as they played in the sand and took in the sun.

The range of criteria would have also included social context, which, in the case at hand, was also a spatial context, or more specifically a racialized spatial context.[102] Because Copacabana and Ipanema were at the time were predominantly upper- and upper middle-class beaches, they were also "white" beaches.[103] Bathers who frequented those beaches would have, in many cases, belonged to the same white social circles. When they encountered deeply tanned moreno bathers at the same beaches whom they did not know, such as those mentioned in the 1939 *Correio da Manhã* article, they could take it for granted that those bathers should be regarded as being white. The same was true of other social contexts that constituted racialized white spaces, such as the Bife de Ouro restaurant in the Copacabana Palace Hotel, a diplomatic reception, an opera performance at the Municipal Theater, or a dance at the country club in Ipanema or at one of the city's other exclusive clubs. To be sure, both at the beach and elsewhere, there would have been limits. Thus, a dark-skinned bather who, in all or nearly all other social contexts, would have been considered a pardo, an afro-mestiço, a mulatto, or a Black would not, presumably, have been seen as merely having a deep tan.

Nevertheless, the social context of Rio de Janeiro's oceanfront beaches in the 1920s, 1930s, and 1940s, like other racialized contexts and spaces, allowed wealthy and well-to-bathers to develop a new "visual 'common sense'" to discern a distinction "between 'racial colour' and 'tanned colour'" even in the case of those (white) men and women who otherwise might "pass for mestiços." They came to see that distinction as "natural," and that distinction, which continues to be regarded as "natural," persists even today. A phrase that Patrícia Silveira de Farias uses as the title of the third chapter of her study, which focuses mainly on Ipanema in the 1990s, neatly summarizes that now-"natural" distinction: "*a cor que se pega e a cor que se tem*," which translates (awkwardly) as "the color that one gets and the color that one has."[104]

It is, however, also necessary to examine from a different angle the complex implications for notions of color and race that the adoption of tanning at Rio de Janeiro's beaches entailed. That, in turn, requires examining the word *moreno* (or *morena* in the feminine), which lacks any exact equivalent in English and which is polysemous; that is, it has multiple meanings. Sources from the 1920s, 1930s, and 1940s regularly use *moreno*—alongside *bronzeado* (bronzed) and *dourado* (golden)—to designate, without the slightest ambiguity, the color that results from suntanning. Less often, amorenado—that is, tanned—appears in those sources. Sources from the same decades also frequently use *amorenar-se* (to make oneself moreno) as a synomym for *bronzear-se* (to bronze oneself, i.e., to tan) and *amorenamento* to refer to the practice of tanning and, more generally, to the process of becoming moreno. For instance, in 1928, the *Revista da Semana* informed its readers that "fashion has prescribed sun-bathing to give the satin-like white skin of lady a warm and moreno coloring." Five years later, *Beira-Mar* observed that "the majority [of bathers in Copacabana] eagerly awaited the sun" because the color "moreno" had become the "ideal." A 1936 advertisement, addressed to women, for Dagelle made even more explicit the relationship between moreno and tanning when it claimed that, by using that lotion, "you can now become morena without [risking a] sunburn."[105]

Yet, the term had and has other meanings.[106] It can be used to describe someone with black or dark brown hair, a fair complexion, and either light- or dark-colored eyes. It also describes individuals with black or dark brown hair, a darker-hued (white) complexion, and, more often than not, dark-colored eyes. In both cases, *moreno* stands in contrast to *louro* (blond). That contrast often figures prominently in, for instance, discussions of Hollywood starlets in the 1920s and 1930s. *Moreno*, in these two accepted definitions, has nothing to do with tanning or with miscegenation (at least not with acknowledged miscegenation). Rather, it is a "subcategory" of *white*.[107] The accepted definitions of *moreno* do not end there. Since at least the early nineteenth-century, it has served to designate the color of an afro-mestiço. When employed with that meaning, *moreno* roughly corresponds to *mulato* and to the category *pardo*, long used in Brazilian censuses.[108]

Moreno's polysemy and its semantic elasticity gain greater significance when we recall that, in the very same decades that tanning took hold at Rio de Janeiro's oceanfront beaches, debates about "race," miscegenation, and national identity once again intensified in Brazil. Those debates were not restricted to a handful of intellectuals. On the contrary, as Tiago de Melo Gomes has demonstrated, in Rio de Janeiro, popular theatrical revues took up the issues at stake in those debates. The revues, it is worth noting, counted on the participation of composers, actors, and other artists "of color," such as those who made up the successful Companhia Negra de Teatro de Revista (Black Theater Revue Company). Through theatrical revues and other cultural media, discussions about "race," miscegenation, and national identity reached a broad public.[109] The debates of the 1920s and 1930s ended up producing a new ideological paradigm that assigned a new positive value to miscegenation and that found in Gilberto Freyre (1900–1987) its most important and most influential representative. Freyre was apparently the first Brazilian scholar to insert tanning into a discussion of race and color. In his view, tanning as practiced in Copacabana confirmed his arguments about miscegenation and the absence of racism in Brazil.[110] One can, it should be stressed, reject Freyre's arguments, and at the same time, acknowledge that, in part as a result of his influence, prevailing racial ideologies in Brazil underwent significant changes, especially with regards to miscegenation, between the 1920s and the mid-twentieth century. In summarizing the ideological paradigm that resulted from those changes, Nelson do Valle Silva writes, "The mestiço defines physically the Brazilian nation and constitutes the demonstration of the [nation's] democratic essence. Yet, going beyond miscegenation," Silva adds, "Brazilian racial democracy would reach its culmination in the final abolition of distinctions based on color." Those distinctions and the identities linked to them would then meld in to a single, "all-inclusive and fluid" category: "the morenos."[111]

Within the new paradigm, the practice of tanning and of making oneself moreno (amorenar-se) took on potential meanings that the very same practice did not have in either Europe or the United States. It allowed beach-goers in Copacabana and Ipanema to participate in an ideological project that defined Brazil as on its way to becoming a moreno nation, forged physically and culturally through miscegenation. Thus, they could see their *amorenamento*—that is, their becoming morenos—at the beach as a contribution to what a 1933 *Beira-Mar* article called "the *aurora morena* [moreno dawn] of the nation's flesh [*a carne nacional*], awaiting the miracle of a strong race." In that "aurora morena," anaemic men, with sickly "very white skin" and "soft bellies," were giving way, on the sands of Copacabana, to a new generation of "healthy and strong young men, displaying the sun-tanned bodies of discus-throwers" and of equally healthy young women. In those tanned young women and men who frequented the beach, the author foresaw the "future of my people and the grandeur of my nation [*pátria*]." Miscegenation at the same time would "lighten" darker-skinned Afro-Brazilians through a process of amorenamento that did not depend on the action of the sun and that would transform them into ever fairer morenos. Miscegenation in that way would, together with social policies based in part on neo-Lamarckian eugenics, also contribute to the creation of "a strong race" in Brazil.[112]

An interpretation along those lines comes close to matching arguments that Gilberto Freyre put forth in the early 1970s. In his view, a double process of "amorenamento" characterized Brazilian society: on the one hand, an "anthropological" amorenamento as a result of miscegenation, which was producing new generations of lighter-skinned Afro-Brazilians; and, on the other, a "semantic" amorenamento, which was leading to the ever-more common use of the term *moreno* to describe not only "white morenos, as in the past, but [also] pardos of varying degrees of *morenidade* (moreno-ness) from light to dark, as a consequence of miscegenation, and [even] blacks." He also detected a third process at work: the amorenamento of "whites who seek out the tropical sun of Copacabana and other beaches," where, through exposure to the sun's rays, they became morenos. The general result of the three processes would, according to Freyre, be the "negation" of all racial distinctions in Brazil and the "affirmation" of a single "meta-race" composed of "morenos."[113]

If they so chose, white beach-goers in Copacabana and Ipanema might interpret their ability to tan at the beach, instead of merely burning or becoming lobster red, as the result of miscegenation that, as Patrícia Farias puts it in a similar context, "possibly occurred in the past."[114] To be sure, from the point of view of those white beach-goers, it would be best if that possible miscegenation belonged to a past so remote that it had become lost in time. Yet, those beach-goers knew that miscegenation was historically widespread in Brazil. Since the nineteenth century, Brazilian intellectuals had given considerable attention to "the mixture of races." Although their interpretations differed, they all saw that "mixture" as a characteristic feature of Brazil's population.[115]

None of this meant that upper- and upper middle-class (white) bathers surrendered their white identity.[116] With that identity intact, the amorenamento of bathers at the beach in Copacabana and Ipanema was fully compatible with a racial hierarchy. Contrary to what Freyre believed, tanning in no way represented a step toward the elimination of color and racial distinctions. Whites "toasted dark brown" by the sun would continue to see themselves as white, and together with those white beach-goers who, for whatever reason, avoided the sun, they would remain at the top of the racial hierarchy. The practice of tanning did not result in an end to racism or an end to the profound racial inequalities that still plague Brazilian society.

The rapid spread of tanning among bathers in Copacabana and Ipanema starting in the mid-1920s intersected with the influences of eugenics, heliotherapy, and foreign fashion. The practice ended up producing a new "visual 'common sense'" that recognized as "natural" a distinction "between 'racial colour' and 'tanned colour.'" At the same time, the rise of tanning coincided with broader changes in views about race and nation in Brazil. Those changes, in turn, led to the emergence of a new ideological paradigm that heralded Brazil as a mestiço and, hence, moreno nation. Together with that paradigm, tanning brought into existence a new aesthetic ideal: a moreno complexion (whether as a consequence of mixed ancestry or, preferably, exposure to the sun) replaced fair skin as the ideal among large segments of the Brazilian population. Of all the changes that accompanied the spread of tanning in Copacabana and Ipanema from the mid-1920s onward, one is easily overlooked: namely, that the new fashion required spending time not in the water but, instead, on the sand and "beneath the blazing sun." That, in turn, meant that, increasingly, the sand replaced the water as the main locus of activity and sociability among bathers who frequented the beaches along Rio de Janeiro's Atlantic shore.

The development of beach-going in Copacabana and Ipanema in the 1920s and 1930s resulted from a mix of public and private investment in utilities, technological changes, patterns of urbanization, the growth of Rio de Janeiro's upper and upper middle classes, real estate speculation, as well as the influence of heliotherapy, eugenics, and foreign fashion. The different and, indeed, disparate elements in that mix can be reduced to four main factors: the growth and development of Copacabana and Ipanema as predominantly upper- and upper middle-class neighborhoods in the early decades of the twentieth century, the tremendous increase in car ownership by wealthy and well-to-do Cariocas after the First World War, the establishment of an effective municipal lifeguard service, and lastly, the prevalence of tanning, a fashion imported from Europe and the United States. In the years after the early 1930s, the same factors continued to encourage wealthy and well-to-do Cariocas to seek out Rio de Janeiro's broad and sandy oceanfront beaches and to engage in beach-going as a daily or weekly leisure activity.

The importance of the breadth, and also for that matter, the length of those beaches may not be immediately obvious, but it is hardly mysterious. Those beaches could accommodate more bathers from the city's expanding upper and upper middle classes, and they provided those bathers with the physical room needed to develop the range of activities that Cariocas have come to associate with beach-going. Copacabana and Ipanema, thus, differed in a crucial way from Flamengo, which had stood out in the 1910s and early 1920s as Rio de Janeiro's most fashionable beach.

The four factors listed above worked in combination to bring about the rise of a recognizably modern form of beach-going in Rio de Janeiro. No one of the four factors by itself would have sufficed. Here, it is fitting to end by returning to the two royal visits to Copacabana that opened this chapter, for many of the elements that came into play in the transformation of sea-bathing into beach-going in Rio de Janeiro's Atlantic oceanfront neighborhoods are present in those two visits. Thus, in 1920, a motorcar, not a horse-drawn carriage, took King Albert I of the Belgians from Guanabara Palace, where he was staying, to Copacabana for his early morning bathing excursions. There, he put on his suit at the beachfront palacete owned by the local director of the Rio de Janeiro Tramway, Light & Power Company, Ltd. Three lifeguards from the recently reorganized and expanded lifesaving service accompanied the king in the water while he exercised his skills as a swimmer. After leaving the water, the Belgian monarch took brisk walks along the paved Avenida Atlântica, which, like the municipal lifeguard service, was the result of public investment. The electric lighting that the avenue boasted was, in turn, the product of investments made by a private utility firm, the Rio de Janeiro Tramway, Light & Power Company, Ltd. Lining the Avenida Atlântica at the time were large single-family houses and palacetes comparable to the one where Albert I changed out of his street clothes. Whoever chose Copacabana as the location for the king's daily sea bath undoubtedly knew that that beach was gaining in prestige precisely because it bordered the fast-growing upper- and upper middle-class neighborhood of the same name.

The prestige that Copacabana and its beach had already acquired explains why Otávio Guinle chose to build there the imposing Copacabana Palace, which, even today, remains Rio de Janeiro's most renowned hotel. The 1923 opening of the hotel, in turn, only added to Copacabana's prestige.[117] In 1931, eight years after it opened, the hotel hosted Prince George, later George VI of Great Britain. By then, Copacabana's first "skyscraper" apartment buildings, the result of ongoing real estate speculation, had already begun to alter the neighborhood's built landscape. Several of them, located near the hotel, are visible in Peter Fuss's photograph from the mid-1930s (figure 4.4). Others at the time were under construction in a fast-growing neighborhood that, except in name, had barely existed in 1895 when the prince was born. That neighborhood continued to benefit from disproportionately generous investments in infrastructure by the municipal government and the privately owned utility firms. When the future monarch went to the beach in Copacabana, he simply crossed the Avenida Atlântica, already wearing his bathing suit, and also in all certainty, a robe or perhaps a sport coat. He did not arrive before seven in the morning as Albert I had done but, rather, after eleven when the "blazing sun" stood high in the tropical skies over Rio de Janeiro. After a quick plunge into the waves, Prince George, unlike the Belgian king, did not go for a walk. Instead, he returned to the sand, had a member of his entourage spread lotion on his back and shoulders, and took in the sun for an hour or so; that is, he tanned himself, or, as a Brazilian might have put it, he let the sun make him moreno. Many of the well-to-do and wealthy Cariocas who happened to be at Copacabana's beach that warm autumn day in April would have also spent much of their time not in the ocean but on the sand, where they, too, hoped to darken their complexions by exposure to the sun's rays.

Some of those Cariocas would have surely read, five years before, the article in the *Revista da Semana* in which the writer Clara Lúcia remarked favorably on the nascent craze for tanning at Rio de Janeiro's beaches. In the same 1926 article, she called attention to the small revolution in habits that the new fashion was bringing about among bathers at Rio de Janeiro's Atlantic beaches. "The chief, essential condition of modern bathing," she wrote, "is to remain on the sand. It [has become] necessary, absolutely obligatory 'to beach [*praiar*].'" Now, "in the most up-to-date present," it was on the sand that, while taking in the sun and "wearing as little as possible," bathers met each other and spent time together. "Today," she concluded, "sea-bathing is done mainly—on land."[118] Although Clara Lúcia's interesting neologism—the verb "praiar" or, in English, "to beach"—never gained acceptance, the practice of beach-going that she described has persisted into our times and has made Rio de Janeiro a city with a "vocation for the beach."

5

Measuring Maillots and Chasing Shirtless Men

The Police and the Beaches

IN 1948, RIO DE JANEIRO'S POLICE AUTHORITIES were busy. As the Cold War intensified internationally and the elected government of Eurico Gaspar Dutra became increasingly reactionary, they focused much of their attention on Communists (the Communist Party had been banned in 1947) and on other "subversive elements" whom they considered "disturbers of order," breaking up strikes and watching over unions. As always, they also had to worry about common crimes like robberies, murders, theft, and now also illegal gambling (casinos had been banned in 1946). The Federal District's feared Divisão de Polícia Política e Social (Division of Social and Political Police or DPPS), later renamed the Departamento de Ordem Política e Social (Department of Political and Social Order or DOPS) later infamous for its repression during the 1964–1985 dictatorship, seemingly had its hands full. Nevertheless, that summer General Antônio José de Lima Câmara, the Federal District's police chief, ordered the DPPS to deploy its agents on Copacabana and Ipanema beaches. Their mission was to impose morality on those beaches and, particularly, to bring to heel the male bathers who defied his 1948 prohibition on leaving the beach without donning a shirt.

The decision to send DPPS agents to Copacabana and Ipanema was yet another police effort to discipline and moralize Carioca beaches. The police had, as we have seen, always patrolled the city's beaches with greater or lesser diligence to maintain order and ensure "decent" behavior. The focus of this chapter is not, however, the normal police presence on the beaches but the specifically moralizing campaigns undertaken by authorities from the 1920s to the 1940s to control bathers' dress. These campaigns are notable in part because, though large-scale efforts, they constitute an almost completely forgotten chapter in the city's history. Many residents of Rio de Janeiro would today be surprised to learn that the police once concerned themselves with these matters. Indeed, scholarship on the city in the twentieth century contains only a few passing references to the police's repeated efforts to impose moral order and social discipline on the beaches.[1] Perhaps even more important, these campaigns stand out because they were not directed exclusively or even principally against lower-class bathers and beach-goers; rather, their main target was the usually well-off and even wealthy bathers who frequented the city's "elegant" and "aristocratic" beaches. Hence, they prompted extensive debates and deep controversy, which filled the pages of the main newspapers and local magazines and revealed disagreements about the meaning of concepts like "morality" and "civilization." They also raised questions about class and identity, privileges based on social standing, the acceptable uses of public space, and the new symbolic geography delineated in Rio de Janeiro after the 1920s.[2] In addition, the controversies demonstrate the divisions in the upper reaches of Carioca society. While some sectors of the upper- and upper middle class embraced the new practices of beach-going, other more conservative sectors rejected them, or at least had grave reservations about them. Similar differences of opinion divided journalists, writers, and other intellectuals.[3]

Rio de Janeiro's peculiar political status as the Federal District and the national capital also shaped these campaigns. The president of the republic, through the Ministry of Justice, appointed Rio de Janeiro's police chiefs, who thus enjoyed a measure of autonomy vis-à-vis local political and social elites. Sometimes they did not even have enduring ties to Rio de Janeiro. Police chiefs, moreover, enjoyed considerable independence when it came to deciding how to carry out their duties, particularly regarding order, morality, and decorum in public space; thus, in 1914, Henrique Valadares prohibited afternoon bathing at Flamengo, allegedly because his family lived in a hotel overlooking that beach.[4] Within their jurisdictions, district delegates, likewise enjoyed similar freedom of action.

"For the Sake of Morality"

Debates about the propriety of bathing attire on Flamengo beach in the 1910s, discussed in chapter 3, served as the prelude to similar controversies that led to waves of police repression in the next decades. For example, in the early 1920s, major newspapers requested on more than one occasion that the police put an end to the "abuses" of those who bathed at city beaches. Those who frequent Rio de Janeiro's beaches today will recognize some of these "abuses."

Journalists complained that some bothered their fellow bathers by taking dogs to the beach or by playing sports—football and shuttlecock (*peteca*)—on the sand. Another cause for complaint, less familiar today, was the presence of rowboats in waters used by bathers (see figures 2.4 and 3.4). Editorials and other articles also criticized the "very skimpy" and "immoral" outfits that many bathers wore. These critics, however, did not limit themselves to what those in the water and on the sand wore; they also targeted the "spectacle" of bathers on city streets. Thus, the *Gazeta de Notícias*'s Binóculo declared in 1920 that "this spectacle is only seen in Rio de Janeiro." He claimed that there was no other "city in a civilized country in which people walk on public streets dressed in this way." Two years later, in February 1922, Coelho Neto addressed the same issue in a front-page article in *A Noite*. He condemned "the scandalous strolling of bathers" who, "in skimpy diving dress," took over the streets—even "the busiest ones during rush hour"—when they went to the beach and returned home. For this writer, this habit, which was neither "right" nor "decent," would only give foreigners a bad impression of the city.[5]

At the beginning of that year, the police imposed strict regulations to discipline sea-bathers and moralize the city's beaches. These measures coincided with preparations for the international exhibition to celebrate Brazil's independence centenary, which would take place later that year. The moralizing campaign continued under a new police chief, Marshal Manoel Lopes Carneiro da Fontoura, who held office from 1922 to 1926. In this campaign, the police paid little attention to the beaches of the North Zone and the suburbs such as Caju, Porto de Inhaúma, and Ramos. Rather, they focused on the downtown beaches of Santa Luzia, Virtudes, and Calabouço, and especially the "elegant beaches" of Flamengo, Urca, and Copacabana.[6]

Authorities began their surveillance of these beaches by insisting that bathers keep their robes "hermetically closed, with no gaps" while they were on the streets. The also prohibited women from wearing short bathing dresses, especially maillots. The police were no less strict with the men; in 1923, in the name of "morality," they demanded that male bathers wear shirts that covered their biceps and shorts that covered their knees. Tom Aam, an American staying at the Hotel Glória (one of the city's most expensive) apparently did not know of these rules. In November 1923, he went out on Copacabana beach wearing shorts that did not reach his knees. A guard "called him to order" but Aam resisted verbally and physically; unsurprisingly, he was arrested.[7]

At the beginning of the following year, the district delegate whose jurisdiction included Flamengo beach issued slightly less strict instructions for sea-bathing. Male bathers "of average height" should wear shorts long enough that "the end of the hem is no more than four fingers (eight centimeters) above the knee." The delegate also permitted men to wear shirts without sleeves as long as the "armholes do not reveal the chest or too much of the back." The shirt could not be tucked into the shorts and had to be worn "over the trunks, stretching below them and long enough" to cover them. The delegate was less concerned about "ladies'" attire, merely demanding that they wear bathing "dress as decent as that demanded of men." By contrast, his instructions were quite specific when it came to "going to and from bathing"; on the streets, bathers should be "wrapped in large towels" or wear completely closed robes. If they wanted, men could opt for jackets, but in this case, the jacket had to be "completely buttoned up" in such a way that it covered the "bathing dress from the waist to the bottom of the shirt."[8] Long shirts and closed jackets sought to completely hide the male body's midsection. In his instructions, the delegate also prohibited football on Flamengo beach. The following year, the delegate responsible for Copacabana and Ipanema beaches "absolutely" prohibited football at the lifeguard posts. He also ordered that the police of his district continue to employ "maximum energy" in their campaign against bathers who wore outfits "that, by their exaggerated design, offend public morality." The *South American Handbook* noted the Copacabana police restrictions; while citing Copacabana beach as the preferred place for sea-bathing in its 1925 edition, it took care to warn its readers that the rules about bathing dress were "strict," perhaps thinking of Tom Aam's experience.[9]

The *Gazeta de Notícias* applauded the measures taken by the police since 1922. In a January 1924 editorial, it affirmed that there was no reason to be "upset" at the police chief's decision to reissue the regulations of previous years, for they merely meant to ensure "morality and decency among bathers" on the city's "elegant beaches." The editorial noted that "gallant and distinguished little ladies and elegant moneyed lads went bathing" there, so "nothing [was] more right for the scorching summer and for the honest and entertaining display of attractive and highly modern fashion." One of the police's great duties, added the *Gazeta de Notícias*, was to "protect public decorum"; for this reason, it could not let "gentlemen and *demoiselles* in shorts that reveal half of the thigh or in indiscreet and scandalous *maillots* turn public streets into an extension of their private quarters."[10]

Binóculo, the newspaper's social columnist, did not entirely share this view.

FIGURE 5.1. Changing Female Bathing Dress, 1908 and 1930. *Careta* (8.2.1930), 15.

To be sure, back in 1922, he had insisted that "not even in China" was it permitted to "walk on streets and squares" in bathing dress, but at that time he noted that, "when it comes to morality, it is important to avoid petty misunderstandings. On the beach itself, maillots or revealing outfits [toilettes *muito pouco* drapées] should not be considered crimes." "In all of the world's beaches," he continued, "the morality of dress [*castidade das* tenues] is no cause for concern, so long as they are in areas designated for bathing." Binóculo was not the only journalist to have doubts about the police efforts. Others criticized the police's "itch for modesty [*pruridos de pudicícia*]," which led them to impose "draconian restrictions on bathing dress." In 1925, even *Vida Polícial*, a magazine published in part for police personnel, judged these measures excessive.[11]

The police ultimately ended up accepting the maillot. "For sunbathing" on Copacabana sands and "for bathers' convenience," the *Correio da Manhã* observed in 1925, "the maillot is the most suitable and simple outfit." Two years later, Binóculo could declare that the maillot had "definitively" triumphed in Rio de Janeiro.[12] By this time, Marshal Fontoura had stepped down as the Federal District's police chief and the president named as his replacement Coroliano de Araújo Góes Filho, a much younger man. While the new police chief did not entirely abandon the policing of bathing and beach-going, he was less concerned about it than his predecessor. In early 1930, *Careta* used a cartoon to call attention to the relaxation of beach policing. One frame, set in

1908, shows a guard arresting a bather for baring her arms on the beach. The other frame shows a scene from 1930, in which a woman in a short maillot, cut to reveal her back, walks on a beachside sidewalk while a smiling guard looks on. The caption proclaimed that the police now "supported the cocktail dress maillot" (fig. 5.1).[13]

This relaxation of police vigilance prompted many bathers to return to what, in 1927, the *Jornal do Brasil* called an "unreasonable and indecorous" habit, namely walking on city streets with open robes or unbuttoned jackets, or even without anything to cover their bathing attire. Other abuses that Marshal Fontoura's police had fought against, including beach football, also returned.[14] Indeed, just one year after the marshal left his post, some young residents of Copacabana and Ipanema founded the Liga de Amadores de Football de Areia (Amateur Sand [Beach] Football League). On Copacabana's "aristocratic" beach, many women exposed their bodies to the sun, while wearing daring maillots. Some young men, "almost all considered lads from good families," were even bolder on Copacabana and Ipanema beaches: they rolled down their shirts or took them off altogether, going bare-chested on the sand (figure 5.2). On Ipanema, then a less busy beach than Copacabana, it was not just lads that did this; when they lay facedown on the sand, some female bathers lowered the tops of their maillots to tan their backs.[15]

FIGURE 5.2. Topless Men on Copacabana Beach, 1929. *Careta* (16.11.1929), 37.

The police reaction to these daring displays and other abuses came right after the Revolution of 1930, which brought Getúlio Vargas to power in November of that year. In January 1931, João Batista Luzardo, newly appointed Federal District police chief, issued a new regulation to moralize and discipline the city's beaches. Although it applied to all of the city's beaches, newspaper reports make clear that authorities were most concerned with Copacabana and that police measures prompted the most resistance there. By contrast, the new regulation appears to have been well received at some suburban beaches.[16] It prohibited riding horses on beaches during bathing hours, banned dogs from the sand, and ordered boats belonging to rowing clubs and private owners to stay away from beaches. According to another article, bathers should avoid "shouting and yelling"—unless they were calling for help—so as not to alarm others. Offenders could be fined Rs.20$000, which would be doubled for a second offence. Those unable to pay the fine were subject to prison sentences of twenty-four or forty-eight hours.

Batista Luzardo reinstated the ban on football and extended it beyond the areas around the posts at bathing time; it now applied to the entire beach and to all times of day. The regulation also prohibited "any gymnastics exercises that may inconvenience bathers." The new police chief, moreover, ordered his men to strictly enforce the ban on bathing outside of the official hours. Thus, from Mondays to Saturdays in the summer, bathing was permitted only from seven to eleven in the morning and from four to seven in the evening. On Sundays and holidays, morning bathing hours were extended for one additional hour, as was already established. The ban on after-hours bathing was poorly received. Many bathers only arrived at Copacabana beach around eleven in the morning on Sundays, so they scarcely had time to go into the water and to chat with friends on the sand. Worse yet, the police not only insisted that people leave the water at eleven but also required them to clear the beach at that time. The afternoon bathing hours did not please businessmen and liberal professionals, many of whom did not leave work until six o'clock. Thus, they scarcely had time to get changed at home and to rush to the beach to refresh themselves in Copacabana's waves after a long day in un-air-conditioned offices.[17]

Even more controversial than the ban on football or the restricted bathing hours were the measures that aimed to moralize the beaches. The 1931 regulation, for example, reinstated the requirement to wear closed robes or buttoned, "sufficiently long" jackets on the streets. It also prohibited women from wearing maillots with short bottoms or with too much cut away in the

FIGURE 5.3. Police-Approved Bathing Dress, 1931. *Malho* (7.2.1931).

front or the back. The ban on "overly short" trunks also applied to men. And, even more strictly, the police banned men from going topless. They claimed that "respectable ladies [*senhoras de família*]" did not know where to look when young men took off their shirts on Copacabana beach.[18] For the same reason, the regulation banned the use of shirts made from lightweight or light-colored cloth for, when wet, they became transparent. To enforce these new measures, Batista Luzardo mobilized a small army of "civil guards, secret agents, delegates and acting delegates," and even mounted police. He dispatched police vans to Copacabana and other beaches to cope with the expected number of arrests.[19]

"On the beach," as the *Jornal do Brasil* would recall some two years later, "the police presence was so large that many ladies were frightened."[20] Regardless of whether they were actually afraid, these ladies and their daughters were placed in an uncomfortable situation. Before setting foot on the sand, they had to open their robes so that a guard could inspect their maillot. If the guard did not approve of what he saw, he sent them home. If they wanted to enjoy the sun and the sand the next day, the best thing to do was to buy a new bathing dress that was acceptable to the police. For this reason, *Casa Alemã* announced in January 1931 that, "to better orient the public," it was displaying the swimwear "styles banned by the police," and that it would sell only approved bathing outfits. For its part, *O Malho* illustrated two styles "approved" by the police so that "beautiful bathers" could frequent the beaches "without fear" (figure 5.3).

Neither of these outfits, however, was a maillot, and, indeed, they were considerably more conservative than the maillots that many Cariocas had been wearing since the late 1920s.[21]

A flurry of critical articles and editorials did nothing to reduce the police pressure on beach-goers.[22] Humorous criticisms also appeared in 1931's Carnival. In February of that year, a group of costumed bathers took to Copacabana beach singing, "with deliberate emphasis," Noel Rosa's 1929 samba, "Com que roupa vou?" (What Clothes Will I Wear?). One of the revelers arrived at the beach wearing a "black robe [*baeta*], long pants, and a high-collared [shirt]." On his back, a sign proclaimed: "1910 Model—Permitted by the Police." He also carried a birdcage containing a maillot with a sign, "Banned by the Police."[23] Like the articles published in the press, this creative protest had no effect on the police. Not even the actions of Britain's future King George VI were sufficient for Batista Luzardo to reconsider his moralizing campaign. As we saw in chapter 4, after enjoying the water, "he took off his shirt, spread oil on his body and remained naked from the waist up until after 1:00 pm, under the police's watchful eyes." For obvious reasons, the police did not arrest the prince. But they also did not arrest a nearby Brazilian who, following the prince's example, "dared" to take off his shirt: when a guard tried to arrest him, he said a few words in English and thus passed for a member of the royal entourage.[24]

Facing these criticisms of his regulations, Batista Luzardo conceded two points. On the request of Copacabana residents, he extended morning bathing hours until noon and evening bathing hours to half past seven on summer weekdays. He also approved the request of some "lads" from a Santa Luzia rowing club who pointed out that it was impractical for them to wear a jacket while they carried their shells across Santa Luzia Street, which separated their headquarters from the beach. The police agreed to excuse them from the requirement to wear jackets, but only if they wore bathing attire of the sort that their fathers or grandfathers would have worn: "long cashmere shorts [extending] to the knees and a knit sport shirt." Authorities even suggested that all male bathers should dress in this way.[25]

At this time, the press frequently referred to the new campaign as an effort to combat "nudism," the same expression that it would use to describe later campaigns. On the surface, *nudism* may seem like hyperbole to describe maillots and topless male bathers. However, in the late 1920s and the first half of the 1930s, Carioca newspapers published reports about the nudist movement in Europe and the United States, reports that took the movement and its growth seriously.[26] At the same time, discussions about the city's beaches freely mixed, with often alarming results, references to nudism strictly speaking (naturalism) and the "nudism" of Carioca bathers. One of the better examples of this alarmist rhetoric is found in a January 1931 article by Pilar Drumond, who defended Batista Luzardo's measures. Drumond began by calling attention to "integral [or total] nudism," a "sort of medical-religious sect that originated in North America" and subsequently spread to Scandinavia (where, due to the climate, most people knew better than to go about naked), to Germany, and "even" to France. He affirmed that this sect's adepts were employing more and more aggressive tactics to promote "integral nudism" and offered several examples. In Nelson, Canada, "some one hundred nudists appeared in public without the slightest bit of clothing to cover themselves, obliging the armed forces to intervene and filling the prisons with men and women." In another incident, "more than three hundred American women" allegedly landed in Lisbon and explored the city "in very skimpy outfits," probably short, sleeveless dresses with low necklines. Worse yet, the Americans wore no stockings. Drumond concluded his article by commenting on sunbathing and women's dress on Carioca beaches before the new police measures: they wore maillots that shamelessly revealed "the whole [lower] leg, all of the knees, and a bit more" to boot. "If we add to this their naked arms, neck, and a good part of the back, we have to conclude that these women are well on their way to integral nudism."[27]

Batista Luzardo, however, would not long remain the Federal District's police chief. He fell out with Vargas over other issues and resigned in early 1932. The new chief, João Alberto Lins de Barros, loosened Batista Luzardo's restrictions. In May 1932, he lifted the ban on football on Copacabana and Ipanema beaches in areas away from the posts. Local youth immediately organized a new sand football league. No doubt, too, some of these young men were among the bathers who took advantage of the new regime to take off their shirts on the beach, a practice that nevertheless remained illegal.[28] Finally, in December 1933, the police gave in and allowed men to go topless. Photographs from Copacabana and Ipanema in the summers of 1933–1934 and 1934–1935 show several bare-chested men; in subsequent years, going topless became generalized among men who frequented these beaches. Most men in a mid-1930s photograph of Flamengo beach are also shirtless (figure 5.4). The post–Batista Luzardo police also demonstrated more toleration for women's dress; in the mid-1930s, they permitted one-piece maillots (*maiôs de frente única*). The police, however, continued to insist that bathers wear

FIGURE 5.4. Beach-Goers on Flamengo Beach, Mid-1930s. Fuss, *Brasilien*, plate 94. Arquivo Images2You.

a robe or, in the case of men, a jacket or at least a shirt while they were on the districts' streets (a man at the water's edge in the center of figure 5.4 is wearing such a robe).[29]

It did not take long, however, for new complaints about "nudism" on beaches and adjoining streets, as well as about other "abuses," to appear in the press.[30] At least in part in response to these complaints, the police launched other campaigns to moralize the beaches in the late 1930s and early 1940s. For example, in December 1936, at the start of one of these campaigns, the delegate responsible for the Zona Sul's oceanfront neighborhoods, announced that he was placing "all of Copacabana beach under police supervision." He deployed fifty civil guards, aided by detectives, to "clean up and moralize" that beach. Besides limiting beach sports, these men targeted the "shamelessness" of bathers who wore revealing shorts or "highly indiscreet maillots."[31]

Press complaints, however, make it clear that these campaigns, like their predecessors, produced no lasting results.[32] It is not difficult to explain this lack of success. As a guard who had worked for several years in Copacabana explained in 1931, "it would be necessary [to deploy] at least twenty guards at each post" to enforce the police orders. For this reason, in the 1920s and 1930s, the police apparently adopted the strategy of launching a crackdown during the first weeks of summer, in the hope that this would be enough to modify bathers' habits for good.[33] As soon as the police efforts slackened, beach-goers resumed the "abusive" practices condemned by authorities.

War on the Beaches?

The second half of the 1940s saw another wave of police repression, the last great effort to moralize and discipline the city's beaches. Certainly the most violent of these campaigns, it coincided with the Dutra government's increasingly repressive turn. Already in 1946, Alarico de Freitas advised in an official police publication that authorities should closely monitor Copacabana to stop the immoral acts that took place "under the full sun's bright rays" and "on the soft white sands." There, he observed, "under the shade of their beach tents . . . , young women, apparently still virgins," wearing two-piece maillots, exchanged "ardent kisses" with their boyfriends. Sometimes, one of these girls would even let her little boyfriend rest his head on "her completely naked stomach." Freitas suggested that the duties of policing the beach be assigned to "special agents or detectives" in civilian dress and "partially undressed," in other words in bathing attire; they should have a "beach tent (or umbrella) as well as the indispensable [items] for beach sports: the birdie for shuttlecock and a volley-ball ball." As he made clear, his main concern was not the lower class's public behavior but that of the "middle or bourgeois sector [*camada intermediária ou burguesa*]"; he was also concerned about the "highest social classes'" exaggerated luxury and "moral poverty [*miséria moral*]."[34]

Less than two years later, in the summer of 1947–1948, the police launched another campaign to discipline and moralize the beach, which would last until the first months of 1950. In November 1947, police authorities severely restricted the playing of football on Copacabana, Leme, Ipanema, and Leblon beaches. In January 1948, they turned to bathing attire. Once again, as in the previous campaigns, police actions were not limited to the beach itself; they also encompassed Copacabana and Ipanema streets. They banned residents of these elite and upper middle-class neighborhoods from making purchases at street markets dressed in only maillots or maillots and a short cover-up (*saída-de-praia*). They also demanded that male bathers, outside of the sandy

FIGURE 5.5. Male Beach-Goers on Avenida Atlântica, 1940s.
Photograph by Geneviève Naylor. Arquivo Images2You.

areas, wear at least a buttoned-up shirt. There was one exception. Men could go shirtless on the avenues that faced the beach, and during bathing hours, sit shirtless at the open-air tables that these streets' bars put out, provided that their owners approved. These exceptions also implied that men who lived in beach-facing apartments could leave home shirtless and cross the street to the beach (figure 5.5). In practice, however, guards did not always allow these exceptions.[35]

To enforce these new measures, General Antônio José de Lima Câmara, the Federal District's police chief, mobilized not only civil guards and regular police but also men from the Polícia Especial (Special Police or PE), a sort of riot police. Established in the early 1930s, the PE recruited tall and strong men; many had been drawn from among the members of sporting clubs. The PE's athletes soon earned a reputation as especially violent, specializing in breaking up political demonstrations and roughing up strikers, university students, and "leftists."[36]

"Copacabana's aristocrats [*grã-finos*]" did not welcome the new measures and instead expressed "general discontent." They were upset both at the measures themselves and at the "arbitrary and excessive ways" that the police enforced them. As the *Diário da Noite* pointed out, on the very first Sunday that the new measures would go into force, the police "abused their power aggressively and rudely"; the men who "should keep order . . . turned themselves into the cause of disorder and unrest." In Copacabana, there were "police incursions [*correrias*] and disagreeable conflicts"; unhappy bathers, whose dignity was offended, used the only means left to them—"jeers, derision . . . , and lively and irreverent mockery" of the police. Discontent only mounted when ocean beach-goers learned, through rumor and from newspaper articles, about an incident that took place on that Sunday at Post 2. The PE's detachment, brandishing nightsticks, stormed the post to arrest some boys of twelve or thirteen years who had been playing with a football on the sand. All escaped, except one whom the police seized. The boy then smiled at the policeman who held him, which provoked the soldier's rage; he beat his hapless prisoner. Other nearby bathers jeered the soldier, and when one attempted to intervene on the boy's behalf, he was arrested. The PE released him as soon as he identified himself as an army major.[37]

The following year, in the summer of 1948–1949, The DPPS assigned sixty-three men—an inspector, two detectives, and sixty investigators—to the "quite thankless" task of patrolling Copacabana and other beaches to chase down shirtless men who left the sand. This amounted to more than 10 percent of the entire DPPS personnel.[38] The *Jornal do Brasil* praised the decision to continue the moralizing campaign, arguing that the campaign would "put an end to the libertine and almost lascivious spectacles [that took place] on the beaches" in direct contradiction to "our population's traditions of morality." The editors lamented that Christian Dior's New Look—the long, ankle-length dresses that changed women's fashion in the late 1940s—had not had any effect on maillots; rather, "today's bathing customs" had made them "smaller than Adam's fig leaf." The police chief's initiative thus deserved applause for it would prevent "the spread of pagan sensibilities" and ensure that Rio de Janeiro did not turn into "an immense nudist colony."[39]

The PE, meanwhile, continued to deploy men dressed in bathing suits on these beaches. PE personnel had learned that they needed to be ready to pursue offenders who tried to escape arrest by diving into the water. Nevertheless, once on the sand, these PE "athletes," with their distinctive red bathing trunks, could not control "their Don-Juanesque tendencies"; rather than pursue those who failed to obey the regulations, they spent most of their time watching the prettiest female bathers, flirting with them, or whistling at them. On top of this, PE men violated the prohibition on going topless outside of the beaches. Wearing just their trunks, they rode in an open transport vehicle between their downtown headquarters and Copacabana.[40]

Furthermore, the PE continued to resort to violence, as is clear from two incidents that took place on Leme beach, which had nothing to do with moralizing the beach. On Christmas Day 1948, two lifeguards at Post 1 were taking care of a drunken bather, known to them, when a PE Radio Patrol car arrived in response to a complaint about two army soldiers urinating in public. The two soldiers had already been seized by the army police, so the Radio Patrol turned its attention to the drunk, whom they insisted on arresting. The lifeguards protested, explaining that this was unnecessary, for the drunk was not bothering anyone; they promised to watch him and, as soon as their shift ended, take him home. The police reacted to the lifeguards' protests by punching them, shocking nearby bathers. Renato Dantoni, one of the lifeguards, retaliated by punching the detective in charge of the Radio Patrol in the face. Unsurprisingly, the two lifeguards were arrested but they quickly made bail. They were back at work at their post the next morning, when the PE returned to "take revenge." A Radio Patrol vehicle pulled up at about ten, when the beach was already full; its men ran out onto the sand and began "beating"

Dantoni. Nearby bathers jeered them. Before long, five more Radio Patrol vehicles pulled up, along with two contingents of riot police. Brandishing their nightsticks, they advanced onto the beach. Chaos reigned as the PE men threw tear gas canisters and continued their attacks. According to the *Diário da Noite*, "none" of the bathers escaped "the police's blows. Old and young, women and children, were indiscriminately beaten." When some bathers tried to defend themselves "by throwing handfuls of sand at their aggressors," the PE soldiers "redoubled their furious attack." Rubem Braga sarcastically observed that those who frequented Post 1 had been beaten that Sunday for the "horrible crime of going sea-bathing."[41]

In spite of this incident, General Lima Câmara did not give up his moralizing campaign. In the first week of December 1949, he advised the press that his work would continue, and once again, the Radio Patrol and the PE returned to the beaches. Even before this announcement, the new Sears store calculated that many Carioca bathers would give up elegance in favor of personal safety. In November 1949, it advertised a conservative cover-up with the slogan, "Don't worry about the Radio Patrol."[42] Upon learning that Lima Câmara intended to continue his campaign, journalist Joel Silveira predicted "war" on the beaches. This was only to be expected in light of what had happened in previous years. Nevertheless, the summer of 1949–1950 passed without serious incident. It was not that the PE's men had suddenly become less strict—quite the contrary. They continued to stop men who left the beach without donning a shirt, among other things. Nevertheless, no significant conflicts between the police and bathers were registered that summer.[43] By then, President Dutra's term was ending and the campaign for the October 1950 elections was underway. Getúlio Vargas would win this election and, upon taking office, he named General Ciro Rio-Pardense Resende as the Federal District's new police chief. Unlike his predecessor, Resende was not interested in making a priority of beach policing. Lima Câmara's campaign was the last great effort to moralize Rio de Janeiro's beaches.

Male and Female Bodies: Morality, Modernity, and Civilization

One consistent theme of morality campaigns on Rio de Janeiro's oceanfront beaches was anxiety over the perceived modesty, or lack thereof, of young women. Police efforts to restrict "nudism," stemmed, in part, from long-standing concerns about the presence of women in public. These anxieties intensified in the first half of the twentieth century as women in Rio de Janeiro and other large Brazilian cities gained greater visibility in the public space. Growing numbers of women, including those from the middle and upper classes, took on paid work outside of the home. Women embraced new forms of recreation, which enabled new types of sociability and public interaction.[44] Beach-going was one of these new forms of recreation, but unlike most others, it required that women appear partly undressed in a public space. Unsurprisingly, beach-going prompted numerous questions about public morality. As beach fashion changed and as beachwear became ever more revealing, authorities periodically had to determine what level of "nudism" was acceptable on the city's beaches.

In addition to these general concerns about women's presence in public, there was the centuries-old conservative position of the Roman Catholic Church regarding women. Women, especially young women, should be modest in their behavior and dress lest they lose their reputation as honest and respectable.[45] The rapid changes in fashion and customs, as well as the growing public presence of women in Brazil (and elsewhere in the world) in the 1910s and 1920s, heightened the Church's concern over women's chastity. Thus, already in 1920, the magazine *Selecta* reminded its (female) readers that the Pope, Brazil's bishops, the archbishop of Paris, and Britain's Anglican clergy had all condemned modern fashion's "excesses." It further advised the "living flowers of Flamengo and Copacabana" to heed the Church's admonitions and to avoid revealing bathing dress. All that was needed was "a few fingers-worth of cloth above, below, and at the sides." *A Cruz*, published by the Confederação Católica do Rio de Janeiro (Catholic Confederation of Rio de Janeiro), regularly addressed the same issues. Following Pope Benedict XV's 1921 encyclical *Sacra Propedium*, *A Cruz* criticized "the indecent maillots" and "nudism" on the beaches, explaining that "sea-bathing constitute[ed] the greatest danger for our youth." Unsurprisingly, *A Cruz* supported the police campaigns of the early 1920s and early 1930s.[46]

Similar views appeared in *A Ordem*, a magazine published by Ação Católica (Catholic Action), which enjoyed considerable influence among Catholic intellectuals. On more than one occasion in the 1930s, *A Ordem* called attention to the lack of "morality" on the city's beaches. For example, in 1936, it declared that it was "difficult to distinguish, by their dress, on the beaches and even on the [Rio Branco] Avenue, the daughter of a respectable family [*filha-família*] from a *demi-mondaine*." It concluded by asking, "How can Catholic fathers and husbands reconcile their Christian duty and their authority in the home with the effective paganism of their daughters and wives?" Two years later, Monsignor Conrado Jacarandá went further in an article published in the *Jornal do Brasil*: "The scandalous nudism that fill[ed] the beaches and streets" of Rio de Janeiro, he argued, was not just "shamelessness" and "moral decadence"; it resulted from a "Bolshevik" plot. Based on what he saw on the city's beaches and streets, he concluded that communism was already "winning" in Brazil.[47]

Jacarandá would have been pleased with an initiative launched by São Paulo's Juventude Feminina Católica (Female Catholic Youth, JFC), supported by Ação Católica and the archdiocese. In 1943, the JFC requested the support for its campaign to "moralize the beaches" from Jônatas Serrano, a Catholic editor and journalist in Rio de Janeiro. The campaign exclusively targeted women's bathing dress, for a "young woman who cultivated the Catholic virtue of chastity" could not wear "the maillots [now] in fashion" and protect "the bulwarks of her purity." The JFC proposed designs for bathing dress that combined "Christian modesty and good taste." They had high necklines, long sleeves, wide straps, and a skirt that covered two-thirds of the thigh. And to completely protect the JFC members' "purity," the patterns included a sort of shorts, stitched to the waistband, that could not be lowered, either in the water or on the sand. The JFC further advised its members to wear these outfits "only and exclusively for sea-bathing"; for "playing" on the sand, they should wear a robe or a modest cover-up.[48]

The Paulista JFC's initiatives did not produce results satisfactory to conservative Catholics in Rio de Janeiro, as is clear from a 1947 pastoral letter from Cardinal Jaime de Barros Câmara, the city's archbishop. He lamented the "public vices" that undermined moral order in the city. The first of these consisted of the "offenses against public and private morality" practiced on the city's beaches, and he lamented that the previous police efforts had failed to impose morality. "What can be said," he asked, "about the seductions begun or completed during sea-bathing, which washes the body but stains the soul?" As far as the cardinal was concerned, these "seductions" only served to prove that a large part of Carioca society had "dissipated its morals."[49]

Two years later, the worries of Cardinal Câmara, a fierce anticommunist, were echoed in "Os inimigos da família" (The Family's Enemies), an article published in the *Jornal do Brasil* by Baltasar da Silveira. He railed against "nudism" on Carioca beaches, which, reprising Monsignor Jacarandá's arguments, he judged a "satanic custom" and therefore one of the "means by which those who dream of annihilating the Religion of Calvary [ensure] that disgusting Communism triumphs." He added that "sensible young men will not choose for wives those who do not respect themselves by exposing [their bodies] to beach-goers' sinful eyes." That year, the *Jornal* also published an article by the historian Hélio Silva, who declared that "often, the first spectacle of nudity that a child sees is that of his or her own mother who lacks modesty [*compostura*] at home or on the beaches." He asked, "What can be expected by the parents of a young couple dating [*namorados*] when they spend the morning on the beach in extremely short maillots, and at night, go out in the automobile?" He even insinuated that a mother who let her daughter go to Copacabana beach alone should not be surprised if she lost her virginity to a married man without feeling any shame about it. To make his point, he cited a case of this that involved "one of those young women of Copacabana." It apparently never occurred to Silva to blame the married man for having "seduced" (or even raped) the "young woman" from Copacabana. Nor did he note that a married man who had sex with a minor was committing a crime, according to the criminal code. Rather, for Silva, the fault lay with the mother for having failed to control her daughter and with the daughter for not having maintained an appropriate level of modesty.[50]

Many conservative Catholics like Silveira, Silva, and JFC members in São Paulo and other states no doubt joined the Legião de Decência (Legion of Decency) founded by Cardinal Câmara in the late 1940s. Inspired by an organization of the same name founded in the United States, the Legião sought to defend the "Brazilian family's moral patrimony." To this end, it attacked "exhibitions of nudism," among them the "highly immoral spectacle" of the beaches, which revealed "the rotting corruption of the Brazilian family's morality."[51]

The efforts to regulate women's bathing attire reflected traditional Catholic concerns over women's bodies and chastity and are thus unsurprising. What is surprising is the amount of attention paid to the male body. In all their campaigns, the police demonstrated considerable concern with what men did or did not wear. In some cases, authorities were explicit about their motives when they specified which parts of the male body should be covered or partially covered "for the sake of morality" or to ensure "decency"; these included the chest and the thighs, as well as the groin. Thus, in 1924, Flamengo's delegate banned men from wearing shorts that did not cover most of the thighs (at least down to four fingers above the knees) and demanded that they wear shirts that "not reveal the chest, nor too much of the back." João de Freitas Ferreira, a resident of Copacabana, criticized such prohibitions in a letter to the *Diário da Noite*. Besides declaring that men's bathing shirts were becoming obsolete, he added that police concern with the length of shorts was misplaced. "Shorts," he explained, could be "short *and* decent [italics mine]." "Decency" did not depend on their length but on the quality of the wool cloth from which they were made. When wet, long shorts, and especially those made from inferior material, stuck to the body in revealing ways. Worse yet, long trunks tended to be "loose," and for this reason, when a bather sat on the sand, he risked "a disaster!"[52]

Whence this focus on male bathing attire? If police authorities were concerned about homoeroticism, they said nothing about it in their orders.[53] Nor can these concerns be attributed to the Church, for conservative Catholics who condemned "nudism" on the beaches focused almost exclusively on women's dress. The main explanation for the recurring concern with the male body lies in the period's gender norms. According to those norms, it was entirely acceptable for men to stare (more or less discreetly) at women's bodies in public, on beaches and elsewhere. Newspaper articles frequently touted the possibility of seeing dozens and even hundreds of minimally dressed women as one of the main attractions that Copacabana and Ipanema offered to men. Indeed, Ipanema beach owes much of its international fame to a song about a man who cannot take his eyes off a beautiful young bather (in fact, much younger than him), "A Garota de Ipanema" (The Girl from Ipanema, 1962), by Tom Jobim and Vinícius de Moraes.

Some journalists, indeed, supported the police restrictions on male bathing dress, but opposed efforts to prohibit skimpy maillots. The male body, they explained, was "ugly," especially when the man was hairy. Thus, the presence of partially undressed men on the beach violated "the laws of esthetics." The same journalists, moreover, argued that bodies of young and beautiful women represented "the supreme expression of art" and, consequently, could not be "immoral." The true "crime" was obliging young beauties to wear less revealing attire, therefore preventing "enraptured" men from contemplating their bodies.[54]

At the same time, from the point of view of police authorities, modesty required a completely different comportment on the part of "respectable" women when faced with male bodies. Instead of admiring the minimally dressed male form, they should blush and turn their eyes. Better yet, they should be protected from seeing male bodies in the first place. Therefore, the police should prohibit men from going topless and from wearing short swimming trunks. Those who denounced the "immorality" of male bathing dress frequently mentioned the need to protect women and girls. These complaints, which more than once called on the police to intervene, sometimes alleged that men in revealing attire were offending "families [*famílias*]." In other cases, these complaints explicitly declared that the men in "indecent" attire "scandalize[d]" "ladies" and "little ladies [*senhorinhas*]." In 1929, a *Beira-Mar* editorial bluntly declared that shirtless male bathers demonstrated a lack of "respect" for "ladies" and young women. It denounced the "licentious spectacle" of "almost totally naked men circulating" among the female beach-goers as "indecorous and immoral" and concluded by reminding the men that these women were "their mothers, wives, brides, sisters, [and] daughters."[55] The recurring concern about male dress and male bodies in fact had much to do with women. Men, or at least those who supported the restrictions on male bathing attire, believed them necessary to prevent "their" women from seeing the bodies of other men.

For their part, the critics of the moralizing campaigns did more than just mock the police's "draconian measures" as a "fit of moral hysteria" or the product of extreme and even hypocritical "prudery." They did not fail to remind the police that they had more important tasks at hand like preventing robberies and murders or tracking down real "criminals."[56] They described the city's beaches, especially those on the open ocean, as "stadiums," "forges of athleticism," "open-air gymnasiums," and "schools of eugenics." There, young men and women improved their health through vigorous physical activities and by exposing their bodies to the sun's "beneficent rays." The combination of sports on the sand and tanning would give rise to a new "eugenic" "race" of "healthy" and "strong" Brazilians, "gilded [*dourados*]" by the sun. Obtaining these benefits, however, required that bathers and beach-goers wear minimal attire that did not impede their movements. In these senses, beach "nudism" was moral for it contributed to hygiene and eugenics, and the police efforts to restrict beach sports and to control bathing attire actually harmed "public health" and impeded efforts to improve the country's "racial health."[57]

Critics also called attention to the "scandals" and "disturbances" that the police provoked on the beaches—such as when policemen regularly measured the length of female bathing dress in the 1920s and 1930s. Sometimes, according to the critics, they did not wait for the bathers to open their robes; rather, they "roughly" opened them. Such actions gave a male "stranger," the policeman, the chance to examine closely a woman's body in public; when measuring the length of her attire, he could also touch her naked thigh. Many women considered these inspections "annoyance[s]" and "humiliation[s]," and judged the policemen "uppity" and "insolent." In 1931, *Beira-Mar* held up the measuring of maillots as proof that the police were "undermining morality [*desmoralizando a moralidade*]."[58]

It was not just women who were offended by police actions; their husbands, fathers, brothers, and boyfriends likewise considered them offensive. Few accepted that a male "stranger" might examine, closely and in public, the bodies of "their" women. These examinations represented a challenge to their patriarchal authority. As *Para Todos* explained in 1925, the police "turned themselves into fathers and husbands" and "infringed on the private duties of heads of family." Six years later, a group of Copacabana beach-goers argued that, "if a father or a brother takes respectable young women [*moças de família*] wearing short maillots [to the beach], it is because he thinks that this is fine." They added that "the police ultimately do not have the right to interfere in these matters." That same year, a petition signed by more than one hundred and fifty Copacabana residents made the point that the neighborhood's "fathers of families . . . had always known how to ensure that the members of their households dressed and behaved decently." For this reason, it was "highly upsetting to them to see that authorities felt it necessary to use force to compel bathers" to wear certain kinds of beach attire.[59]

Police inspected the bathing outfits of children, even those as young as three or four, going to the beach with their parents. One Copacabana resident confessed in a 1931 interview with *Beira-Mar* that he had to contain his "indignation" when the police admonished his little children for not wearing a robe while they were on their way to the beach. As the resident recognized, if he had reacted, he would have been arrested. To ensure that his authority as a father and a husband was not again challenged in public, this man resolved that he and his family would, for the time being, cease going to the beach.[60]

Class and Space: Copacabana's Claim to Distinctiveness

The police responsible for moralizing the beaches faced not only rival claims to patriarchal authority but also the force of social hierarchies and demands for privileged treatment based on social position. The press almost completely ignored the women subject to clothing inspections at the downtown beaches that attracted lower middle-class and working-class bathers. Rather, journalists stressed that the women subject to inspection were those who frequented Copacabana and other "elegant" beaches. These were, according to the press, ladies of "quality," "position," or "the highest distinction" who therefore deserved "greater circumspection and respect." The *Diário de Notícias*, which initially supported Batista Luzardo's campaign, soon had a change of heart, and a week later, lamented that policemen dared inspect even "ladies" of "high society" who belonged to "the most noble families."[61]

The press sometimes alluded indirectly to the police personnel's social origins when they highlighted their errors in speaking Portuguese, their mistakes in following orders, and their lack of politeness and tact. Thus, according to a commentary published in 1924 in the magazine *Fon-Fon!*, the policemen assigned to patrol the beaches lacked "the most rudimentary notions of sociability"; they dared address "ladies with the same nearly savage rudeness [*fúria*] with which they spoke to elements of *other* social classes with whom they are [more] familiar." In the same year, *Careta* raised a question that the press generally avoided when it came to criticizing the police: the color of the policemen. It described the men responsible for inspecting the beaches as "representatives of low morality" and also "a bunch of thick-lipped blacks with tangled hair [*negrada de gaforinha e beiçola*]." *Careta* did not need to add that the "ladies" of "high society" who frequented "elegant" beaches considered themselves white and respectable, and therefore, that they believed that the policemen, and especially those of darker color, should treat them with deference and respect.[62]

Critics also accused the police of failing to demonstrate deference when they dealt with the men who frequented these beaches. For example, in 1924, Álvaro de Penalva, a *Gazeta de Notícias* columnist, recounted the case of a "young university student, from a respectable family," who had violated the police instructions about bathing attire but had managed to escape their clutches; apparently, he had gone to the beach without a robe or a jacket. Later that day, the police arrested him and took him to jail as if he were, in Penalva's words, "any common person [*desclassificado*]." The young man's friends would have quickly secured his release had it not been for the "manly pride with which he reacted against the rude words that the commissioner directed at him as a reprimand." The next day, a judge, also a friend of the young man, obtained his release; the judge, explained Penalva, was "angry at the arbitrary actions" of the police.[63]

Seven years later, a January 1931 editorial in *O Jornal* alleged that, "charged with the stupid task of persecuting bathers . . . on the beaches where the cream of Carioca society gathers," the police were insufficiently "polite." They insisted on stopping "even respectable men to measure their trunks." *O Jornal* offered the example of an incident in Copacabana in which policemen threatened to take a "high-ranking army officer" to the station because he was wearing briefs that were too short. Bystanders' intervention spared the officer the indignity of a ride in a police van. According to another editorial, the police were treating even "the most respectable persons," as if they were "ruffians from Saúde Hill," the location of a favela.

The law, in other words, was not equal for all. With a reputation for violence that dated back to the nineteenth century, the Carioca police resorted to often brutal force when dealing with members of the lower class and those whom they defined as troublemakers from the favelas. When interacting with people of means, however, this very same police force had to demonstrate "politeness" and "respect." In a report about the first days of Batista Luzardo's crackdown, the *Diário da Noite* noted that Copacabana was a "beach frequented by the elite," so the police had "to act with more diplomacy." At the same time, the *Correio da Manhã* observed that, "although it may appear a paradox, Copacabana was the beach that gave the police more difficulty." "The elegant folks," explained the newspaper, "do not like to be bothered, and for this reason, disregard the orders that they receive."[64] All of this brings to mind the classic, indignant challenge, "Do you know who you're talking to?" This question, though not unique to Brazil, has deep roots in Brazilian culture. Those who resort to it seek to use their actual or claimed social position or their connections (real or not) with more powerful figures to get around bureaucratic requirements or to escape equal application of the law. Copacabana and Ipanema bathers, in effect, deployed this question in their confrontations with the police in the 1930s and 1940s.[65]

It is easy to see the attitudes that lay behind this question in a comic protest against General Lima Câmara's campaign organized by a group of Zona Sul "playboys," which reprised some aspects of the April 1917 protest on Flamengo beach (chapter 3). One sunny Sunday in December 1949, the playboys—dressed, in addition to their bathing trunks, in shirts, ties, tailcoats or tuxedo jackets, and in some cases, top hats—paraded in convertibles down Avenida Atlântica, accompanied by young women with "foxes" and other "millionaires' furs" draped over their maillots. They chanted, "Fewer shirts!" and in an improvised cancan, declared that they were determined to "give" not their lives but "their bodies for the freedom of customs." "The freedom of customs," in this case, obviously had a double meaning. They then took part in a game of beach volleyball after which some of them—still in white or black tie—entered the water. It was likely no coincidence that this protest took place on the very same day, 11 December, that many conservative Catholics were attending the Legião da Decência's official founding.[66]

Despite the almost carnivalesque tone of this protest, the playboys took care to make it clear that they belonged to the well-heeled. Nobody could doubt this upon seeing their "elegant" convertibles, the playboys themselves dressed "in the perfect style of the upper bourgeoisie," and their female friends with costly furs draped over their maillots. Any lingering doubts would have been dispelled by their extravagant gesture of diving into Copacabana's waves and thereby ruining their tailcoats and tuxedo jackets. During their procession, they had provocatively asked the policemen whom they encountered, "Is this good?" But the police did not react to the provocation; rather, an "instinctive movement of respect" took hold of them and the *Diário da Noite* explained that the "top hat has always been something that inspired much respect among the majority of Christians, especially police authorities, for whom social importance is a sort of fetish." Indeed, according to the *Diário*, "the worst and fiercest commie [*comuna*] can attend . . . the most violent subversive rally," and if he wears a top hat and tailcoat, "the police will not lay a hand on him."[67] While the *Diário* may have exaggerated the police's tolerance for well-dressed subversives, the newspaper got its analysis of the protest right: through their clothes and their automobiles, the playboys invoked class distinctions to challenge the police and to place themselves, in their day-to-day activities, above the authorities.

For Rio de Janeiro's middle and upper classes, the main purpose of the police was to control the poor and the working class, thereby keeping "order." This did not include interfering in the leisure activities of "noble" and "distinguished" families from the "cream of society." Any meddling with them by definition constituted a lack of "respect" that would inevitably result in "scandals," "excesses," "arbitrary acts," and "violence."[68] When it came to beach-going, the police were interfering in a leisure activity that had become an important focal point for the social life of Rio de Janeiro's upper and upper-middle classes. Police measures limited their "freedom" to amusing themselves with family members and friends on the sands of Copacabana and Ipanema and to demonstrating their social standing when they were seen on those beaches. These measures also threatened to ruin the "festival of sun and sea" and the "parade of elegance" that Copacabana offered during the summer months. During these campaigns, the presence of numerous police agents and their prison wagons gave the beach "a warlike appearance" that drove away many beach-goers.[69]

Police restrictions on bathing dress also prevented those who frequented the "elegant" beaches from following European and North American fashions, another way of demonstrating social status. The "ladies" of "high society" and their daughters who went to the beach wearing revealing outfits could argue that their maillots were identical to those seen on the pages of *Vogue* and *Harper's Bazaar*. The "nudism" practiced by Copacabana and Ipanema bathers was thus "modern" and also "civilized." Binóculo also made the connection between smaller bathing suits and "modernity" and "civilization" in 1927, when he declared that only a "fossil" could oppose the maillot, for "as in all the civilized cities of the world that have beaches, the maillot had also triumphed in Rio de Janeiro." Beach-going men could make similar arguments. In the 1920s and 1930s, when they wore "speeding suits" with short trunks and cutaway shirts like those sold by Jantzen, when they adopted the "American system" and wore unbuttoned shirts that thus revealed the chest, or even when they took their shirts off altogether, they could claim that they were doing nothing more than following the latest fashions from European and North American beaches. They gained an important ally in 1931, when Prince George took off his shirt on Copacabana beach. The *Correio da Manhã* explained the topless prince by noting that he "was certainly accustomed to bathing at civilized beaches, whose patrons can freely take the sun. Hence he took off his shirt."[70]

Ultimately, as far as Copacabana and Ipanema bathers were concerned, men and women alike, beach-going was a "civilized" and "modern" activity. With its "parade of elegance," Copacabana represented "the most fascinating and civilized spectacle" of Rio de Janeiro in the summer. The same commentators saw in this "spectacle" proof that Copacabana and later Ipanema rivaled the beaches of the most famous bathing resorts of Europe and the United States. Thus, Binóculo affirmed in 1928 that "when it came to bathing beaches," Rio de Janeiro had reached "the same level of civilization . . . [as that of] Lido, Ostende, Atlantic City, etc. Copacabana's chic posts truly followed the same standards . . . as those of Biarritz and the like." Tetrá de Teffé, for example, declared in 1936 that "beach life" in "modern Copacabana" had "overthrown old

Rio" de Janeiro. She would certainly have agreed with Wanderley Pinho. In an essay published in 1945, this historian departed from a narrow consideration of beach-going and beach "nudism" to discuss the wide-ranging changes in customs and habits that had transformed Carioca "high society" "social life" since the 1890s and especially since the First World War.[71]

Of course, conservative moralists, whether linked or not to the Catholic Church, denounced the new beach customs—especially the fact that partially undressed young women mingled freely with seminude men on the sand. They saw threats to the "family" and to traditional morality in these customs. A series of articles published in 1928 and 1929 in the magazine *O Cruzeiro* used the fictional example of Lúcia, an "emancipated" young woman, to lay out these threats. Sporting red lipstick, Lúcia goes to the beach at Copacabana's Post 4 with her boyfriend, Jorge, owner of a late-model Nash automobile. Wearing a "futurist maillot" that makes her resemble the movie star Clara Bow, Lúcia lets herself get sunburned (which is "good for her health"), flirts, plays shuttlecock, downs "cocktails," and smokes. "Cigarettes," explains a certain "Miss Dean," are "indispensable for a modern young woman." To Lúcia, Post 4 looks like a "movie scene." "One of Jorge's friends, who has been to the United States," tells her that she and her friends could have been "lifted [straight] from Atlantic City," "the great beach of New York [sic], which always appears in the movies." But Jorge and Lúcia's unsupervised outings are not limited to mornings at the beach. They play tennis at the country club in Ipanema. They also attend balls there and in other exclusive clubs where, pretending to resist, Lúcia lets Jorge kiss her. On these occasions, the "emancipated" young woman again smokes and drinks cocktails, in addition to joining Jorge in "modern dances" like the shimmy, the Charleston, and the foxtrot, to the sounds of jazz bands. Lúcia's aunt warns her that the likely outcome of her "flirtation with Jorge" is not "a good marriage" but "a bad movie"; Lúcia pays her no attention for, after all, these are new times. Unsurprisingly, it does not take long for Jorge to try to take advantage of her. One night, leaving a club to go for a drive along the beaches, they end up at his "love nest [*garçonnière*]" where Lúcia narrowly escapes losing her virginity. Unintentionally, moral panic narratives like this one ended up promoting the new beach-going customs when they linked them to other equally "modern" habits and behaviors.[72]

Defenders of the new beach customs saw no signs of "moral corruption" in them; rather, they considered the more or less explicit sexual connotations of beach-going as signs of the elite's and the middle class's growing sophistication and modernity. Thus, in the 1936 article in which Teffé declared that modern Copacabana had overthrown the old Rio de Janeiro, she also approvingly described the beach's "vibrant *sex-appeal*," using the English expression. By the time that she published this article, Copacabana's women, young and old alike, increasingly had a reputation for being "free of the restrictions" that remained in the city's "more conservative" districts. Their "advanced" comportment and their visibility in public spaces—on the beach, in the streets, in restaurants, in the open-air bars along Avenida Atlântica, and in nightclubs—contributed in important ways to creating Copacabana's image as Rio de Janeiro's most "modern" and "cosmopolitan" neighborhood.[73]

The police were not just interfering with upper- and upper middle-class leisure activities; they were also invading those classes' space. As far as the well-off beach-goers of Copacabana and Ipanema were concerned, their beaches were different from the others, for theirs were socially exclusive spaces. The one hundred and fifty or more Copacabana residents who signed the 1931 petition against Batista Luzardo's regulations supported the police chief's measures for the downtown beaches but not for Copacabana. Their neighborhood was "eminently balneary" and "inhabited exclusively by families." More important, Copacabana differed from Virtudes, Santa Luzia, Calabouço, or Flamengo beaches, which attracted "people of all social classes." Other critics of the police campaigns implicitly invoked similar arguments when they highlighted that those who frequented Copacabana were "the cream of society" and belonged to "noble" and "distinguished" families.[74]

Assis Chateaubriand, owner of the Diários Associados newspaper chain, who lived at that time in a mansion on Copacabana's Avenida Atlântica, was one of the signatories of the 1931 petition. In a front-page editorial in his *Diário da Noite*, he compared Copacabana beach to a private club—a "sumptuous" one and, indeed, "the best and most beautiful club in Rio" de Janeiro. Unfortunately, however, the police were preventing the members of the "Copacabana Club" from enjoying their association's facilities. That same day, *O Globo* published a letter from Frederico Dompré, the spokesman for a group of young men who hung out at Post 6 and demanded that Batista Luzardo revoke some of his instructions. Dompré explained that "the beach did not belong to him [the police chief]"; rather, "it is ours, it is Carioca." Wanderley Pinho made an almost identical observation in his 1945 essay: for many in

Copacabana, "the beach was their parlor." According to this point of view, the beach was a socially exclusive, semiprivate, quasi-domestic space that should not fall under police jurisdiction.[75]

The police repeatedly sought to control "nudism" not only on the sand and in the water but also on the streets. Those who supported the police efforts judged the custom of walking on the streets in bathing dress as "scandalous" and incompatible with Rio de Janeiro's status as the "civilized" capital of a "civilized country." They feared that this "indecent" spectacle would undermine the city's reputation among foreign visitors. However, there is almost no evidence that foreign visitors expressed shock or dismay at seeing partially undressed bathers on the streets. Rudyard Kipling, for one, considered the presence of men and women in bathing attire on Flamengo streets to be one of the neighborhood's charming features in 1927.[76]

The obvious solution, as journalists and editorialists noted, would be to build facilities on the beaches so that bathers could change their clothes before entering or leaving the sand.[77] Rudimentary changing facilities existed at the time on Virtudes and Calabouço beaches downtown, as well as at Caju, Maria Angu (Ramos), and Penha beaches in the Zona Norte and the suburbs. Some Flamengo pensions rented rooms in the 1920s to bathers so that they could put on their bathing dress. Indeed, as late as the late 1940s, Flamengo bathers could still rent "rustic booths [*cabines*]" behind a house close to that beach.[78] Of course, lower-income bathers would have thought twice about spending their hard-earned money on renting a place to change clothes, especially if they lived only a few kilometers from the beaches; in this case, they could don their bathing dress at home and go to the beach without spending any money. To rent a cabana for Rs.1$000 for four Sundays would mean spending what it cost to buy two kilograms of meat, one kilogram of rice, and two kilograms of beans at official prices in 1930. Even if cost were not a factor, the number of cabanas was insufficient for those who sought out the downtown and suburban beaches. There were fewer than ninety on Virtudes beach in 1930. In 1930, *O Globo* calculated that, daily, between five and ten o'clock in the morning, Virtudes attracted three thousand bathers, with double that number on Sundays and holidays, the majority of whom went to the beach on foot, already dressed in bathing attire. Thus, they occupied downtown streets, and even some of the principal avenues of the city's center.[79]

As we saw in chapter 3, since the late nineteenth century, there had been proposals to build a large European- or North American–style luxury bathing station in Copacabana or Ipanema, but none of these came to fruition. Even the more modest efforts to supply Copacabana with simple booths or tents for changing failed. The shortage of changing facilities, however, in no way prevented well-off Cariocas from frequenting this beach from the 1920s onward. As we saw in chapter 4, those who lived far from the ocean beaches could take their own automobiles to go to the beach. And as *O Cruzeiro* explained in 1928 when discussing the lack of bathing stations on Rio de Janeiro's beaches, for those who lived in the neighborhood, their residences were their "changing booths."[80]

Articles published in *Beira-Mar* in 1931 suggest that many upper middle- and upper-class Cariocas agreed with the police's efforts to restrict the presence of bathers on downtown streets.[81] It was not just the case that downtown beaches attracted primarily lower middle-class, working-class, and poor bathers. More important was the fact that these beaches were downtown, where, at the time, the best cinemas, stores, theater, and confectionaries were found. Downtown was also home to the Senate, the Chamber of Deputies, the Supreme Court, government ministries, the stock exchange and the city's main cultural institutions like the Teatro Municipal, the Biblioteca Nacional, the Academia Brasileira de Letras, and the Museu Nacional de Belas Artes. Those who could afford to do so dressed up to go downtown, even if it was just for window-shopping or to stroll along Avenida Rio Branco.

By contrast, Copacabana and Ipanema were simultaneously elegant and "balneary neighborhoods." To live there conferred status.[82] Before the second half of the 1940s, the few lower middle-class or working-class Cariocas from the Zona Norte and the suburbs who made it to Copacabana only did so after a long journey in second-class streetcars that also carried baggage and parcels. These streetcars, known as *taiobas*, allowed passengers in bathing dress so long as they wore a robe, or in the case of men, a jacket or later a shirt. There were no direct streetcar lines from the Zona Norte and the suburbs to Copacabana and Ipanema. The only route lay via downtown, where passengers had to walk a few blocks to catch another streetcar. Thus, in 1949, *O Cruzeiro* could observe correctly that, even for "Cariocas. . . , Copacabana is a privilege. The worker who lives in the suburbs," added the magazine, "only has second-hand knowledge of [Copacabana] beach, or from a much-discussed Sunday expedition with the entire family." But he probably never entered its waters.[83] After all, when the suburban worker finally made it to Copacabana with his family, he would find no place to change into bathing attire. But he and his family could see residents of the neighborhood leave their houses and apartment buildings, dressed in bathing attire, walking to the beach.

This clarifies the significance of the simple act of walking in the streets wearing bathing attire for well-off residents of Copacabana and Ipanema. The act publicly signaled that they lived in Copacabana and Ipanema and that they therefore belonged to the privileged sectors of Carioca society who enjoyed easy access to the beaches every day of the week. Many years later, Renato Sérgio, referring to Rio de Janeiro before the 1980s, would note that the "true Carioca, from the Zona Sul, liked the beach that was close to home; good beaches were those to which one could go on foot [while] the rest were picnics [*convescote*]."[84] For Sérgio, true Cariocas were those who lived in the ocean neighborhoods. Their place of residence enabled them to go to the beach on foot and thereby distinguished them from the majority of Rio de Janeiro's inhabitants who lived in districts sometimes many kilometers away.

In a 1931 editorial, the *Jornal do Brasil* proclaimed: "There must be a difference between bathing beaches and the street." Lamentably, however, "the exhibitionist mania" of Carioca bathers threatened to erase this difference; thus, the newspaper supported the campaign that Batista Luzardo launched that year.[85] In other words, the police should prevent the beach from invading the city. Between 1920 and 1950, the Federal District's police regularly intervened to limit the presence of bathers on city streets. These efforts, however, achieved no lasting success. Whenever the police relaxed their vigilance, bathers returned to the streets, wearing bathing attire that was more revealing and wearing less over their beach dress. Today, men in briefs or swim trunks and women in bikinis with only a light wrap (*canga*) freely mingle on the streets of Copacabana, Ipanema, and Leblon with people in sober professional dress, with fully dressed shoppers, and with children and teenagers in school uniforms. This mixture, which reflects the current integration of the beach into the city's ambit, amply demonstrates the police campaigns' failures.

The history of these campaigns, however, is an example of how, despite restrictions, practices of daily life can change norms that govern the acceptable use of urban public space.[86] In Rio de Janeiro, beach-going as a regular, daily activity steadily undermined the distinction that, according to the authorities and those who supported them, ought to delimit clearly the street and the beach. It modified other spatial distinctions. Thus, in 1953, only a few years after the end of General Lima Câmara's campaign, an article in *Manchete* magazine called Copacabana "an independent and half-naked city." Milton Pedrosa, the article's author, through word and accompanying photographs, highlighted the presence of partially undressed bathers on the neighborhood's streets. Unlike the inhabitants of other districts, Copacabana's residents seemed to spend "half of their lives . . . [dressed] in trunks, shorts, or maillots." "From Leme to the Jardim de Alá [from the start of Copacabana to the end of Ipanema]," Pedrosa concluded that "life mixes together the kitchen, the office, and the beach." The "half-naked" residents of Copacabana had no compunctions about going from the kitchen and the dining room to the beach and back again; wearing bathing dress or shorts, they shopped at the local bakeries and butcher shops, enjoyed drinks in bars or outside, went to the barber or the dentist, and even sold automobiles and real estate.[87]

The bathers whom Pedrosa saw on Copacabana's streets in 1953 no doubt remembered Lima Câmara's campaign; many probably also knew of the earlier ones. Today, however, the history of these campaigns has been completely erased from collective memory. Already in the 1970s—unless they were more than forty or fifty years old—many of Renato Sérgio's "true Cariocas from the Zona Sul," for whom "good beaches were those to which one could go on foot," assumed that they had always had the "right" to walk the streets of Copacabana, Ipanema, and Leblon wearing only swimming trunks in the case of men or bikinis or maillots in the case of women. Few of them knew that, for almost two decades, their parents and grandparents had had to defy the police to win this "right." However, in contrast to other better-known conflicts over public space, this resistance came from bathers who belonged to the well-off and even wealthy sectors of society. When they demanded deference from the police; when they challenged policemen with the question, "Do you know who you're talking to?"; or when, like the 1949 playboys who grandly ruined their tailcoats and tuxedo jackets in Copacabana's waves, the wealthy and well-off bathers claimed privileges on the basis of their social class.

In the debates prompted by the police campaigns, questions of social class and privilege merged with discussions about health, the body, and eugenics, as well as conceptions of morality and civilization. Both defenders and the critics of the campaigns invoked "morality" and "civilization." But, for the critics, "modernity" and social class influenced understandings of civilization and morality. By attacking the police measures, the critics spelled out important elements of the sociocultural identity that important sectors of a rising bourgeoisie and a new upper middle class were constructing for themselves. They defended the new beach customs, including "nudism," as "moral," "civilized," and "modern." They specifically associated these "modern" and "civilized" customs with Copacabana and Ipanema, the beaches favored by the upper and upper middle classes. For the Cariocas who belonged to this new middle class, going to these beaches, tanning themselves there, and meeting with friends on the sand—along with the more or less explicit emphasis on sexuality on the beaches and the ever-greater visibility of women in public space—came to symbolize their cosmopolitan modernity. Going to the beach in Copacabana and Ipanema, in short, constituted a mark of social distinction; it formed part of a broader sociocultural identity that many upper- and upper middle-class Cariocas used to distinguish themselves from the rest of the city's population.

The construction of this identity also contributed to the creation of a new symbolic geography in Rio de Janeiro in which the Zona Sul neighborhoods, and especially those along the seashore, came to represent more than just a place of residence for the elite. Copacabana and, later, in their own ways, Ipanema and Leblon came to symbolize all that was deemed glamorous cosmopolitan, and modern. The *Diário da Noite* resorted to this symbolic geography in its report on the 1949 playboy protest. Copacabana was, according to the newspaper, Rio de Janeiro's "first truly cosmopolitan neighborhood." It had escaped the "old and sullen provincialism" that characterized the rest of the city. With "its tanned [*moreno*] population," it was simultaneously an "international," "Brazilian," and "viscerally Carioca" neighborhood. The *Diário* saw in the playboys' protest evidence of the emergence of a "new urban Brazilian civilization."[88]

Perhaps the best way to end this chapter is to cite an article that Lúcia Benedetti published in 1949 in the *Revista de Copacabana*. Criticizing Lima Câmara's campaign, Benedetti judged it "shocking" to try to impose "dress codes [*roupismo*] with Radio Patrols and nightsticks" on Copacabana's residents. "We," she declared as a Copacabana resident herself, "are not like the residents of Andaraí [a solidly middle-class Zona Norte neighborhood], who do not show their bodies except when they dress for balls. We show our bodies every day." For Benedetti, residents of Copacabana, as "honorable beach denizens [*praianos*]," constituted a "special" sort of people, different from, for example, residents of Laranjeiras and Tijuca. Anywhere in the city, residents of Copacabana were identifiable "by their dress," "their gait," and perhaps most important, "the [effects of the] sun on their skin." But now, amid Lima Câmara's campaign, "young women don't know whether the length of their *short* is decent or not." And "those who used to go to the movies in shirt sleeves, with a most Copacabanesque smile [on their faces], now go out looking over their shoulders, cautiously, like thieves." The writer, in short, argued that if the police managed to impose their dress code on the neighborhood's residents, everything would change: "We who live in Copacabana will lose the particular way of life [*jeito*] of those who live on this side of the tunnel."[89] Benedetti's comments brought together many of the issues raised by the police campaigns between 1920 and 1950. Her remarks also clearly point to the sociocultural identity's links with practices of beach-going and places of residence and, therefore, also implicitly social class. This identity defined the city's new symbolic geography.

Epilogue

Beach-Going in the Zona Sul, 1950s–1980s

BRYAN MCCANN

BERT BARICKMAN HAD THE UNCANNY ABILITY to stand on any street corner in Rio de Janeiro and peer into the past. He could readily tell you what happened in 1964, or 1922, or 1871. For this reason, my favorite place to stroll with Bert was in the *centro*, the old downtown, where the urban palimpsest has the most layers. Bert loved to point out sewer covers and other street fixtures, many of them decades old, and decipher their obscure lettering, placing them precisely by political regime, urban planning initiative, and other contexts. But he could also see a hidden past, the kiosks, and streetcars of the early twentieth century, as well as the tenement houses and stables of the nineteenth.

For this reason, it initially seemed odd to me that Bert chose the beach as an incessant topic of research. He was not much of a beach-goer himself, though he loved to sit at a beachside bar and argue the finer points of history. And it was in the course of these discussions that I realized that he understood the beach as a privileged site for reflecting on the grand progress of Carioca history and, indeed, of Brazilian history more generally. Movements on the beach suggested a larger history. They did not always easily reflect the vicissitudes of Brazilian political history, as regimes often came and went without any apparent manifestation on the beach. But changes in beach-going habits exemplified deep processes in the transformation of social life, driving Bert's interest.

In 1997, when he learned that I was researching popular music of the 1930s and 1940s, he casually remarked that there were not many songs about the beach written before the mid-1940s, and he had me stumped. I struggled to name a few *marchas*, inevitably thinking of several from the late 1940s and early 1950s ("Chiquita Bacana" [Cool Chiquita], "Biquini de Filó" [String Bikini], and a few others). Bert scoffed when I remembered "Praia Maravilhosa"

(Marvelous Beach), the ersatz version of the classic "Cidade Maravilhosa" (Marvelous City), sung by the adherents of the failed 1935 Communist uprising, celebrating their attempt to seize the garrison at Praia Vermelha. Exactly his point. Before the 1940s, songs mentioning Rio de Janeiro beaches were, for the most part, not about beach-going.

Bert gave me partial credit for "Deixa a Lua Sossegada" (Leave the Moon in Peace), the Braguinha and Alberto Ribeiro marcha of 1935, whose narrator imagines a kiss "beginning in Realengo, heating up in Flamengo, and finishing in Leblon," an early reference both to automobile travel from the Zona Norte to the Zona Sul, and to the discreet Hotel Leblon at the far end of that beach, often considered the city's first love motel. This led to a longer discussion about how the automobile changed both middle-class beach-going and the geography of popular music, bringing us back around to Dick Farney's majestic 1946 recording of "Copacabana," the "Princess of the Sea." It was only through talking with Bert that I could hear that old chestnut anew, as an evocation of a vision of beachside glamour that was beginning to change Rio de Janeiro in the second half of the 1940s. "Copacabana" began an explosion of beach-themed popular songs, one that would carry Brazilian popular music through the first wave of bossa nova in the late 1950s and beyond.

In later years, our beachside and beach-focused conversations often turned to the *farofeiros* controversy of the mid-1980s. *Farofa* is toasted manioc meal, a staple of the popular Brazilian diet. Farofeiro was initially a disparaging epithet that middle-class residents of Ipanema lobbed at Zona Norte beach-goers who lived too far away to go home for lunch and who could not afford to go to Poli's, a block from the beach, for a filet sandwich with fries. The farofeiros brought their lunch to the beach, a gaffe that middle-class Ipanema residents, accustomed to strolling down to the sand wearing the bare minimum, viewed as unforgivable. The residents of Ipanema were predominantly white, while the Zona Norte visitors were mostly Black and brown, so the elite disdain of farofeiros was always as much about race as it was about class.

This became a political flashpoint in the mid-1980s when, during his first term as governor (1983–1987), Leonel Brizola created a state-operated bus company in Rio de Janeiro, partly with the goal of enabling working-class residents of the Zona Norte to get to Zona Sul beaches. Brizola inaugurated several bus lines starting in the Zona Norte and ending in Ipanema (a trajectory that offered a downmarket, 1980s version of the romantic automobile ride described by Braguinha and Alberto Ribeiro in 1935—albeit coming through the new Rebouças Tunnel, opened in 1967, rather than along Flamengo Beach). These were not the first bus lines linking the Zona Norte and the Zona Sul, but their route was for more direct than previous lines, and they terminated at the beach, rather than a block or two inland, making the journey more convenient and practical. Clashes between Ipanema residents and farofeiros heated up the summer of 1984, until the Zona Norte visitors claimed the term as a badge of pride, organizing demonstrations, carrying signs reading "Farofeiro Pride" and "The Beach Belongs to Everyone." João Batista de Melo, who made the beachward trek from the Zona Norte housing project of Cidade Alta, penned the Farofeiro Manifesto, declaring, "We are farofeiros because we have learned to stretch our measly salaries. Rather than submit to the extortion of local commerce, that by its prices seems to have been created exclusively for foreign tourists, we prefer snacks brought from home."[1]

Bert tipped me off to that fascinating source and to many others. His knowledge was encyclopedic. Where was the Dom Manuel beach? Adjacent to Praça XV, covered by landfill in the early twentieth century. When did the Rua Montenegro become the Rua Vinícius de Moraes? Before Google existed, you could ask Bert. It was in 1980, shortly after Vinícius's death. We discussed the renaming of this toney Ipanema street as another symbolic transition—when bossa nova–era Rio de Janeiro became part of a past to be commemorated rather than an everyday state of being.

No one was more attuned to these changing patterns of Carioca social life than Bert. In an ideal world, he would have carried through his fine-grained history of beach-going through the 1980s, as planned. But as we lack Bert's deeply grounded research, a more episodic overview of changes beginning in the 1940s must suffice. I have incorporated Bert's draft and notes into this epilogue.

Copacabana's "Golden Age"

Automobiles, tunnels, and asphalt dramatically changed access to Zona Sul beaches over the course of the twentieth century.[2] The Alaor Prata Tunnel, popularly known as the Old Tunnel, linking Botafogo and Copacabana, was inaugurated in 1892, and was used primarily for streetcars during the first forty years of its existence. The early tunnel linking Botafogo and Leme was also primarily used for streetcars. The inauguration of the Marques Porto Tunnel, popularly known as the New Tunnel, in 1947, changed travel to the Zona Sul.

The New Tunnel—really a series of two tunnels under Pasmado and Babilônia Hills—was designed for automobiles, enabling drivers to get from the historic downtown to Copacabana in fifteen minutes (this was long before the traffic jams that now characterize this route).[3]

New tunnels and the roads that went with them helped make Leme and Copacabana—and later Ipanema and Leblon, farther along the oceanfront—desirable neighborhoods for middle-class residence. The nighttime ride from Realengo to Leblon described in "Deixa a Lua Sossegada" was still largely the stuff of popular fantasy when that marcha came out in 1935. With the inauguration of the New Tunnel, commuting from Copacabana to downtown, or driving from older, central middle-class neighborhoods like Tijuca to Copacabana on the weekend, became common practice.

In the 1950s and 1960s, Copacabana had more private passenger cars per thousand inhabitants than any other "administrative region" in the city: 79 in 1957 and 124.8 in 1964. The corresponding ratios for Rio de Janeiro as whole stood at 21.3 and 37.5. Even other generally affluent "administrative regions," such as Botafogo (which included Flamengo and Laranjeiras), Lagoa, and Tijuca displayed much lower rates of car ownership than Copacabana. As late as 1964, the number of cars per thousand inhabitants in those "administrative regions" did not surpass 90. Given the rate of car ownership in Copacabana, it should come as no surprise that average household income in the neighborhood in 1966 was 49 percent higher than in Rio de Janeiro as whole and 59 percent higher than in the greater metropolitan region.[4]

New apartment buildings sprang up to accommodate the newly mobile middle class. When the gleaming white Copacabana Palace Hotel was inaugurated in 1923, it towered above humble bungalows nearby, the only building on the entire beachfront taller than two stories (with the possible exception of the spire of Nossa Senhora da Copacabana Church). By the 1950s, the hotel itself was overshadowed by neighboring apartment towers. Many of Brazil's most politically powerful figures lived in Copacabana. Six of the eight men who governed Brazil as president between 1946 and 1964 had private residences in the neighborhood. Among them was (João Fernando Campos) Café Filho, who, while serving as president between August 1954 and November 1955, even allowed himself to be photographed in a pair of trunks at the beach. Other nationally prominent politicians, such Carlos Lacerda, Horácio Lafer, Tancredo Neves, and Field-Marshal Henrique Lott, also chose to live in the neighborhood.[5]

Some of Rio de Janeiro's best-known and most expensive stores and confeitarias, recognizing the purchasing power of Copacabana's residents, opened branches in the neighborhood. Numerous other stores that targeted an upscale market established their first and only locations in Copacabana. Growing numbers of doctors and dentists set up offices in the neighborhood. As a result, Copacabana became an increasingly mixed residential and commercial neighborhood.[6]

In many ways, the late 1940s, 1950s, and even early 1960s represented a "golden age" in Copacabana's history. Dick Farney's "Copacabana" was a siren song luring beach-goers, nightclubbers, tourists, and new residents to the neighborhood. In the years following the release of Farney's recording of the song, the image of Copacabana as a neighborhood different from the rest of city became even more firmly established. In a 1953 crônica that more than once refers to beach-going, Henrique Pongetti argued that Copacabanenses constituted a distinct "ethnicity," entirely different from the inhabitants of other areas of Rio de Janeiro and of the rest of Brazil. He, therefore, jokingly suggested that the neighborhood declare its independence. His proposed "Republic of the United States of Copacabana" would include, as states, the beachfront neighborhoods of Ipanema and Leblon.[7] But, paradoxically, at the same time, Copacabana became ever more so than before an icon of a specifically Brazilian modernity. As Carlos Lessa has pointed out, the neighborhood, unlike Pereira Passos's Rio de Janeiro, was not a "tropical copy of Paris." It was, instead, seen as expressive of Brazil's own "national originality." In the imagination of Cariocas and many Brazilians elsewhere in the country, Copacabana figured as a "magical place," filled with "glamour," where those with the necessary income could combine sun-filled mornings at the beach with "the sophistication of formal dress [required by the neighborhood's] night clubs and candle-lit dinners" at elegant restaurants.[8]

Indeed, after 1940, Copacabana, which almost from its very first days could claim some nighttime attractions, replaced Lapa as the main center of nightlife in the city. Sophisticated bars, nightclubs, and restaurants sprang up in the beachside neighborhood. Leaving behind the beer halls and cabarets of Lapa, located on the edges of central Rio de Janeiro, writers and other intellectuals made Copacabana's bars their drinking headquarters. Men and women whose names routinely appeared in social columns patronized the neighborhood's nightclubs and bars. So, too, did nationally known politicians, as well as famous recording artists and the stars of radio, cinema, theater, and, later, television.

In 1951, Dorival Caymmi and Carlos Guinle translated the dream of a "good night in the neighborhood" into song in their "Sábado em Copacabana" (Saturday in Copacabana). The same dream in 1957 served as the theme of Wilson Batista's and Jorge Castro's "Copacabana à Noite" (Copacabana at Night), which mentions well-known nightspots by name.[9]

Prostitution was not uncommon. As far back as 1930, the police kept an eye on four establishments in the neighborhood suspected of serving as bordellos. One of the four may have been the Hotel e Bar 20, in Ipanema, which, in the 1920s and 1930s, was accused of promoting prostitution (*lenocínio*). In 1937, *Beira-Mar* complained about the prostitutes who, at night, plied the Avenida Atlântica, especially the stretch in front of Post 2. One year later, the authorities classified the Hotel do Leme as a brothel in all but name.[10] But, as Copacabana became the city's nightlife center from the 1940s onward, prostitution gained greater space and visibility in some parts of the neighborhood. In the precinct encompassing Copacabana and Ipanema, police detained for questioning twenty-eight women suspected of being prostitutes in October 1948 alone. Although prostitution was, and is, not a crime in Brazil, that did not prevent authorities from harassing women who may have earned their living through the sex trade. Less than a decade after the police questioned those twenty-eight women, the striptease clubs (*inferninhos*) lining the Rua Prado Júnior in Copacabana were already flourishing; there, men interested in exchanging money for sex could easily find women willing to accept payment.[11]

Transformations in Beach-Going

The new mode of beach-going favored by Copacabana's residents at midcentury emphasized fitness, youth, and display of the body. That display was markedly more reserved than the fashions that became common in the 1980s and later. As discussed in chapter 5, Carioca women generally wore one-piece suits that would look conservative by today's standards, while men wore swim trunks. But styles for both women and men grew more form-fitting and revealing in the 1950s, paving the way for widespread adoption of the bikini for women and briefs for men in the late 1960s.[12]

In these same years, a stretch of sand in front of the Copacabana Palace became known by *entendidos*, or insiders, as a place where gay men could see, be seen, and socialize without harassment. The spot became known as the Bolsa de Valores, or stock exchange, a nickname that endured well into the

1960s. The open secret of the Bolsa de Valores seemed to capture the spirit of daring, modern Copacabana.[13]

Hedonistic youth toasted their skin on the beach by day and frolicked in nightclubs after dark. That was the popular image, at least, one both invoked and mocked by author Rubem Braga in a classic 1958 journalistic essay titled "Ai de Ti, Copacabana" (Woe unto You, Copacabana). The essay is a satirical, pseudobiblical imprecation against heathen Copacabana, warning its louche denizens of the coming tidal wave that will wash away its many sins. "Woe unto you, Copacabana," Braga warned, in the voice of the Almighty:

> Because they called you the Princess of the Sea, and garlanded your front with a crown of lies, and you let out besotted and vain laughter in the bosom of the night. . . . Your maidens stretch out on the sand and rub aromatic oils on their bodies to toast their epidermis, and your young men use their motor scooters as instruments of concupiscence. Lament, young men, and beseech, young ladies, and roll in the ashes, because your days are finished, and I will destroy you.[14]

The reality was usually more prosaic: While Copacabana boomed as a diverse neighborhood of commerce, entertainment (including risqué nightclubs), and upper middle-class residence, Leme, Ipanema and Leblon remained overwhelmingly residential. And while Ipanema cultivated its own style of liberated sensuality in the 1960s, Leme and Leblon remained relatively staid until the 1980s.

In popular cultural depictions, however, the celebration of a Zona Sul lifestyle of sun, sand, and sea was extended from Leme to Leblon. This was the sentiment evoked in "Teresa da Praia" (Teresa from the Beach), a 1954 samba by Tom Jobim and Billy Blanco, for example. In the original recording by singers Dick Farney and Lúcio Alves, the singers trade wistful invocations of the eponymous green-eyed beauty who enchants and ultimately frustrates all her admirers on the beach in Leblon. The samba is a forerunner of "A Garota de Ipanema" (The Girl from Ipanema), the bossa nova standard that Jobim would compose with Vinícius de Moraes eight years later (writing the initial verses at a bar on the Rua Montenegro, as it happens). Both songs—along with dozens of others written in that fertile period—celebrated the Zona Sul beaches and their inhabitants as the epitome of effortless allure.

If few Zona Sul residents were as relentless in their pursuit of pleasure as those described by Rubem Braga, they did develop new practices of beach-going. *Futebol da praia*, or beach soccer, became common for men—and remained almost exclusively male until the twenty-first century. Beach volleyball also became common and was more open to female participation (although women remained a minority among beach volleyball players until the early 1980s, when their participation expanded dramatically). Beach soccer and volleyball emphasized improvisation, lunges and dives across the sand, and competition with an adversary who generally remained friendly, but the game occasionally heated up into *bate-boca*, or public argument, itself a kind of sport.[15]

Transformations in Copacabana

Even as the image of golden-age Copacabana became a staple of Brazil's cultural industry, the neighborhood continued to change rapidly. By the 1960s, it was made increasingly dense and diverse, the latter socially and economically; the population more than tripled between 1940 and 1960, increasing from less than 75,000 to nearly 235,000. Single-family houses continued to disappear, replaced by seemingly endless rows of apartment buildings by 1960. Copacabana grew much faster than the city as whole in the two decades after 1940. By 1960, it already had the highest population density of any district in Rio de Janeiro.[16]

Real estate firms continued to tout new apartment buildings, particularly those along Avenida Atlântica, to the wealthy. Construction of buildings with medium-sized and large apartments, with tiny bed- and bathrooms for a domestic servant, destined for a growing number of middle- and upper middle-class families, remained common. Developers also continued to put on the market new buildings with large, luxury apartments intended for sale to wealthy buyers. Those apartments, in some cases, boasted four bedrooms, one or two spacious living rooms (*salas*), two bathrooms, a foyer, and a lunchroom (*saleta de almoço*), as well as a kitchen and pantry (*copa*) and quarters (with bathroom) for at least two live-in domestic servants. For instance, with four-hundred-square-meter apartments, the Edifício Chopin, on the Avenida Atlântica next to the Copacabana Palace Hotel, dates from 1955. President João Goulart (1961–1964), a millionaire rancher, had an apartment in the Chopin, which remains one of the most famous addresses in the city; today, socialites live there. Buildings with luxury apartments would still be built in the neighborhood in the 1970s.[17]

From the mid-1940s and the 1950s, however, buildings with studio apartments, known as *conjugados* or *kitchenettes*, and small one-bedroom apartments also began to form part of Copacabana's urban landscape. Those apartments met a demand for housing in the neighborhood from young professionals and also from middle- and lower middle-class families who exchanged spacious houses in the Zona Norte and in the suburbs for cramped quarters in Copacabana.[18] For them, Copacabana held out various attractions: the convenience of all kinds of shops and professional services on hand; entertainment possibilities not limited to nightclubs, bars and cinemas; its reputation as the most modern and cosmopolitan neighborhood in Rio de Janeiro; and, of course, easy access to the beach.

They were, in some cases, also drawn to Copacabana by the oft-touted live-and-let-live attitude of its inhabitants. Unlike residents of other parts of the city, Copacabanenses reportedly did not busy themselves with what their neighbors did or did not do, nor did they take notice if a married woman or a teenaged girl wore slacks on the street. Beyond all that, they sought the prestige that came with being able to say that they lived in Copacabana and that thus they, too, had "conquer[ed] their place in the sun."[19]

Wealthy and well-to-do Copacabanenses came to share their neighborhood with a growing number of middle- and even lower-class residents. As a result, a much larger and more heterogeneous public gained easy access to Copacabana's once "elegant" beach. Also contributing to the greater heterogeneity of that public was the growth of the six favelas flanking Leme and Copacabana: Chapéu Mangueira, Babilônia, Ladeira dos Tabajaras, Morro dos Cabritos, Pavão, and Cantagalo. These favelas grew in conjunction with the middle-class apartment buildings, providing cheap accommodation for the maids, nannies, cooks, handymen and other low-wage workers that enabled the apparent ease of the middle-class lifestyle.[20]

Favela residents used the beach as well, of course, and it is common to hear senior citizens from both favela and asfalto—the asphalt, or middle-class sections with paved streets—fondly reminisce about a simpler time when favela and middle-class residents supposedly shared greater common ground than they do in twenty-first century Rio de Janeiro. These reminiscences almost invariably center on beach soccer, the favored location for cross-class camaraderie. In other ways, however, the beach was divided. When they went to the beach, favela residents often did so to work, selling packages of Biscoitos Globo, for example; this airy cookie, which crumbles to dust at the slightest pressure, has constituted a staple of Carioca beach culture for nearly a century (a staple with greater cultural than nutritional value). Apart from soccer, those at the beach eager for hard-won leisure activities tended to have relatively little interaction with middle-class beach-goers. Favela and middle-class residents generally occupied different stretches of sand.[21]

The putatively golden age of Copacabana reached its apogee, but also its inflection point, with the massive expansion of both the beach and beachfront Avenida Atlântica at the end of the 1960s. Although Copacabana was always much broader than any of the main bayshore beaches, it did not have an especially wide expanse of sand. By the late 1950s, the line of apartment buildings along the Avenida Atlântica, which were no more than twelve stories high, cast shadows across nearly the entire beach, as far as the water's edge after two in the afternoon (see, for an earlier example, figure 4.5). In a late and only partially successful attempt to offer some semblance of underground, piped-sewage service to the Zona Sul beachfront neighborhoods, Governor Francisco Negrão de Lima (1965–1971) supervised a project expanding Avenida Atlântica from two lanes in either direction to three, with a generous median, and sewage pipes and chambers hidden underneath. A broad *calçadão*, or promenade, ran parallel to the avenue. To protect both the avenue and the plumbing from erosion, the state government pumped in tons of sand to expand the width of the beach. Copacabana Beach went from a golden strip some twenty-five to fifty meters in width to a dazzling field of sand one hundred meters wide. The broadened beach enabled substantial expansion of areas reserved for beach soccer and volleyball, further consolidating Copacabana's association with fitness and leisure.[22]

Landscape architect Burle Marx designed the stone mosaic for the promenade and the median on Avenida Atlântica. For the promenade, he used a variation on the previously existing undulating waves of black and white stones. For the median, he created bold, abstract modernist designs. The undulating waves of the promenade symbolically connected the avenue to the ocean, while the abstract designs on the median gave cool Brazilian modernism one of its most visible and most accessible manifestations. The inauguration of the broad avenue and the newly expanded beach in 1970 capped a thirty-year process in the making of modern Copacabana.[23]

The more diverse public that Copacabana's beach attracted after the mid- and late 1940s did not only result from changes in the social composition of the neighborhood's population. Those years also saw the gradual erosion of porous but real barriers that had long prevented the majority of Cariocas from frequenting Copacabana, Ipanema, and Leblon. As those barriers eroded, the city once again began to invade the beach. Now, however, the invasion came from the city "beyond the tunnels [*além-túneis*]"—that is, from the Zona Norte and the suburbs, from the favelas in those areas, and even from the Baixada Fluminense.

More Tunnels and More Cars

After the mid-1940s and especially during the 1950s and 1960s, the local government carried out a series projects aimed at easing movement between different parts of the city by opening new avenues, building viaducts, and boring tunnels through mountains. Of those projects, three are especially relevant here. The first is the Aterro do Flamengo, a large landfill extending along the southern shore of Guanabara Bay from the city's center to the far end of Botafogo. Constructed in the late 1950s and early 1960s, the landfill not only altered the shape of the bay's shoreline but also allowed for the creation of a park with more than one million square meters and, running through the park, an expressway (see map 3.1). Motorists could now avoid the Avenida Beira-Mar, with its numerous traffic lights, and quickly reach Botafogo and, from there, Copacabana.[24]

Shortly after the Aterro do Flamengo's expressway opened to traffic, local authorities inaugurated the 1.3-kilometer Santa Bárbara Tunnel between Catumbi, in the Zona Norte, and Laranjeiras, in the Zona Sul. Next came the opening of the two-galleried Rebouças Tunnel in 1965 and 1967. Constructed in two segments, with a total length of 2.8 kilometers, the tunnel burrows under the Morro dos Prazeres (Prazeres Hill) and the Christ-topped Corcovado Mountain between the neighborhoods of Rio Comprido and Lagoa. The two tunnels provided a direct link between the Zona Norte and the Zona Sul. Beach-going motorists who lived in Tijuca or Grajaú in the Zona Norte or in the suburbs could now bypass the city's center altogether on their way to Copacabana, Ipanema, or Leblon.[25]

The construction of these two tunnels also redefined the meaning of expressions such as "*aquém-túneis* [on this side of the tunnels]" and "*além-túneis* [beyond the tunnels]," variants of which appear in the sources as early as the 1920s. Until the 1960s, *tunnels* in those expressions referred to the Old and New Tunnels, and "on this side of the tunnels" meant specifically Copacabana and, by extension, Ipanema. Afterwards, "on this side of the tunnels" came to refer to the entire Zona Sul, and, in turn, "on the far side of the tunnels" came to designate generically the Zona Norte and the suburbs. Residents of the Zona Sul would, for their part, begin to refer to beach-goers from the Zona Norte and the suburbs as bathers "from beyond the tunnel [*dalém-túnel*]."

Only a small minority of Rio de Janeiro's residents of "beyond the tunnels," however, owned automobiles, even into the mid-1960s. To go to the beach in Copacabana or Ipanema, they had to rely on public transportation. As discussed in chapter 5, regulations against riding streetcars—and later buses—in bathing attire made this more difficult for residents who could not simply walk to the beach. Even after the elimination of these rules, Zona Norte residents faced a long and complicated trek to the beach. While streetcars remained the dominant mode of public transportation, no direct tramlines linked the Zona Norte and the suburbs with Copacabana and Ipanema. To reach the city's oceanfront beaches, a resident of the Zona Norte or the suburbs had to change trams in the city's center, and thus, an outing to Copacabana or Ipanema required paying four fares.

The municipal government would, in any event, eliminate all but one tramline in the 1960s. That left buses as the only option for residents of the Zona Norte and the suburbs who wished to spend a morning at the beach in Copacabana, Ipanema, or Leblon and who did not own their own cars. Those residents faced two problems. First, as late as 1945, only one bus connected the Zona Norte and the Zona Sul, departing the middle-class neighborhood of Tijuca and following a winding route through the city's center toward Ipanema. Thus, for most residents of the Zona Norte or the suburbs, an excursion to the beach meant taking at least two buses each way. By 1957, eleven bus lines provided direct connections between the Zona Norte and the suburbs, on the one hand, and Copacabana, Ipanema, and Leblon, on the other. In contrast to the state-run lines created by Governor Brizola in 1984, however, these lines did not terminate on the beachfront but at least a block or two inland.[26]

The second problem was that in 1966 authorities once again prohibited riding the bus in bathing attire. Older teenage boys in the upper- and upper middle-class Zona Norte neighborhood of Tijuca resented the prohibition. In a 1966 interview with a reporter from the *Correio da Manhã*, they explained that having to wear street clothes over their suits and, then, undress at the beach made them look like "hicks [*roceiros*]" in the eyes of Cariocas from the Zona Sul.[27] The boys did not need to wait long before they could go to Copacabana or Ipanema without any risk of being seen as "hicks." This prohibition would gradually fall by the wayside, and by the 1970s, buses heading to the oceanfront beach neighborhoods routinely transported passengers in nothing more than bathing suits and, in the case of women and girls, a garment to cover up or a towel wrapped around their waists.

The expansion in the number of bus lines and the lapse in the prohibition against riding buses in bathing suits would allow residents of the suburbs and the Zona Norte to frequent the oceanfront beaches in growing numbers. Already in 1959, one Copacabana dweller noted that, until recently, "only the residents" of Copacabana had been "able to enjoy" the neighborhood's beach. But now, she added, the new bus lines brought bathers from all parts of Rio de Janeiro to that beach. The number of such bathers would increase in the years after 1959.[28]

The increasing presence of bathers from the Zona Norte and the suburbs would, in turn, foster and help consolidate one of the most cherished notions in contemporary Carioca culture, namely, the idea that Rio de Janeiro's beaches constitute a "democratic space," open to all, where social distinctions disappear because everyone is wearing a bathing suit. The same Copacabana resident who noted the arrival of new beach-goers from the Zona Norte described that beach as "the most democratic in the world." "The bus lines," she proclaimed, "have democratized Copacabana." Yet, perhaps despite herself, the resident acknowledged that social distinctions did not disappear on the sand. She found it easy to identify beach-goers who were not from the Zona Sul. "They arrive," she wrote, "looking like picnickers, carrying all sorts of packages, satchels, [and] bags, wearing beneath their skirts or their long trousers maillots and bathing trunks, bikinis, and strange home-made suits." Once at the beach, "they set themselves up on an empty spot of sand, [and] undress as though they were behind closed doors." With their folded clothes deposited on the sand, "they throw themselves, with wild joy, into Copacabana's sea and sun."[29] Such reactions were a foreshadowing of the full-blown farofeiros controversy that emerged when the presence of Zona Norte beach-goers intensified in the early 1980s. Copacabana's wealthier residents viewed the beach's "democratization" with ambivalence.[30]

Despite these changes, the number of Zona Norte and suburban bathers on Zona Sul beaches remained modest through the 1970s. Although the new direct bus lines did make it much easier for lower middle- and working-class residents of the Zona Norte, suburbs, and Baixada to reach Copacabana, Ipanema, and Leblon, it was still a long trip, which might, depending on the point of departure, last an hour or more in often overcrowded buses. Catching a ride on one of those buses on a hot, sunny Saturday or Sunday might entail, first, queuing up for as long as an hour. And, for many, a weekend excursion to the beach in Copacabana, Ipanema, or Leblon began with a ride in a hot, crowded car on one of Rio de Janeiro's commuter trains to the center, where they caught a bus to the beach. Working- and other lower-class Cariocas would have also needed to consider the cost of an excursion to beach. Even if the excursion required taking only one bus each way, for a family of four, that would amount a total of eight bus fares; this did not, of course, include any expenditures on food or drink at the beach.

Equally important, residents of the Zona Norte and the suburbs who wished to spend a weekend morning at the beach had other options closer at hand, such as Ramos, which journalists described as the "Copacabana of the suburbs."[31] *Suburbanos*, as Flávio Tavares notes, "took pride" in their beaches. Just like residents of the Zona Sul, they, too, had one that was easy to reach.[32] Ramos, which gained its large, modern balneário in 1948, was in the 1940s, 1950s, and even the early 1960s still a relatively clean beach. However, due to lack of maintenance, the balneário would be in ruins by 1960. Although Ramos would suffer from increasingly severe pollution problems after the 1960s, many residents of the Zona Norte, suburbs, and Baixada continued to flock to the beach. Photos from the early 1970s show the beach jammed with bathers.[33] And, in 1980, Afranio Melo, Oswaldo Melo, and Ivony Miranda would compose "Praia de Ramos" (Ramos Beach). The song, recorded by Dicró, celebrates a suburban family's outing to Ramos. The family—husband, wife, children, and mother-in-law—rent a truck for a day at the beach. At the time, if any member of that family lacked a bathing suit, they could rent one from some of the many improvised stalls at the beach, which served primarily as bars.

Although suburbanos may have taken pride in their "Copacabana," articles in the press repeatedly stressed the difference between, on the one hand, Ramos and, on the other, Copacabana and Ipanema. The articles and the photographs that accompanied them point to the out-of-date suits worn by beach-goers in Ramos, their general lack of "sophistication," and the less-than-trim bodies on display—as if every beach-going resident of Copacabana or Ipanema could claim an ideal physique.

Dictatorship, Desbunde, and the Pier

Negrão de Lima's expansion of Copacabana Beach happened under the watchful gaze of the military regime that had seized power in 1964 and would not relinquish it until 1985. (He was part of the moderate, centrist opposition tolerated by the dictatorship.) In the late 1960s and early 1970s, the regime sought to stoke the kind of middle-class consumerism typified by the Zona Sul lifestyle. The construction of apartment buildings in Leme and Leblon accelerated, increasing the number of Cariocas on the beach. But the repressive mechanism of the dictatorship had its own influence, as crackdowns on public displays of same-sex affection disrupted the Bolsa de Valores, driving its former visitors to more covert redoubts. Responses to the dictatorship also drove a wedge into Rio de Janeiro's bossa nova youth. One politicized faction argued that celebrations of sun, sand, and sea were vapid and misleading in a context that demanded popular resistance, while another continued to aspire to the kinds of easy-going sensuality celebrated in songs like "A Garota de Ipanema."[34]

These debates gained new resonance in the early 1970s, in conjunction with another sewerage project. This time, Ipanema was the favored neighborhood, with the construction of a set of underwater pipes designed to carry sewage far out to sea. (This was the dark side, and the environmental cost, of dense occupation of the beachfront in the second half of the twentieth century.) Construction of the sewage pipes required a temporary pier from the middle of Ipanema out into the sea. The pier altered the flow of waves and currents, leading to unusually intense waves near its pilings, and to the rise of sand dunes on the adjacent beach.[35]

Changes in the water and on the sand coincided with social changes, as many Zona Sul youth rejected both the avid consumerism of their parents (at least temporarily) and the militant activism of the politically engaged left. Instead, they pursued a politics of *desbunde*, a local slang term which roughly means dropping out, letting go, and pursuing personal transformation, often sensory or esoteric in nature. Desbunde was a Carioca variation on post-1960s counterculture, one shaped by life under the dictatorship and frustration with apparently failed political responses.[36]

The dunes adjacent to Ipanema's pier became the epicenter of desbunde. As with the Bolsa de Valores twenty years earlier, it was a Zona Sul beach location where the normative expectations of mainstream society were relaxed. Indeed, the *desbundados* of Ipanema's dunes exalted sexual ambiguity in ways that echoed the attitudes of the Bolsa de Valores. Sexual questioning accompanied other forms of experimentation. Kids hung out and smoked pot. They cast aspersions on the dictatorship but not too vigorously. And they always stopped to celebrate each day's sunset with a round of applause. Their hair grew longer as their swimsuits grew more daring, albeit in a relaxed and earthy way: macramé and crochet were in style. The hangout became known as the Dunas da Gal, in honor of singer Gal Costa, whose 1971 live album *Fa-tal: Gal a Todo Vapor* (Fa-tal: Gal Full Speed Ahead) was the unofficial soundtrack of desbunde. The scene in the Dunas da Gal was a forerunner of redemocratization—a process that would be shaped by suspicion of old hierarchies and new forms of identity politics. The pier was removed in 1975. Not coincidentally, desbunde lost the limited power of cohesion it had briefly held, dissipating like a receding wave across the sand.[37]

Changing Residential Patterns

The buildings with studio and other minuscule apartments constructed from the mid-1940s on would give rise to what João Antônio (Ferreira Filho), an author who dedicated himself to chronicling life in the neighborhood, called Copacabana's "*civilização de quarto-e-sala*"; that is, its "one-bedroom civilization." In coining the expression, João Antônio cited as an example "the old 200 [*o antigo 200*]."[38] An immense, twelve-story building, with more than five hundred studio and small one- and two-bedroom apartments, "the old 200" dates from 1959 and is located on the Rua Barata Ribeiro, a few blocks from the beach and from the Chopin. The young professionals and middle- and lower middle-class families who initially occupied the building would, over time, come to share it with janitors, seamstresses, cleaners, bellhops and other hotel staff, hairdressers, delivery boys, salesclerks, and other poorly paid service workers who might have to hold down two jobs just to scrape by. They also came to share the building with *o pessoal da noite* (the night people)—women who in the United States would be known as exotic dancers and other employees of striptease clubs, as well as sex workers.

To live in "the old 200," bellhops, sex workers, hairdressers, and the like did not need to own or lease an apartment there; they could, instead, flop in a rented bed or on a rented couch in someone else's apartment (*morar de vaga*, as it was known). "The old 200" earned such a notorious reputation that some of its residents, ashamed of stating where they lived, successfully lobbied to have its address officially changed from 200 Barata Ribeiro to 194 Barata Ribeiro. The change did not improve its reputation. This was the setting for "Kátia Flávia," the 1987 hit by Carlos Laufer and Fausto Fawcett. The lyrics describe femme fatale Kátia Flávia, a devilish blonde ("*louraça Belzebu,*" "*louraça Satanás*"), who, with her "Exocet panties [*calcinha Exocet*]" (a reference to anti-ship missile technology), openly defied the police while hiding out in a tenebrous apartment in Copacabana.

From Leme to Pontal

As redemocratization gathered steam in the early 1980s, beach-going practices continued to evolve. The beaches along the oceanfront past Leblon—São Conrado, Barra da Tijuca, and even Recreio dos Bandeirantes—became the favored areas for speculative real estate growth. The *emergentes*, or newly minted members of the middle-class, who purchased apartments in these areas aspired to an ideal of South Beach rather than Zona Sul. *Scarface* (the 1983 Al Pacino version set in Miami) and *Miami Vice* were the operative cultural referents, rather than "Copacabana" and "Teresa da Praia."[39] The soundtrack for this transition was BRock, the branding term for a new generation of Brazilian Rock. Lulu Santos captured the mood with his 1983 hit "Como uma Onda" (Like a Wave). Santos's Brazilian yacht rock was mellow and seductive, its lyrics redolent of sun, sea, and sand that had characterized the first generation of bossa nova but with a rock beat and a slick 1980s production.

This was the context for the farofeiros controversy of 1984. The farofeiros had history on their side. Self-identification as a proud farofeiro was emblematic of the identity politics of the moment, breaking down barriers and expanding access to formerly elite strongholds. They had the governor on their side, also, for Brizola not only rejected calls to eliminate the new bus lines but took particular relish in snubbing Ipanema's upper middle-class residents. By the late 1980s, the farofeiros had shown that the beach belonged to them as much as it belonged to residents of Ipanema's expensive apartments.

But Zona Norte day-trippers were not the only population transforming the beach. International tourists came by the jet-load, also, and were even less likely to understand the unwritten codes of Zona Sul beach-going. Automobile ownership expanded progressively over the 1980s, giving ever greater numbers of Cariocas and domestic tourists ready access to the beach. And while Brizola had upset the coconut cart with three bus lines connecting the Zona

Norte directly to Ipanema beach in 1984, by the end of the 1980s, dozens of lines jockeyed for position on the main thoroughfares of the Zona Sul after winding their way through the city. The city's deliberately opaque system of transportation concessions gave private operators incentives to compete with one another where the population was most dense, and few places in the world were as densely populated as Copacabana. If most beach-goers in Ipanema of the 1960s were locals, by the 1990s they came from all over the city, all over the region, and indeed from the rest of the world.

Inevitably, the beaches grew more crowded, chaotic, and diverse in both population and use, continuing the long transition described throughout this book. By the end of the 1980s, the sands of Zona Sul beaches were the focus of myriad activities, commercial, social, and recreational. The term farofeiro, while still occasionally levied in disdain or proclaimed in pride, soon lost all meaning, as eating on the beach became common practice for nearly all beach-goers regardless of class or origin. Newly expanded *barracas*, or beach-stands, offered grilled sausage, skewered shrimp, and endless quantities of stupidly cold beer. Beach volleyball shared space with *futevôlei*, the homegrown variety played with no hands. *Frescobol*, or paddleball—a pastime pursued with equal fervor by men and women—provided the thwack-thwack rhythm of a day at the beach. City government and private promoters regularly took over vast stretches of beach to erect temporary stages and stadia for concerts and sporting events. Some Cariocas still dipped into the sea but usually not for long, and many beach-goers never bothered. The social life was on the sand, and it was irrepressible and ultimately untamable.

Brazilian soul singer Tim Maia captured the new mood with his 1986 classic "Do Leme ao Pontal," whose title and refrain evoke the long stretch of golden beaches from Leme to the Pontal in Recreio dos Bandeirantes: Leme, Copacabana, Ipanema, Leblon, São Conrado, Barra da Tijuca, Recreio, and Pontal. Most of the song consists of Maia and backing singers grooving on this refrain as if reveling in the ecstasy of beach-hopping through an endless Carioca summer.

In the *breque*, or bridge, Maia reminds listeners of the beaches of earlier generations: Calabouço, Flamengo, Botafogo, Urca, and Praia Vermelha. Flamengo, Urca, and Praia Vermelha all remain heavily frequented, in their way, albeit not nearly as heavily as the stretch from Leme to Pontal, and without the social cachet. Botafogo beach, though a strikingly beautiful crescent of brilliant sand, is both polluted and cut off from the fabric of the city by no fewer than *eighteen* lanes of hectic traffic, and as a result is lightly frequented. But the real surprise on Maia's list is Calabouço, a downtown beach that had not existed for sixty-five years by the time the song was written, formerly adjacent to a colonial-era fort that now serves as the National Historic Museum. Calabouço beach was eliminated by the destruction of Morro do Castelo (Castle Hill) and the ensuing landfill projects that extended the downtown waterfront in 1920. The beach was gone long before Tim Maia was born. The reference to Calabouço grounds the song historically as well as geographically, connecting listeners to a long history of Carioca sea-bathing and beachgoing, one that started on the narrow beaches adjacent to the colonial core and gradually extended southward and westward.

"Do Leme ao Pontal" was a showstopper for Maia, one of the highlights of his legendary live shows. Not surprisingly, it was one was one of Bert's favorites, and mine as well. There is no more fitting way to end this epilogue than with Tim Maia's immortal celebration of the glittering stretch of Carioca beachfront: "Do Leme ao Pontal. Não há nada igual." From Leme to Pontal. There is nothing like it.

Notes

Introduction

1. B. J. Barickman to João José Reis, 25 June 2015 (email).
2. This photograph is available from the BN Digital, icon. 1450894.
3. João A. L. Barros, *Memórias*, 230.

A Note on Orthography and Currency

1. See "Padrão monetário brasileiro: histórico das alterações," http://www.debit.com.br/moedas.php (accessed on 7.5.2012).
2. In quoting prices in Brazil's post-1942 currencies, I have followed the English-language convention of using a period (rather than a comma) as the decimal point.
3. For pound sterling exchange rates, I have relied on Leff, *Development*, 1:246; and on Brazil, IBGE, "Cotações mensais da libra esterlina em relação à moeda nacional—1901–1930," https://seculoxx.ibge.gov.br/economicas/setor-externo/tabelas.html (accessed by editors on 3.8.2021). For dollar exchange rates, I have relied on Lawrence H. Officer and Samuel H. Williamson, "Measuring Worth," http://www.measuringworth.com/datasets/exchangeglobal/ (accessed by editors on 3.8.2021), which provides annual average rates.

Chapter One

1. Melville, *White Jacket*, 205; *South American Handbook* (1933), 105; Matschat, *Seven Grass Huts*, 154. It would be easy to multiply these three examples. For a guide to nineteenth-century travelers to Rio, see Berger, *Bibliografia*.
2. Brazilian municipalities typically consisted of both urban and rural districts.
3. Cavalcanti, "Reordenação"; Lessa, *Rio*, 77, 95; Florentino, *Em costas*, 51.
4. The literature on slavery in nineteenth-century Rio is extensive. See, e.g., Karasch, *Slave Life*; Algranti, *Feitor*; Chalhoub, *Visões* and *Força*; Frank, *Dutra's World*; Farias, Soares, and Gomes, *Labirinto*; Soares, "*Povo*."
5. Brazil, Ministerio dos Negocios da Agricultura, Commercio e Obras Públicas, *Relatorio* (1888), 24. Unfortunately, the ministerial report, which provides the

results of the 1886–1887 national slave registry and lists a total of 7,488 slaves for the city of Rio, does not distinguish between urban and rural parishes. On epidemics, see Chalhoub, *Cidade*; S. Graham, *House*, 110–11.

6. Luccock, *Notes*, 41, 79. See also Albuquerque, *Almanak*, 114–63, 165–206.
7. The following discussion draws on Lobo, *História*, the most comprehensive economic history of Rio. Valuable information on the city's nineteenth-century economy can also be found in Frank, *Dutra's World*; Lessa, *Rio*, chaps. 3–6; Sweigart, "Financing."
8. Arruda, *Brasil*, 136, 182, 185–89, 287; Stein, *Vassouras*, 53; R. Graham, *Britain*, 15; Sweigart, "Financing," 164–66, 222–23, 302; Frank, *Dutra's World*, 87; Love, *São Paulo*, 37–38; Holloway, *Immigrants*, 3–34.
9. Frank, *Dutra's World*, 8 and chaps. 2–5; Owensby, *Intimate Ironies*, 18–29; Holloway, *Policing*, 228, 272, 274–75, 282; Hahner, *Poverty*, esp. chap. 1; Meade, *"Civilizing" Rio*, 50; Popinigis, *Proletários*. On the city's elite, see Needell, *Tropical Belle Époque*.
10. Mauricio Abreu, *Evolução*, 37–54; Schultz, *Tropical Versailles*, 106–7; Burke and Staples Jr., *Business*, 40, 58. On eighteenth-century Rio, see Cavalcanti, *Rio de Janeiro*, esp. pt. 1.
11. Maurício Abreu, *Evolução*, 37–53 (quotation, 37); F. Santos, *Meios*, 1:257–393, 2:215–37, 259–64; M. Silva, *Transportes*, 44 (1907 trackage).
12. Needell, *Tropical Belle Époque*, 103; Maurício Abreu, *Evolução*, 42, 54–55; Marcelo Motta, "Centro."
13. Calculated from Soares, "*Povo*," 381. This percentage, which takes into account the number of inhabitants in the parishes of Candelária, São José, Santa Rita, Sacramento, Santo Antônio, and Santana, refers only to the population in the city's urban parishes. On tenements and other types of housing available to Rio's poor, see Chalhoub, *Cidade*, chap. 1; Benchimol, *Pereira Passos*, 112–36, 150–66; Meade, *"Civilizing" Rio*, 67–74; Hahner, *Poverty*, 25–30; Adamo, "Broken Promise," 32.
14. Maurício Abreu, *Evolução*, 37, 41–43, 45–47; Needell, *Tropical Belle Époque*, 142–43, 152; El-Kareh, "Quando os subúrbios"; Lemos, "Posição," 18–28; Hahner, *Poverty*, 28; Ribas, *Botafogo*, 30–31; Aluísio Azevedo, *Cortiço*.
15. Morales de los Rios Filho, *Rio*, 130; Schultz, *Tropical Versailles*, chap. 4; Holloway, *Policing*, 31–43.
16. Lessa, *Rio*, 133, 143–44, 148–49, 166; S. Graham, *House*, 24; Burke and Staples Jr., *Business*, 40–41; Morales de los Rios Filho, *Rio*, 116; Needell, *Tropical Belle Époque*, 22–26; Maurício Abreu, *Evolução*, 61 (illustration).
17. For a few examples, "Os banhos de mar," *Mosquito* (26.12.1869), n.p.; "Os banhos de mar," *RI* (3.3.1878), 3, 6; *GN* (27.1.1893), 2; and *ACM* (1 June–28 Aug. 1912), 67. The sources occasionally mention bathing at other times of the day

and night. See, e.g., Ouseley, *Description*, 50; A. Carvalho, ed., *Ministério*, 195; *DRJ* (24.12.1875), 2; and some of the drowning reports cited below.

18. Holloway, *Policing Rio*, 23, 46–47, 257–58; Chazkel, "Lado escuro"; Bunbury, "Narrativa," 18; Kidder and Fletcher, *Brazil*, 124–26; W. Pinho, "Cinqüenta anos," 38; Debret, *Viagem*, 1:195; Renault, *Rio*, 136, 248–49. On the theater, see, e.g., S. Souza, *Noites*. On kiosks, Ermakoff, *Augusto Malta*, 23–26. On nightlife, see Edmundo, *Rio*, 1:142–43, 165; 2:292–93, 407–26; 3:469–90, 605–6; Coaracy, *Memórias*, 127–30, 134, 138, 196–98; Meade, *"Civilizing" Rio*, 41–43.
19. Ebel, *Rio*, 98; Fletcher and Kidder, *Brazil*, 166, 173; "Praça do mercado," *RS* (8.11.1903), n.p. *RS* (15.11.1903), n.p. See also Ewbank, *Life*, 186, 199; S. Graham, *House*, 48.
20. Costa, *Ordem*, 118–19; Freyre, *Sobrados*, 318; Alencastro, "Vida," 86–87. See also J. T. Santos, "De pardos." On the sometimes-tenuous line separating whites and those of mixed ancestry, see Barickman, "'Passarão por mestiços.'"
21. *CMe* (24.2.1864), 2; Alencastro, "Vida privada," 86–87.
22. Costa, *Ordem*, 118–19; Freyre, *Sobrados*, 318.
23. Carpenter, *Round about Rio*, 318. This work is a novel, but, from the wealth of details about customs and institutions that it presents, it is clear that Carpenter had ample familiarity with Carioca society.
24. Kidder and Fletcher, *Brazil*, 91; *DRJ* (3–4.2.1857), 1.
25. Numerous paintings, engravings, and photographs confirm that the beaches were quite narrow, Ermakoff, *Paisagem*, 44, 74, 99, 145, 175, 240, 262, 282–83, 286–87, 306–7, 318, 323, 351–57.
26. *CP* (1830), 23; *CP* (1854), 36–37; *BICM* (Oct.–Dec. 1880), 3; *BICM* (April–June 1885), 70; *BICM* (July–Sept. 1885), 48, 159; *BICM* (Oct. –Dec. 1885), 112; *BICM* (Oct. –Dec. 1886), 98; *BICM* (July–Sept. 1887), 3, 38, 47, 135.
27. Francisco Filinto de Almeida and João Gateli de Solá, "Memorial" (1907), AN, PI, 4610.
28. Brand, *Journal*, 305; *CMe* (17.12.1857), 1; *CMe* (29.11.1858), 2; *DRJ* (9.3.1869), 1; *DRJ* (29.11.1870), 2; *DRJ* (1.2.1877), 1; *GN* (28.1.1878), 1; *GT* (13.12.1882), 2; *GN* (4.1.1897), 2.
29. *CMe* (7.9.1867), 1; *DRJ* (25.11.1871), 1; *DRJ* (25.2.1876), 2–3; A. Souza, *Bahia*, 137, 140; "Banhos de mar," *OP* (8.2.1896), 2; Morales de los Rios Filho, *Rio*, 366–67.
30. Ouseley, *Description*, 47, 50 (Botafogo); *JC* (2.12.1848), 3 (Caju); "Os banhos," *CS* (23.3.1871), 3 (Saudade).
31. Joaquim Mello, *Generalidades*, 35; "Asseio e salubridade publica," *CMe* (14.3.1851), 2; "Um bairro abandonado," *CMe* (6.3.1854), 2; "Limpeza da cidade," *CMe* (24.12.1854), 2; Freyre, *Sobrados*, 195.

32. *BICM* (Oct.–Dec. 1876), 8–9, 19; *CP* (1894), 245; *JC* (6.11.1879), 2; *DRJ* (20.11.1874), 3; *JC* (1.2.1880), 2; Sedrez, "Bay," 88. On trash collection, see Aizen and Pechman, *Memória*, esp. 42–66; I. Gomes, "Questão," chaps. 2–3.
33. *O Brasil Illustrado* (30.6.1855), 64; "Ora o lixo!" *RI* (19.12.1876), 3, 6. On pollution in the bay, see Sedrez, "Bay."
34. Bunbury, "Narrativa," 16; *SI*, 3 (Jan. 1861), 21; *SI*, 5 (Jan. 1861), 36; *SI* (30.11.1862), 818; *FL* (1877), xxvi–xxvii; Alencastro, "Vida," 71; Chalhoub, *Cidade*, esp. 29–59; Benchimol, *Pereira Passos*, esp. chap. 6; Meade, *"Civilizing" Rio*, 74–94. On other cities, see, e.g., Melosi, *Sanitary City*, chap. 1; Alewitz, *"Filthy Dirt"*; Corbin, *Miasme*; Cohen and Johnson, eds., *Filth*, pt. 2.
35. Karasch, *Slave Life*, 131; *CP* (1830), 13–14.
36. Kidder and Fletcher, *Brazil*, 89–91. See also "Um bairro abandonado," *CMe* (6.3.1854), 2; "Limpeza da cidade," *CMe* (24.12.1854), 2; Ewbank, *Life*, 88.
37. "Banhos de mar," *OP* (8.2.1896), 2; "Cheiros de Botafogo," *OP* (26.1.1896), 2; "Praia do Russell," *JC* (22.4.1877), 5. On the sewer system, see I. Gomes, "Dois séculos," 56–61; R. Graham, *Britain*, 116; Sedrez, "'Bay,'" 86–90, 218.
38. *ACM* (2 April–31 May 1912), 147. The *intendente* (city councilor) Leite Ribeiro read the article to the municipal council.
39. Sedrez, "Bay," 230–32; Hassan, *Seaside*, 50, 125–26, 140, 145–47. See also Booth, *Australian Beach Cultures*, 166. On bathers at polluted beaches in Brazil in recent times, see "Botafogo: 'Se a praia está aí, por que não?'" *JB* (5.2.1970), cad. B, 4; "Praia, sol e esgoto," *Veja* (20.1.1999), 60–65; "Flamengo: poluição 90 vezes acima do limite," *OG* (13.2.2005), 25; "Banhistas ignoram toxina e mergulham na Barra," *OG** (29.1.2007).
40. See, e.g., R. Kaz, "Das coxias," 22; Gerson, *História*, 158; T. Azevedo, "A praia," 90; C. Gaspar, *Orla*, 79, 81; Disitzer, *Mergulho*, 30; F. Veríssimo et al., *Vida*, 152. See also L. Garcia, "Casa." My description of the contraption used by the prince is based on the Casa de Banho de Dom João VI's exhibits (visited on 12.7.2000).
41. Cavalcanti, *Crônicas*, 81–82; *GRJ* (27.5.1812), 4.
42. *GRJ* (2.1.1811), 4; *GRJ* (23.1.1811), 4; *GRJ* (22.11.1815), 4. Between 1813 and 1817, the average price of an *alqueire* (36.27 liters) of *farinha* in Rio was Rs.$781, Johnson Jr., "Preliminary Inquiry," 272. Thus, Rs.$160 roughly corresponded to the price of a fifth of an alqueire (7.25 liters) of farinha. In late eighteenth- and early nineteenth-century Bahia, a quarter alqueire of farinha every ten days (i.e., 9.07 liters, or 0.907 liters per day) was regarded a standard adult ration, Barickman, *Bahian Counterpoint*, 46–47. On farinha consumption in Rio, see Brown, "Internal Commerce," 67–69, 111.
43. Luccock, *Notes*, 48, 284; Schlichthorst, *Rio*, 83–84; Brand, *Journal*, 305; Ouseley, *Description*, 50–52. See also Bougainville, *Journal*, 1:611; Leithold, "Minha

excursão," 70. Pedro also bathed at Flamengo and Botafogo, G. Cruls, *Aparência*, 1:286; Dunlop, *Rio*, 1:35; Ouseley, *Description*, 47–48; Bösche, "Quadros," 204–5; Ebel, *Rio*, 152.

44. See, e.g., Langsdorff, *Diário*, 153–54; Kidder and Fletcher, *Brazil*, 90–91; Wilberforce, *Brazil*, 41; Burton, *Life*, 1:437; Andrews, *Brazil*, 34; Carpenter, *Round about Rio*, 317–18; Ewbank, *Life*, 199.
45. *JC* (1.12.1848), 4; *CMe* (15.11.1860), 4; *CMe* (3.11.1861), 3; *CMe* (25.2.1863), 4; *CMe* (4.12.1863), 3; *CMe* (17.12.1863), 4; *DRJ* (22.1.1865), 4; *AL* (1868), N, 44; *VF* (14.12.1872), 1233; *AL* (1873), N, 68; *AL* (1875), N, 95; *GN* (21.1.1878), 1; *O Besouro* (25.5.1878), 56; *AL* (1880), N, 71; *JC* (16.10.1882), 3; *GN* (9.12.1882), 4; *AL* (1906), 639.
46. *JC* (7.12.1848), 3; *CMe* (18.12.1857), 3; *JC* (8.10.1864), 4; *JC* (11.11.1880), 7; *JC* (13.11.1882), 3, *JC* (24.11.1885), 6; *JC* (6.1.1886), 3; *GN* (13.12.1882), 3; *GN* (24.1.1887), 3; *JC* (31.1.1893), 9; *CMe* (20.8.1857), 3; *JC* (21.11.1885), 4; *Correio da Tarde* (3.2.1862), 3.
47. *JC* (13.8.1842), 4; *AL* (1850), 404; *AL* (1859), 698; *JC* (28.11.1873), 5; *AL* (1883), 578, 1,986–87; *AL* (1883), 1989; *AL* (1885), 2013; *GN* (9.11.1894), 5.
48. *DRJ* (19.1.1875), 3; *DRJ* (9.11.1871), 1; *DRJ* (5.12.1871), 1; *GN* (26.10.1903), 2; *CMa* (11.2.1904), 2; *JC* (6.1.1886), 1; *DRJ* (9.3.1869), 1; *DRJ* (19.12.1876), 2; *DRJ* (13.12.1870), 2; *Correio da Tarde* (15.1.1862), 2; *CMe* (19.1.1861), 3; *JC* (16.1.1880), 1; *JC* (1.12.1880), 2; *DRJ* (1.2.1868), 2; *JC* (7.11.1879), 2. The sources cited here refer explicitly to drownings that occurred while the victim was bathing; they do not include accidental deaths by drowning or suicides, the latter common among slaves, Karasch, *Slave Life*, 317.
49. Official data, available for 1970–1973, 1980, 1983–1984, 1990, and 1992, indicate that lifeguards rescued more than 41,600 bathers, 75 percent of whom were male. More than three-fifths (63 percent) of the rescued victims were between the ages of 15 and 29. Unfortunately the data are not broken down by both sex and age, Guanabara, Secretaria de Planejamento e Coordenação Geral, *Anuário Estatístico* (1973), 324; (1974), n.p. (tabela 4.7.5.1); PCRJ, *Informações* [1983], 283; PCRJ, *Informações . . . 1983/1984*, 283; PCRJ, *Anuário* (1991), 128; PCRJ, *Anuário* (1993), 266.
50. Luccock, *Notes*, 180–81; "Escola de natação," *OP* (20.6.1886), 1 (emphasis in the original). On the 1876 contract, see "Melhoramentos," *Figaro* (16.9.1876), 298–99; *DRJ* (13.1.1877), 2; Conselho de Estado, consulta (22.9.1882), AN, cx 559, pacote 4, doc. 50-A.
51. Kidder and Fletcher, *Brazil*, 91.
52. A. Carvalho, ed., *Ministério*, 195; Machado de Assis, *Dom Casmurro*; "A chave" [1878–79], 841–42; Lopes [Ferreira], *Vida*, 203. Although *Dom*

Casmurro was published in 1899, Machado states that Escobar died by drowning in March 1871.

53. "Chronicas fluminenses," *RI* (15.1.1881), 2; Renault, *Dia-a-dia*, 102; "Sport," *D de Not* (2.1.1885), 1; *D de Not* (5.12.1885), 4; "Sport," *D de Not* (8.12.1885), 1; *D de Not* (10.12.1885), 4; *D de Not* (1.1.1886), 6; "Sport," *D de Not* (7.1.1886), 1; "Sport," *D de Not* (18.1.1886), 1. See also *FL* (1855), 12; "No banho," *D. Pedro V* (27.7.1873), n.p.; Taunay, *Memórias*, 22. Contemporary cartoons published in local magazines occasionally portray bathers who are swimming (figure 1.1). See, e.g., *Mosquito* (26.12.1869), 4; "No Boqueirão," *O Binoculo* (22.10.1881), n.p. According to Lenček and Bosker, knowledge of how to swim became more common in Europe starting in the late eighteenth century; see *Beach*, 172–87.
54. In addition to figures 1.1 and 1.2, see *FL* (1855), 12; *FL* (1859), 25; *FL* (1888), 47–48. On the depiction of bathing in Rio by cartoonists more generally, see Alvarus, "Do Boqueirão do Passeio ao Castelinho," *Crz.* Ed. comemorativa do IV centenário [da fundação do Rio] (Nov. 1965), 83–89.
55. José Mattoso Duque Estrada Carneiro, "Descripção" (27.1.1876), AN, PI, 6907; dec. no. 6.463 (18.1.1877), AN, DPE, PI, cx 9, maço 16A; Antonio Augusto dos Santos Luzes, "Banheiros fluctuantes" [1890], AN, PI, 44; Luzes, "Descripção" (17.6.1890), AN, PI, 527. The most common meaning of *banheiro* today is *bathroom*. But, here and in similar contexts, I have translated the term as bathing pool. Neither the *Aurélio* nor the *Houaiss* registers for the word any definition that could be construed as referring to a pool. But the *Caldas Aulete* does list *banheira* (bathtub) as one possible definition of *banheiro*. *Aurélio*, s.v. *banheiro*; *Houaiss*, s.v. *banheiro*; *Dicionário contemporâneo da língua portuguesa Caldas Aulete*, s.v. *banheiro*. Apparently, in nineteenth-century Rio, a bathing pool was seen as something akin to a very large bathtub.
56. João Gonçalves Ferreira Tito, "Relatorio" (1891), AN, PI, 6217; André Cateysson, "Relatorio" (5.4.1904), AN, PI, 6464; Cateysson, "Memorial" (10.6.1904), AN, PI, 8715.
57. *JC* (1.10.1848), 4; *JC* (5.11.1848), 3; *JC* (19.12.1848), 3; *JC* (26.12.1848), 3; *JC* (28.12.1848), 4; *AL* (1849), 334; João Batista da Silva (comptroller) to Manoel Vieira Tosta (Navy Minister) (14.1.1850) and encls., AN, XM, maço 253; *CMe* (7.2.1851), 3; *JC* (21.11.1852), 3; Kidder and Fletcher, *Brazil*, 91; Paranhos, *Cartas*, 56.
58. Dec. no. 922 (28.2.1852), AN, DPE, PI, cx 7, maço 13A; *CMe* (15.11.1853), 2; *CMe* (5.1.1854), 1, 2; *CMe* (15.1.1860), 1; *CMe* (11.2.1862), 1; *CMe* (12.2.1862), 2; *CMe* (14.2.1862), 2; *CMe* (14.11.1863), 4; *JC* (9.10.1864), 3; *AL* (1867), 593; *AL* (1869), 638. In the sources consulted, I did not locate references after 1855 to

the second barge. In 1855, Carvalho sold his Companhia de Barcas de Banhos, *CMe* (23.11.1855), 2.

59. *JC* (16.11.1873), 4; *JC* (19.11.1873) 6; *JC* (20.11.1873), 6; *JC* (23.11.1873), 6; *JC* (28.11.1873), 6; *JC* (30.11.1873), 4, 7; "Dous melhoramentos uteis," *VF* (29.11.1873), 1699; *Mosquito* (3.12.1873), 8; *AL* (1875), 854. The barge is listed in *AL* (1885), 433, but not in any later editions of this almanac, which also do not mention any other bathing barges. Apparently, Salubridade had operated another bathing barge anchored at one of the city's quays in 1871. See *SI* (16.7.1871), 4421; *SI* (15.10.1871), cover. According to Renault, a bathing barge also functioned in Botafogo Cove, *Dia-a-dia*, 200–1, but I have been unable to locate any contemporary references to it.
60. DRJ (5.1.1873), 2; JC (16.11.1873), 4; JC (29.11.1873), 5; SI (6.2.1873), cover; JC (30.11.1873), 4. On bathing masters and maîtres baigneurs, see Lenček and Bosker, Beach, 126–27; Urbain, Sur la plage, 113–14. The Houaiss includes as one definition of banheiro the equivalent of bathing master in English. Banhista, at the time (just as today), could also mean bather. Yet, well into the 1940s, it was commonly used as a synonym for guarda-vidas (lifeguard). Both the Houaiss and the Aurélio list guarda-vidas as one possible definition of banhista. Houaiss, s.vv. *banheiro*, *banhista*; Aurélio, s.v. *banhista*.
61. The only edition of the Gazeta do Banho that I was able to locate is the inaugural one, dated 25 Dec. 1881. In articles written in 1904 and 1911, João do Rio reported that the "establishment owned by Dordeau, which date[d] from 1870" was the first casa de banho to open at Boqueirão do Passeio beach. He also identified "Dordeau" as a French immigrant. Dordeau, it is safe to assume, represented a corruption of d'Ordan. That surname appears in four requests that "Francisco Affonso [sic] Cot d'Ordan" submitted, between 1874 and 1885, to the treasury, the captaincy of the ports, and Rio's municipal council, all of which had to do with properties that he owned adjoining Boqueirão do Passeio beach. One of these requests was for permission to build "diving dock" "at his bathing establishment." In the mid-1890s, the establishment was still known as "a casa francesa" ("the French [bath] house"), João do Rio, "Velhos aspectos," GN (16.9.1904), 2; João do Rio, "Os banhos de mar," GN (26.6.1911), 1; BICM (Feb. 1874), 7; BICM (Oct.–Dec. 1880), 26; BICM (July–Sept. 1881), 60; BICM (April–June 1882), 48; BICM (July–Sept. 1885), 123; "Folhetim," GB (25.12.1881), 1; D de Not (5.12.1885), 4; "Os banhos de mar," OP (28.1.1896), 2.
62. Testamento e contas testamentárias de Francisco Affonso Cot d'Ordan (1886), AN, Juízo da Provedoria, cx 361, no. 261; Zephyr Frank, personal communication (28.4.2006). Editors' note: Frank provides further analysis on wealth-holding in *Reading*, 142–43.

63. João do Rio, "Velhos aspectos," *GN* (16.9.1904), 2. See also João do Rio, "Os banhos de mar," *GN* (26.6.1911), 1. On João do Rio (1881–1921), whose full real name was Paulo Emílio Cristóvão dos Santos Coelho Barreto, see, e.g., Rodrigues, *João do Rio*.
64. *GN* (3.11.1879), 4; *GN* (6.11.1879), 6; João do Rio, "Velhos aspectos," *GN* (16.9.1904), 2.
65. AGCRJ, cód. 43-1-8, fols. 3, 8–9, 11–13, 15–18, 20–21, 23–28, 30–31, 33–34; AGCRJ, cód. 43-1-9, fols. 2, 4–5, 7–8, 11–12, 15–24; AGCRJ, cód. 43-1-13, fols. 1–5, 9–10, 12, 16–18, 19, 22–23, 24, 27–28; AGCRJ, cód. 46-2-74, fols. 1–9; AGCRJ, cód. 50-1-2, fols. 1–3. These requests were regularly evaluated by the city council; see *BICM* (1872–1889), *Boletim da Intendencia Municipal* (1892), *A do CM* (1893–1905).
66. *BICM* (Jan.–March 1877), 17; *BICM* (April–June 1877), 6; *JC* (2.12.1877), 4; *BICM* (Oct.–Dec. 1884), 42; Theodulo Pupo de Moraes and Theophilo Rufino Bezerra de Menezes, req. (19.3.1888), AGCRJ, cód. 43-1-9, fols. 15–16. In 1819, Leithold claimed that "sharks not only bite the toes of bathers [in Rio], but also sometimes even devour them," "Minha excursão," 70. Other travelers insisted that bathing was safe, Ouseley, *Description*, 50–52; Wilberforce, *Brazil*, 41; Kidder and Fletcher, *Brazil*, 91.
67. Eugenio Carrier, req. (26.1.1885), AGCRJ, cód., 43-1-9, fol. 5; *BICM* (Jan.–March 1885), 31. On renting tents to bathers, see *BICM* (Oct.–Dec. 1884), 57; *BICM* (July–Sept. 1885), 107; *BICM* (Jan.–March 1886), 11.
68. Ousely, *Description*, 50; Burton, *Life*, 1:437. On bathing machines in Europe, Montevideo, and Guarujá, see Lenček and Bosker, *Beach*, 70–72, 82, 84–86, 116, 125, 135, 138; Frizell and Greenfield, *Sight-seeing*, 177; "Montevideo capital do verão," *RS* (6.3.1915), n.p.; Peck, *South American Tour*, 280; N. Cunha, "Gestión," 131; "Fon-Fon! em S. Paulo," *FF* (2.11.1912), s.n.; Ferrreira, *Banho*, 76–77.
69. Apart from Carrier's request, I located only three other references to bathing machines. All three come from proposals that never materialized and involved installing bathing machines at the oceanfront beaches, which were much wider than those along the bayshore, so parking and maneuvering them would have presented no problems, Effiseo Cogliate, "Memorial" (25.9.1891), AN, PI, 918; Samuel Pelitzer, req. (24.3.1915), AGCRJ, ano 1915, pasta 44, no. 2586; *ACM* (5 June–28 Aug. 1916), 203.
70. The number of bathing establishments is calculated from *AL* (1894–1904); João do Rio, "Velhos aspectos," *GN* (16.9.1904), 2; "Policia sanitaria—2ª circunscripção," in "Relatorio semestral (julho a dezembro de 1896)," 488. See also AGCRJ, ano 1899, pasta 33, doc. 86; AGCRJ, cód. 262, fols. 189–90;

AGCRJ, ano 1899, cx 08, doc. 20; AGCRJ, ano 1894, pasta 46, doc. 332; "Os banhos de mar," *OP* (28.1.1896), 2.

71. *BIM* (Oct.–Dec. 1896), 8–9. See also *ACM* (6 Nov. 1896–7 Jan. 1897), 5, 28, 39–40; PDF, *Consolidação das leis e posturas municipaes*, 2:174. The law seems to have been based, at least in part, on orders issued by the municipal Diretoria Geral de Higiene e Assistência Pública (General Directorate of Hygiene and Public Assistance) in mid-1896. See "Circular no. 950, 1ª Secção, em 21 de julho de 1896," in "Relatorio da Directoria Geral de Hygiene e Assistencia Publica," in PDF, *Relatorios . . . 1897*, 448. See also the complaints about the lack of lifesaving equipment at the city's bathing establishments: "Os banhos de mar," *OP* (28.1.1896), 2; *OP* (31.1.1896), 2; *OP* (8.2.1896), 2.
72. *CLMV*, 1: 39–40 (dec. no. 1.231, de 14.10.1908) and 41–43 (dec. no. 717, de 11.1.1909); *ACM* (29 Aug.–31 Oct. 1908), 220, 223; *ACM* (1 Nov. 1908–4 Jan. 1909), 78, 86; *BIM* (Oct.–Dec. 1908), 9–10; *BIM* (Jan.–July 1909), 5–8. Barbosa ("Dona Filó," 539) and Sevcenko ("Capital," 572–73) transcribe parts of the 1909 decree but incorrectly date it to 1906 and wrongly claim that it was the first law to regulate the city's casas de banhos.
73. Sevcenko, "Capital," 573. See also Saliba, "*Belle époque*," 83.
74. [João do Rio], "A cidade," *GN* (26.10.1903), 2. In 1897 and 1898, the city's Diretoria Geral de Higiene e Assistência inspected the bathing establishments at Boqueirão do Passeio and Santa Luzia beaches, but apparently not those in Flamengo. References to such inspections disappear from the available sources after 1899. See Dr. Celso dos Reis (chefe, 1º Distrito Sanitário) to the Diretor Geral de Higiene e Assistência Pública (30.11.1897), and "Policia sanitaria," encl. in Dr. Bento Geraque Murta (chefe, 3º Distrito Sanitário) to the Diretor Geral de Higiene e Assistência Pública (1.12.1897), both in AGCRJ, cód. 8-4-28, fols. 47–51, 81; "Relatorio semestral—julho a dezembro [de 1898] . . . 3º Districto Sanitario" (10.1.1899), AGCRJ, cód. 38-2-42, fol. 117; "Relatorio semestral, julho de 1898, pelo chefe do 1º Distº Sanitº" and "Relatorio do 2º semestre de 1898 . . . 1º districto sanitario," both in AGCRJ, cód. 38-2-42, fols. 1–25; "Relatorio sobre os serviços de Hygiene e Assistencia Publica" (1904), AGCRJ, cód. 38-3-15, fols. 4, 6; and the documentation in AGCRJ, códs. 38-3-1, 38-3-7, 38-3-13, 38-3-14, 38-3-16, 38-3-17, 38-3-18, 38-3-20 (fols. 39–41).
75. *AL* (1885), 433, 1855; AGCRJ, ano 1894, pasta 46, doc. 332; João do Rio, "Velhos aspectos," *GN* (16.9.1904), 2. See also the photos of a bathing establishment at Santa Luzia beach, in AGCRJ, Icon., pasta 414, 1642; pasta 685A, 3024/07, which are reproduced in Ermakoff, *Augusto Malta*, 132–33. Unfortunately, the photos, which probably date from the years 1900–1909, show only the back entrance to the establishment and one of its side façades. Cf. the

photos of casas de banhos in *RS* (20.2.1902), 622; *RS* (29.1.1905), 1992. The second photo is reproduced in Cohen, Fridman, and Siqueira, *Rio*, 23.

76. João do Rio, "Velhos aspectos," *GN* (16.9.1904), 2. See also "Folhetim," *GT* (26.10.1882), 1, according to which "thousands of persons" in the early 1880s bathed at Boqueirão do Passeio beach; "Varias noticias," *JC* (16.4.1905), 3; *ACM* (1 June–28 Aug. de 1912), 67.
77. João do Rio, "Velhos aspectos," *GN* (16.9.1904), 2; *GN* (19.10.1879), 2; Andrews, *Brazil*, 34.
78. *GN* (3.11.1879), 4; *GN* (14.12.1882), 2; *AL* (1883), 1856; *Guia do viajante*, 96; *AL* (1890), 1908. See also *DRJ* (5.1.1873), 2. The same prices were also cited in Theodulo Pupo de Moraes and Theophilo Rufino Bezerra de Menezes, req. (19.3.1888), AGCRJ, cód. 43-1-9, fol. 16v. By 1896, the price of a single bath had increased to Rs.$300. A proposed 1909 law authorizing the construction of a new bathing establishment specified Rs.$500 as the price of a single bath and Rs.10$000 as the price of a subscription for thirty baths. Nine years later, an establishment in Santa Luzia charged Rs.60$000 for a "monthly subscription," "Banhos de mar," *OP* (31.1.1896), 2; *ACM* (30 March–31 May 1909), 56; "O eterno trambolho," *GN* (5.2.1918), 1.
79. *JC* (6.1.1886), 1.
80. See, e.g., "Os banhos de mar," *Museu Litterario* (30.4.1878), 3; Machado de Assis, "A chave," 841–42. See also Ouseley, *Description*, 50; Kidder and Fletcher, *Brazil*, 90; *DRJ* (10.2.1865), 3; "Banhos de mar," *Mosquito* (26.12.1869), n.p.; Karasch, *Slave Life*, 59; S. Graham, *House*, 35.
81. *DRJ* (20.1.1877), 1. See also, e.g., *DRJ* (25.1.1875), 2; *DRJ* (4.3.1877), 3; Burton, *Life*, 1:437; "Banhos de mar," *GN* (31.1.1893), 3. João do Rio, in recalling Boqueirão do Passeio before 1904, noted that poor bathers undressed at the beach, "Velhos aspectos," *GN* (26.6.1911), 2. See also "Os tradicionaes banhos de Santa Luzia," *OG* (13.1.1930), ed. das 17 horas, 3. But cf. the discussion of an 1885 incident in chap. 2 below.
82. *DRJ* (27.2.1876), 2 (emphasis in the original); *DRJ* (3.3.1876), 2 (emphasis in the original). See also, e.g., *DRJ* (7.3.1868), 2; *DRJ* (26.2.1869), 1; *DRJ* (4.3.1877), 3; *O Pandego* (30.4.1880), n.p. (cartoon); *FL* (1888), 45–46. In the early twentieth century, *banhista* (bather) "in the slang used by Carioca delinquents" referred to a thief who stole bathers' belongings while they were in the water, *Guia do Districto*, 265. On "beach rats," see, e.g., "Perigo: com a chegada do verão aparece o 'rato de praia,'" *Crz* (31.12.1960), 102–5; "Verão violento transforma praias," *JB* (8.1.1984), 14; "Patrulha ostensiva não detém 'ratos de praia,'" *JB* (9.1.1984), 5.
83. *JC* (20.11.1885), 1; Kidder and Fletcher, *Brazil*, 90; A. Carvalho, ed., *Ministério*, 195; Carpenter, *Round about Rio*, 318; João do Rio, "Velhos

aspectos," *GN* (16.9.1904), 2. See also José Antônio José [João do Rio], "A paixão pelo mar," *RS* (11.3.1916), n.p

84. "Os banhos de mar," *OP* (16.2.1896), 2.
85. On José Antônio de Oliveira and Manoel Cabinda, see *DRJ* (13.12.1870), 2; *DRJ* (1.2.1868), 2. On Michel Calógeras's father, see the biographical note in A. Carvalho, ed., *Ministério*, 9–18. The German-born Fleiüss often used the character of Doutor Semana to portray himself in cartoons in his magazine. Several show Doutor Semana bathing; hence my conclusion that Fleiüss went sea-bathing (figure 2.2). On Fleiüss, see Guimarães, "Henrique Fleiüss."
86. João do Rio, "Velhos aspectos," *GN* (16.9.1904), 2; "Os banhos de mar," *GN* (26.6.1911), 1–2; "A cidade," *GN* (24.12.1903), 2.

Chapter Two

1. Edmundo, *Rio*, 4:841. The second edition of Edmundo's book, cited here, does not specify the time period covered by the work, but it can be found in the *Correio da Manhã*, in which Edmundo originally published his memoirs as a series of articles. See, e.g., Edmundo, "O Rio de Janeiro do meu tempo (1901–1912)," *CMa* (6.1.1935), sup., 1.
2. Sevcenko, "Capital," 572–73; R. Kaz, "Das coxias," 23; O'Donnell, "Rio," 89, 115–21. See also Mauad, "Sob o signo," 54; G. Cruls, *Aparência*, 2:540; Alencastro, "Vida," 52; Disitzer, *Mergulho*, 43; Wehrs, *Rio*, 20; MacLachlan, *History*, 59; Rosa Araújo, *Vocação*, 321; C. Gaspar, *Orla*, 32, 34; Villaça, "Points," 30; A. Pinho, "Bonde"; Huguenin, "Praias," 20–21; T. Azevedo, "Praia," 89–92; Maul, *Rio*, 209–10; San Martini, ed., *Copacabana*, 90–91; Eneida, "Introdução," 10; Boechat, *Copacabana Palace*, 23; S. Garcia, *Rio*, 153–54; Lago, ed., *Praias*, 71; Pinheiro and Pinheiro, *Encantos*, 180–81; Poerner, *Leme*, 16–17. Besides Luiz Edmundo's memoirs, the other main source for the argument appears to be Barbosa, "Dona Filó," 537–40. Both authors, in fact, provide information suggesting that bathing was *not* a strictly therapeutic activity.
3. "Praia só com ordens médicas," *OG* (20.1.2000), *ZS*, 4. See also, e.g., "Ai de ti, Avenida Atlântica," *OG* (27.7.2006), *ZS*, 23; "O Rio antes do Cristo," *Veja Rio* (25.8.2010), 18–19; Joaquim Ferreira dos Santos, "Gente Boa," *OG* (10.12.2012), 2° cad., 3.
4. Corbin, *Território*, 69–85; Hassan, *Seaside*, 15–20; Lenček and Bosker, *Beach*, 71–89; Urbain, *Sur la plage*, 103–22 (quotation, 111); Machado, *Construção*, 61, 119–27.
5. Paulo Barbosa da Silva (chief steward) to Sebastião do Rego Barros (Minister of War) (25.9.1860, 24.10.1860, 30.10.1860), AN, cód. 572; J. R. Barros, "Reminiscencias," 93; Schwarcz, *Barbas*, 219.

6. *JC* (19.11.1849), 2; *AL* (1865), N, 8; *AL* (1874), N, 134. See also *CMe* (16.12.1856), 4; *CMe* (8.12.1862), 4; *DRJ* (10.1.1865), 5 (advertisements for the following private hospitals: São Sebastião, Nossa Senhora da Glória, and Godinho e Bezerra).
7. Durão, *Breves considerações*, 16, 20 (quoted passages); J. Sá, *Structura*, esp. 63–65; H. Lima, *Do emprego*, 1–2, 21; Claparède, *Estudos*, esp. 8–9; *A Reforma* (11.3.1876), [3]; *DRJ* (17.12.1877), 4; *DRJ* (25.1.1878), 4 (advertisements announcing the book). See also, e.g., Vieira, *Quaes as modificações*, 1–15; Manoel Motta, *Que influencia*, 3–6; E. Paiva, *Como se deve proceder*, 25–30; L. Araujo, *These*, 39–41; José Mello, *Do emprego*, esp. 24. In 1843, a physician in Pernambuco had already recommended sea baths to prevent hydrocele (swelling of the scrotum); see Teixeira, "Sobre as causas," 73. On cold water and thermal shocks, see Corbin, *Território*, 75–82, 86; Lenček and Bosker, *Beach*, 73–81.
8. Durão, *Breves considerações*, esp. 5, 6, 9; Vieira, *Quaes as modificações*, 8–10; Claparède, *Estudos*, 30–31. On drinking seawater, see also Hassan, *Seaside*, 16–17, 38.
9. Aluísio Azevedo, *Girândola*, 126–27, and *Casa*, 93–94; Artur Azevedo, "Banhos," 77–85.
10. *JC* (21.12.1873), 3; *JC* (23.12.1873), 5.
11. Here I borrow the idea of a "mystery" from H. Vianna, *Mistério*. There is an interesting parallel between, on the hand, the historiography of sea-bathing and beach-going in Rio and, on the other, most academic discussions dealing with the history of samba. Those discussions generally describe samba before 1930 as a disdained genre, whose practitioners the police persecuted. Then, supposedly, after 1930, samba suddenly and "mysteriously" became elevated to the status of Brazil's "national" music and gained official support. But, as Vianna shows, the secondary literature tends to exaggerate the disdain in which samba was held before 1930 and to ignore cultural interactions between upper- and lower-class groups in the nineteenth and early twentieth centuries. See also Hertzman, *Making Samba*; T. Gomes, *Espelho*; M. Cunha, *Ecos*.
12. Braggs and Harris, *Sun*; Hassan, *Sand*; Lenček and Bosker, *Beach*; Sterngrass, *First Resorts*; Urbain, *Sur la plage*; Walton, *English Seaside Resort*.
13. Álvarez, *Mar del Plata*, 79 (the number of summer visitors); Pastoriza and Torre, "Mar del Plata"; Fagnani, *Ciudad*, 15–56; N. Cunha, *Montevideo*; Góngora, "De jardín," 302–9, 320–21; Pastoriza, ed., *Puertas*.
14. *BICM* (July–Sept. 1877), 4 (session of 15 Sept.); *Skating-Rink: Jornal Humoristico e Litterario* (24.7.1878–29.8.1878); "Skating-Rink," *O Besouro* (11.1.1879), 10; *JC* (16.10.1882), 8; *GN* (3.11.1882), 2; "No Club-Rink," *GT* (9.12.1885), 1; *A Semana* (21.6.1886), 211; *AL* (1886), 1529; "Bellodromo," *RI* (12.1892), 7; Táti,

Mundo, 179; Rainho, *Cidade*; Needell, *Tropical Belle Époque*, esp. chap. 5; Schetino, *Pedalando*; L. Pereira, *Footballmania*, chap. 1. On rowing, see below.

15. Binzer, *Alegrias*, 110–13; Reis Filho, *São Paulo*, 50–59 (p. 50, quoted passage); Christoffoli, *História*, 48–49; Pinheiro, "Fundação." See also Octavio, *Elos*, 46–47; Lanna, *Cidade*, 97–98, 101, 150. On beaches in Olinda and Recife (Pernambuco), see "Carta . . . do Sineiro da Sé," *Diario de Pernambuco* (3.1.1866), 8; Rita Araújo, *Praias*, 249–97. On Newport, see Sterngass, *First Resorts*, chaps. 2, 6.
16. See, e.g., Alencastro, "Vida"; Sevcenko, "Capital"; Mauad, "Sob o signo"; Lessa, *Rio*; S. Kaz, *Jeito*.
17. "Banhos de mar," *BM* (4.2.1938), 2 (interview with Caldeira); "Hotel Balneario da Urca," *GN* (9.1.1925), 4; Joel Silveira, "Muito sol sôbre o espaço vital," *D de N* (7.1.1948), 2ª seção, 1; *Thalassotherapia*; Almeida, *Technica*.
18. F. Gontijo, "*Carioquice*," 52–53, 75.
19. L. Cruls, *Clima / Climat*, 9, 23; "Inverno tem o dia mais quente do ano," *JB* (9.9.1999), 18; "Primeiro dia de verão," *OG** (22.12.2000); "A capital mais quente do país," *OG** (11.2.2001); "O Rio tem o dia mais quente do ano," *OG** (16.2.2001); "Dia mais quente do ano," *JB** (23.1.2006); e "Areia molhada," *OG** (25.1.2006). On the Tijuca Forest, forests in the city more generally, and historical changes in Rio's climate, see Maurício Abreu, "Cidade"; Brandão, "Alterações," esp. 161–269; Heynemann, *Floresta*.
20. Schwarcz, *Barbas*, 231–44; Needell, *Tropical Belle Époque*, 149–50; Chalhoub, *Cidade*; Alencastro, "Vida," 67–68.
21. See, e.g., "Em familia," *Illustração do Brazil* (18.1.1877), 202; "Chronicas fluminenses," *RI* (18.12.1880), 2; "Pequenas chronicas," *RI* (27.1.1883), 2; "Medidas urgentes," *DRJ* (28.12.1867), 2; *Gde N* (28.11.1882), 1.
22. Electric table fans were available for purchase by the 1910s: *A Noite* (17.1.1912), 4; *CMa* (12.2.1915), 11; *A Noite* (10.1.1916), 4; *A Noite* (29.1.1916), 5; *A Noite* (13.12.1916), 5.
23. "Relatorio da commissão sanitaria" (30.12.1879), AGCRJ, cód. 8-4-24, fol. 40; F. Veríssimo and Bittar, *500 anos*, 89–90; *DRJ* (24.1.1877), 2.
24. "O calor," *VF* (1.2.1868), 54–55. On men's and women's clothing, see Kidder, *Sketches*, 2:162; "Fragmento," *SI* (14.1.1872), 4630; *FL* (1877), xiv; Leclerc, *Cartas*, 47–48; Rainho, *Cidade*; Needell, *Tropical Belle Époque*, 168–71; W. Pinho, "Cinqüenta anos," 36–37; S. Gontijo, *80 anos*, 10–22. Cf. also *RI* (13.1.1883), cover; *RI* (11.2.1882), 4–5.
25. A. S. Peck, *South American Tour*, 312; "O calor continúa a fazer victimas," *CMa* (1.2.1917), 1, 3. See also "Que calor!" *A Noite* (24.1.1917), 3; "Sem paletot," *A Noite* (27.1.1917), 2; "A canicula," *JB* (31.1.1917), 1; "As victimas," *JB*

(31.1.1917), 6. For women's fashions in the 1920s and 1930s, see S. Gontijo, *80 anos*, 26–50.

26. "O paletot do Sr. Lopes," *GN* (31.12.1924), 2; Alvaro Penalva, "Pela rama," *GN* (7.1.1925), 2; "Hygiene," *JB* (11.1.1920), 5; "Bin," *GN* (21.1.1925), 4; "Bin," *GN* (10.1.1930), 5; "EN: A indumentaria," *JB* (29.12.1932), 5; "EN: Heróis da indumentaria," *JB* (26.1.1938), 5; "Cc," *JB* (15.12.1939), 6.
27. *CMe* (15.1.1863), 1; *VF* (7.12.1872), 1221; *GN* (15.12.1882), 1; "T&N: O tempo," *CMa* (16.1.1904), 1; "O rigor," *Careta* (29.1.1916), n.p.
28. As late as 1943, Franck noted that Cariocas preferred not to discuss the city's heat with foreigners, thinking that it would reflect poorly on the country; see *Rediscovering*, 332. See also, e.g., "Echos," *OI* (3.2.1917), 2; "Cc," *JB* (14.1.1938), 6; Yvonne Jean, "A praia maravilhosa," *CMa* (8.1.1950), 11.
29. Pedro II, *D. Pedro II*, 384 (quotation) and 372; "Os banhos de mar," *OP* (28.1.1896), 2.
30. "Folhetim," *GT* (26.10.1882), 1; *RI* (30.11.1883), 8; *RI* (2.1893), 3; [João do Rio], "A cidade," *GN* (6.12. 1903), 2; "Varias noticias," *JC* (16.4.1905), 3; Morales de los Rios Filho, *Rio*, 346; "Echos e Factos: A impossibilidade do banho," *OP* (25–26.12.1922), 4.
31. Vigarello, *Propre*; Ashenbug, *Dirt*; Smith, *Clean*; Lessa, *Rio*, 154; F. Veríssimo and Bittar, *500 anos*, 98–106; *JC* (23.11.1873), 5; *GN* (14.12.1882), 3.
32. *RI* (30.11.1883), 8. See also "EN: A falta d'agua," *JB* (6.12.1928), 5; "Zona Sul," *Crz* (6.3.1954), 30–31; "Com calor," *Crz* (20.3.1954), 46–47. On the problems with water supply, see, e.g., Maurício Abreu, "Cidade"; Lessa, *Rio*, 153–55.
33. Austen, *Northanger Abbey*; Dostoyevsky, *Gambler*. Studies on nineteenth-century mineral spas in Europe and the United States include Sterngass, *First Resorts*, chaps. 1, 4, 5; Mackaman, *Leisure Settings*; Blackbourn, "Fashionable Spa Towns"; Walton, "Health." On Poços de Caldas, see Marras, *A propósito*; João do Rio, *João do Rio*.
34. Durão, *Breves considerações*. See also, e.g., J. Sá, *Structura*, 64; "Barca," *CMe* (28.1.1855), 2; "Hygiene," *O Brasil Illustrado* (30.6.1855), 64; *DRJ* (9–10.12.1872), 2; "Ora o lixo!" *RI* (19.12.1876), 3, 6; "Hygiene," *GB* (25.12.1881), 2; *OP* (2.12.1884), 1; and the proposals for bathing establishments cited in chap. 1.
35. See, e.g., Costa, *Ordem*; Bourdelais, ed., *Hygiénistes*; La Berge, *Mission*. The only definition of *hygiene* supplied by the *OED* is "that department of knowledge or practice which relates to the maintenance of health; a system of principles or rules for preserving or promoting health; sanitary science," *Oxford English Dictionary*, s.v. *hygiene*. See also *Aurélio*, s.v. *higiene*; *Houaiss*, s.v. *higiene*. The current common association of hygiene with cleanliness no doubt stems from the fact that eighteenth- and nineteenth-century proponents of

hygiene argued that cleanliness was *one* means to promote and maintain good health.

36. Durão, *Breves considerações*, 12, 27. See also Joaquim Mello, *Generalidades*, 35.
37. Costa, *Ordem*; Chalhoub, *Cidade*, 29–56; Gondra, *Artes*; Reis, *Morte*, chaps. 10–11.
38. Gondra, *Artes*, 187–190, 284–350, esp. 333–50; Costa, *Ordem*, 184–87; Coutinho, *Esboço*, 15. See also Joaquim Mello, *Generalidades*, 32–35; Silva and Melo, "Fabricando o soldado."
39. *AL* (1859), 476–77 and N, 21–22; *CMe* (6.1.1859), 3; *AL* (1883), 1980; *JC* (4.1.1838), 4; *CMe* (11.2.1860), 1; *SI* (19.1.1868), 2962.
40. Sevcenko, "Capital," 568–71; L. Pereira, *Footballmania*, chap. 1; V. Melo, *Cidade*; Jesus, "Construindo." See also Costa, *Ordem*, esp. chap. 6. Closely related to this "sporting fever" was the development of new conceptions of masculinity in Brazil; see Beattie, *Tribute*.
41. Mendonça, *Historia*, 3. On rowing and its prestige, see V. Melo, *Cidade* (which also discusses its links with sea-bathing), esp. 93–106; L. Pereira, *Footballmania*, chap. 2; Sevcenko, "Capital," 569–71; Edmundo, *Rio*, 4:835–36.
42. V. Melo, *Cidade*, 47, 67–69.
43. Gerson, *História*, 255; Mendonça, *Historia*, 231, 202; *AL* (1897), 437; *AL* (1904), 828–29, 833; *AL* (1908), 920–21; Edmundo, *Rio*, 4:836; V. Melo, *Cidade*, 100.
44. See, e.g., Lopes, *Vida*, 204; João do Rio, "Os banhos de mar," *GN* (26.6.1911), 1; "A hora do banho no Flamengo," *Careta* (29.1.1916), n.p.; "As praias cariocas: Flamengo," *Selecta* (20.1.1917), n.p.; "O verão no Rio: a praia de Santa Luzia," *Selecta* (10.2.1917), n.p.
45. Edmundo, *Rio*, 4:841; Mendonça, *Historia*, 207, 235, 259, 367, 369; "Um aspecto . . . depois de ser disputado o 'Campeonato Brasileiro de Natação,'" *RS* (14.12.1912), n.p.; "A temporada de 1913," *RS* (14.2.1914), n.p.; "Sport," *OP* (14.12.1915), 7; "Campeonato Brasileiro de Natação," *OP* (11.12.1916), 8. See also João do Rio, "Os banhos de mar," *GN* (26.6.1911), 1; "As praias," *DN* (29.12.1931), 3. On Provenzano's participation in the 1932 Olympics and his work as a lifeguard, see Confederação Brasileira de Remo, https://www.remobrasil.com/remo/remo-nos-jogos-olimpicos (accessed by editors on 3.8.2021); *BPDF* (Jan.–March 1939), 64.
46. Although frequently misspelled, the English term *sportsman* and its plural are often found in the sources.
47. The example of football is relevant here. L. Pereira shows that, in the early twentieth century, the discourses both for and against the game produced by intellectuals completely ignored the meanings that working-class men in

Rio assigned to football. Those intellectuals did not recognize the possibility that football fostered forms of sociability that could reinforce class-based solidarities. Nor could they even conceive of the possibility that more and more workers took up the game because they found playing football fun; see *Footballmania*, chap. 3.

48. *CMe* (8.11.1862), 1. See also *DRJ* (3–4.2.1857), 1. Cf. Wiltse's discussion of the long history of skinny-dipping by boys in the United States, in *Contested Waters*, 10–14.
49. The percentage of illiterate people refers only to the population in Rio's urban districts. The 1872 census did not collect information on literacy by age, but it did reveal that, regardless of age, 60 percent of all residents in the city's urban parishes were illiterate; see Brazil, *Recenseamento* (1906), 112–13; Brazil, *Recenseamento* (1872), [21]: n.p. (parish population tables).
50. In 1872, less than one percent of the 37,567 slaves in the city's urban parishes knew how to read and write; see Brazil, *Recenseamento* (1872), [21], n.p. (parish population tables).
51. Consider the fascinating case of a slave named Romão, who in 1873 fled a sugar plantation in Pernambuco (in Northeastern Brazil) and went to Recife to take sea baths to alleviate his rheumatism; see Holanda, "Barão de Lucena," n.p.
52. See, e.g., Robert Slenes's discussion of Central Africans' understandings of water spirits, in "Great Porpoise-Skull Strike." Editors' note: For a discussion of African aquatic cultures, see Dawson, *Undercurrents*, esp. chaps. 1–5 on swimming.
53. "As praias," *DN* (29.12.1931), 3. On folk healers, see Pimenta, "Terapeutas"; Sampaio, *Nas trincheiras*; Karasch, *Slave Life*, 263–65.
54. Corbin, *Território*, 94–99, 279. See also Walton, *English Seaside Resort*, 9–11.
55. Tollenare, *Notes*, 1:235; Machado, *Construção*, 49; Brazil, *Recenseamento* (1872), [21]: n.p. (parish population tables); Brazil, *Recenseamento* (1906), 22, 126.
56. Léry, *Journal*, 267–68; Sousa, *Notícia*, 50.
57. Machado de Assis, *Dom Casmurro*; "Questão de vaidade"; "A chave". Nothing in the novel and the short stories indicates that the main characters bathed because they were sick. On the eve of his death, Escobar even showed off his biceps to Bentinho (Machado de Assis, *Dom* Casmurro, 181). See also Lopes, *Vida*, 203. Michel Calógeras represents a nonfictional example pointing in the same direction. According to his father, Michel went bathing in 1865, but *not* because he was sick; instead, his father described him as "robust" and as a "vigorous athlete"; see A. Carvalho, ed., *Ministério*, 195.
58. Ouseley, *Description*, 50; Kidder and Fletcher, *Brazil*, 90–91.

59. "Chronicas," *RI* (15.1.1881), 2; "Canhenho," *RI* (23.12.1882), 6; "A vida," *RI* (6.1.1883), 3; *FL* (1888), 45.
60. Francisco de Sales Torres Homem, req. (9.7.1888), AGCRJ, cód. 43-1-9, fol. 1l. On piers at English resorts, see, e.g., Walton, *English Seaside Resort*, 163–66, 173–74.
61. *JC* (23.11.1873), 6; *AL* (1875), 854; *AL* (1885), 433; *Mosquito* (3.12.1873), 8. The word *anfibicrobático* (amphibicrobatic) does not exist in Portuguese; the cartoonist coined it for the occasion.
62. *AL* (1885), 433, 1855. The expression *high life* was already common by the early 1880s. See, e.g., "Os theatros," *RI* (1.12.1876), 3; "Salpicos," *Mosquito* (22.1.1876), n.p.; "High-Life," *DRJ* (6.5.1878), 2; "Chronicas fluminenses," *RI* (18.12.1880), 2; "Corte e High-Life," *O Brazil* (6.11.1881), 3.
63. "Folhetim," "Pescaria," and "Ichtygraphia," *GB* (25.12.1881), 1–3; "Folhetim," *GT* (26.10.1882), 1; [Artur Azevedo], "De palanque," *D de Not* (1.12.1885), 1; "Os banhos," *OP* (16.2.1896), 2; João do Rio, "A cidade," *GN* (24.12.1903), 2; João do Rio, "Velhos aspectos," *GN* (16.9.1904), 2; João do Rio, "Parada"; João do Rio, "Os banhos," *GN* (26.6.1911), 1; Lopes, *Vida*, 203–4.
64. *RN* (5.9.1903), 5; AGCRJ, ano 1894, pasta 46, doc. 332; João do Rio, "Velhos aspectos," *GN* (16.9.1904), 2; "O Rio precisa de banhos de mar," *A Noite* (17.12.1912), 1.
65. *Guia do viajante*, 96; "Uma aventura na praia," *RN* (5.9.1914), 5; *AL* (1883), 1856; *AL* (1886), 1980; *AL* (1890), 1908.
66. "Hygiene do banho," *GB* (25.12.1881), 2; Parente e Monte-Mór, eds., *Rio*, 62; the cartoons cited in chap. 1; João do Rio, "Velhos aspectos," *GN* (16.9.1904), 2. On diving docks, see also *SI* (6.2.1873), cover; "Os banhos de mar," *OP* (31.1.1896), 2.
67. Octavio, *Elos*, 264.
68. "Folhetim," *GB* (25.12.1881), 1; João do Rio, "Velhos aspectos," *GN* (16.9.1904), 2; João do Rio, "Os banhos de mar," *GN* (26.6.1911), 2 (which deals with Boqueirão do Passeio beach before 1905); *AL* (1886), 1980; *JC* (13.11.1879), 2; *AL* (1883), 1856.
69. "Folhetim," *GB* (25.12.1881), 1, 2. João do Rio, "Velhos aspectos," *GN* (16.9.1904), 2; João do Rio, "Os banhos," *GN* (26.6.1911), 1; João do Rio, "A cidade," *GN* (24.12.1903), 2. See also Lopes, *Vida*, 202–3.
70. "Os banhos," *OP* (16.2.1896), 2.
71. "Os banhos," *Museu Litterario* (30.4.1878), 3; "Folhetim," *GB* (25.12.1881), 2. See also figure 1.1; *Mephistopheles* (26.9.1874), 4–5; "Os banhos," *RI* (3.3.1878), 3, 6; "Os banhos," *Carbonario* (4.1.1888), 1; "Os banhos," *GN* (23.3.1907), 3; "Vida alheia," *OP* (3.3.1918), 2; João do Rio, "Parada."
72. *O Brasil Illustrado* (30.6.1855), 64; *SI* (26.1.1868), 2972; *SI* (19.3.1871), 4289;

SI (5.1.1873), capa; *SI* (6.2.1873), cover; *SI* (12.12.1876), 6333; *Mosquito* (26.12.1869), 4; *Mosquito* (29.1.1870), 4; *Mosquito* (21.1.1871), 4; figure 2.6; *Mephistopheles* (26.9.1874), 4–5; *Mephistopheles* (17.10.1874), 4–5; *Mequetrefe* (28.1.1875), 4–5; *Mequetrefe* (10.11.1882), 4; *Mequetrefe* (20.11.1883), 4; figure 2.7; *Mequetrefe* (20.1.1887), 4–5; *RI* (11.5.1878), 4–5; "Gracejos policiaes," *O Telephone* (12.5.1878), 18-19 (quoted passage); *O Pandego* (30.4.1880), n.p. (cartoon); *RI* (7.1.1882), 4–5; *RI* (11.2.1882), 4–5; *RI* (13.1.1883), cover; *RI* (31.12.1885), betw. pp. 6 and 7; Machado de Assis, "Chave," 842 (quoted passage). On fabrics, see *GN* (4.12.1887), 6. It is also quite possible that some men went bathing in their underwear; see "Os banhos," *CS* (23.3.1871), 3.

73. See also, e.g., *RI* (13.1.1883), cover; "Os banhos," *OP* (16.2.1896), 2. On the Alcazar Theater, see Macedo, *Memorias*, 243–45.
74. Freyre, *Sobrados*, chap. 2; DaMatta, *Casa*, 33–70; Rosenthal, "Spectacle," 57; S. Graham, *House*, esp. chaps. 2–3; Needell, *Tropical Belle Époque*, 134–37; Abreu Esteves, *Meninas*, esp. chaps. 1–2; Caulfield, *In Defense*, esp. chaps. 2–4; Besse, *Restructuring*, esp. chap. 1. See also Kraay, "'Barbarous Game'"; Rago, *Prazeres*. Restrictions on women's access to public spaces were by no means unique to Brazil; see, e.g., Walkowitz, *City*; Deutsch, *Women*.
75. Schlichthorst, *Rio*, 83; Kidder and Fletcher, *Brazil*, 91. See also, e.g., Bougainville, *Journal*, 1:611; Carpenter, *Round about Rio*, 318; Andrews, *Brazil*, 34; Karasch, *Slave Life*, 59; S. Graham, *House*, 35.
76. Lenček and Bosker, *Beach*, 137–38; Corbin, *Território*, 296; Urbain, *Sur la plage*, 126; Travis, "Continuity"; A. S. Peck, *South American Tour*, 280. See also Booth, *Australian Beach Cultures*, 32–36; Fagnani, *Ciudad*, 43; Désert, *Vie*, 176.
77. *JC* (21.11.1852), 3. See also *GRJ* (19.9.1812), 4; *JC* (19.12.1848), 3; *CMe* (14.11.1863), 4; *CMe* (28.11.1863), 4; *JC* (9.10.1864), 3; *JC* (23.11.1873), 6; *JC* (30.11.1873), 4. A short-lived barge that opened in 1854 admitted only male bathers, who, nevertheless, had to wear "drawers [ceroulas]." *CMe* (15.11.1853), 2; *CMe* (5.1.1854), 1; chap. 1, n. 60. The regulations allowed slave maids (*servas*) to enter cabins with their mistresses. The maids, however, were not supposed to bathe. Other sets of regulations did not mention slaves. The barges that operated in the 1860s and 1870s offered large tubs specifically designated for "families," in which, presumably, husbands and wives could, with their children, bathe together, *CMe* (14.11.1863), 4; *JC* (9.10.1864), 3; *JC* (23.11.1873), 6.
78. I located only two references to segregation by sex at Rio's beaches, and there is much more evidence pointing to a lack of such segregation. A 1913 law allowed the municipal government to impose segregation by sex at the city's oceanfront beaches, but there is no evidence that authorities ever implemented this; see "Queixas," *OP* (31.1.1916), 6; Hermeto Lima, "O carioca e os

banhos de mar," *RS* (23.10.1926), 31; *CLMV*, 1:46. An absence of segregation by sex was also the rule at the main US seaside resorts (Sterngass, *First Resorts*, 57, 60–61, 109–10), while segregation by sex was common at US public bathing pools even though the pools were frequented mostly by children (Wiltse, *Contested Waters*, 22, 32, 48, 52, 65, 76, 78, 82).

79. Schlichthorst, *Rio*, 83. On spectators, see *CMe* (11.2.1860), 1; "Folhetim," *GB* (25.12.1881), 1; *A Vida Fluminense* (19.12.1889), cover; *RN* (12.12.1903), 5; [João do Rio], "A cidade," *GN* (24.12.1903), 2; João do Rio, "Velhos aspectos," *GN* (16.9.1904), 2; [Maciel], *Memórias*, 189.
80. "Folhetim," *GT* (26.10.1882), 1; Machado de Assis, "A chave," 842–43. See also *FL* (1859), 25; Duque, "A estética," 97; "Deu o burro," *RS* (10.5.1903), 575. But cf. Doyle, "'Salt Water,'" 94–108, esp. 99.
81. "Livro da porta," *RI* (31.1.1880), 2. See also *SI* (26.1.1868), 2972; "Carta . . . Sineiro da Sé," *Diario de Pernambuco* (3.1.1866), 8; "Decepção," *RS* (19.8.1900), 110.
82. João do Rio, "Os banhos de mar," *GN* (26.6.1911), 1; *VF* (24.2.1872), 895–96; *RN* (1.11.1899), 1; *RN* (7.1.1903), 8. See also *Mequetrefe* (30.1.1885), 8; João do Rio, "Parada." On "respectable" forms of courtship, see, e.g., T. Azevedo, *Regras*, chaps. 1–2; Martha Abreu Esteves, *Meninas*, esp. chaps. 1–2; Rosa Araújo, *Vocação*, 97–124.
83. *FL* (1888), 47 (emphasis in the original); *Mephistopheles* (26.9.1874), 4–5; *Mephistopheles* (17.10.1874), 4–5; "No Boqueirão," *O Binoculo* (22.10.1881), n.p.; *A Vida Fluminense* (19.12.1889), cover. Among *RN*'s many cartoons and short stories, see *RN* (1.11.1899), 1; "A minha francezinha," *RN* (5.4.1913), 6; "Uma aventura na praia," published in *RN* (5.9–26.9.1914. On *Rio Nú*, see C. Pereira, "Sexo."
84. "O eterno trambolho," *GN* (5.2.1918), 1; Edmundo, *Rio*, 4:837; "Queixas," *OP* (31.1.1916), 6.
85. Brand, *Journal*, 305; Bösche, "Quadros," 204–5; Ebel, *Rio*, 152; Schlichthorst, *Rio*, 83–84. On male nudity at seaside resorts in England and other parts of Europe, see Walton, *English Seaside Resort*, 193; Walvin, *Beside the Seaside*, 69–71; Lenček and Bosker, *Beach*, 84, 134; Hassan, *Seaside*, 42; Corbin, *Território*, 96; Travis, "Continuity."
86. The ordinance remained in force for the rest of the century; see *CP* (1830); *CP* (1854), 48; *CP* (1860), 46; *CP* (1870), 20; *CP* ([1889]), 49; *CP* (1894), 25.
87. *CMe* (20.1.1857), 3; *DRJ* (3–4.2.1857), 1; *CMe* (8.2.1857), 2; *CMe* (12.1.1864), 1; *JC* (16.11.1885), 1.
88. "Um banho," *OI* (27.1.1914), 6; "Em trajes de Adão," *CMa* (4.1.1915), 4; "Casos de policia," *OP* (1.3.1918), 6; "Por causa do calor," *GN* (28.1.1923), 3; Franck, *Working*, 185.

89. Karasch, *Slave Life*, 35 (on recently arrived slaves). On the police and their efforts to discipline the population, see Holloway, *Policing*; Bretas, *Guerra* and *Ordem*. Gilbero Freyre was, it seems, the first author to mention efforts to prohibit nude bathing in Brazilian cities; see *Sobrados*, 225, 420.
90. *DRJ* (27.1.1877), 2; *RI* (11.5.1878), 4–5; "Gracejos policiaes," *O Telephone* (12.5.1878), 18–19; *O Pandego* (30.4.1880), n.p. (cartoon); *RI* (7.1.1882), 4–5; *RI* (11.2.1882), 4–5; *Mequetrefe* (10.11.1882), 4; *RI* (31.12.1885), betw. pp. 6 and 7; *Mequetrefe* (20.1.1887), 4–5.
91. Luiz Barreto Corrêa de Meneses (police chief) to the Câmara Municipal. (17.9.1880), AGCRJ, cód. 43-1-8, fl. 7; Brazil, *Codigo criminal*, 333 (parte IV, cap. I, art. 280); Brazil, *Codigo penal*, 151 (liv. II, tít. VIII, cap. V, art. 282).
92. [Artur Azevedo], "De palanque," *D de Not* (1.12.1885), 1; "Canhenho," *RI* (23.12.1883), 6; *DRJ* (25.11.1877), 2; *JC* (7.11.1879), 2; *JC* (16.11.1885), 1; João do Rio, "Velhos aspectos," *GN* (16.9.1904), 2; João do Rio, "Os banhos," *GN* (26.6.1911), 1; On Senhor dos Passos Street, see Gerson, *História*, 133. According to Edmundo (*Rio*, 4:840), after seven in the morning, "the families" left Boqueirão do Passeio beach because a "*senhora de qualidade* [lady of quality]" would not appear in public alongside the "*cocottes*" and the "rowdy young men" who went bathing there after that hour. However, Artur Azevedo's observations and other sources cited in this chapter make it clear that there was no strict "family" hour at that beach.
93. *DRJ* (31.1.1872), 1; *DRJ* (9–10.12.1872), 2; *JC* (20.12.1873), 4.
94. *CMe* (1853–1862); *JC* (25.3.1861), 4; *CS* (27.10.1870), 2; *CS* (16.2.1871), 3; *CS* (23.3.1871), 3 (emphasis in the original); *GN* (25.1.1878), 1; *JC* (19.12.1879), 1; *JC* (31.1.1880), 1; *O Cruzeiro* (10.12.1882), as quoted in Renault, *Dia-a-dia*, 163–64; *DRJ* (2.20.1850); *Corsario* (18.1.1883), 2; *Gazeta Operaria* (21.2.1885), 1; *OP* (2.12.1884), 1; *GN* (26.12.1886), 2; *GN* (31.1.1893), 3; *Tagarela* (17.1.1903), 2.
95. On the incident, see *GT* (19.11.1885), 1, 2; *GT* (21.11.1885), 2; *GT* (24.11.1885), 2; *JC* (20.11.1885), 1, 2; *JC* (21.11.1885), 3, 4; *JC* (22.11.1885), 2; *JC* (23.11.1885), 3; *JC* (24.11.1885), 4; *GN* (21.11.1885), 3; *GN* (23.11.1885), 3; *OP* (20.11.1885), 2; *OP* (21.11.1885), 2; "É boa!" *Carbonario* (23.11.1885), 1; "Pequenos echos," *RI* (30.11.1885), 3; [Artur Azevedo], "De palanque," *D de Not* (1.12.1885), 1. All the quotations are from the sources cited here.
96. The subdelegado did *not*, at least in his published responses to the bathers, invoke the municipal ordinance that required all persons, while on the city's streets, to wear "decent clothing."
97. Andrews, *Brazil*, 34.
98. João do Rio, "Os banhos de mar," *GN* (26.6.1911), 1; "Bin," *GN* (14.1.1928), 5; Peregrino, "A festa," *OJ* (3.1.1930), 14, and (12.1.1930), 14; Peregrino,

"Block-Notes," *Careta* (7.3.1931), 36; R. Magalhães Junior, "As praias," *CMa* (8.11.1934), 6.

Chapter Three

1. João do Rio, "Os banhos," *GN* (26.6.1911), 1–2; "A paixão pelo mar," *RS* (11.3.1916), n.p.; "A praia maravilhosa," *OP* (22.5.1917), 3; Rodrigues, *João do Rio*, 221–22.
2. E. Silva, "Law," 451; Conrad, *Destruction*, 298.
3. Máximo, *Cinelândia*, 73–84; PCRJ, *Guia . . . Art Déco*, 29, 27–30, 32, 34–41.
4. Soares, "*Povo de Cam*," 382; Adamo, "Broken Promise," 13–19, 15–24; Fischer, *Poverty*, 51–55; Brazil, *Recenseamento* (1940), série regional, pt. 16, p. 54; Maurício Abreu, *Evolução*, 99; Brazil, IBGE, *Características*, 81–87.
5. Owensby, *Intimate Ironies*, 27; Brazil, *Recenseamento* (1960), série regional, vol. 1, t. 12, pt. 2, p. 22. By 1960, some employees of the national government had already taken up residence in Brasília, the new capital.
6. Sweigart, "Financing," 222–23; Lobo, *História*, 2:448; Welch, *Capital Markets*, 97, 104–5; Lévy, *História*; H. Melo, "Trajetória," 224; Guanabara, *Mensagem*, 59. Percentage of imports calculated from Lobo, *História*, 566–67.
7. H. Melo, "Trajetória," 225; Carone, *República*, 2:77; Hahner, *Poverty*, 194–95.
8. Thorp, "Reappraising," 184; Baer, *Brazilian Economy*, chaps. 3–6.
9. T. Jordan, "Contesting," 13–14; H. Melo, "Trajetória," 226–27.
10. H. Melo, "Trajetória," 225; Marly Motta, "Fusão," 27; T. Jordan, "Contesting," 14–15; Mauricio Abreu, *Evolução*, 125; Lessa, *Rio*, 347–48, 350, 352.
11. Hahner, *Poverty*; Meade, *"Civilizing" Rio*; T. Jordan, "Contesting"; Chalhoub, *Trabalho*; Fischer, *Poverty*; Owensby, *Intimate Ironies*.
12. Unfortunately, no study of Rio's elite after 1920 comparable to Needell's *Tropical Belle Époque* exists. The composition of the city's upper class, therefore, must be inferred from information about changes in the economy. Cf. Lemos "Posição."
13. Fischer, *Poverty*; Valladares, *Invenção*; B. McCann, *Hard Times*; Maurício Abreu, *Evolução*, 87–90, 105–8, 126–29.
14. The following discussion is based on Benchimol, *Pereira Passos*; Needell, *Tropical Belle Époque*, 33–51; Meade, *"Civilizing" Rio*, chap. 3; Hahner, *Poverty*, chap. 5; Maurício Abreu, *Evolução*, 59–67; Fischer, *Poverty*, 34–38; Chalhoub, *Cidade*, 97–185.
15. PCRJ, *Guia . . . eclética*, 31–33, 35, 40–41; M. Ferrez, G. Ferrez, and Santos, *Album*; Ermakoff, *Rio*, 220, 222–23.
16. On the housing shortage, see also L. Ribeiro, *Dos cortiços*, 169–83.

17. Sevcenko, *Revolta*; Meade, "'Civilizing' Rio de Janeiro," 311 (quotation); J. Carvalho, *Bestializados*, chap. 4; Needell, "*Revolta*," 33–69; Chalhoub, *Cidade*, 97–185.
18. In what follows, I rely primarily on Maurício Abreu, *Evolução*, 59–147; Meade, *"Civilizing" Rio*, chaps. 2–3; Fischer, *Poverty*, pts. I and IV; Cardoso, "Estrutura," 73–88; Fernandes, *Rapto*; the sources cited in table 3.1.
19. Soares, "*Povo de Cam*," 381; Brazil, *Recenseamento* (1960), vol. 1, série regional, t. 12, pp. 68–70.
20. The terms *Zona Norte* (North Zone) and *Zona Sul* (South Zone) did not come into widespread use until the mid-twentieth century; see Cardoso, "Invenção," 37–58. But because some of the social differences that they connote were already present in the first half of the century and because they are so common today, I use them here. On the Zona Norte, see Rito and Souza, eds., *Zona Norte*.
21. Lemos, "Posição," 23–26, 48; Pochmann et al., eds., *Atlas*, 3:157–59; F. Oliveira, "*Habitus*."
22. The growth of the suburbs along the railway lines is clearly shown in "Distribuição da população em 1920" and "Distribuição da população em 1960," both in Guanabara, *Mensagem . . . 1961–1965*, n.p. On Rio's suburbs, see the sources, cited above, as well as Oliveira and Fernandes, eds., *150 anos*; Maurício Abreu, *Evoluçao*, 30; Fischer, *Poverty*, 31.
23. Ralston, "Social Change," chap. 2.
24. Cardoso, "Invenção"; Lemos, "Posição," 27–35, 48–52, 58–71; Pochmann et al., eds., *Atlas*, 3:156–59.
25. [United Nations], PNUD, "Distribuição," 1–20; "Abismo crescente entre pobres e ricos," *JB** (12.10.2003); Pochmann et al., eds., *Atlas*, 2:110–19 and 3:156–59. For average incomes in 2010, see "Censo revela abismo entre bairros ricos e pobres," *OG* (17.11.2011), 15 (which cites IBGE data). On income disparities in earlier years, see, e.g., Maurício Abreu, *Evolução*, 29.
26. Brazil, *Recenseamento* (1940), série regional, pt. 16, pp. 52, 157. See also Pinto, *Negro*, chap. 3. The 1920 census did not collect information on color.
27. Maurício Abreu, *Evolução*, 82, 99–101; Hahner, *Poverty*, 194–95; Brazil, *Recenseamento* (1940), série regional, pt. 16, pp. 52, 157; Pinto, *Negro*, 134–36 and (on domestic servants) 117–19. On Afro-Brazilian women as maids in Copacabana, see also "Copacabana," *Crz* (17.11.1945), 8–13; "Dona Zezé do '33' Ministro Viveiros de Castro," *RC* (Sept. 1949), 63–65.
28. Pinto, *Negro*, 136–41 (quotation, 138), who discusses the racial composition of favela populations. On the same matter, see Fischer, *Poverty*, 4. On favelas in the Zona Sul, see Fischer, *Poverty*, 71–81, 214–301; B. McCann, *Hard Times*;

Perlman, *Myth*, 25–32, 195–240; Maurício Abreu, *Evolução*, 89–90, 105, 107, 129. More generally, see also Pochmann et al., eds., *Atlas*, 2:110–19, 3:133, 156–59.

29. Although in the past, most favelas had few, if any, paved streets or alleys, this is no longer the case in older, better-established favelas. Nevertheless, Cariocas still frequently draw a contrast between morro and asfalto.
30. Maio, "Costa Pinto," 19; Frederick Simpich, "Gigantic Brazil and Its Glittering Capital," *National Geographic* (Dec. 1930): 733; Rotherby, *South America*, 247. See also Bell, *Beautiful Rio*, 23–24. On the construction of the avenue, see PDF, *Mensagem . . . 2 de abril de 1904*, 13–14; Benchimol, *Pereira Passos*, 236–37; Kessel, *Vitrine*, 108.
31. Varias noticias," *JC* (16.4.1905), 3; João do Rio, "Velhos aspectos," *GN* (16.9.1904), 2; "Recordações do Passeio," *Malho* (14.12.1907), n.p.; "Reclamações," *CMa* (25.1.1911), 5; "Quasi morreu afogado," *GN* (25.1.1917), 2; "Os banhos de mar," *A Noite* (7.11.1911), 1.
32. Panoramic photos of Flamengo taken shortly after the opening of the Avenida Beira-Mar show absolutely no sand at that beach; see Ermakoff, *Augusto Malta*, 222. The same holds true for some later photos; see L. Vianna, *Rio*, 65, 67, 75, 77. Yet by the mid- and late 1910s a small and narrow stretch of sand existed at the southern end of Flamengo (figure 3.8).
33. "Sereias e tritões," *RS* (14.3.1914), n.p.; R. Castro, *Carmen*, 17–18; *JB* (11.1.1934), 31; *AL* (1906), 459, 2751; *AL* (1908), 654; *AL* (1910), 783; *AL* (1913), 1:981; *AL* (1921), 1887; "O eterno trambolho," *GN* (5.2.1918), 1; "O Rio precisa de banhos," *A Noite* (17.12.1912), 1; "A falta de policiamento," *A Noite* (18.2.1914), 4; "Os banhos," *A Noite* (7.12.1915), 6; "Exploração e abuso," *JB* (11.12.1919), 7. See also *ACM* (30.3–31.5.1909), 102; *ACM* (1.6–28.8.1909), 44, 56, 78, 81, 86, 96.
34. On Virtudes, see "Quando nadava," *GN* (2.12.1927), 4; "Praias," *Rio Illustrado* (Dec. 1928), 54–55; "Pereceram," *CMa* (2.1.1930), 6; "Os tradicionaes banhos," *OG* (13.1.1930), ed. das 17 horas, 1, 3; "As praias," *DN* (28.12.1931), 2; "As praias," *DN* (29.12.1931), 3; "Dois casos," *OJ* (2.1.1930), 5; "Chegou a vez," *BM* (2.1.1932), 3; "As praias," *DN* (7.1.1932), 1, 2; "As barracas," *BM* (18.7.1936), 1; Henrique Pongetti, "Carne e areia," *BM* (6.2.1937), 9; "Nosso amigo," *RS* (3.3.1945), 22. On Calabouço, see "Morreu o vigia," *JB* (31.12.1926), 21; "Escapou de afogar-se," *JB* (27.12.1932), 13; "Cc," *JB* (14.11.1934), 6; "EN: Um habito incabivel," *JB* (15.1.1927), 5. Curiously, in her "historical guide" to Rio's beaches, C. Gaspar (*Orla*, 119–281) does not mention Virtudes or Calabouço.
35. Malamud, *Recordando*, 34; AGCRJ, Icon., pasta 402, 1585/02 and 1588/17 (photos of bathers in the water near the market from the late 1910s or early

1920s). On Caju, see "Noticiario," *JB* (2.2.1917), 5; "A 'fauna' da praia do Cajú," *FF* (8.3.1924), 40; "Praias," *Rio Illustrado* (Dec. 1928), 54–55; "Taba de Anhangá," *BM* (11.1.1931), 3; "Praia do Cajú," *BM* (22.2.1931), 1.

36. "Banho fatal," *JB* (10.1.1921), 7; "Banho funesto," *OP* (5.12.1922), 6; "Supplemento suburbano," *JB* (11.12.1927), 16; "O suburbio pittoresco," *OJ* (3.1.1929), 8; "Pereceu afogado," *CMa* (16.12.1930), 8; "Quando se banhava," *JB* (3.1.1930), 9; "O policiamento nas praias," *JB* (11.1.1931), 11; "O domingo na Policia," *DN* (4.1.1932), 4; "Como se improvisa um pic-nic na Penha," *Light* (Sept. 1932), 7–8; "EN," *JB* (28.1.1934), 5; "Percorrendo as praias," *BM* (16.2.1935), 1; "Inaugurado o Balneario de Ramos," *A Noite* (6.12.1948), 9. Penha and Porto de Inhaúma no longer exist as beaches.

37. *ACM* (17 Feb.–4 March 1905), 110–11; *ACM* (17 Nov.–31 Dec. 1905), 136–37; *ACM* (30 March–31 May 1906), 78; *BIM* (July–Sept. 1906), 2.

38. PDF, *Mensagem . . . 27 de abril de 1911*, 12; *ACM* (4 Sept.–31 Oct. 1911), 139, 162–64, 185, 245; *ACM* (2 April–31 May 1912), 102–3, 147, 156; *ACM* (1 June–28 Aug. 1912), 15, 66–67, 87, 92, 160–61, 167, 194–96; *CMLV*, 1:44–45; PDF, *Mensagem . . . 2 de abril de 1913*, 8. See also "O Rio precisa de banhos," *A Noite* (17.12.1912), 1; "Quem paga os loucos?" *A Noite* (19.12.1912), 1; "EN," *A Noite* (30.12.1919), 2.

39. For a few examples, see C. Arno Gierth and J.H. Lowndes, req. (1.9.1909), AGCRJ, cód. 44-2-35; Fernando Mendes de Almeida (pres., Automóvel Club do Brasil), req. (27.2.1915), AGCRJ, ano 1915, pasta 44, doc. 2.588; Samuel Pelitzer, req. (24.3.1915), AGCRJ, ano 1915, pasta 44, doc. 2586; *ACM* (1 Nov. 1908–4 Jan. 1909), 113–14. Additional proposals were discussed in *ACM* (1909–1920).

40. PDF, *Mensagem . . . 5 de abril de 1915*, 36.

41. Boechat, *Copacabana Palace*, 22–23; MacLachlan, *History*, 59; Bartelt, *Copacabana*, 57; "Passeios pelo mirante do azul," *OG** (2.12.1999), *ZS* (which cites the "historian Milton Teixeira"); Novaes, "Cem anos," 51–52 ; A. Pinho, "Bonde"; R. Castro, *Carnaval*, 229. I examined all the editions published during Bernhardt's stay in Brazil (27.5–12.7.1886) of the following Rio periodicals: *OP*, *Gazeta de Noticias*, *Jornal do Commercio*, *A Semana*, and *Revista Illustrada*. I did not find any mention of Bernhardt and Copacabana. James Green, who has researched Bernhardt's visit to Rio, states that he also has not found references to her excursion to Copacabana; personal communication (23.5.2006). It is also hard to see how she could have shocked Carioca society by remaining on the sand after seven in the morning unless there were other people at the beach. On access to Copacabana before 1892, see San Martini ed., *Copacabana*, 28–29, 37–40.

42. Debret, *Viagem*, 2:342; M. Graham, *Journal*, 297; Schlichtorst, *Rio*, 174–75;

Landseer, *Charles Landseer*, 122; Rugendas, *Viagem*, 1:9 and plate 1/1; Kidder, *Sketches*, 2:133; Renault, *Rio*, 156–57.

43. *JC* (30.11.1878), 1; *GN* (10.11.1879), 4; *JC* (15.11.1879), 5; *JC* (6.1.1880), 4. See also Domingos José Freire (pres., Junta Central de Higiene Pública) to José Ferreira Nobre (pres., Câmara Municipal) (12.1.1884), AGCRJ, cód. 8-4-22, fol. 45; *BICM* (Jan.–March 1884), 42, 46, 61; Gerson, *História*, 317–19. See also the rather blurry 1882 sketches of Figueiredo Magalhães's "chalet" in Mendes, *América*, 21–22. Note that in the sources the doctor's surname appears as *de Figueiredo Magalhães* and not as *Figueiredo de Magalhães*, the name of the street in Copacabana that today honors him.

44. AGCRJ, cód. 55-1-2; Visconde de Lages and Francisco Teixeira de Magalhães, req. [1872], AGCRJ, cód. 43-1-8, fol. 3; *BICM* (Aug. 1872), 5; *RI* (12.1.1881), 8; "Piruetas," *RI* (19.11.1881), 6; *RI* (26.11.1881), 4–5; "Pequena Chronica," *RI* (26.11.1881), 6; *O Brazil* (6.11.1881), 5–6; Pimentel, *Sr. Ministro*; Niemeyer, *Questão*; Dunlop, *Apontamentos*, 2:61–65, 100, 105-8, 121, 123, 135–38.

45. AGCRJ, códs. 55-4-7 and 55-4-10; Dunlop, *Apontamentos*, 2:173–74, 187–89, 199–203, 233–36, 274–78, 301–2.

46. Ricardo Domingues & C., req. (1891), AGCRJ, 46-2-74, fols. 1–9; "Companhia da Cidade da Gavea: planta de uma parte da zona . . . na qual se pretende edificar importante cidade balnearia" (1891), AN, 4Y, no. 530; *GN* (19.11.1891), 3; "Cidade da Gavea," *RI* (12.1892), 6; "Cidade," *GN* (23.1.1893), 1; "Cidade," *RI* (2.1893), 3–5; "Varias noticias," *JC* (23.1893), 2.

47. Iracema, "Copacabana praia elegante," *RS* (31.10.1914), n.p.; Iracema, "A vida na praia," *RS* (21.11.1914), n.p. See also "A mesa de chá na praia," *RS* (12.12.1914), n.p.

48. "Bin," *GN* (8.2.1915), 4; "Bin," *GN* (27.2.1915), 4; "Bin," *GN* (1.3.1915), 4; Fernando Mendes de Almeida (pres., Automóvel Club do Brasil), req. (27.2.1915) and encls., AGCRJ, ano 1915, pasta 44, doc. 2.588; "Idéas," *GN* (7.3.1915), 5. See also "Bin," *GN* (8.3.1915), 4; "Bin," *GN* (11.3.1915), 4; "Copacabana," *CMa* (10.3.1915), 3; Iracema, "A vida," *RS* (27.2.1915), n.p.; "Sorrisos," *RS* (6.3.1915), n.p.; Iracema, "A vida," *RS* (20.3.1915), n.p.; "Topicos," *JC* (24.11.1914), ed. da tarde, 3; "Copacabana," *CMa* (10.3.1915), 3; Iracema, "As nossas praias," *RS* (6.1.1917), n.p.; Iracema, "O banho," *RS* (15.12.1917), n.p. The Binóculo cited here was not (Alberto) Figueiredo Pimentel, who, under the same pseudonym, wrote the *Gazeta*'s social column for many years but who died in early 1914. In the late 1920s, Waldemar Bandeira was responsible for the column; see "A morte de um jornalista," *A Noite* (6.2.1914), 1; "A cidade do amor," *FF* (3.12.1927), n.p. I have been unable to determine whether he took over the column immediately after Figueiredo Pimentel's death.

49. "Além do projecto de construcção do Automovel Club," *CMa* (13.3.1915), 3;

ACM (5 June–28 Aug. 1916), 7, 203–204, 208, 237; *ACM* (4 Sept.–31 Oct. 1916), 458; Samuel Pelitzer, req. (24.3.1915), AGCRJ, ano 1915, pasta 44, doc. 2586.

50. See the sources, cited above, and "O Rio de Janeiro não tem uma praia de banhos," *OI* (5.1.1913), 1; "Echos," *OI* (17.1.1914), 2; "Noticiario," *JB* (28.4.1914), 5; "Ns," *OI* (5.12.1915), 5; "Pé de columna," *A Noticia* (27–28.11.1916), 2; "Semana elegante," *RS* (13.10.1917); "EN," *A Noite* (19.1.1918), 2; "O que são e que é preciso que sejam as nossas praias atlanticas," *RS* (8.6.1918)," n.p.
51. PDF, *Mensagem . . . 4 de abril de 1905*, 20–21.
52. Théo-Filho, *Praia*, esp. 13, 47–48, 59, 112. On Raul Kennedy de Lemos, see Peixoto et al., *Villa Ipanema*, 202. The biographical information about Théo-Filho provided by Ruy Castro is untrustworthy; see "Prefácio" and *Ela*, 371–73. Castro states that, in 1930, Théo-Filho founded the neighborhood newspaper *Beira-Mar*, published in Copacabana, and that he wrote his last novel in 1936. On the one hand, the first edition of *Beira-Mar*, founded by Manoel Nogueira de Sá, is dated 28 Oct. 1922. Théo-Filho collaborated with the paper in the 1920s and then became its chief editor. After 1936, he published *Ao sol de Copacabana*, among other novels. On Théo-Filho and *Beira-Mar*, see Baptista, "Introdução," chap. 1, esp. 16–25; Baptista, "Rumo."
53. "Hotel Balneario da Urca," *GN* (9.1.1925), 4; PCRJ, *Urca*, 38; "Urca," *JB* (14.11.1934), 11. On Urca in the mid- and late 1920s, see M[aria] E[ugenia] C[elso], "Femina," *JB* (22.1.1926), 9; Benjamim Costallat, "Chronica," *JB* (24.1.1926), 5; "Praias do Rio," *Rio Illustrado* (Oct. 1928), 23.
54. PDF, *Mensagem . . . 1º de junho de 1922*, 26; "Interesses municipaes," *JB* (26.1.1922), 6; *BPDF* (July–Dec. 1922), 242–43; *BPDF* (Jan.–Dec. 1923), 100; "Bin," *GN* (24.1.1923), 4; *CMa* (28.1.1923), 8; *BM* (4.1.1923), 8; *BPDF* (Jan.–June 1924), 243–45. With one exception, the last references to the cabanas that I located date from 1930: *BPDF* (July–Dec. 1930), n.p. ("Directoria de Estatistica e Archivo: Casas commerciaes licenciadas . . . 1928"); PDF, *Mensagem . . . 1º de junho de 1930*, 408. The one exception is a short excerpt from a novel published in *Beira-Mar* in 1931: Celestino Silveira, "Os intoxicados," *BM* (15.8.1931), 6. Presumably, the author wrote the novel before the cabanas were closed. I was unable to locate a copy of the novel or even to determine whether it was ever published. By contrast, repeated references to the restaurant appear in sources dated after 1930.
55. On the hotel, see Boechat, *Copacabana Palace*; Nina, "Jorge Guinle," 39–45; Guinle with Silva, *Século*, esp. chap. 6. The original plans for the hotel included the construction of 250 cabanas, but only a handful were ever built. "O deslumbramento," *A Noite* (18.8.1923), 7; "EN: As praias de banho," *JB* (22.12.1928), 5. In 1935, a second casino opened in Copacabana, the Cassino

Atlântico; see "Inaugurou-se," *BM* (23.3.1935), 3. Both were closed in 1946 when the government banned gambling.

56. *South American Handbook* (1925–1941); Orazi, *Rio*, 124–25; Orazi, *Rio . . . arredores*, 124–25. See also "'Beira-Mar' visita os hoteis de Copacabana," *BM* (21.9.1930), 1; "Hoteis de Copacabana," *BM* (5.5.1934), 10; "Hoteis de Copacabana," *BM* (19.5.1934), 2; "Movimento dos hoteis em Copacabana," *BM* (28.7.1934), 8. In 1938, the district of Copacabana (which, at the time, included Ipanema) had twelve hotels with a total of 720 rooms; see Brazil, IBGE, *Anuário*, 362.
57. On this matter, see Iracema, "O banho no Flamengo," *RS* (15.12.1917), n.p.; "Nossas praias," *Crz* (15.12.1928), 2; "Balnearios," *OJ* (19.12.1926), 2ª seção, 6; "O maior derivativo," *OJ* (15.1.1930), 3.
58. "EN: Visita," *JB* (8.11.1928), 12; "O maior derivativo," *OJ* (15.1.1930), 3. See also, e.g., "Turista," *OJ* (29.1.1928), 4; "Num cruzeiro," *CMa* (25.1.1934), 5; "Visita," *CMa* (17.1.1935), 5.
59. Scattered references in the sources suggest that, though not especially numerous, Argentines formed the largest single group of foreign tourists in the interwar years. See, e.g., "O Rio o maior centro," *A Noite* (6.1.1922), 2; "As possibilidades do Brasil," *Crz* (3.10.1931), 3; "Copacabana-Palace-Hotel," *FF* (25.12.1925), n.p.; Hudson, *South by Thunderbird*, 323.
60. Brazil, IBGE, *Anuário*, 363; Hassan, *Seaside*, 263–64.
61. Barickman, "Not Many Flew," 232.
62. Brazil, IBGE, *Anuário*, 363; "Num cruzeiro," *CMa* (25.1.1934), 5; Touring Club of Brazil, *Rio*; PDF, *Anuário . . . 1941*, 476.
63. See, e.g., Kane, *South America*, 115; "The People of Rio," *Look* (4.6.1963), 54–64; "A Glance Over the Carioca Beaches," *Jornal de Turismo* (20.2–20.3.1967), 1; "Eu disse 'Calma' . . . I said, 'Be Calm,'" *Jornal de Turismo* (20.2–19.3.1968), 1; Fodor, ed., *Fodor's Guide*, 470, 472–74, 498, 504; Botting and the Editors of Time-Life Books, *Rio*, 120–31; Goslin, *Rau tchu bi a carioca*, 46–47, 81–95; Pickard, *Rio*, F9–F13; Camus and Manoncourt, *Brésil*, 81–86; Taylor, ed., *Insight Guides*, 41–47 and passim. Ipacom Travel, *Insider's Guide*; R. Castro, *Carnaval*, 227–53. See also "Os turistas e as praias," *BM* (17.9.1938), 1.
64. See, e.g., Reid, *Seeing South America*, 39–41; "Aunt Jessie's Chat," *Cidade Maravilhosa* (Sept.–Oct. 1936), 44–45; "Praias cariocas," *Cidade Maravilhosa* (Sept.–Oct. 1936), 38–39; Gibson, *Rio*, 8–10; "Copacabana," *Guanabara—The Tourist's Magazine* (Summer 1939), 18–19; Brazil, Department of Press and Propaganda, *Rio*.
65. C. Castro, "Narrativas"; Perrotta, "Desenhando"; Freire-Medeiros and Castro, *Destino*, 3–19. For an example of a map of the type described by Castro, see Arthur Duarte Ribeiro, "Planta informativa da cidade do Rio de Janeiro,

especialmente organisada para o Guide Briguiet" (1929), BN, Cartografia, ARC 25.6.7.

66. Dec. 3816 (March 1932), typed copy (1940), in AGCRJ, FDP, HD, cx 172; "A 1ª temporada," *CMa* (10.1.1932), 10; "As possibilidades," *Crz* (3.10.1931), 3. See also "As questões," *OP* (11.11.1922), 3, which describes Rio as "above all else a winter city"; "O nosso turismo e o inverno," *JB* (23.11.1926), 6; "Visita," *CMa* (17.1.1935), 5. On early official efforts to promote tourism, see *BPDF* (July–Dec. 1927), 128–29; *BPDF* (Jan.–June 1928), 6; PDF, *Mensagem . . . 1º de junho de 1930*, 8–9, 453–56; *BPDF* (April–June 1934), 120–21; PDF, *Mensagem . . . 3 de maio de 1936*, 7.
67. Brazilian Representation, *Travel*, 17–33, 87, 116, 127, 153–54, 163. The book does, it is true, mention in passing Rio's "superb beaches" (5) in its preface and does include a photograph of the Copacabana Palace Hotel (33). However, from the photo, no one unfamiliar with Rio would know that it was a beachfront hotel. By contrast, it includes photos of the beaches in Santos and Guarujá, which were and are seaside resorts (56–57).
68. Frederick Simpich, "Gigantic Brazil and Its Glittering Capital," *National Geographic* (Dec. 1930): 732–78 (reference to bathing, 776); W. Robert Moore, "Rio Panorama," *National Geographic* (Sept 1939): 283–324 (photos, plates VII and XIX; discussion of beach-going, 290, 299).
69. Freeland, dir., *Flying Down to Rio*; Hitchcock, dir., *Notorious*. Note that both films include locally filmed establishing shots and that most of the scenes showing Rio's beaches in *Flying* are shot from the air. There is more than one possible explanation for why the beach as shown in *Notorious* is entirely empty. It may have been shot during hours in which bathing was prohibited. Or it could have been filmed on a cold, though sunny, day. *Notorious* also includes background shots of Copacabana's beach at night. On the two films, see Freire-Medeiros, *Rio*, 11–17; Amancio, *Brasil*, 51–52, 67–68. On the first film, see also Schwartz, *Flying Down*, esp. 7–19.
70. Barickman, "Not Many Flew," 235–37.
71. "A Cidade de Copacabana I," *Crz* (15.1.1949), 13, 16. See also Henrique Pongetti, "O oceano onírico," *Manchete* (12.1.1957), 3; Lessa, *Rio*, 245–46; S. Kaz, *Jeito*; S. Pereira, "Anos." The statement about nationally circulating magazines is based on an examination of various periodicals, including *Careta*, *Revista da Semana*, *Fon-Fon!*, *O Cruzeiro*, and *Manchete*.
72. Tad Szulc, "Rio Sight-seeing Still on a Do-It-Yourself Basis," *New York Times* (11.11.1956), X21; "O Rio não está capacitado," *JB* (14.1.1968), 26.
73. My discussion of the magazines draws on Mauad, "Sob o signo," esp. chap. 4; Oliveira, Velloso, and Lins, eds., *Moderno*.
74. Mauad, "Sob o signo," 34 and 340–63. The term *footing*, borrowed from

English by way of French, was used at the time. On the footing in Flamengo, see the sources cited below.

75. The statements in the text are based on an examination of all the available editions of *Careta* and the *Revista da Semana* for the months November through March, from January 1910 to December 1920.

76. Iracema, "O banho no Flamengo," *RS* (15.12.1917), n.p.; "Bin," *GN* (7.11.1920), 4; "Bin," *GN* (11.1.1923), 6; "Bin," *GN* (16.12.1917), 6; "Bin," *GN* (27.1.1918), 6; "Bin," *GN* (31.1.1918), 6; "Bin," *GN* (10.11.1920); "Bin," *GN* (5.12.1920), 4; "Bin," *GN* (22.1.1922), 7. See also, e.g., "Nem nas praias," *A Noite* (15.1.1915), 4; "As praias cariocas: Flamengo," *Selecta* (20.1.1917), n.p.; "Um sorriso para todas," *Careta* (3.1.1920), n.p.; "No Flamengo: o 'footing' e o banho de mar," *FF* (21.1.1922), n.p.; "Manhãs e tardes de verão," *Malho* (6.2.1923), n.p.

77. "Vida elegante," *Careta* (25.12.1915), n.p.; "Os costumes novos," *PT* (25.1.1919), 12; "Aspectos do Rio: no Flamengo," *RS* (5.1.1918), n.p (figure 3.8). See also "EN," *A Noite* (30.12.1919), 2; "No Flamengo: o 'footing' e o banho de mar," *FF* (21.1.1922), n.p. On the footing in Flamengo, see, e.g., Iracema, "A vida," *RS* (21.11.1914), n.p.; "A semana elegante,"*RS* (4.12.1915), n.p.; "Bric-à-brac," *Cta* (22.1.1916), n.p.; "Notas e comentarios," *RS* (9.12.1916), n.p.; "Bin," *GN* (15.1.1917), 3; "Bin," *GN* (15.12.1919), 4; "Bin," *GN* (20.12.1921), 4. On "doing the Avenue" and published photos of women, see also Bell, *Beautiful Rio*, 22, 192. On promenading more generally, see, e.g., Scobey, "Anatomy."

78. "Galeria," *RS* (19.12.1916), n.p. On Carmen Lydia, see "As interessantes provas," *GN* (20.12.1915), 3; "Uma nadadora," *RS* (1.1.1916), n.p.; "Carmen," *Careta* (5.2.1916), n.p.; "Carmen," *RS* (19.2.1916), n.p.; "Ns," *Imp* (10.2.1916), 6. See also "Um grande escandalo," *GN* (19.1.1917), 3; "Ns," *OI* (11.1.1917), 8; "Uma nota," *A Noite* (18.1.1917), 1. In some of these sources, Carmen Lydia appears as Carmen Sylvia. On Kellerman, see Lenček and Bosker, *Making Waves*, 36.

79. "Ns," *OI* (23.12.1913), 6; "Ns," *OI* (24.11.1914), 6; "Quando teremos?" *A Rua* (30.1.1915), clipping attached to petition of Automovel Club do Brasil (27.2.1915), AGCRJ, pasta 44, doc. 2.588; Iracema, "Vida," *RS* (27.2.1915), n.p.; Iracema, "O banho," *RS* (15.12.1917), n.p.; "T&N," *CMa* (26.1.1915), 2; "Artes," *Careta* (30.1.1915), n.p.; "Bin," *GN* (1.3.1915), 4; "As praias," *A Noite* (28.1.1916), 2; "Ns," *OI* (31.1.1916), 5; "Noticias," *RS* (27.1.1917), n.p. and (10.3.1917), n.p.; "Ns," *OI* (26.11.1917), 6; "Vida," *OP* (3.3.1918), 2; "O Rio cidade," *RS* (9.3.1918), n.p.; AGCRJ, ano 1915, pasta 44, doc. 2.588. See also "Ns," *OI* (23.12.1913), 6; "Topicos," *JC* (23.11.1914), afternoon ed., 3; *JC* (24.11.1914), afternoon ed., 3; João do Rio, *Crónicas*, 84–85; "Uma reclamação," *A Noite* (22.1.1916), 4.

80. A. S. Peck, *South American Tour*, 313; Cooper, *Brazilians*, 128.

81. "Policia," *JC* (14.3.1917), 3, (21.3.1917), 3, (23.3.1917), 4; "P&R," *CMa* (14.3.1917), 1; "Os abusos," *GN* (14.3.1917), 3; "Pela decencia!" *A Noite*

(14.3.1917), 3; "Os rowers," *OI* (14.3.1917), 10; "Ns," *OI* (15.3.1917), 8; "Ainda," *JB* (23.3.1917), 8; "Noticiario," *JB* (25.3.1917), 5; "Policia de costumes," *Malho* (26.3.1917), n.p.; "Os taes," *JB* (26.3.1917), 8; Bretas, *Ordem*, 139. On the Spanish flu, which struck some 66,000 Cariocas or 5.7 percent of the population, and killed about 15,000, see Goulart, "Revisitando," 105.

82. "A vida elegante," *Careta* (16.1.1915), n.p.
83. Burke and Staples Jr., *Business*, 40.
84. Hahner, *Poverty*, 194, 168–69; Ribeiro, *Dos cortiços*, 186–93; "Bin," *GN* (7.11.1920), 4; "Bin," *GN* (11.1.1923), 6; "Bin," *GN* (26.1.1922), 4; "Bin," *GN* (5.2.1922), 4.

Chapter Four

1. Caufield, *In Defense*, 48–79, esp. 51; Baptista, "Tem rei." For press coverage of the king's excursions to Copacabana, see, e.g., *CMa*, *GN*, *OP*, and *JB* for 21 Sept.–16 Oct. 1920, as well as "Os banhos de el-Rey," *D. Quixote* (13.10.1920), n.p.; "O rei sportsman," *RS* (2.10.1920), n.p.
2. "O Principe de Galles e o Principe Jorge," *CMa* (9.4.1931), 1; "Prince George," *New York Times* (10.4.1931), 27; "Os principes inglezes," *CMa* (7.4.1931), 1; "A visita," *JC* (7.4.1931), 4; "Realizou-se hontem," *CMa* (27.3.1931), 1; "Welcome!" *BM* (5.4.1931), 10.
3. The local government artificially widened Copacabana's beach in 1969–72, but as is evident in numerous photographs, even before the widening, it was much broader than any of the main bayshore beaches at the time.
4. *BICM* (June 1874), 5; Alexandre Speltz, "Nova planta indicadora da cidade do Rio de Janeiro" (1877), BN, Cartografia, ARC 012.09.008; Cardoso et al., *História*, 34–40; Berger, "História," 71–91. See also O'Donnell, "Rio," 37; "Praia de Copacabana, 1880," AGCRJ, Icon., pasta 930B, 5925; G. Ferrez, *Photography*, 83. I have borrowed the expression "an immense expanse of sand [*um imenso areal*]" from Eneida, "Introdução," 5. On the tunnel, see AGCRJ, 50-3-45; Berger, "História," 64–65.
5. Berger, "História," 67–68 and photo between 56 and 57 (which shows an original ticket stub with one of the verses); Dunlop, *Apontamentos*, 2:302–3. *O Copacabana* regularly reprinted the verses between 1907 and 1912.
6. Dunlop, *Apontamentos*, 2:301–2; San Martini, ed., *Copacabana*, 54; *Copacabana* (15.6.1907), 4; Efegê, "Mère Louise"; *Copacabana* (1.7.1907), 3; *Copacabana* (15.6.1907), 4; *Copacabana* (1.7.1907), 4. By 1901, a restaurant had also opened in Ipanema; see *RS* (17.11.1901), 653. Théo-Filho describes the functioning of Copacabana's early pensions through the fictional example of the Pensão das Janelas Verdes in *Ao sol*, 9–22. By 1912, Copacabana boasted

at least one establishment that called itself a hotel: the Hotel Miramar e Babilônia; see *Copacabana* (13.10.1912), 2. Ipanema had such an establishment as early as 1907, *Copacabana* (1.7.1907), 4.

7. [João do Rio], "A cidade," *GN* (6.12.1903), 2; "Impressões," *Copacabana* (1.7.1907), 3; "Passeiando," *Copacabana* (3.5.1908), 1; "O verão," *Copacabana* (19.2.1911), 1; "Copacabana," *Copacabana* (4.2.1912), 1; "Ns," *OI* (9.2.1913), 7; "Ns," *OI* (13.1.1914), 9; Chrysanthème, "Palestra," *OP* (11.11.1915), 3; "Notas e commentarios," *RS* (22.1.1916), n.p.; João do Rio, *Crónicas*, 79–88; "As nossas praias," *RS* (19.2.1916), n.p.; "Do Leme a Copacabana," *RS* (31.3.1917), n.p.; "Bin," *GN* (3.1.1918), 6; "O verão á beira-mar," *Malho* (2.2.1919), n.p.; "Bin," *GN* (5.1.1922), 4.
8. "No Leme," *FF* (25.12.1914), n.p.; "Trepações," *FF* (9.1.1915), n.p.; "Trepações," *FF* (6.3.1915), n.p.; "Trepações," *FF* (13.3.1915), n.p.; "Trepações," *FF* (9.3.1912), n.p.; "Trepações," *FF* (25.12.1914), n.p.; "Trepações," *FF* (27.2.1915), n.p.; "O Rio noctívago," *RS* (27.1.1912), n.p; "Felizes," *PT* (15.3.1924), 17.
9. E. Oliveira, *Fossas*, 6; Dunlop, *Apontamentos*, 2:276n14.
10. Fernandes, *Rapto*, esp. 56–64, 109–19, 135–41; El-Kareh, "Quando os subúrbios."
11. *ACM* (29 Aug.–30 Oct. 1894), 193; *BIM* (April–June 1898), 9; *ACM* (18–25 Feb. 1899 and 28 Feb.–29 April 1899), 82, 92; *BIM* (Oct.–Dec. 1902), 19. See also O'Donnell, *A invenção*, 50–51.
12. E. Oliveira, *Fossas*, 6; "O dia," *OP* (13.4.1905), 2. On the early growth of favelas in Copacabana, see "No Morro," *CMa* (2.6.1907), 1, 2; "A Babylonia," *A Noite* (25.12.1911), 1; Fischer, *Poverty*, 241–43.
13. PDF [Francisco Pereira Passos], *Mensagem . . . 4 de abril de 1905*, 20–21; *BIM* (July–Sept. 1905), 3; PDF [Francisco Pereira Passos], *Mensagem . . . 5 de setembro de 1906*, 27. On the sidewalk's pattern as a well-known symbol of Copacabana, see S. Kaz, "Jeito," 206–10, 218–29.
14. These statements are based on an examination of all available editions of *Copacabana* and *Beira-Mar*. On *Copacabana*, see O'Donnell, *Invenção*, 70–80, and "Rio," 81–95. According to O'Donnell, the paper ceased publication in 1919; see "Rio," 82, n. 24. In February 1908, the paper adopted the name *Copacabana—O Novo Rio. Beira-Mar*, a publication with serious journalistic and literary pretensions, was founded in 1922 by M. N. de Sá, the owner of a grocery store in Copacabana. *Beira-Mar*, in contrast with its predecessor, defined its area of interest as embracing not only Copacabana and Leme, but also Ipanema and, later, Leblon as well. On *Beira-Mar*, see Baptista, "Rumo."
15. *Copacabana* (16.4.1908), 3.
16. See the photographs reproduced in Ermakoff, *Augusto Malta*, 235, 236–39, and *Rio de Janeiro*, 98–99, 101–2; C. Gaspar, *Orla*, 211; as well as those from

1916 to 1923 in L. Vianna, *Rio de Janeiro*, 91, 93, 95, 99, 101, 103, 105, 107, 109, 111.

17. *ACM* (7 Jan.–28 March 1914), 47; *ACM* (2 April–30 May 1914), 173, 177; Brazil, *Recenseamento* (1920), vol. 5, pt. 1, pp. 6–7.
18. Brazil, *Recenseamento* (1940), vol. 1, série regional, pt. 16, p. 51.
19. These statements are based on an examination of all available editions of *O Copacabana* and *Beira-Mar*. See also O'Donnell, "Rio," 89–90; Baptista, "Rumo," 89–93.
20. [Afonso Henrique de] Lima Barreto, "O prefeito e o povo" (1921), in *Toda crônica*, 2:294–95; Maurício Abreu, *Evolução*, 74–79; Cardoso et al., *História*, 44–52; Meade, *"Civilizing" Rio*, 80–81, 175; Kessel, *Vitrine*, 15, 17–18, 53–56; Fischer, *Poverty*, 26–32; Berger, "História," 25; Ermakoff, *Augusto Malta*, 244; S. Garcia, *Rio*, 106–7; C. Gaspar, *Orla*, 252. An official map shows that most streets in Leblon were, as late as 1928, still merely planned and had not yet been opened; see PDF, Directoria Geral de Obras e Viação, *Planta da cidade do Rio de Janeiro. . .*, *AG*CRJ, Icon., 2/7/4: a, b.
21. The data presented in this and the following paragraph are found in Brazil, Ministerio do Trabalho, Commercio e Industria, *Estatistica predial*, 222–29 (data for Copacabana); Fischer, *Poverty*, 31 (data for all other districts).
22. Brazil, *Recenseamento* (1940), vol. 1, série regional, pt. 16, p. 51.
23. See the collection of Malta photographs in the Museu da Imagem e do Som.
24. Mesquita, *De Copacabana*, 80–83, 88, 92–93, 99, 116, 133–34; Ângela Porto, personal communication (24.3.2015); photo of Sérgio and his brother sitting on the front wall of the family's house (c. 1930), private collection of Ângela Porto; José Raimundo Vergolino, personal communication (29.3.2015). See also Sérgio Porto's nostalgic memoir of his childhood and early adolescence, *Casa*. On bungalows in Copacabama, see Cardoso et al., *História*, 169–71; O'Donnell, *Invenção*, 169–73.
25. On the Guinles, see Needell, *Tropical Belle Époque*, 99–100, 102–3, 111; Guinle with Silva, *Século*.
26. The 1940 census does not allow for an accurate estimate of the number of domestic servants who worked and lived in Copacabana because it included them in a broader category, "domestic employment [and] school activities"; see Brazil, *Recenseamento* (1940), vol. 1, série regional, pt. 16, p. 59.
27. On local businesses in Copacabana, see Cardoso et al., *História*, 84–85. Reports on drownings and near drownings sometimes supply the names and addresses of service workers and domestic servants; see, e.g., "Quando se banhava," *JB* (20.1.1925), 12; "Pereceu," *GN* (27.11.1925), 4; "Quando se banhava," *GN* (22.12.1925), 4; "Pereceu," *BM* (7.3.1926), 4; "Ia morrendo," *BM* (4.4.1926), 3.

28. On the growth of favelas in Copacabana, Ipanema, and Leblon, see "Morar de graça," *OI* (20.1.1920), 1; "Morar de graça," *D. Quixote* (28.1.1920), n.p.; "As chagas," *BM* (4.10.1925), 1, See also Cardoso et al., *História*, 172–76; Fischer, *Poverty*, 243–46.
29. Ministerio do Trabalho, Commercio e Industria, *Estatistica*, 222–29. See also "Palacios e cortiços," *D de N* (2.12.1934), 8; "Ainda existem barracões," *BM* (29.1.1938), 1. All of the houses located in avenidas in Copacabana were, according to the 1933 survey, built of brick and mortar. On avenidas, see F. Veríssimo and Bittar, *500 anos*, 27; Hahner, *Poverty*, 166.
30. *Nossa Sociedade*, 9–147. On Copacabana as an elite neighborhood, see also, e.g., Lemos, "Posição social," 49–51.
31. "As grandes iniciativas," *BM* (28.10.1923), 4. On the use of reinforced concrete, see O'Donnell, *Invenção*, 196; Maurício Abreu, *Evolução*, 112. On the early history of the apartment building in Rio, see Vaz, *Modernidade*. On the law, see Ribeiro, *Dos cortiços*, chap. 7; Freeman, "Face to Face," 104–5.
32. Ministerio do Trabalho, Industria e Commercio, *Estatistica*, 222–29.
33. "O Rio," *CMa* (20.1.1937), sup., 3; Vaz, *Modernidade*, 77–83, esp. 77. On apartment buildings in Copacabana in the 1930s, see also "Copacabana!" *BM* (27.4.1930), 6; "Copacabana!" *BM* (11.5.1930), 7; "O Leme," *BM* (8.8.1931), 1; O'Donnell, *Invenção*, 195–210; Cardoso et al., *História*, 158–69; Baptista, "Introdução," chap. 4.
34. *CMa* (12.11.1944), 23. On doorways and foyers, see Vaz, *Modernidade*, 136; Cardoso et al., *História*, 106, 181; PCRJ, *Guia . . . Art Déco*, 74, 82. 84–85.
35. Franck, *Rediscovering South America*, 331, 368; "Copacabana," *JB* (22.12.1942), 5; "Copacabana," *Crz* (17.11.1945), 10; E. Veríssimo, "Passeios por aí" (1945), in *Rio de Janeiro*, 71; "Cidade de Copacabana II," *Crz* (22.1.1949), 15; Ribeiro, *Dos cortiços*, 268, 268 n.17. On European refugees, see, e.g., Lesser, *Welcoming the Undesirables*; Koifman, *Quixote*.
36. Freeman, "Face to Face," 104–5; Ribeiro, *Dos cortiços*, 276.
37. See, e.g., *CMa* (16.1.1944), 25; *CMa* (23.1.1944), 19; *CMa* (14.1.1945), 25.
38. With a good dose of nostalgia for Copacabana in the 1920s, Théo-Filho, the long-time editor of *Beira-Mar*, chronicles the neighborhood's rapid growth and transformation between the mid-1910s and the mid-1940s in his 1948 novel *Ao sol*. See also Pôrto, *Casa*.
39. PCRJ, *Guia . . . Art Déco*, 72–98; Cardoso et al., *História*, 181–82. Population density calculated from the 1920 and 1940 censuses, cited above, and the district's area (8.0183 square kilometers), PDF [Alfred Agache], *Cidade*, 98.
40. "O banho de sol," *Illustração Brasileira* (Feb. 1925), n.p.
41. See, e.g., *CMa* (5.1.1915), 5; *CMa* (8.12.1927), 14; *JB* (11.1.1934), 31; *CMa*

(19.11.1944), 11; *JB* (12.12.1954), 13; See also Bilac et al., *Brésil*, 194; E. Oliveira, *Fossas*, 6; "Pró Copacabana," *Copacabana* (11.4.1909), 1.

42. Meireles, *Rute*.
43. Editors' note: This is an issue that Barickman intended to examine at length in the chapter projected to appear between this and the next chapter.
44. Wolfe, *Autos*, 14–15, 24–25; "Directoria de Estatistica. . .: Automoveis licenciados, 1903 e 1924," in *BPDF* (July–Dec. 1925), n.p.
45. Wolfe, *Autos*, 64–65; Downes, "Autos," 570–71; "Directoria de Estatistica. . .: Automoveis licenciados, 1903 e 1924," in *BPDF* (July–Dec. 1925), n.p.; PDF, Secretaria do Prefeito, Departamento de Geografia e Estatística, *Anuário Estatístico . . . 1941*, 194.
46. José Antônio José [João do Rio], "A paixão pelo mar," *RS* (11.3.1916), n.p.
47. *BPDF* (Oct.–Dec. 1915), 60; Wolfe, *Autos*, 21–22 (on the employment of chauffeurs); José Antônio José [João do Rio], "A paixão pelo mar," *RS* (11.3.1916), n.p.; "Pela moralidade," *GN* (26.11.1927), 1; Alvaro de Penalva, "Pela rama," *GN* (26.11.1927), 2.
48. *Guia official do trafego*; *Código nacional de trânsito* (1947) (which reprints the 1941 code); *Código nacional de trânsito: decreto-lei no. 3651*; *Código nacional de trânsito* (1980) (which reprints the 1972 code). The 1934, 1941, 1956, and 1972 traffic codes, it should be pointed out, did not include any dress requirements for private motorists, which seem to have been imposed by the police. The 1972 code did prohibit driving barefoot. Otherwise, the codes included requirements only about the dress of drivers of "collective vehicles" (i.e., buses and trams), which also, presumably, applied to taxi drivers. Yet, numerous Brazilian acquaintances have told me that they understood that, in the case of men, driving without a shirt violated the law. In 1969, the *Jornal do Brasil* pointed out that, even though the then-current code did not include any prohibition against shirtless driving, the police had imposed that prohibition; see "Código não exige," *JB* (9.1.969), 5.
49. "Carta de mulher," *Crz* (15.12.1928), 24; "Um passeio," *BM* (11.4.1929), 1; Edschmid, *South America*, 345; "Ns," *JB* (30.11.1932), 12; Peregrino, "Um sorriso," *Careta* (16.11.1935), 28–29; Hoffmann-Harnisch, *Brasil*, 21.
50. "Para a condução," *BM* (7.5.1932), 1; "Os intoxicados," *BM* (15.8.1931), 6; Nohara, *Brasilien*, 129. As early as 1915, *Careta* published a photo showing women in bathing attire entering a taxi in Flamengo; see "O banho de mar," *Careta* (30.1.1915), n.p. On the number of taxis, see "Directoria de Estatistica. . .: Automoveis licenciados, 1903 e 1924," in *BPDF* (July–Dec. 1925), n.p.; PDF, *Anuário . . . 1941*, 194.
51. Wolfe, *Autos*, 107–9; Joel Wolfe, personal communication (4.4.2012); PDF,

Secretaria Geral do Interior e Segurança, Departamento de Geografia e Estatística, *Anuário Estatístico . . . 1947*, 2:49.

52. PDF, Secretaria Geral do Interior e Segurança Pública, Departamento de Geografia e Estatística, *Anuário Estatístico . . . 1950*, 2:62. On car ownership by class, see Owensby, *Intimate Ironies*, 115.

53. See, e.g., "Carioca," *JB* (8.1.1969), 3; "Rio Makes Life-Saving Gain," *New York Times* (7.9.1958), 120.

54. "O banho no Flamengo," *RS* (16.12.1916), s.n.; "O horrivel desastre," *A Noite* (9.12.1912), 2. The second society incorporated in its name the French term *sauvetage* (lifesaving), often used in local sources well into the 1920s. On rescues by fishermen, see the sources cited below.

55. "Ultimo banho!" *CMa* (26.3.1911), 2–3; "Uma grande desgraça," *OP* (26.3.1911), 3; "Ainda a tragedia," *CMa* (27.3.1911), 3; "Sinistra catástrofe," *Copacabana* (15.4.1911), 1; "Postos," *Copacabana* (5.11.1911), 1.

56. *CLMV*, 1:45–46; PDF [Rivadavia da Cunha Correia], *Mensagem . . . 3 de abril de 1916*, 17; PDF [A.A. de Azevedo Sodré], *Mensagem . . . 4 de setembro de 1916*, 97; "O serviço," *OI* (27.1.1916), 6; C. Gaspar, *Orla*, 47; Baptista, "Rumo," 178; O'Donnell, *Invenção*, 103; Disitzer, *Mergulho*, 42–43. Not taking into account the 1913 legislation, all these sources assert that Rio's municipal lifesaving service was created in 1917.

57. See, e.g., "Quasi afogado," *JB* (12.1.1914), 4; "Tres vidas," *GN* (13.12.1914), 7; "Notas e Noticias," *GN* (14.12.1914), 1; "Ultimo banho," *JB* (13.12.1914), 13; "O triste espectaculo," *OI* (13.12.1914), 6.

58. "Na voragem," *A Noite* (1.3.1917), 2; "A tragica morte," *GN* (2.3.1917), 1; "O dr. Mauricio França," *CMa* (2.3.1917), 3; "O sorvedouro," *CMa* (3.3.1917), 3; "Varias noticias," *JC* (2.3.1917), 4; "Na praia," *OI* (2.3.1917), 3; "O lamentável desastre," *OI* (4.3.1917), 3; "Mais uma victima, " *OP* (2.3.1917), 4.

59. "Echos e Factos: Providencias," *OP* (2.3.1917), 1; "Varias noticias," *JB* (2.3.1917), 4; "T & N," *CMa* (4.3.1917), 1; *CLMV*, 1:46–47; Amaro Cavalcanti (pref.) to the Chefe de Polícia (31.5.1917), AN, IJ^6 617; "Inauguram-se hoje," *A Noite* (1.6.1917), 1; "A 'sauvetage,'" *GN* (2.6.1917), 3; "Copacabana," *CMa* (2.6.1917), 3; "Para maior segurança . . . : A installação de telephones," *BM* (27.2.1932), 1; PDF [Carlos Cesar de Oliveira Sampaio], *Mensagem . . . 1922*, 26, 95; "No Posto," *BM* (24.4.1928), 1; "O 'Dia do Banhista,'" *CMa* (27.12.1936), sup., 9, 11.

60. The available sources sometimes make it difficult to trace with precision the expansion of the lifesaving posts at Rio's oceanfront beaches. Cf. "A victima," *BM* (21.1.1923), 1; "Foram inaugurados," *BM* (22.6.1930), 1; "Vae de vento em pôpa," *BM* (20.3.1937), 1; "Foi inaugurado," *BM* (25.1.1936), 1. On Post 0, see "O famoso Posto 2," *BM* (15.2.1936), 3; "Serão finalmente inauguradas," *BM*

(7.3.1936), 3. Post 2½ already existed by 1930. See "Sob o esplendor," *CMa* (21.1.1930), 3; "Bazar," *DN* (14.12.1931), 4. On the establishment of lifeguard posts at bayshore beaches, see "Para proteger," *BM* (27.2.1937), 2; "O banho," *RS* (27.2.1937), 34; "Inaugurado," *BM* (6.3.1937), 3. A post was operating in Flamengo by late 1939; see "Os que iam perecendo," *JB* (7.11.1939), 10.

61. PDF [Antonio Prado Junior], *Mensagem . . . 1º de junho de 1929*, 254; "O 'Dia do Banhista,'" *CMa* (27.12.1936), sup., 9, 11; "Ainda bem!" *BM* (14.9.1935), 1; "Até que enfim!" *BM* (18.1.1936), 1; "Notas de modernismo," *BM* (25.1.1936), 1; "Os postos," *BM* (8.8.1936), 1; "As torres," *BM* (6.2.1937), 3; "Curso de botinho," *CMa* (3.1.1968), 9; "Salva-vidas," *CMa* (30.1.1968), 3; "Praias ganham novos postos," *OG* (16.4.1978), 15; "Trânsito atrasa," *JB* (19.11.1979), 16. Le Corbusier visited Rio in 1936 and thus may have seen some of the first new art deco observation towers; see Durand, "Negociação."

62. Leme is the exception because that area of the beachfront neighborhood already had a name before the construction of the posts, and it has always been known as Leme rather than as Post 1.

63. *Instrucções para o uso dos banhos de mar nas praias do Leme e de Copacabana* (May 1917), copies of which can be found enclosed in Amaro Cavalcanti (pref.) to the Chefe de Polícia (31.5.1917) and in Paulino Werneck (Diretor de Higiene e Assistência Pública) to the Chefe de Polícia (12.9.1917), both in AN, IJ^6 617. Some of Rio's major papers also reprinted the instructions in their editions for 2 June 1917. For the May 1917 decree, see *CLMV*, 1:46–47. On the organization of the lifesaving service, see also *CMLV*, 2:262–64. Neither the instructions nor the decree specifies the length of the stretch of beach that corresponded to a post at the time. But that information can be found in "Copacabana," *CMa* (2.6.1917), 3. O'Donnell (*Invenção*, 103) claims that the May 1917 decree required bathers on their way to and from the beach to wear robes or, in the case of men, at least sport coats. The police in later years would impose that requirement (chap. 5). But neither the decree nor Werneck's instructions includes any such requirement.

64. Kobel, *Great South Land*, 168.

65. Paulino Werneck (Diretor de Higiene e Assistência Pública) to Chefe de Polícia (12.9.1917, 18.9.1917), AN, IJ^6 617; *CMLV*, 2:262–64; "Dous banhistas," *JB* (12.1.1926), 10; *ACM* (June–July 1927), 657–58.

66. "O horário," *A Noite* (17.12.1949), 8; "Serviço," *D de N* (17.12.1949), 2ª seção, 1; "Para maior segurança," *CMa* (3.1.1950), 5; "Deve o público ser instruído," *D de N* (5.12.1950), 2ª seção, 1.

67. See, e.g., "Natal," *BM* (8.1.1928), 13; "Ipanema homenagêa," *BM* (22.1.1928), 1; "O maior derivativo," *OJ* (15.1.1930), 3; "Sob o esplendor," *CMa* (21.1.1930),

3; "Heroes de todo dia," *BM* (4.1.1936), 1; "O 'Dia do Banhista,'" *CMa* (27.12.1936), sup., 9, 11.

68. "Heroes de todo dia," *BM* (4.1.1936), 1; Edschmid, *South America*, 346; Nohara, *Brasilien*, 130. In the early 1940s, Henry Vallotton interviewed one of Copacabana's lifeguards, João Piracuru, whom he called a "black giant," *Brésil*, 67–69. Photos reveal that many lifeguards were not Black: "O inimigo," *Crz* (30.1.1954), 54–55, 72; "Êles vivem," *Crz* (3.1.1959), 58–64; "Em Copacabana," *CMa* (11.12.1959), cad. Singra, 4–5.
69. Lt. Col. Artur Leão dos Santos, "Um pouco de história . . . ," on the Grupamento Marítimo's official site, www.gmar.rj.gov.br/historico.html (accessed on 31.3.2004) (Editors' note: This site appears to be defunct, and its successors do not include this article. See http://www.cbmerj.rj.gov.br/93-1-gmar and https://www.cbmerj.rj.gov.br/95-3-gmar [accessed by editors on 13.8.2021]); "O 'Dia do Banhista,'" *CMa* (27.12.1936), 11; "Voltando aos bons tempos: China!" *O Calçadão* (May 1976), 9; "Sports," *BM* (29.12.1929), 8; *BPDF* (Jan.–March 1939), 64; "Pondo um ponto final," *BM* (14.9.1935), 1; PDF [Antonio Prado Junior], *Mensagem . . . 1º de junho de 1930*, 357; "Um socorro," *BM* (3.4.1937), 5; "Em festa," *BM* (23.12.1939), 4; "O inimigo do mar," *Crz* (30.1.1954), 54–55, 72; "A officialidade," *BM* (28.11.1936), 5; "Premiados," *BM* (21.8.1937), 10.
70. See, e.g., "Festa," *BM* (24.12.1932), 17; "O Dia do Banhista," *JB* (29.12.1935), 6; "O 'Dia do Banhista,'" *CMa* (27.12.1936), sup. 9, 11; "Uma manhã," *CMa* (29.1.1936), 7; "As grandes commemorações," *OI* (29.12.1936), 13; "Cidade," *DN* (28.12.1959), 3; "Dia do Guarda-Vidas," *JB* (28.12.1968), 7.
71. "Figuras," *CMa* (28.7.1957), 7° cad., 19; "Prefeitos," *Crz* (11.2.1961), 22–29 (quotation, 28). See also R. Lima, *Antigo Leblon*, 55–57; "A sauvetage," *A Noite* (10.1.1921), 2; "O serviço," *A Noite* (10.1.1921), 2d ed., 1.
72. "Em Copacabana," *CMa* (11.12.1959), cad. Singra, 4–5; and, for the value of the minimum wage in 1959, Guanabara, Secretaria de Planejamento e Coordenação Geral, *Anuário Estatístico* (1971), 250.
73. I deal in greater detail and at greater length with the issues addressed in the following pages in Barickman, "'Passarão por mestiços.'"
74. "Echos e Factos: Providencias," *OP* (2.3.1917), 1; *CMLV* 2:247.
75. M[aria] E[ugenia] C[elso], "Femina," *JB* (9.1.1924), 7 (emphasis in the original).
76. On the rise of tanning as a fashion in Europe and the United States, see Lenček and Bosker, *Beach*, 201–4; Hassan, *Seaside*, chap. 4; Carter, *Rise*, 20–95; Peiss *Hope*, 150–51; Braggs and Harris, *Sun*, chap. 6; Segrave, *Suntanning*, esp. 27–42; Hansen, "Shades," chaps. 2–3.
77. "O tempo estival," *PT* (23.2.1924), 10 (which also includes photos of women

sheltering themselves under towels and beach umbrellas); "Na linda praia," *PT* (12.12.1925), 29; Clara Lucia, "Banhos de mar," *RS* (9.1.1926), 2. The first explicit reference to tanning that I located in a Carioca publication dates from 1924; curiously, it is in Spanish and refers to River Plate beaches; see "Agitación veraniega," *FF* (19.1.1924), n.p. Baptista ("Rumo," 150–57) and O'Donnell (*Invenção*, 166–69) also identify the 1920s and early 1930s as the moment when tanning became fashionable in Rio.

78. "Os perigos dos banhos de sol," *O Estado* (Florianópolis) (14.1.1930), 1 (which, citing the Carioca press, refers to Copacabana); "O grave perigo," *JB* (4.1.1930), 9; "Um aviso aos banhistas," *OJ* (7.1.1930), 3; "Um aviso," *OJ* (9.1.1930), 3; "Um aviso," *OJ* (11.1.1930), 3; "A longa permanencia," *OJ* (14.1.1930), 3 (interviews with Renato Kehl, and Drs. Artur Moncorvo Filho, Júlio Monteiro, A. Austregésilo, and Eduardo Rabelo). But cf. "Os banhos de sol," *GN* (4.12.1926), 1; "A longa permanencia," *OJ* (21.1.1930), 3 (interviews with Drs. Carlos Sá and Manoel de Abreu).
79. "Ns," *JB* (6.12.1933), 12.
80. *BM* (10.3.1934), 5; *Crz* (19.12.1936), 5; *BM* (11.1.1936), 3; *Crz* (9.1.1937), 3; *Cop M* (Feb. 1938), 12; *BM* (5.2.1938), 7; *BM* (19.3.1938), 7.
81. "Bin," *GN* (16.12.1927), 5; "Por que modificaram?" *BM* (11.1.1931), 4; "Os banhos," *C de M* (23.12.1926), 8. See also "Março," *BM* (23.3.1930), 1.
82. "Praias," *Crz* (15.12.1928), 52; "Praias," *Rio Illustrado* (Oct. 1928), 22 (squatting in Flamengo). On the narrow Flamengo and Virtudes beaches, see chap. 3. Even in the early 1930s, when many bathers arrived at the beach in Copacabana only at eleven in the morning, most bathers who frequented Virtudes and who generally belonged to the working and lower middle classes, did so between five and ten in the morning; see "Os tradicionaes banhos," *OG* (13.1.1930), ed. das 17 horas, 3.
83. "O banho de sol," *Illustração Brasileira* (Feb. 1926), n.p. For an analysis of tanning in the 1920s with regards to racial and color hierarchies in Brazil, focusing on São Paulo, see Schpun, *Beleza*, 113–18.
84. Exposure to the sun served as a justification for male toplessness in the late 1920s and early 1930s. See, e.g., "Nem tanto," *BM* (29.12.1929), 1; "O maior derivativo," *OJ* (15.1.1930), 3; "Para que seja modificada," *OG* (19.1.1931), ed. das 16 horas, 6; "Copacabana," *BM* (2.9.1933), 2.
85. Hassan, *Seaside*, 82–87; Segrave, *Suntanning*, 13–26; Lenček and Bosker, *Beach*, 213–14; Carter, *Rise*, chaps. 3–5; Randle, "Suntanning," 461–62.
86. Moncorvo Filho, *Primeiros ensaios*, *Cura*, and *Em favor*; as well as *Historia*, esp. 335, 347, 349 e 353. On Moncorvo Filho, see Wadsworth, "Moncorvo Filho."
87. Renato Kehl, "Remedio N° 1," *RS* (18.11.27.1929), 20; Kehl, "Remedio N° 2," *RS* (10.12.1927), 17; Kehl, "O sol do Brasil," *OJ* (11.1.1929), 4. See also Kehl,

Formulario, 222. On Kehl and eugenics in Brazil in general, see Stepan, *Hour*, 46–54, 89–90, 99–100, 126–28, 153–69; Schpun, *Beleza*, 118.

88. See, e.g., "Os banhos de sol," *GN* (4.12.1926), 1; "Nossas praias," *Crz* (15.12.1928), 2; "Manhãs," *BM* (8.6.1930), 1; "Copacabana," *BM* (1.3.1931), 1; "Sereias," *BM* (5.4.1931), 3; "Para que seja modificada," *OG* (19.1.1931), ed. das 16 horas, 6; "Policia," *BM* (28.5.1932), 6; "Volta á natureza," *Crz* (7.1.1933), 15–16; "Copacabana," *BM* (2.9.1933), 2; "Banhos de sol," *BM* (7.4.1934), 3.
89. It could be that, in some cases, invoking eugenics, hygiene, or heliotherapy was mainly a pretext for adhering to the new fashion. But it is equally possible that many bathers saw no need for a pretext; in their minds, as a 1927 article claimed, "fashion" went "hand in hand with hygiene"; see "De elegancia," *PT* (22.10.1927), 42. For other bathers, "fashion" went "hand in hand" with heliotherapy or with eugenics or, conceivably, with hygiene, heliotherapy, and eugenics.
90. "Agitación veraniega," *FF* (19.1.1924), n.p.; "Banhos de sol," *BM* (7.4.1934), 3; Randle, "Suntanning," 462; Carter, *Rise*, 103–4; Braggs and Davis, *Sun*, 49; O'Donnell, *Invenção*, 166. See also J. Melo, *Memórias*, 259; Farias, *Pegando*, 131–32.
91. Stoler, "Racial Histories," 186; Grin, "Desafio," 109, 166.
92. Ahmed, "Tanning," 38; Ahmed, "'It's a Sun Tan.'" See also Fry, *Persistência*, chap. 6; Hanchard, "Black Cinderella?"
93. See, e.g., Telles, *Race*, 82–85; Sansone, "Nem somente preto ou branco." J. T. Santos demonstrates that the use of multiple categories dates back to the colonial period, "De pardos."
94. N. Silva, "Cor," 146. The seven most common "colors" were *branca*, *preta*, *amarela*, *parda*, *clara* (light or fair), *morena*, and *morena clara* (light morena), all in the feminine because *color* (*cor*) in Portuguese is a feminine noun. For the definition of *morena*, see the discussion later in this chapter. For a complete list of the 135 answers, see "Veja a definição de cor do brasileiro," *Folha de São Paulo* (25.6.1995), cad. especial "Racismo cordial," 5. The survey in question was the IBGE's 1976 PNAD (Pesquisa Nacional por Amostra de Domícilos).
95. Telles, *Race*, 79.
96. Unlike *mestizo*, its Spanish cognate, the Portuguese term *mestiço* designates someone of *any* mixed racial background, *Aurélio*, s.v. *mestiço*; *Houaiss*, s.v. *mestiço*. Context often suffices to indicate the specific mixture. Greater precision, where needed, can be achieved by attaching a prefix such as *afro*, as in *afro-mestiço*.
97. "De elegancia," *PT* (22.10.1927), 42; "Os perigos," *O Estado* (Florianópolis) (14.1.1930), 1. On Baker and the *tumulte noir*, see Blake, *Tumulte*; Baker and Chase, *Josephine*, esp. 132–223; Stovall, *Paris Noir*, esp. 49–56.

98. Chermont de Brito, "Elegancias," *JB* (28.12.1935), 8.
99. *Canticum canticorum*, 1:4. Although many specialists today believe that the queen was from what is now Yemen, the idea that she was Black and African persists. See, e.g., Madden, *In Her Footsteps*.
100. Chermont de Brito, "Elegancias," *JB* (31.1.1938), 9. If "I." in the other article had fair hair and fair eyes, Chermont de Brito surely would have mentioned their color. Note also that the change in "Mme. Z's" coloring makes her the object of sexual desire. In the columnist's eyes, she had been "whiter than a lily," and hence, pure—a woman only to be admired. But once deeply tanned, she resembled not merely a mestiça, but specifically a "delicious mulatta." On the eroticization of the mulatta in Brazil, see Corrêa, "Sobre a invenção."
101. "Os que reprovam a heliotherapia," *CMa* (20.1.1939), sup., 1 (emphasis in the original). Here, it is interesting to note that, at least in recent decades and in contrast with common practice in the United States, beach-going Carioca women and teenaged girls, while tanning, often studiously seek to obtain a visible "*marca* (or *marquinha*) *de biquíni*"; that is, literally, a bikini mark, but better translated as a bikini tan line. They then show off the tan lines by wearing low-cut blouses and dresses when not at the beach. One of the messages conveyed by the bikini tan lines is, "Yes, I am dark. But it is the result of suntanning. The strap lines show you my natural, or racial, color." I discuss tan lines in "'Passarão por mestiços,'" 190–91, 200.
102. Authors from diverse disciplines have employed the concept of racialized space. See, e.g., E. McCann, "Race"; Penha-Lopes, "Racialização"; Vargas, "Apartheid"; Calmore, "Racialized Space." Implicitly, the concept of racialized space is used by Chalhoub, *Visões*, chap. 3; and by F. Gomes, *Histórias*, esp. 34–52, when they analyze, respectively, the *cidade negra* (Black city) and the *campo negro* (Black field).
103. Photos of Copacabana and Ipanema from the 1920s through the 1970s published in major illustrated magazines only very rarely show bathers who can with any real measure of certainty be identified as Black. Likewise, with one exception, none of the bathers who frequented Ipanema in the 1970s and whom Farias (*Pegando*, 70–71) could interview recalls any Blacks at the beach at the time. The one exception recollected the presence of Antônio Pitanga, a famous Afro-Brazilian actor.
104. Farias, *Pegando*, 119.
105. "A alleluia," *RS* (27.10.1928), n.p.; "Entre a variante," *BM* (27.5.1933), 1; *Crz* (19.12.1936), 5. See also *Houaiss*, s.vv. *moreno* and *amorenar*; *Aurélio*, s.v. *moreno*.
106. Stephens, *Dictionary*, 614–21; *Houaiss*, s.v. *moreno*. It is common to characterize *moreno* as "extremely ambiguous." See, e.g., N. Silva, "Cor," 146; Telles,

Race, 84. I, however, prefer to characterize the word as polysemous (i.e., having multiple meanings) and as semantically elastic. To understand the nonambiguity of moreno in a given context requires drawing on the concepts of pragmatic meaning and indexation used in linguistic anthropology. See, e.g., Mertz, "Beyond Symbolic Anthropology"; A. J. B. Silva, "Indexing."

107. See, e.g., "Mais devagar," *Crz* (11.11.1933), n.p.; "A Cidade de Copacabana," *Crz* (15.1.1949), 16 (reference to the "*moreninhas* [little morenas] *de Paris*"); "Uma festa," *CMa* (18.12.1927), 6; "Louras ou morenas?" Here, *moreno* might be translated as *brunet* or *brunette* or as *dark* as in the expression "tall, dark, and handsome."
108. A. M. Silva, *Diccionario*, s.vv. *moreno* and *pardo*; I. Lima, *Cores*, 89; "Chronicas fluminenses," *RI* (27.11.1880), 2; Nascimento, "Reduto," 298; Pierson, *Negroes*, 136–40; Pinto, *Negro*, 200; J. T. Santos, "De pardos," 127, 129–30, 135–36.
109. Skidmore, *Black*, chap. 6; Martínez-Echazábel, "Culturalismo"; Schwarcz, *Espetáculo*, esp. 239–50; T. Gomes, *Espelho*.
110. Gilberto Freyre, "Raça e classe," *Crz* (2.1.1954), 48; Freyre, *Seleta*, 120. Freyre was also one of the first authors to comment on the fashion of tanning at Rio's beaches, in "Suggestões do Rio," *Diario de Pernambuco* (25.3.1926), 3.
111. N. Silva, "Morenidade," 81. Farias (*Pegando*, 203–13) also analyzes tanning at Rio's beaches in the 1990s in light of more recent versions of the same ideological paradigm.
112. "Copacabana," *BM* (2.9.1933), 2. On social policies in the 1920s, 1930s, and 1940s intended to "improve the race," see Dávila, *Diploma*; Stepan, *Hour*, 162–69.
113. Freyre, *Seleta*, 120. See also Freyre, "Raça e classe," *Crz* (2.1.1954), 1; Freyre, *Modos*, 39; Gilberto Freyre, "O amplo espectro da morenidade brasileira," *Folha de São Paulo* (25.2.1982), 29). In turn, drawing on his research in Salvador, Bahia, in 1935–37, Pierson (*Negroes*, 136) noted that, "the *moreno*, many Bahians say, is the new physical type which Brazil is developing." With regards to "the morena . . . [seen as] the 'ideal type' of Bahian femininity," he wrote, "typically, she has dark-brown eyes and dark hair, quite wavy, perhaps even curly, and Caucasian features; her color is *café com leite* [i.e., café-au-lait] . . . like that of one 'heavily tanned.'"
114. Farias, *Pegando*, 206, 134–39.
115. Skidmore, *Black*; Schwarcz, *Espetáculo*; Seyferth, "Paradoxos"; "A nossa côr," *Careta* (1.2.1930), 3. On whites who admitted to having distant Indigenous and African ancestry, see also "Looping the Loop," *Careta* (23.4.1938), 13.
116. In a 2000 survey carried out in Rio de Janeiro state, 52 percent of all respondents who classified themselves as white believed that they had some

non-European ancestors (either Indigenous or African); 38 percent believed that they had "some African ancestry"; see Telles, *Race*, 93.

117. See, e.g., PDF [Agache], *Cidade*, 197.
118. Clara Lucia, "Banhos de mar," *RS* (9.1.1926), 2.

Chapter Five

1. O'Donnell, "Rio," 195–97, 209; Baptista, "Rumo à praia," 162–75; Bartelt, *Copacabana*, 149–51; Cardoso et al., *História*, 115–17, 119–20; San Martini, ed., *Copacabana*, 91; Bretas, *Ordem*, 139; C. Gaspar, *Orla*, 47; T. Gomes, *Espelho*, 244–47.
2. See Thompson, *Making* and *Customs*; Bourdieu, *Distinction*; Gunn, "Spatial Turn," 9.
3. While similar restrictions were imposed on beaches in Europe, the United States, and elsewhere, there are few studies about them. See, however, Booth, *Australian Beach Cultures*, chap. 2; Huntsman, *Sand*, 57–76; Walton, "Policing," 145–58; Pack, *Tourism*, 78–80, 144–45; Horwood, "'Girls,'" 653–73.
4. "Os banhos," *A Noite* (19.1.1914), 4; "Policia," *OI* (26.1.1914), 5.
5. "Bin," *GN* (15.12.1920), 4; Coelho Neto, "Proh pudor!" *A Noite* (2.2.1922), 1.
6. On police repression between 1922 and 1926, see, e.g., "Moralisando," *GN* (9.1.1922), 2; "Bin," *GN* (10.2.1922), 6; "Bin," *GN* (12. 2.1922), 4; "Nota da semana," *Malho* (18.2.1922), n.p. I have found no references to police repression at the Zona Norte and suburban beaches. A 1924 article, in fact, referred to the lack of policing at Caju beach: "A 'fauna,'" *FF* (8.3.1924), 40.
7. "Echos e Factos: A impossibilidade," *OP* (25–26.12.1922), 4; "Bin," *GN* (25.1.1923), 4; "Genero," *CMa* (9.11.1923), 3.
8. "A policia," *GN* (19.1.1924), 2; "A policia," *CMa* (19.1.1924), 3.
9. "Os banhos," *CMa* (6.12.1925), 3; "Os banhos," *GN* (6.12.1925), 4; *South American Handbook* (1925), 113.
10. "A decencia," *GN* (18.1.1924), 2.
11. "Bin," *GN* (12.2.1922), 4; "EN: De sobrecasaca," *JB* (31.1.1926), 5; "A moral," *RS* (27.1.1923), n.p.; "As praias de banho," *Vida Policial* (13.12.1925), n.p. On *Vida Policial*, see Caulfield, "Getting into Trouble."
12. "Copacabana," *CMa* (18.12.1925), 5; "Bin," *GN* (13.1.1927), 5.
13. "A evolução," *Careta* (8.2.1930), 15.
14. "EN: Um habito," *JB* (15.1.1927), 5; "É preciso," *GN* (23.11.1927), 10; "EN: Os banhos," *JB* (23.11.1927), 5; "A praia," *BM* (18.11.1928), 12; "Bin," *GN* (12.1.1929), 4; "EN: Policiamento," *JB* (28.12.1929), 5; "T&N: A policia," *CMa* (1.1.1930), 4; "Pedem policiamento!" *OG* (6.1.1930), 2nd ed., 2; "Onde está?" *OG* (7.1.1930), 5; "EN: O policiamento," *JB* (10.1.1930), 5; "T&N: Praias," *CMa* (12.1.1930), 4;

"T&N: Banhistas," *CMa* (14.1.1930), 4; "Echos e Factos: O banho," *OP* (19.1.1930), 3; "Os cavallos," *BM* (11.5.1930), 3; "Abusos," *BM* (29.6.1930), 1; "EN: Disciplina," *JB* (23.11.1930), 5; "Um perigo," *CMa* (14.12.1930), 7; "Os perigos," *BM* (21.12.1930), 2; "T&N: Football," *CMa* (26.12.1930), 4.

15. "Estavam!" *GN* (5.1.1927), 4; "EN: Os banhos," *JB* (23.11.1927), 5; "Bin," *GN* (17.1.1928), 5; "Nem tanto," *BM* (29.12.1929), 1; "Bin," *GN* (31.12.1929), 3; "O maior derivativo," *OJ* (15.1.1930), 3; "Sob o esplendor," *CMa* (21.1.1930), 3; "Copacabana," *BM* (6.4.1930), 1. On the establishment of the Liga de Amadores de Football de Areia (originally the Liga de Amadores de Foot-ball na Praia [Amateur Beach Football League]), see [Baptista], "'Foot-ball.'"
16. On the 1931 regulation and the first weeks of its enforcement, see, e.g., "Nos banhos," *JC* (7.1.1931), 6; "Vae terminar," *OJ* (7.1.1931), 7; "O policiamento," *OJ* (11.1.1931), 9; "Em benefício," *CMa* (7.1.1931), 3; "T&N: As praias," *CMa* (7.1.1931), 4; "Regulamentando," *CMa* (9.1.1931), 5; "O primeiro dia," *CMa* (13.1.1931), 3.
17. "Porque modificaram?" *BM* (11.1.1931), 4; "A policia," *OJ* (16.1.1931), 2; "T&N: A acção," *CMa* (17.1.1931), 4; "A guerra," *BM* (18.11.1931), 1; "Manhãs," *BM* (25.1.1931), 1.
18. Authorities in several parts of the United States also prohibited men from going topless on beaches and in public swimming pools in the first half of the 1930s; see Lenček and Bosker, *Making Waves*, 70–71.
19. In principle, as the police chief explained in 1924, authorities could arrest scantily dressed bathers for violating Article 282 of the 1890 penal code ("public indecency"), "Os trajes," *BM* (20.1.1924), 3. But it appears that these arrests rarely led to police inquiries, charges, or trials. Violations of this article resulted in only three trials in the entire city in 1925 and 1926, but these trials were not necessarily related to bathing attire. Similarly, despite the rigorous 1931 campaign, authorities laid no charges for "public indecency" in these districts. Instead of being indicted, those arrested in the 1920s typically received a "lecture" at the police station and were ordered to send for their clothing, after which they were freed. In the 1930s, the police generally appear to have adopted the same policy, with one difference, the imposition of a fine. Once the fine was paid, they released the offenders, provided that their clothes had arrived. Those who could not pay might remain under arrest for twenty-four hours (or forty-eight for a second offence). The police adopted a different policy in the campaign that they launched in the late 1940s: male bathers who left the beach without putting on a shirt were taken to the station and only released at six in the evening. See "Inqueritos-crimes," in "Annexos ao Relatorio" (1923), AN, IJ^{6}, maço 396; Angelo F. Bittancourt (Secretaria da Polícia do Distrito Federal) to Diretor (25.2.1932) and anexos, and "Mapa comparativo

das infrações penaes processados . . . durante os anos de 1925 a 1931," AN, IJ^6, maço 401; "A policia," *GN* (19.1.1924), 2.

20. "Ns," *JB* (2.12.1932), 12.
21. *OG* (17.1.1931), 5; *A Noite* (19.1.1931), 3; *OJ* (20.1.1931), 13; "Para o banho," *Malho* (7.2.1931), 4. Sources on the police repression in the 1920s and in 1931–1932 frequently allude to the police's use of tape measures to determine the length of bathers' maillots. However, other than the orders issued in 1924 by the delegate whose district included Flamengo, no later regulation specified the precise length of acceptable bathing attire.
22. See, e.g., "P&R," *CMa* (9.1.1931), 2; "T&N: Os banhistas," *CMa* (9.1.1931), 4; "O nú," *CMa* (13.1.1931), 6; M. Paulo Filho, "A policia," *CMa* (16.1.1931), 4; "P&R," *CMa* (15.1.1931), 2; "T&N: A acção," *CMa* (17.1.1931), 4; "Modelos 1931," *CMa* (18.1.1931), 1; "Ora!" *CMa* (9.4.1931), 5; "Modas," *CMa* (11.4.1931), 5; "O policiamento," *OJ* (13.1.1931), 4.
23. Peregrino Junior, "Dona," *Crz* (14.2.1931), 38–39; Peregrino Junior, "Banhos a fantasia," *OJ* (10.2.1931), 10.
24. "O Principe de Galles e o Principe Jorge," *CMa* (9.4.1931), 1; "Prince George," *New York Times* (10.4.1931), 25.
25. "Os banhos," *CMa* (15.1.1931), 8; "A policia," *OG* (16.1.1931), 3; "As praias," *CMa* (17.1.1931), 6; "Nas praias," *OJ* (18.1.1931), 6; "O policiamento," *DN* (17.1.1931), 2nd ed., 3; "A policia," *DN* (19.1.1931), 2nd ed., 3 (which included a picture showing the pattern for an outfit for members of rowing clubs, with trunks that reached two centimeters above the knees). Cf. "Manhãs," *BM* (25.1.1931), 1, 5.
26. See, e.g., "A policia," *CMa* (27.1.1926), 6; "Bin," *GN* (8.1.1930), 5, (8.1.1930), 5, (11.1.1930), 5, and (15.1.1930), 3; "O nudismo," *CMa* (8.1.1930), 4; "Notas," *OJ* (19.12.1930), 10; "Nudismo," *BM* (4.1.1931), 5; "Contra o nú," *Malho* (21.2.1931), 8, 23; "O nudismo," *CMa* (7.1.1933), 5; "Volta," *Crz* (7.1.1933), 16–17; "A opinião," *DC* (1.1.1933), 7; "A influencia, *DC* (1.1.1933), 10; "O nudismo," *DC* (7.2.1933), 5; "O frio," *OG* (2.11.1934), 4; "A moral?" *BM* (25.5.1935), 1–2; "P&R," *CMa* (26.12.1936), 2. "Os 'dilettanti,'" *BM* (23.1.1937), 2.
27. Pilar Drumond, "Banhos," *CMa* (14.1.1931), 2. It bears noting that the incident in Nelson, British Columbia, had nothing to do with spreading nudism. Rather, it was a demonstration of Doukhobors, members of a dissident Russian Orthodox sect, who disrobed in their protests against authorities; for them, nudity signified their disdain for material possessions; see Woodcock and Avakumatov, *Doukhobors*. I thank Glenn Avent for calling my attention to these protests.
28. "Copacabana!" *BM* (17.9.1932), 1; "A alegria," *RS* (29.10.1932), n.p.; "EN: Os banhos," *JB* (10.11.1932), 5; "Ns," *JB* (2.12.1932), 12; "Sports," *BM* (30.4.1932),

8, (7.5.1932), 8, (14.5.1932), 10, (11.6.1932), 10 e (16.7.1932), 8; "Banhos," *BM* (21.5.1932), 1; "A policia," *BM* (22.10.1931), 1; "A barraca," *RS* (28.2.1933), n.p.; "Copacabana," *Careta* (1.7.1933), 22; "EN: Nas praias," *JB* (21.12.1933), 5. On Batista Luzardo's dismissal, see Pandolfi, "Anos," 24.

29. "A indumentária," *JB* (7.12.1933), 11; "Attenção!" *BM* (9.12.1933), 12; "Policiamento," *BM* (23.12.1933), sup., 1; "Manhãs," *BM* (19.8.1933), 1; "Vida," *BM* (9.12.1933), 3; "Zona Sul," *BM* (24.3.1934), 1; "O verão," *RS* (12.1.1935), 26–27. On the spread of male topless bathing, see "O primeiro dia," *RS* (28.3.1936), 26–27; "Copacabana," *Crz* (21.11.1936), 13–15; "O verão," *RS* (16.1.1937), 26–27; "Copacabana," *BM* (24.7.1937), 1. By contrast, male topless bathing only became common in the United States as of 1937; see Lenček and Bosker, *Making Waves*, 70. Carioca stores were already selling maillots *de frente única* as of late 1934, *OG* (21.11.1934), 5; *CMa* (1.12.1935), sup., 4; *CMa* (23.12.1936), 7 (ads of O Camizeiro, Casa Simões and A Capital).

30. See, e.g., "Os cães," *BM* (2.9.1933), 1; "Providencias," *BM* (13.1.1934), 1; "Cc," *JB* (8.11.1934), 6; "EN: Que coisa!" *JB* (16.1.1935), 5; "Criminalidade," *JB* (27.1.1935), 27; "Policia," *JB* (15.11.1935), 11; "Cc," *JB* (24.11.1935), 6; "EN: Os banhistas," *JB* (4.12.1935), 5; "Pelo decoro," *JB* (8.12.1935), 10; "EN: Nudismo," *JB* (21.12.1935), 5; "Cães," *BM* (11.1.1936), 1; "Arestas," *BM* (18.4.1936), 1; "Sereias," *BM* (2.5.1936), 5; "Os cães," *BM* (9.5.1936), 1; "T&N: Entre dizer," *CMa* (10.12.1936), 4; "P&R," *CMa* (11.12.1936), 2; "O nudismo," *JB* (11.12.1936), 5; "EN: A repressão," *JB* (5.1.1937), 5.

31. "A praia," *JB* (2.11.1934), 13; "A praia," *CMa* (2.11.1934), 7; "P&R," *CMa* (3.11.1934), 2; "T&N: Nada," *CMa* (3.11.1934), 4; "A policia," *JB* (11.11.1934), 23; "Cc," *JB* (13.11.1934), 6; "Moralizando," *CMa* (13.11.1934), 8; "T&N: A policia," *CMa* (4.12.1934), 4; *BS* (8.12.1936), 1; "P&R," *CMa* (2.12.1936), 2; "Cc," *JB* (2.12.1936), 6; "P&R," *CMa* (8.12.1936), 2; "Pela tranquillidade," *A Noite* (8.12.1936), n.p.; "Vistam," *DN* (8.12.1936), 6; "Toda a praia," *OI* (9.12.1936), 13; "Banhistas," *JB* (9.12.1936), 11; "EN," *A Noite* (11.12.1936), n.p.; "O nudismo," *JB* (13.12.1936), 5; "Os sem camisas," *JB* (25.12.1936), 6; "Hontem," *OI* (27.12.1936), 5; "Policiando," *BM* (2.1.1937), 3; "Copacabana," *BM* (9.1.1937), 1; "O inimigo," *BM* (27.3.1937), 10; "Calções," *BM* (9.10.1937), 2; "EN: O policiamento," *JB* (3.12.1937), 5; "Que calor!" *CMa* (3.12.1937), 7; "T&N: O policiamento," *CMa* (15.12.1937), 4; "Cc," *JB* (18.1.1938), 6; "Proibido," *D de N* (25.11.1941), 2nd section, 1; "Proibidos," *CMa* (26.11.1941), 7; "Na policia," *JB* (26.11.1941), 16; "Coisas," *D de N* (30.11.1941), 2nd section, 11; "Os banhistas," *D de N* (12.1.1944), 2nd section, 7; "O policiamento," *CMa* (12.1.1944), 2; "Policia," *D de N* (13.1.1944), 4.

32. See, e.g., "Policiamento," *BM* (2.10.1937), 3; "EN: O escandalo," *JB* (7.12.1937), 5; "EN: O nudismo," *JB* (11.12.1937), 5; "EN: Contra o nú," *JB* (4.1.1938), 5.

33. "Acabou-se," *DN* (7.1.1931), 2; [Untitled Article], *Malho* (5.1.1924), n.p.; "EN," *JB* (31.1.1926), 5; "Os intoxicados," *BM* (15.8.1931), 6; "Policia," *BM* (28.5.1932), 6; "Policia," *BM* (27.3.1937), 3; "Contra o nú," *D de N* (6.9.1938), 2nd section, 7.
34. Alarico de Freitas, "A assistência," *Arquivos do Departamento Federal de Segurança Pública* 3, no. 7 (Jan.–March 1946), 55, 60.
35. On the police repression of the late 1940s, see, in addition to the sources cited in the notes below, "Aviso," *BS* (21.11.1947), 5 and (3.12.1947), 4–5; "Delegacia," *BS* (3.1.1948), 5; "Para o conhecimento," *BS* (6.1.1948), 1; "Na polícia," *JB* (3.1.1948), 7; "A Policia," *DN* (3.1.1948), 8; "T&N: Hábitos," *CMa* (4.1.1948), 4; "A defesa," *DC* (6.1.1948), 4.
36. On the Polícia Especial, see Cancelli, *Mundo*, 65–66; Rose, *Uma das coisas*, 46–47.
37. "Mal recebida," *DN* (5.1.1948), 1, 2; "Dia," *DN* (5.1.1948), 4; "Violências," *D de N* (6.1.1948), 2nd section, 1; "Os banhistas," *D de N* (7.1.1948), 4; "Vida," *D de N* (18.1.1948), 3rd section, 1.
38. "O dia," *JB* (20.11.1948), 8; "Policiamento," *DN* (20.11.1948), 6; "O crime," *DC* (21.11.1948), 12; Maj. Adauto Esmeraldo (Director, Divisão de Polícia Política e Social) to Gen. Antônio José de Lima Câmara (Chefe de Polícia, Distrito Federal) (22.12.1948) and attachment (carbon copies), APERJ, FDPPS, 13.012, no. 2801; Esmeraldo to Chefe da Seção de Pessoal da Divisão de Administração (4.1.1949) and attachment (carbon copies), APERJ, FDPPS, 13.002, no. 29. The second letter indicates that the DPPS then had a total personnel complement of 582.
39. "O policiamento," *JB* (21.11.1948), 4.
40. "Polícia Especial," *BS* (24.11.1948), 7 and *BS* (1.12.1948), 9; "Um pouco," *CMa* (5.12.1948), 31.
41. "Os choques," *DN* (27.12.1948), 2nd ed., 1, 6; Rubem Braga, "Natal," *D de N* (29.12.1948), 3.
42. Joel Silveira, "Guerra," *D de N* (10.12.1949), 2; "Começou," *DN* (12.12.1949), 1, 6; "P&R," *CMa* (13.12.1949), 4; Sears advertising, *CMa* (6.11.1949), 17; *D de N* (6.11.1949), 5th section, 5.
43. Joel Silveira, "Guerra," *D de N* (10.12.1949), 2; "Polícia," *D de N* (28.2.1950), 2. I found no references to confrontations between the police and bathers in the summer of 1949–1950.
44. See, e.g., Martha Abreu Esteves, *Meninas*; Caulfield, *In Defense* and "Getting"; Besse, *Restructuring*.
45. See, e.g., Marcílio, ed., *Família*, especially the chapter by Azzi, "Família."
46. "Modus," *Selecta* (14.2.1920), 17; Bento XV, *Sacra propediem* (1921), https://www.vatican.va/content/benedict-xv/en/encyclicals/documents/hf_ben-xv_enc_06011921_sacra-propediem.html (accessed by editors on 5.8.2021);

"Noticias de toda a parte," *A Cruz* (4.6.1922), 3; "Baile," *A Cruz* (25.6.1922), 2; "A moda," *A Cruz* (4.10.1925), 4; "Pela moral," *A Cruz* (13.9.1925), 6; "A música," *A Cruz* (20.12.1925), 5; "Os concursos de belleza," *A Cru* (7.9.1930), 1; "Pró & contra," *A Cruz* (21.9.1930), 3, (4.1.1931), 3, (11.1.1931), 3 and (1.2.1931), 3; "Repressão," *A Cruz* (18.1.1931), 3; "O nudismo," *A Cruz* (28.12.1930), 4.

47. "Ainda fora," *A Ordem* (March 1934), 171; "Prazer," *A Ordem* (April 1936), 288–300; "A alegria," *A Ordem* (July–Aug. 1936), 129; "A moda," *A Ordem* (Nov.–Dec. 1936), 464; Mons. Conrado Jacarandá, "A moral," *JB* (28.1.1938), 6.
48. Adalgisa Giordano (Vice President, Juventude Feminina Católica, S. Paulo) to Jonathas Serrano (May 1943) and attachments, AN, Arquivo Privado de Jonathas Serrano, R2, cx 7. It appears that the São Paulo clergy, even more so than their counterparts in Rio, were concerned about women's physical education and the partially unclothed female body; see "Pastoral coletiva do Episcopado . . . de São Paulo," *Ação Catholica* (Feb. 1941), 5; *Ação Catholica* (Jan. 1942), 9–10.
49. Câmara, *Exame*, 24.
50. Alfredo Balthazar da Silveira, "Os inimigos," *JB* (16.11.1949), 4; Hélio Silva, "A propósito," *JB* (15.12.1949), 5.
51. "A Legião," *JB* (10.12.1949), 6; "Concentração," *JB* (10.12.1949), 6; "Instalada," *JB* (13.12.1949), 9; "Para moralizar," *RS* (24.12.1949), n.p.; "Campanha," *JB* (13.12.1949), 5; "Moda," *A Noite* (14.12.1949), 4; "Pela decência," *A Noite* (17.12.1949), 2.
52. A polícia," *CMa* (19.1.1924), 3; "O policiamento," *DN* (17.1.1931), 2nd ed., 3.
53. New gender conventions were, in fact, a matter of concern to some in the 1920s and early 1930s. They considered the "new woman" and the *melindrosa* (flapper) to be overly masculinized, while the *almofadinha* (the male dandy) was sometimes considered effeminate. The *Diário de Notíticas*'s social chronicler remarked on the 1931 police instructions: "As is well known, elegant Carioca society is divided into three perfectly defined sexes—the masculine, the feminine, and the *almofadinha*." The police had determined how masculine and feminine bathers should dress, but the "great unknown" was what the almofadinha should wear, "Bric-à-brac," *D de N* (15.1.1931), 2nd section, 15. This is the only reference to homosexuality that I have found in the coverage of these police campaigns; neither of the two principal studies of male homosexuality in Brazil mentions the police campaigns on the Carioca beaches; see Green, *Beyond Carnival*; Trevisan, *Devassos*.
54. "Bric-à-brac," *D de N* (10.1.1931), 2nd section, 15; "O nú," *CMa* (13.1.1931), 6; "A campanha," *BM* (8.2.1931), 5.
55. "Policia," *JC* (14.3.1917), 3; "Ns," *OI* (26.11.1917), 6; "Vida," *OP* (3.3.1918), 2; "Notas e Noticias," *GN* (24.1.1920), 1; "Attentado," *Malho* (10.4.1926), 18;

"EN: Os banhos," *JB* (23.11.1927), 5; "T&N: A policia," *CMa* (1.1.1930), 4; "Nem tanto," *BM* (29.12.1929), 1; "Pelo decoro," *JB* (8.12.1935), 10.

56. A moral," *RS* (27.1.1923), n.p.; "As sereias," *RS* (14.2.1925), 20; "As praias," *Vida Policial* (13.12.1925), n.p.; "T&N," *CMa* (9.12.1925), 4; "EN: De sobrecasaca," *JB* (31.1.1926), 5; "Os banhos," *GN* (4.12.1926), 1; "Elegancias," *JB* (10.12.1926), 11; "Bin," *GN* (13.1.1927), 5; "O policiamento," *OJ* (13.1.1931), 4; M. Paulo Filho, "A policia," *CMa* (16.1.1931), 4; "O policiamento," *DN* (17.1.1931), 2nd ed., 3.

57. "Chroniqueta," *BM* (21.1.1923), 1; "Os banhos," *GN* (4.12.1926), 1; "Maillots," *BM* (18.4.1926), 1; "Nossas praias," *Crz* (15.12.1928), 2; "O maior derivativo," *OJ* (15.1.1930), 3; "A longa permanencia," *OJ* (21.1.1930), 3; "As praias," *A Noite* (2.1.1931), 1; Peregrino Junior, "Um sorriso," *Careta* (7.3.1931), 21; "O banho," *JB* (13.1.1931), 6; "O policiamento," *OJ* (13.1.1931), 4; M. Paulo Filho, "A policia," *CMa* (16.1.1931), 4; "Para que seja," *OG* (19.1.1931), 4:00 pm edition, 6; Bandeira, "De nudez," 39–40; "Policia," *BM* (28.5.1932), 6; "Caixinha," *BM* (29.8.1931), 5.

58. "Panos," *OP* (19.1.1923), 3; Alvaro Penalva, "Pela rama," *GN* (27.1.1924), 2; "Policia selvagem," *FF* (2.2.1924), n.p.; "Looping," *Careta* (2.2.1924), n.p.; "Caixa," *PT* (14.2.1925), 14–15; "Acabou-se," *DN* (6.1.1931), 10; "O policiamento," *OJ* (13.1.1931), 4; "O excesso," *D de N* (14.1.1931), 1; "O policiamento," *DN* (17.1.1931), 2nd ed., 3; "A policia," *DN* (19.1.1931), 2nd ed., 3; "Notas,'" *OJ* (24.1.1931), 4; "O decrescimo," *BM* (8.3.1931), 1; "Desmoralisando," *BM* (3.10.1931), 1; "Instantaneos," *CMa* (29.12.1931), 7.

59. "Caixa," *PT* (14.2.1925), 14–15; "Acabou-se," *DN* (6.1.1931), 10; "A policia," *DN* (19.1.1931), 2nd ed., 3; *Dicionário eletrônico Houaiss*, q.v., *pai*.

60. "Policia selvagem," *FF* (2.2.1924), n.p.; "O policiamento," *OJ* (13.1.1931), 4; M. Paulo Filho, "A policia," *CMa* (16.1.1931), 4; "A campanha," *BM* (8.2.1931), 5; "O decrescimo," *BM* (8.3.1931), 1; "Na praia," *CMa* (13.12.1949), 22.

61. "Panos," *OP* (19.1.1923), 3; Alvaro Penalva, "Pela rama," *GN* (27.1.1924), 2; "As praias," *Vida Policial* (13.12.1925), n.p.; "O policiamento," *OJ* (13.1.1931), 4; "O policiamento," *DN* (17.1.1931), 2nd ed., 3; "A policia," *D de N* (9.1.1931), 2; "O excesso," *D de N* (14.1.1931), 1; "Desmoralisando," *BM* (3.10.1931), 1.

62. "Policia selvagem," *FF* (2.2.1924), n.p.; "Looping," *Careta* (2.2.1924), n.p.; "Desmoralisando," *BM* (3.10.1931), 1.

63. Alvaro Penalva, "Pela rama," *GN* (27.1.1924), 2.

64. "Desmoralisando," *BM* (3.10.1931), 1; "Acabou-se," *DN* (12.1.1931), 2; "O primeiro dia," *CMa* (13.1.1931), 3. On the police, see Holloway, *Policing*; Bretas, *Guerra* and *Ordem*.

65. "Nas praias," *A Noite* (12.1.1931), 3; "Iniciou-se," *OG* (12.1.1931), 3;

"Copacabana," *BM* (29.1.1938), 3; "Tomara," *D de N* (28.11.1948), 2nd section, 3. On "Do you know who you're talking to?," see the oft-cited essay, DaMatta, *Carnavais*, chap. 4.

66. "Começou," *DN* (12.12.1949), 1, 6; "Peles," *DN* (12.12.1949), 2nd ed., 12; Millôr Fernandes, "A verdade," *Crz* (31.12.1949), 12–19. Boechat (*Copacabana Palace*, 73–74) labels the women who participated in the parade as "prostitutes." While this is not implausible, contemporary reports never insinuated it. The *Correio da Manhã* called them "high-society [girls], young women, and budding adolescents [*granfas, garotas e brotinhos*]," "P&R," *CMa* (13.12.1949), 4. According to Ruy Castro, Millôr Fernandes did more than just report on the protest; he also helped organize it; see *Ela*, 255–56.
67. "Peles," *DN* (12.12.1949), 2nd ed., 12.
68. With the exception of the abuses of the Policia Especial in the late 1940s, the only other explicit reference to police violence dates from December 1937, when policemen stopped a shirtless bather leaving Santa Luzia Beach. They ordered him to don his shirt, but he refused, saying that it was too hot. In response, the police "beat" him and wounded him with a pistol shot. "Que calor!" *CMa* (3.12.1937), 7; "A policia," *OJ* (16.1.1931), 2; "Echos," *OG* (17.1.1931), 2; "T&N: A acção," *CMa* (17.1.1931), 4; "O nú," *DN* (14.1.1931), 2nd ed., 1.
69. "Panos," *OP* (19.1.1923), 3; "As praias," *Vida Policial* (13.12.1925), n.p.; "Notas," *OJ* (15.1.1928), 2nd section, 7; Peregrino Junior, "Block-Notes," *Careta* (7.3.1931), 36–37; Peregrino Junior, "Um sorriso," *Careta* (25.4.1931), 28; "O policiamento," *OJ* (13.1.1931), 4; "A policia," *OJ* (16.1.1931), 2; "Para que seja," *OG* (19.1.1931), 4:00 pm edition, 6; "A policia," *DN* (19.1.1931), 2nd ed., 3; "O decrescimo," *BM* (8.3.1931), 1; "EN: Os banhos," *JB* (10.11.1932), 5; "Ns," *JB* (2.12.1932), 12; "Ronda," *RC* (Sept.–Oct. 1948), 4; "Vida," *D de N* (18.1.1948), 3rd section, 1.
70. "Bin," *GN* (25.1.1927), 5; "Bin," *GN* (13.1.1927), 5; "Panos," *OP* (19.1.1923), 3; "Os maillots," *BM* (18.4.1926), 1; Peregrino Junior, "Calor," *OJ* (29.12.1928), 12; Peregrino Junior, "Um sorriso," *Careta* (14.3.1931), 28; Peregrino Junior, "Modas," *OJ* (11.4.1931), 11; "O Principe de Galles e Príncipe Jorge," *CMa* (9.4.1931), 1.
71. "O policiamento," *OJ* (13.1.1931), 4; Peregrino Junior, "Calor," *OJ* (29.12.1928), 12; "Bin," *GN* (17.1.1928), 5; "38° á sombra!" *Crz* (18.1.1930), 11; Tetrá de Teffé, "Magia," *CMa* (19.1.1936), sup., 3; W. Pinho, "Cinqüenta anos," 36.
72. "Carta de mulher," *Crz* (24.11.1928–2.2.1929), 49. On the "modern girl," see Barlow et al., "Modern Girl."
73. Tetrá de Teffé, "Magia," *CMa* (19.1.1936), sup., 3; A. M. Peck, *Round about South America*, 314.

74. "A policia," *DN* (19.1.1931), 2nd ed., 3; "O policiamento," *OJ* (13.1.1931), 4; "Desmoralisando," *BM* (3.10.1931), 1; "O excesso," *D de N* (14.1.1931), 1.
75. Assis Chateaubriand, "Policia," *DN* (19.1.1931), 2nd ed., 1; "Para que seja," *OG* (19.1.1931), 4:00 pm edition, 6; "Os indesejaveis," *BM* (26.2.1938), 2; "Defendamos," *BM* (17.4.1937), 1; W. Pinho, "Cinqüenta anos," 41.
76. Kipling, *Brazilian Sketches*, 19–20. See also Faris, *Seeing South America*, 54; Edschmid, *South America*, 345–46; Durtain, *Imagens*, 65; Harnisch, *Brasil*, 21–22; A. M. Peck, *Round about South America*, 313; Nohara, *Brasilien Tag*, 129–30. Kipling's travel account was quickly translated; see "Paysagens," *OJ* (20.1.1928), 3.
77. See, e.g., "Quando teremos?" *A Rua* (30.1.1915), clipping attached to petition of Automovel Club do Brasil, (27.2.1915), AGCRJ, pasta 44, doc. 2.588; "Interesses," *JB* (3.2.1922), 7; Coelho Neto, "Proh pudor!" *A Noite* (2.2.1922), 1; "EN," *JB* (21.1.1925), 5; "T&N," *CMa* (19.12.1926), 4.
78. On Virtudes and Calabouço beaches' cabanas, see "Pereceram," *CMa* (2.1.1930), 6; "Dois casos," *OJ* (2.1.1930), 5; "Foi," *JB* (27.11.1934), 16; "Chegou," *BM* (2.1.1932), 3; "Morreu," *JB* (31.12.1926), 21. On the cabanas at Caju, Penha, and elsewhere, see "Praias," *Rio Illustrado*, (Dec. 1928), 54–55; "Iniciou-se," *OG* (12.1.1931), 3; "O primeiro dia," *CMa* (13.1.1931), 3. On Flamengo, see *JB* (11.12.1921), 3; *JB* (11.12.1921), 22; *JB* (14.12.1922), 4; Joel Silveira, "Muito sol," *D de N* (7.1.1948), 2nd section, 1.
79. "Os tradicionaes," *OG* (13.1.1930), 5:00 pm edition, 3.
80. "Nossas praias," *Crz* (15.12.1928), 2.
81. "A guerra," *BM* (18.1.1931), 1; "A campanha," *BM* (8.2.1931), 5; "A policia," *DN* (19.1.1931), 2nd ed., 3.
82. See, e.g., Velho, *Utopia*; Cardoso et al., *História*.
83. "A Cidade," *Crz* (15.1.1949), 16, 20.
84. Sérgio, *Alma*, 19.
85. "EN: Ordens," *JB* (29.1.1931), 5.
86. See Rosenthal, "Spectacle," 57; Certeau, *Practice*, esp. chap. 7.
87. Milton Pedrosa, "Copacabana," *Manchete* (7.2.1953), 46–47.
88. "Peles," *DN* (12.12.1949), 2nd ed., 12. See also, e.g., Henrique Pongetti, "A República dos Estados Unidos de Copacabana," *Rio* (Aug.–Sept. 1953), 138–39; Lessa, *Rio*, 245–46.
89. Lúcia Benedetti, "Roupismo," *RC* (Dec. 1949), 6.

Epilogue

1. On the farofeiros controversy, see Banck, "Mass Consumption"; J. Melo, *Memórias*; Pravaz, "Tan"; Freeman, "Democracy."

2. Miller, *Street.*
3. Mauício Abreu, *Evolução.*
4. Guanabara, *Mensagem,* 145–46; "Copacabana," *CMa* (10.11.1966), 11. See also Kehren, "Tunnel Vision," 142.
5. San Martini, ed, *Copacabana,* 136; "Em política," *Crz* (9.10.1954), 103 (photo of Café Filho). The six presidents were General Eurico Gaspar Dutra, João Fernando Campos Café Filho, Carlos Coimbra da Luz, Nereu Ramos, Juscelino Kubitschek, and João Goulart. During the military dictatorship, General Emílio Garrastazu Médici (president, 1969–74) also had an apartment in Copacabana. See also "Copacabana," *JB* (20.12.1990), cad. Cidade, 6, which lists other prominent politicians who had private residences in the neighborhood in the 1950s and 1960s; and "Os prédios famosos," *JB* (3.5.1981), *Dom,* 24.
6. Cardoso et al., *História,* 85–96; "Copacabana," *Crz* (17.11.1945), 8–13; "A Cidade de Copacabana II," *Crz* (22.1.1949), 12–20, 26, 76; "Copacabana," *CMa* (10.11.1966), 11.
7. Henrique Pongetti, "República dos Estados Unidos de Copacabana," *Rio* (Aug.–Sept. 1953), 138–39. See also, e.g., "Copacabana vai à feira," *Crz* (24.12.1949), 38–40, 108; "Copacabana," *Manchete* (7.2.1953), 46–47.
8. Lessa, *Rio,* 245–46. See also, e.g., Henrique Pongetti, "O oceano onírico," *Manchete* (12.1.1957), 3; S. Pereira, "Anos"; Lavinas and Ribeiro, "Imagens," 43–56; Cardoso et al., *Copacabana,* 134; "Copacabana, anos 50," *OG* (22.2.1970), cad. Domingo, 2.
9. Martins, *Noturno,* 218–19, 247, 255; H. Sá, *Brazilians,* 48–50; "A cidade de Copacabana III," *Crz* (29.1.1949), 12–20, 22; "Roteiro noturno (de Copacabana)," *Manchete* (4.10.1952), 27–30; "Pelas esquinas da noite," *Manchete* (16.10.1954), 21; "Roteiro noturno de Coapcabana," *CMa* (28.7.1957), 7° cad., 4; "A noite . . . em Copacabana," *CMa* (28.7.1957), 7° cad., 13, 20; San Martini, ed., *Copacabana,* 124–27; "Copacabana, anos 50," *OG* (22.2.1970), cad. Domingo, 2; Lavinas and Ribeiro, "Imagens"; Eneida, "Introdução," 13–15; J. F. Santos, *Homem*; R. Castro, *Chega de saudade.*
10. "Relação das casas de meretricio, ou suspeitas de o serem, conhecidas e fiscalisadas pela Primeira Delegacia Auziliar, existentes em Dezembro dos anos de 1929, 1930 e 1931," in "Dados [para] o Relatorio," AN, IJ[6], 401; "A questão do 'Hotel e Bar 20 de Novembro,'" *DC* (6.11.1938), 8; Peixoto with Câmara, *Ipanema,* 33; "Copacabana reclama," *BM* (3.4.1937), 5; Diretoria Geral de Expediente e Contabilidade da Polícia Civil do Distrito Federal to Prefeito (10.2.1938) and encl., AGCRJ, HD, cx 176.
11. "Delegacia de Costumes . . . Sessão [*sic*] de Repressão ao Meretrício . . . outubro de 1948," *BS* (10.11.1948), 17; Elsie Lessa, "'Aqui outrora retumbaram

hinos,'" *Manchete* (27.11.1954), 22; "Roteiro noturno de Copacabana," *CMa* (28.7.1957), 7º cad., 4; Phelps, *Lost Horizon*, 128. See also "A cidade de Copacabana," *Crz* (22.1.1949), 21 and *Crz* (29.1.1949), 19; Théo-Filho, *Ao sol*, 315; "Pré-advertências," *JB* (1.12.1950), 5; Marques Rebello, "Pequena corografia," *Manchete* (20.1.1957), 30; Cesário Marques, "Copacabana: inocência de saia justa," *DC* (15.8.1965), cad. DC^2, 3; "Copacabana: as duas faces da noite," *CMa* (23.11.1966), 11; "Ai de ti, Avenida Atlântica," *JB* (22.1.1969), cad. B, 4–5; Otto Maria Carpeaux, "Documentos de Copacabana," *Leitura* (June 1963), 10–11; and M. Gaspar, *Garotas*.

12. Ferreira and Serrano, "Evolução," 1–8.
13. Green, *Beyond Carnival*, 156–58.
14. Braga, *200 crônicas*, 222–23.
15. Oliveira and Costa, "Histórias."
16. Cardoso et al., *História*, 73–88.
17. See, e.g., *JB* (25.11.1944), 15; *CMa* (27.1.1946), 9; *CMa* (28.4.1946), 24, 26; *CMa* (28.11.1946), 12; *CMa* (12.11.1947), 21; *DN* (16.1.1950), 8; *CMa* (5.11.1950), 2º cad., 12; *CMa* (21.1.1951), 2º cad., 11; *CMa* (4.11.1951), 3º cad., 16; *D de N* (9.11.1951), 6ª seção, 4; *CMa* (6.1.1952), 3º cad., 17; *UH* (19.11.1952), 10; *UH* (26.11.1952), cad. Imobiliária, 2; *UH* (8.12.1952), 7; "A cidade de Copacabana," *CMa* (28.7.1957), 7º cad., 2; *CMa* (11.11.1962), 3; *JB* (17.7.1973), 3; *JB* (1.2.1976), 23; *OG* (27.1.1979), 19. See also Rangel, "Copacabanas," 49. On the Chopin, see "Aos 50 anos, o edifício Chopin ainda dá samba," *OG** (9.10.2005); and A. Jordan, *Rio*, 47–49, 119.
18. Cardoso et al., *História*, 63–71; Maurício Abreu, *Evolução*, 129; Velho, *Utopia*, esp. chaps. 1–4; Rangel, "Copacabanas," 21–25; "Beleza de Copacabana," *CMa* (6.11.1966), 2º cad., 1.
19. Velho, *Utopia*, esp. chap. 5; "Copacabana ao sol," *Crz* (29.1.1944), 14–17, 26; "Copacabana," *Crz* (17.11.1945), 8–13; "A Cidade de Copacabana II," *Crz* (22.1.1949), 14, 16, 20, 76; "Copacabana vai à feira," *Crz* (24.12.1949), 38–40, 108; Henrique Pongetti, "República," *Rio* (Aug.–Sept. 1953), 138–39; "Copacabana, onde morar exige psicologia," *CMa* (17.11.1966), 11. By 1966, Copacabana had fifteen cinemas, six theaters, fifty-three restaurants, and fifty-two nightclubs (*boates*) and "nighttime bars [*bares noturnos*]." "Beleza de Copacabana," *CMa* (6.11.1966), 2º cad., 1; "Copacabana: um bairro," *CMa* (10.11.1966), 11.
20. B. McCann, *Hard Times*, 45–49, 112–14.
21. [Baptista], "'Foot-ball' na areia."
22. Kehren, "Tunnel Vision," 205–7, 222–26; Cardoso et al., *História*, 81–88.
23. Gregory, "Roberto Burle Marx."

24. Kehren, "Tunnel Vision," 146–50; Freire and Oliveira, *Novas memórias*, 28, 43, 80–81, 128.
25. Kehren, "Tunnel Vision," 29–37; Freire and Oliveira, *Novas memórias*, 26–27, 41.
26. Freire, *Guerra*.
27. "Tijuca: O que pensa a juventude," CM (2.12.1966), 2° cad., 1.
28. Eneida, "Introdução," 11.
29. Eneida, "Introdução," 11.
30. Berger, "História," 47–49.
31. See, e.g., "Nosso irmão, o mar," *RS* (16.2.1946), 14.
32. Tavares, *Dia*, chap. 2, section 1 (no pagination).
33. "Orlas Suburbanas", *O Dia** (21.1.2020).
34. Castro, *Bossa Nova*, 259–73.
35. Dunn, *Contracultura*, 49–50.
36. Dunn, *Contracultura*, 30, 38–40.
37. B. Carvalho, "Mapping"; V. Paiva, "História."
38. [Ferreira Filho], *Ô, Copacabana*, 30. See also "Copacabana, apartamentos conjugados," *OG* (7.10.1973), 12; "Copacabana, apartamento conjugado," *OG* (8.10.1973), ed. final, 14.
39. Jaguaribe, "Barra da Tijuca"; Cezimbra and Orsini, *Emergentes*.

Bibliography

Archives

Arquivo Geral da Cidade do Rio de Janeiro
Fundo do Gabinete da Administração de Henrique Dodsworth
Divisão de Iconografia
Arquivo Nacional
Arquivos da Segunda Delegacia de Polícia Auxiliar, Peças Teatrais
Decretos do Poder Executivo, Privilégios Industriais
Arquivo Público do Estado do Rio de Janeiro
Fundo da Divisão de Polícia Política e Social
Biblioteca Nacional
Divisão de Música, Arquivo da Empresa Paschoal Segreto
Setor de Cartografia
Setor de Iconografia
Centro de Documentação da TV Globo
Centro de Documentação e Disseminação de Informações do Instituto Brasileiro de Geografia e Estatística
Instituto Histórico e Geográfico Brasileiro
Instituto Moreira Salles
Museu da Imagem e do Som

Discography of Recordings Cited in Epilogue

Almirante. "Deixa a Lua Sossegada" (João de Barro and Alberto Ribeiro). RCA Victor, 1934.

Amaral, Ruth. "Biquini de Filó" (João de Barro and Alberto Ribeiro). Todamérica, 1952.

Borba, Emilinha. "Chiquita Bacana" (João de Barro and Alberto Ribeiro). Continental, 1948.

Costa, Gal. "Fa-tal: Gal a Todo Vapor." Phillips, 1971.

Farney, Dick. "Copacabana" (João de Barro and Antônia de Almeida). Continental, 1946.

Farney, Dick, and Lúcio Alves. "Teresa da Praia" (Antônio Carlos [Tom] Jobim and Billy Blanco). Continental, 1954.
Fawcett, Fausto. "Kátia Flávia" (Fausto Fawcett and Carlos Laufer). WEA, 1987.
Gilberto, João, Stan Getz, and Astrud Gilberto. "A Garota de Ipanema" (Antônio Carlos Jobim and Vinícius de Moraes). Verve, 1963.
Maia, Tim. "Do Leme ao Pontal" (Tim Maia). Continental, 1986.
Miranda, Aurora. "Cidade Maravilhosa" (André Filho). Odeon, 1934.
Santos, Lulu. "Como uma Onda" (Lulu Santos and Nelson Motta). WEA, 1983.

Published Primary and Secondary Sources

Abreu, Maurício de Almeida. "A cidade, a montanha e a floresta." In *Natureza e sociedade no Rio de Janeiro*, edited by Maurício de Almeida Abreu, 54–103. Rio: Secretaria Municipal de Cultura, Departamento Geral de Documentação e Informação Cultural, 1992.
———. *Evolução urbana do Rio de Janeiro*. 4th ed. Rio: Instituto Pereira Passos, 2006.
Abreu Esteves, Martha de. *Meninas perdidas: os populares e o cotidiano do amor no Rio de Janeiro da "Belle Époque."* Rio: Paz e Terra, 1989.
Adamo, Sam. "The Broken Promise: Race, Health, and Justice in Rio de Janeiro, 1890–1940." PhD diss., University of New Mexico, 1983.
Ahmed, Sara. "'It's a Sun Tan, Isn't It?': Auto-biography as an Identificatory Process." In *Black British Feminism: A Reader*, edited by Heidi Mirza, 153–67. London: Routledge, 1997.
———. "Tanning the Body: Skin, Colour, and Gender." *New Formations*, no. 34 (Spring 1998): 25–40.
Aizen, Mário, and Robert M. Pechman. *Memória da limpeza urbana*. Rio: Prefeitura da Cidade do Rio de Janeiro, Comlurb, 1985.
Albuquerque, Alexandre José Curado de Figueiredo e. *Almanak da Côrte do Rio de Janeiro para o anno de 1811*. Republished in *Revista do Instituto Geográfico e Histórico Brasileiro*, no. 282 (1969): 97–236.
Alencastro, Luiz Felipe de. "Vida privada e ordem privada no Império." In *História da vida privada no Brasil*, 4 vols., edited by Fernando A. Novais, 1:11–93. São Paulo: Companhia das Letras, 1997–1999.
Alewitz, Sam. *"Filthy Dirt": A Social History of Unsanitary Philadelphia in the Late Nineteenth Century*. New York: Garland, 1989.
Algranti, Leila Mezan. *O feitor ausente: estudos sobre a escravidão urbana no Rio de Janeiro, 1808–1822*. Petrópolis: Vozes, 1988.
Almeida, Serafim Vieira de. *Technica e indicação dos banhos de mar e de sol*. São Paulo: Empreza Graphica da Revista dos Tribunaes, 1937.

Álvarez, Adriana. *Mar del Plata: una historia urbana*. Buenos Aires: Banco de Boston, 1991.
Amancio, Tunico. *O Brasil dos gringos: imagens no cinema*. Niterói: Intertexto, 2000.
Andrews, C[hristopher] C[olumbus]. *Brazil: Its Condition and Prospects*. New York: Appleton, 1889.
Araujo, Luiz de Souza. *These*. . . . Rio: Typ. de G. Leuzinger, 1870.
Araújo, Rita Cássia Barbosa de. *As praias e os dias: história social das praias do Recife e de Olinda*. Recife: Prefeitura do Recife, Secretaria de Cultura, Fundação de Cultura Cidade do Recife, 2007.
Araújo, Rosa Maria Barboza de. *A vocação do prazer: a cidade e a família no Rio de Janeiro republicano*. Rio: Rocco, 1993.
Arruda, José Jobson de A. *O Brasil no comércio colonial*. São Paulo: Ática, 1980.
Ashenbug, Katherine. *The Dirt on Clean: An Unsanitized History*. New York: Random House, 2007.
Assis, [Joaquim Maria] Machado de. "A chave." In *Obra completa*, 3 vols., edited by Afrânio Coutinho, 2:871–85. Rio: Editora José Aguilar, 1959.
———. *Dom Casmurro*. 6th ed. Edited by Massaud Moisés. São Paulo: Cultrix, 1968.
———. "Questão de vaidade." In *Histórias românticas*, 7–90. Rio: W. M. Jackson, 1937.
Austen, Jane. *Northanger Abbey*. Edited by Marilyn Butler. London: Penguin, 2003.
Azevedo, Aluísio. *Casa de pensão*. São Paulo: Livraria Martins Editora, 1965 [1884].
———. *O cortiço*. São Paulo: Livraria Martins Editora, 1959 [1890].
———. *Girândola de amores*. São Paulo: Livraria Martins Editora, 1960 [1882].
Azevedo, Artur. "Banhos de mar." In *Histórias brejeiras*, edited by R. Magalhães Júnior, 77–85. Rio: Edições de Ouro, 1956.
Azevedo, Thales de. *Regras do namoro à antiga*. São Paulo: Ática, 1986.
Azzi, Riolando. "Família, mulher e sexualidade na Igreja do Brasil (1930–1964)." In *Família, mulher, sexualidade e Igreja na história do Brasil*, edited by Maria Luiza Marcílio, 101–34. São Paulo: Edições Loyola and CEDHAL/CEHILA, 1993.
Baer, Werner. *The Brazilian Economy: Growth and Development*. 5th ed. Westport, CT: Praeger, 2001.
Baker, Jean-Claude, and Chris Chase. *Josephine: The Hungry Heart*. New York: Random House, 1993.
Banck, Geert A. "Mass Consumption and Urban Contest in Brazil: Some Reflections on Lifestyle and Class." *Bulletin of Latin American Research* 13, no. 1 (Jan. 1994): 45–60.
Bandeira, Manuel. "De nudez na praia." In *Todos os verões do Rio*, edited by João Alegria, 39–43. Rio: Artensaio, [2002].

Baptista, Paulo Francisco Donadio. "Introdução a uma história da praia no Rio de Janeiro—Problemas de acesso balneário—Beira-Mar, 1930–1939." BA thesis, Universidade Federal do Rio de Janeiro, 2003.

———. "'Foot-ball' na areia e banhos de sol no Rio de Janeiro." *Recorde* 4, no. 1 (June 2011): 1–20.

———. "Rumo à praia: Théo-Filho, beira-mar e a vida balneária no Rio de Janeiro dos anos 1920 e 30." MA thesis, Universidade Federal do Rio de Janeiro, 2007.

———. "Tem rei no mar." *Revista de História da Biblioteca Nacional* 3, no. 3 (July 2008): 79–83.

Barbosa, Francisco de Assis. "Dona Filó é quem diz." In *Rio de Janeiro em prosa e verso*, edited by Manuel Bandeira and Carlos Drummond de Andrade, 537–40. Rio: José Olympio, 1965.

Barickman, B. J. *A Bahian Counterpoint: Sugar, Tobacco, Cassava, and Slavery in the Recôncavo, 1780–1860*. Stanford, CA: Stanford University Press, 1998.

———. "Medindo maiôs e correndo atrás de homens sem camisa: a polícia e as praias cariocas, 1920–1950." *Recorde* 9, no. 1 (Jan.–June 2016): 1–66.

———. "Not Many Flew Down to Rio: Tourism and the History of Beach-Going in Twentieth-Century Rio de Janeiro." *Journal of Tourism History* 6, nos. 2–3 (2009): 223–41.

———. "'Passarão por mestiços': o bronzeamento nas praias cariocas, noções de cor e raça e ideologia racial, 1920–1950," *Afro-Ásia* 40 (2009): 173–221.

Barlow, Tani E., Madeleine Yue Dong, Uta G. Poiger, Priti Ramamurthy, Lynn M. Thomas, and Alys Eve Weinbaum. "The Modern Girl around the World: A Research Agenda and Preliminary Findings." *Gender and History* 17, no. 2 (Aug. 2005): 245–94.

Barreiros, Eduardo Canabrava. *Atlas da evolução urbana da cidade do Rio de Janeiro: ensaio, 1565–1965*. Rio: Instituto Histórico e Geográfico Brasileiro, 1965.

Barreto, [Afonso Henrique de] Lima. "O prefeito e o povo." In *Toda crônica: Lima Barreto*, 2 vols., edited by Beatriz Resende and Rachel Valença, 2:294–95. Rio: Agir, 2004.

Barros, João Alberto Lins de. *Memórias de um revolucionário*. Part 1: *A marcha da coluna*, 2nd ed. Rio: Civilização Brasileira, 1954.

Barros, João do Rêgo. "Reminiscencias de ha 50 annos, de um cadete do 1º regimento de cavallaria," *Revista do Instituto Geográfico e Histórico Brasileiro* no. 152 (1925): 89–98.

Bartelt, Dawid Danilo. *Copacabana: Biographie eines Sehnsuchtsortes*. Berlin: Klaus Wagenbach, 2013.

Beattie, Peter. *The Tribute of Blood: Army, Honor, Race, and Nation in Brazil, 1864–1945*. Durham, NC: Duke University Press, 2001.

Bell, Alured Gray. *The Beautiful Rio de Janeiro.* London: William Heinemann, 1914.
Benchimol, Jaime Larry. *Pereira Passos, um Haussmann tropical: a renovação urbana da cidade do Rio de Janeiro no início do século XX.* Rio: Secretaria Municipal de Cultura, Departamento de Geral de Documentação e Informação Cultural, 1990.
Berger, Paulo. *Bibliografia do Rio de Janeiro de viajantes e autores estrangeiros, 1531–1900.* [Rio]: Livraria São José, [1964].
———. *Dicionário histórico das ruas do Rio de Janeiro: V e VI Regiões Administrativas.* Rio: Fundação Casa de Rui Barbosa, 1994.
———. "História de Copacabana." In *História dos subúrbios: Copacabana,* edited by Eneida [Costa de Morais] and Paulo Berger, 21–93. São Paulo: Departamento de História e Documentação da Prefeitura do Distrito Federal, 1959.
Besse, Susan K. *Restructuring Patriarchy: The Modernization of Gender Inequality in Brazil, 1914–1940.* Chapel Hill: University of North Carolina Press, 1996.
Bilac, Olavo, Guimaraens Passos, and Antonio Francisco Bandeira. *Brésil: Guide des États-Unis du Brésil: Rio de Janeiro, système Boedecker.* Translated by Roberto Gomes. Rio: Bilac, Passos & Bandeira, 1904.
Binzer, Ina von. *Alegrias e tristezas de uma educadora alemã no Brasil.* Translated by Alice Rossi and Luisita da Gama Cerqueira. São Paulo: Editora Anhembi, 1956.
Blackbourn, David. "Fashionable Spa Towns in Nineteenth-Century Europe." In *Water, Leisure, and Culture: European Historical Perspectives,* edited by Susan C. Anderson and Bruce H. Tabb, 2–23. Oxford: Berg, 2002.
Blake, Jody. *Le Tumulte Noir: Modernist Art and Popular Entertainment in Jazz-Age Paris, 1900–1930.* University Park: Pennsylvania State University Press, 1999.
Boechat, Ricardo. *Copacabana Palace: um hotel e sua história.* São Paulo: DBA Artes Gráficas, 1998.
Booth, Douglas. *Australian Beach Cultures: The History of Sun, Sand, and Surf.* London: Frank Cass, 2001.
Bösche, Eduardo Theodoro. "Quadros alternados de viagens terrestres e maritimas, aventuras, acontecimentos politicos, descripção de usos e costumes de povos, durante uma viagem ao Brasil." Translated by Vicente de Souza Queirós. *Revista do Instituto Geográfico e Histórico Brasileiro* no. 137 (1918): 137–241.
Botting, David, and the Editors of Time-Life Books. *Rio de Janeiro.* Amsterdam: Time-Life Books International, 1977.
Bougainville, Baron Hyacinth, Yves Philippe Potentin, Baron de. *Journal de la navigation autour du globe de la frégate* La Thétis *et de la corvette* L'Espérance *pendant les années 1824, 1825 et 1826.* 2 vols. Paris: Arthus Bertrand, 1837.
Bourdelais, Patrice, ed. *Les hygiénistes: enjeux, modèles et pratiques.* Paris: Belin, 2001.

Bourdieu, Pierre. *Distinction: A Social Critique of Judgement and Taste*. Translated by Richard Nice. London: Routledge, 1984.

Braga, Rubem. *200 crônicas escolhidas: as melhores de . . .*, 2nd ed. Rio: Editora Record, 1978.

Braggs, Steven, and Diane Harris. *Sun, Fun, and Crowds: British Seaside Holidays between the Wars*. Stroud, Gloucestershire, UK: Tempus, 2000.

Brand, Charles. *Journal of a Voyage to Peru: A Passage across the Cordillera of the Andes in the Winter of 1827, Performed on Foot in the Snow; and a Journey across the Pampas*. London: Henry Colburn, 1828.

Brandão, Ana Maria de Paiva Macedo. "As alterações climáticas na área metropolitana do Rio de Janeiro: uma provável influência do crescimento urbano." In *Natureza e sociedade no Rio de Janeiro*, edited by Maurício de Almeida Abreu, 143–200. Rio: Secretaria Municipal de Cultura, Departamento de Geral de Documentação e Informação Cultural, 1992.

Brazil. *Codigo criminal do Imperio do Brasil, annot. Araujo Filgueiras Junior*. Rio: Eduardo & Henrique Laemmert, 1873.

———. *Codigo penal da Republica dos Estados Unidos do Brasil, commentado e annotado segundo a legislação vigente até 1901 por Oscar Macedo Soares*. Rio: Typographia da Empreza Democratica, 1902.

———. Department of Press and Propaganda [i.e., Departamento de Imprensa e Propaganda]. *Rio de Janeiro*. [Rio]: n.p., [1940 or 1941?].

———. Directoria Geral de Estatistica. *Recenseamento da população do Imperio do Brazil a que se procedeu no dia 1º de agosto de 1872*. 21 vols. in 22. Rio: Leuzinger & Filhos, 1873–1876.

———. Directoria Geral de Estatistica. *Recenseamento do Brazil realizado em 1º de setembro de 1920*. 5 vols. in 18. Rio: Typ. da Estatistica, 1922–1930.

———. Fundação IBGE. *Censo demográfico 1991: resultados do universo relativos às características da população e dos domicílios*. 28 vols. Rio: Secretaria de Planejamento, Orçamento e Coordenação, Fundação Instituto Brasileiro de Geografia e Estatística, [1994].

———. IBGE. Comissão Censitária Nacional. *Recenseamento geral do Brasil. (1º de setembro de 1940)*. Série regional. 22 vols. Rio: Serviço Gráfico do Instituto Brasileiro de Geografia e Estatística, 1950–1952.

———. IBGE. Conselho Nacional de Estatística. *Características demográficas e sociais do Estado da Guanabara*. [Rio: IBGE, 1966.]

———. IBGE. Conselho Nacional de Estatística. Serviço Nacional de Recenseamento. *VI recenseamento geral do Brasil*. Série regional. 30 vols. Rio: IBGE, Conselho Nacional de Estatística, 1954–1956.

———. IBGE. Departamento de Censos. *VIII recenseamento geral do Brasil—1970: censo demográfico*. Série regional. 24 vols. Rio: [IBGE], 1972–1973.

———. IBGE. Diretoria de Estatística Municipal. *Anuário estatístico do Distrito Federal Ano VI—1938*. Rio: Serviço Gráfico do IBGE, 1939.
———. IBGE. *IX recenseamento geral do Brasil—1980*. 6 vols. Rio: IBGE, 1981–1984.
———. IBGE. Serviço Nacional de Recenseamento. *VII recenseamento geral do Brasil: censo demográfico de 1960*. Série regional. Rio: [IBGE], 1967.
———. Ministerio do Trabalho, Industria e Commercio, Departamento de Estatistica e Publicidade. *Estatistica predial do Distrito Federal*. Rio: n.p., 1935.
———. Ministerio dos Negocios da Agricultura, Commercio e Obras Públicas. *Relatorio apresentado á Assembléa Geral Legislativa na terceira sessão da vigesima legislatura pelo Ministro e secretario de estado dos negocios da guerra Thomaz José Coelho d'Almeida*. Rio: Imprensa Nacional, 1888.
———. Ministerio dos Negocios do Imperio. *Relatorio da Repartição dos Negocios do Imperio apresentado á Assembléa Geral Legislativa na sessão ordinaria de 1838 pelo respectivo ministro e secretario de Estado interino Bernardo Pereira de Vasconcellos*. Rio: Typographia Nacional, 1838.
———. *Recenseamento do Rio de Janeiro (Distrito Federal) realisado em 20 de setembro de 1906*. Rio: Officina de Estatistica, 1907.
Brazilian Representation, New York World's Fair 1939. *Travel in Brazil, Official Publication*. Rio: n.p., [1939].
Bretas, Marcos Luiz. *A guerra das ruas: povo e polícia na Cidade do Rio de Janeiro*. Rio: Ministério da Justiça, Arquivo Nacional, 1997.
———. *Ordem na cidade: o exercício cotidiano da autoridade policial no Rio de Janeiro, 1907–1930*. Translated by Alberto Lopes. Rio: Rocco, 1997.
Brown, Larissa Virginia. "Internal Commerce in a Colonial Economy: Rio de Janeiro and Its Hinterland, 1790–1822." PhD diss., University of Virginia, 1986.
Bunbury, Charles. "Narrativa de viagem de um naturalista inglês ao Rio de Janeiro e Minas Gerais (1833–35)." *Anais da Biblioteca Nacional*, no. 62 (1940): 15–135.
Burke, Ulick Ralph, and Robert Staples Jr. *Business and Pleasure in Brazil*. London: Field & Tuer, 1884.
Burton, [Lady] Isabel. *The Life of Captain Sir Rich[ar]d Burton, K.C.M.G., F.R.G.S.* 2 vols. London: Chapman & Hall, 1893.
Calmore, John O. "Racialized Space and the Culture of Segregation: 'Hewing a Stone of Hope from a Mountain of Despair.'" *University of Pennsylvania Law Review* 143, no. 5 (1995): 1233–73.
Câmara, Jaime de Barros Câmara. *Exame de consciência: sétima carta pastoral*. Petrópolis: Vozes, 1947.
Camus, Dominique, and Chantal Manoncourt. *Brésil*. Paris: Arthaud, 1996.
Cancelli, Elizabeth. *O mundo da violência: a polícia da era Vargas*. Brasília: Ed. da Universidade de Brasília, 1993.

Cardoso, Elizabeth Dezouzart. "Estrutura urbana e representações: a invenção da Zona Sul e a construção de um novo processo de segregação no Rio de Janeiro nas primeiras décadas do século XX." *GeoTextos* 6, no. 1 (July 2010): 73–88.
———. "A invenção da Zona Sul: origens e difusão do topônimo Zona Sul na geografia carioca." *GEOgraphia* 11, no. 22 (2009): 37–58.
Cardoso, Elizabeth Dezouzart, and Grupo de Pesquisa em Habitação e Uso do Solo Urbanao da Universidade Federal do Rio de Janeiro. *História dos bairros, memória urbana.* Vol. 4: *Copacabana.* Rio: João Fortes Engenharia and Index, 1986.
Carone, Edgard. *A República Velha.* 2 vols. 2nd ed., rev. and enl. São Paulo: DIFEL, 1975.
Carpenter, Frank [De] Y[eaux]. *Round about Rio.* Chicago: Jansen, McClurg, 1884.
Carter, Simon. *Rise and Shine: Sunlight, Technology, and Health.* Oxford: Berg, 2007.
Carvalho, Antonio Gontijo, ed. *Um ministério visto por dentro: cartas inéditas de João Batista Calógeras, alto funcionário do Império.* Rio: José Olympio, 1959.
Carvalho, Bruno. "Mapping the Urbanized Beaches of Rio de Janeiro: Modernization, Modernity and Everyday Life," *Journal of Latin American Cultural Studies* 16, no. 3 (2007): 325–39.
Carvalho, José Murilo de. *Os bestializados: o Rio de Janeiro e a República que não foi.* São Paulo: Companhia das Letras, 1987.
Castro, Celso. "Narrativas e imagens do turismo no Rio de Janeiro." In *Antropologia urbana: cultura e sociedade no Brasil e em Portugal,* edited by Gilberto Velho, 80–87. Rio: Jorge Zahar, 1999.
Castro, Ruy. *Bossa Nova: The Story of the Brazilian Music That Seduced the World.* Chicago: A Capella Books, 2000.
———. *Carmen: uma biografia.* São Paulo: Companhia das Letras, 2005.
———. *Carnaval no fogo: crônica de uma cidade excitante demais.* São Paulo: Companhia das Letras, 2003.
———. *Chega de saudade: a história e as histórias da bossa nova.* São Paulo: Companhia das Letras, 1991.
———. *Ela é carioca: uma enciclopédia de Ipanema.* São Paulo: Companhia das Letras, 1999.
———. "Prefácio." In *Praia de Ipanema,* by Théo-Filho [Manoel Theotonio de Lacerda Freire Filho], 7–9. Rio: Dantes Livraria Editora, 2000.
Caulfield, Sueann. "Getting into Trouble: Dishonest Women, Modern Girls, and Women-Men in the Conceptual Language of *Vida Policial,* 1925–1927." *Signs* 19, no. 1 (Oct. 1993): 146–76.
———. *In Defense of Honor: Sexual Morality, Modernity, and Nation in Early-Twentieth-Century Brazil.* Durham, NC: Duke University Press, 2000.

Cavalcanti, Nireu Oliveira. "A reordenação urbanística da nova sede da Corte." *Revista do Instituto Geográfico e Histórico Brasileiro*, no. 436 (July–Sept. 2007): 149–99.
———. *Crônicas: histórias do Rio colonial*. Rio: Civilização Brasileira, 2004.
———. *O Rio de Janeiro setecentista: a vida e a construção da cidade da invasão francesa até a chegada da Corte*. Rio: Jorge Zahar, 2004.
Certeau, Michel de. *The Practice of Everyday Life*. Translated by Steven Randall. Berkeley: University of California Press, 1984.
Cezimbra, Marcia, and Elisabeth Orsini. *Os emergentes da Barra*. Rio: Relume Dumará, 1996.
Chalhoub, Sidney. *Cidade febril: cortiços e epidemias na Corte imperial*. São Paulo: Companhia das Letras, 1996.
———. *A força da escravidão: ilegalidade e costume no Brasil oitocentista*. São Paulo: Companhia das Letras, 2012.
———. *Trabalho, lar e botequim: o cotidiano dos trabalhadores no Rio de Janeiro da Belle Époque*. São Paulo: Brasiliense, 1986.
———. *Visões da liberdade: uma história das últimas décadas da escravidão na Corte*. São Paulo: Companhia das Letras, 1990.
Chazkel, Amy. "O lado escuro do poder municipal: a mão de obra forçada e o toque de recolher no Rio de Janeiro oitocentista." *Revista Mundos do Trabalho* 5, no. 9 (Jan.–June 2013): 31–48.
Christoffoli, Angelo Ricardo. *Uma história do lazer nas praias: Cabeçudas, SC, 1910–1930*. Itajaí: Univali Editora, 2003.
Claparède, Édouard. *Estudos sobre os banhos de mar: conselho aos banhistas pelo Doutor Claparede*. Translated by M. de T. 2nd ed. Lisbon: Typ. Progressista de P. A. Borges, 1874.
Coaracy, Vivaldo. *Memórias do Rio de Janeiro*. Rio: José Olympio, 1955.
Codigo de Posturas da Camara Municipal do Rio de Janeiro. Rio: Typographia Imperial e Nacional, 1830.
Codigo de Posturas da Cidade do Rio de Janeiro. [Rio]: n.p., [1889].
Codigo de Posturas da Illustrissima Camara Municipal. Rio: Typ. Dous de Dezembro de P. Brito, 1854.
Codigo de Posturas da Illustrissima Camara Municipal. Rio: Typographia de F. de Paula Brito, 1860.
Codigo de Posturas da Illustrissima Camara Municipal do Rio de Janeiro. . . . Rio: Eduardo & Henrique Laemmert, 1870.
Codigo de Posturas, Leis, Decretos e Resoluções da Intendencia Municipal do Districto Federal. . . . Rio: Papelaria e Typographica Mont'Alverne, 1894.
Código nacional de trânsito. Rio: Ed. Gráfica Auriverde, 1980.
Código nacional de trânsito. Rio: Ed. Mesbla, 1947.

Código nacional de trânsito: decreto-lei no. 3651, de 25.09.1941. 7th updated ed. Rio: Ed. Alvorada, 1956.

Cohen, Alberto A., Sergio Fridman, and Ricardo Siqueira. *Rio de Janeiro: ontem e hoje 2.* Rio: Ed. do Autor, 2004.

Cohen, William A., and Ryan Johnson, eds. *Filth: Dirt, Disgust, and Modern Life.* Minneapolis: University of Minnesota Press, 2004.

Conrad, Robert. *The Destruction of Brazilian Slavery, 1850–1888.* Berkeley: University of California Press, 1972.

Cooper, Clayton Sedgwick. *The Brazilians and Their Country.* New York: Frederick A. Stokes, 1917.

Corbin, Alain. *Le miasme et la jonquille: l'odorat et l'imaginaire social, XVIIIe–XIXe siècles.* 2nd ed. Paris: Flammarion, 1986.

———. *O território do vazio: a praia e o imaginário ocidental.* Translated by Paulo Neves. São Paulo: Companhia das Letras, 1989.

Corrêa, Mariza. "Sobre a invenção da mulata." *Cadernos Pagu*, no. 6–7 (1996): 35–50.

Costa, Jurandir Freire. *Ordem médica e norma familiar.* 4th ed. Rio: Graal, 1999.

Coutinho, Candido Teixeira de Azeredo. *Esboço de uma hygiene dos collegios aplicadas aos nossos. . . .* Rio: Typ. Universal de Laemmert, 1857.

Cruls, Gastão. *Aparência do Rio de Janeiro (notícia histórica e descritiva da cidade).* 2 vols. Rio: Livraria José Olympio, 1949.

Cruls, L. *O clima do Rio de Janeiro / Le climat de Rio de Janeiro.* Rio: H. Lombaerts, 1892.

Cunha, Maria Clementina Pereira Cunha. *Ecos da folia: uma história social do carnaval carioca entre 1880 e 1920.* São Paulo: Companhia das Letras, 2001.

Cunha, Nelly da. "Gestión municipal y tiempo libre en Montevideo (1900–1940)." In *Las puertas del mar: consumo, ocio y política en Mar del Plata, Montevideo y Viña del Mar*, edited by Elisa Pastoriza, 117–132. Buenos Aires: Biblos, 2002.

———. *Montevideo, ciudad balnearia (1900–1950): el municipio y e el fomento de turismo.* Montevideo: CSIC, Universidad de la República, 2010.

DaMatta, Roberto. *Carnavais, malandros e heróis: para uma sociologia do dilema brasileiro.* 5th ed. Rio: Guanabara, 1990.

———. *A casa e a rua: espaço, cidadania, mulher e morte no Brasil.* Rio: Guanabara, 1987.

Dávila, Jerry. *Diploma of Whiteness: Race and Social Policy in Brazil, 1917–1945.* Durham, NC: Duke University Press, 2003.

Dawson, Kevin. *Undercurrents of Power: Aquatic Culture in the African Diaspora.* Philadelphia: University of Pennsylvania Press, 2018.

Debret, Jean-Baptiste. *Viagem pitoresca e histórica ao Brasil.* Translated by Sérgio

Milliet. 2 vols. Belo Horizonte: Itatiaia; São Paulo: Ed. da Universidade de São Paulo, 1978.

Désert, Gabriel. *La vie quotidienne sur les plages normandes du Second Empire aux Années folles*. [Paris]: Hachette, 1983.

Deutsch, Sarah. *Women and the City: Gender, Space, and Power in Boston, 1870–1940*. New York: Oxford University Press, 2000.

Dicionário contemporâneo da língua portuguesa Caldas Aulete. 3rd Brazilian ed. 5 vols. Rio: Ed. Delta, 1980.

Dicionário eletrônico Houaiss da língua portuguesa. Version 1.0. CD-ROM. São Paulo: Editora Objetiva, 2001.

Disitzer, Márcia. *Um mergulho no Rio: 100 anos de moda e comportamento na praia carioca*. Rio: Casa da Palavra, 2012.

Distrito Federal, Prefeitura [A. A. de Azevedo Sodré]. *Mensagem do prefeito do Districto federal lida na sessão do Conselho Municipal de 4 de setembro de 1916*. Rio: Typ. do *Jornal do Commercio* de Rodrigues, 1916.

——— [Alfred Agache]. *Cidade do Rio de Janeiro: extensão—remodelação—embelezamento*. Paris: Foyer Brésilien, [1930].

——— [Antonio Prado Junior]. *Mensagem ao Conselho Municipal: 1º de junho de 1930*. Rio: Officinas Graphicas do *Jornal do Brasil*, 1930.

——— [Antonio Prado Junior]. *Mensagem do prefeito do Districto Federal lida na sessão do Conselho Municipal de 1º de junho de 1929*. Rio: Off. Graphicas do *Jornal do Brasil*, 1929.

——— [Bento Ribeiro Carneiro Monteiro]. *Mensagem do prefeito do Districto Federal lida na sessão do Conselho Municipal de 27 de abril de 1911*. Rio: Imprensa Nacional, 1911.

——— [Bento Ribeiro Carneiro Monteiro]. *Mensagem do prefeito do Districto Federal lida na sessão do Conselho Municipal de 2 de abril de 1913*. Rio: Typ. do Jornal do Commercio, 1913.

——— [Carlos Cesar de Oliveira Sampaio]. *Mensagem do prefeito do Districto Federal lida na sessão de 1º de junho de 1922*. Rio: Officinas Graphicas do *Jornal do Brasil*, 1922.

——— [Francisco Pereira Passos]. *Mensagem do prefeito do Districto Federal lida na sessão do Conselho Municipal de 2 de abril de 1904*. Rio: Typographia da *Gazeta de Noticias*, 1904.

——— [Francisco Pereira Passos]. *Mensagem do prefeito do Districto Federal lida na sessão do Conselho Municipal de 4 de abril de 1905*. Rio: Typ. da *Gazeta de Noticias*, 1905.

——— [Francisco Pereira Passos]. *Mensagem do prefeito do Distrito Federal lida na sessão do Conselho Municipal de 5 de setembro de 1906*. Rio: Typ. da *Gazeta de Noticias*, 1906.

——— [Olympio de Mello]. *Mensagem apresentada á Camara Municipal do Districto Federal em 3 de maio de 1936 pelo prefeito em exercicio Olympio de Mello.* Rio: Officinas Graphicas do *Jornal do Brasil*, 1936.
——— [Rivadávia da Cunha Correia]. *Mensagem do prefeito do Districto Federal lida na sessão do Conselho Municipal de 3 de abril de 1916.* Rio: Typ. do *Jornal do Commercio* de Rodrigues, 1916.
——— [Rivadávia da Cunha Correia]. *Mensagem do prefeito do Districto Federal lida na sessão do Conselho Municipal de 5 de abril de 1915.* Rio: Typ. do *Jornal do Commercio* de Rodrigues, 1915.
———. Directoria Geral de Obras e Viação. *Planta da cidade do Rio de Janeiro organisada na carta cadastral.* Rio: Directoria Geral de Obras e Viação, Prefeitura do Districto Federal, 1928.
———. Secretaria do Prefeito, Departamento de Geografia e Estatística. *Anuário Estatístico do Distrito Federal 1941.* Rio: Departamento de Geografia e Estatística, 1942.
———. Secretaria Geral do Interior e Segurança, Departamento de Geografia e Estatística. *Anuário Estatístico do Distrito Federal–Ano XI–1947.* 4 vols. Rio: Departamento de Geografia e Estatística, 1948.
———. Secretaria Geral do Interior e Segurança Pública, Departamento de Geografia e Estatística. *Anuário Estatístico do Distrito Federal Ano XIII - 1950.* 4 vols. Rio: Departamento de Geografia e Estatística, 1950.
———. *Consolidação das leis e posturas municipaes.* Vol. 1: *Legislação Federal.* Vol. 2: *Legislação Districtal.* Rio: Impresso nas Officinas Typographicas de Paula Souza, 1904–1906.
Dostoyevsky, Fyodor. *The Gambler and Other Stories.* Translated by Ronald Meyer. London: Penguin, 2010.
Downes, Richard. "Autos Over Rails: How US Business Supplanted the British in Brazil, 1910–28." *Journal of Latin American Studies* 24, no. 3 (Oct. 1992): 570–71.
Doyle, Debbie Ann. "'The Salt Water Washes Away All Impropriety': Mass Culture and the Middle-Class Body on the Beach in Turn-of-the-Century Atlantic City." In *Gender and Landscape: Renegotiating Morality and Space*, edited by Lorraine Dowler, Josephine Carubia, and Bonj Szczygiel, 94–108. London: Routledge, 2005.
Dunlop, C. J. *Apontamentos para uma história dos bondes no Rio de Janeiro.* 2 vols. Rio: Laemmert, 1956.
———. *Rio antigo.* 3 vols. Rio: Editora Rio Antigo, 1955–1960.
Dunn, Christopher. *Contracultura: Alternative Arts and Social Transformation in Authoritarian Brazil.* Chapel Hill: University of North Carolina Press, 2016.

Duque [Estrada], [Luís] Gonzaga. "A estética das praias." In *Graves & frívolos*, 91–103. Rio: Fundação Casa de Rui Barbosa and Sette Letras, 1997 [1906].
Durand, José Carlos. "Negociação política e renovação arquitetônica: Le Corbusier no Brasil." *Revista Brasileira de Ciências Sociais* 6, no. 16 (July 1991): 5–26.
Durão, José Ferraz de Oliveira. *Breves considerações ácerca do emprego hygienico e therapeutico dos banhos de mar*. Rio: Typ. de Texeira, 1845.
Durtain, Luc. *Imagens do Brasil e do pampa*. Translated by Ronald de Carvalho. 2nd ed. Rio: Ariel, 1935.
Ebel, Ernst. *O Rio de Janeiro e seus arredores em 1824*. Translated by Joaquim de Sousa Leão Filho. São Paulo: Editora Nacional, 1972.
Edmundo [de Melo Pereira da Costa], Luiz. *O Rio de Janeiro do meu tempo*. 2nd ed. 5 vols. Rio: Conquista, 1957 [1938].
Edschmid, Kasimir. *South America: Lights and Shadows*. Translated by William Oakley. New York: Viking Press, 1932 [German ed., 1931].
Efegê, Jota [João Ferreira Gomes]. "Mère Louise, velha e pobre, vendeu seu famoso *cabaret*. . . ." In *Meninos, eu vi*, 203–4. Rio: FUNARTE/Instituto Nacional de Música, Divisão de Música Popular, 1985.
El-Kareh, Almir Chaiban. "Quando os subúrbios eram arrebaldes: um passeio pelo Rio de Janeiro e seus arredores no século XIX." In *150 anos de subúrbio carioca*, edited by Márcio Piñon de Oliveira and Nelson da Nóbrega Fernandes, 19–56. Rio: Lamparina, FAPERJ, EdUFF, 2010.
Eneida [Costa de Morais]. "Introdução." In *História dos subúrbios: Copacabana*, edited by Eneida [Costa de Morais] and Paulo Berger, 5–20. São Paulo: Departamento de História e Documentação da Prefeitura do Distrito Federal, 1959.
Ermakoff, George. *Augusto Malta e o Rio de Janeiro: 1903–1936*. Rio: G. Ermakoff Casa Editorial, 2009.
———. *Paisagem do Rio de Janeiro: aquarelas, desenhos e gravuras dos artistas viajantes, 1790–1890*. Rio: G. Ermakoff Casa Editorial, 2011.
———. *Rio de Janeiro, 1910–1930: uma crônica fotográfica*. Rio: G. Ermakoff Casa Editorial 2003.
Ewbank, Thomas. *Life in Brazil, or a Journal of a Visit to the Land of the Cocoa and the Palm*. New York: Harper & Brothers, 1856.
Fagnani, Fernando. *La ciudad más querida: Mar del Plata desde sus orígenes hasta hoy*. Buenos Aires: Editorial Sudamericana, 2002.
Farias, Juliana Barreto, Carlos Eugênio Líbano Soares, and Flávio dos Santos Gomes. *No labirinto das nações: africanos e identidades no Rio de Janeiro*. Rio: Arquivo Nacional, 2005.
Farias, Patrícia Silveira de. *Pegando uma cor: relações raciais na cidade do Rio de Janeiro*. Rio: Secretaria Municipal das Culturas, Departamento Geral de Documentação e Informação, Divisão de Editoração, 2003.

Faris, John T. *Seeing South America*. New York: Flemming H. Revel, 1931.
Fernandes, Nelson da Nóbrega. *O rapto ideológico da categoria subúrbio: Rio de Janeiro, 1858–1945*. Rio: Apicuri, 2011.
Ferreira, Aurélio Buarque de Holanda. *Dicionário Aurélio eletrônico século XXI*, versão 3.0, CD-ROM, Rio: Nova Fronteira, 1999.
Ferreira, Debie, and Rosiane Serrano. "A evolução do biquini no século XX." Paper presented to 8ª Jornada de Ensino, Pesquisa e Extensão (Erechim, Rio Grande do Sul), 8–9 Oct. 2019.
[Ferreira Filho], João Antônio. *Ô, Copacabana*. 2nd ed. São Paulo: Cosac & Naify, 2001 [1978].
Ferrez, Gilberto. *Photography in Brazil, 1840–1900*. Translated by Stella de Sá Rego. Albuquerque: University of New Mexico Press, 1990.
Ferrez, Marc, Gilberto Ferrez, and Paulo Ferreira Santos. *O album da Avenida Central: um documento fotográfico da construção da Avenida Rio Branco, Rio de Janeiro, 1903–1906*. São Paulo: Ex Libris, 1982.
Fischer, Brodwyn. *A Poverty of Rights: Citizenship and Inequality in Twentieth-Century Rio de Janeiro*. Stanford, CA: Stanford University Press, 2008.
Fletcher, James C., and D[aniel] [Parrish] Kidder. *Brazil and the Brazilians Portrayed in Historical and Descriptive Sketches*. 8th ed., rev. and enl. Boston: Little, Brown, 1868.
Florentino, Manolo. *Em costas negras: uma história do tráfico de escravos entre a África e o Rio de Janeiro*. São Paulo: Companhia das Letras, 1997.
Fodor, Eugene. *Fodor's Guide to South America, 1968*. New York: David McKay, 1968.
Franck, Harry A[lverson]. *Rediscovering South America: Random Wanderings from Panama to Patagonia and Back, Reviewing a Continent the Author Covered, Mainly on Foot, a Generation Ago*. Philadelphia: J. B. Lippincott, 1943.
———. *Working North from Patagonia: Being the Narrative of a Journey, Earned on the Way, Through Southern and Eastern South America*. Garden City, NY: Garden City, 1921.
Frank, Zephyr L. *Dutra's World: Wealth and Family in Nineteenth-Century Rio de Janeiro*. Albuquerque: University of New Mexico Press, 2004.
———. *Reading Rio de Janeiro: Literature and Society in the Nineteenth Century*. Stanford, CA: Stanford University Press, 2016.
Freeland, Thornton, dir. *Flying Down to Rio*. Hollywood: RKO, 1933.
Freeman, James Patrick. "Democracy and Danger on the Beach: Class Relations in the Public Space of Rio de Janeiro." *Space and Culture* 5, no. 1 (Feb. 2002): 9–28.
———. "Face to Face but Worlds Apart: The Geography of Class in the Public Space of Rio de Janeiro." PhD diss., University of California, Berkeley, 2002.
Freire, Américo. *Guerra de posições na metrópole: a prefeitura e as empresas de ônibus*

no Rio de Janeiro, 1906–1948. Rio: Núcleo de Memória Política Carioca e Fluminense, 2001.
Freire, Américo, and Lúcia Lippi Oliveira. *Novas memórias do urbanismo carioca*. Rio: FGV Editora, 2008.
Freire-Medeiros, Bianca. *O Rio de Janeiro que Hollywood inventou*. Rio: Zahar, 2005.
Freire-Medeiros, Bianca, and Celso Castro. *Destino Cidade Maravilhosa: turismo no Rio de Janeiro*. Rio: Fundação Getúlio Vargas, CPDOC, 2011.
French, John D. *The Brazilian Workers' ABC: Class Conflict and Alliances in Modern São Paulo*. Chapel Hill: University of North Carolina Press, 1992.
Freyre, Gilberto. *Modos de homem & modas de mulher*. Rio: Record, 1986.
———. *Seleta para jovens*. Rio: José Olympio, 1971.
———. *Sobrados e mucambos: decadência do patriarcado rural e desenvolvimento do urbano*, 12th ed. Rio: Record, 2000 [1936].
Frizell, William G., and George H. Greenfield. *Sight-Seeing in South America*. N.c.: n.p., 1912.
Fry, Peter. *A persistência da raça: ensaios antropológicos sobre o Brasil e a África austral*. Rio: Civilização Brasileira, 2005.
Fuss, Peter. *Brasilien*. Berlin and Zurich: Atlantis-Verlag, 1937.
Garcia, Lúcia Maria Cruz. "Casa de banhos de D. João VI." In *Dicionário do Brasil Joanino: 1808–1821*, edited by Ronaldo Vainfas and Lúcia Bastos Pereira das Neves, 77–78. Rio: Objetiva, 2008.
Garcia, Sérgio. *Rio de Janeiro—passado & presente*. Rio: Conexão Cultural, 2000.
Gaspar, Claudia Braga. *Orla carioca: história e cultura*. São Paulo: Metalivros, 2004.
Gaspar, Maria Dulce. *Garotas de programa: prostituição em Copacabana e identidade social*. 2nd ed. Rio: Jorge Zahar, 1988.
Gerson, Brasil. *História das ruas do Rio*. 3rd ed., edited by Alexei Bueno. Rio: Lacerda Editora, 2000.
Gibson, Hugh. *Rio*. New York: Doubleday, Doran, 1937.
Gomes, Antonio José de Souza. *Que influencia tem tido sobre a saúde publica da Capital os banhos. . . .* Rio: Typ. Universal de Laemmert, 1853.
Gomes, Flávio dos Santos. *Histórias de quilombos: mocambos e comunidades no Rio de Janeiro, século XIX*. Rev. and enl. ed. São Paulo: Companhia das Letras, 2006.
Gomes, Isabelle Macedo. "Dois séculos em busca de uma solução: esgotos sanitários e meio ambiente na Cidade do Rio de Janeiro." In *Rio de Janeiro: formas, movimentos, representações, estudos de geografia histórica carioca*, edited by Maurício de Almeida Abreu, 56–71. Rio: Da Fonseca Comunicação, 2005.
———. "Uma questão fundamental e sempre renovada: a disposição final do lixo na cidade do Rio de Janeiro." BA thesis, Universidade Federal do Rio de Janeiro, 1996.

Gomes, Rodrigo Cantos Savelli. "A mulata e o malandro no samba carioca do início do século XX: um exame das relações de gênero no teatro musicado." Paper Presented at the Seminário Internacional Fazendo Gênero, Florianópolis, 2013.

Gomes, Tiago de Melo. *Um espelho no palco: identidades sociais e massificação de cultura no teatro de revista dos anos 20*. Campinas: Editora UNICAMP, 2004.

Gondra, José. *Artes de civilizar: medicina, higiene e educação escolar na Corte Imperial*. Rio: EdUERJ, 2004.

Góngora, Álvaro. "De jardín privado a balneario popular: veraneando en Viña del Mar." In *Historia de la vida privada en Chile*, 3 vols., edited by Rafael Sagredo and Cristián Gazmuri, 2:305–32. Santiago: Taurus, 2005–2010.

Gontijo, Fabiano. "Carioquice ou carioquidade? Ensaio etnográfico das imagens identitárias cariocas." In *Nu & vestido: dez antropólogos revelam a cultura do corpo carioca*, edited by Mirian Goldenberg, 41–77. Rio: Record, 2002.

Gontijo, Silvana. *80 anos de moda no Brasil*. Rio: Nova Fronteira, 1987.

Goslin, Priscilla Ann. *How to Be a Carioca: The Alternative Guide for the Tourist in Rio*. Rio: TwoCan, 1991.

———. *Rau tchu bi a carioca: o guia alternativo para o turista no Rio*. Translated by Carlos Araújo. Rio: Twocan, 1993.

Goulart, Adriana da Costa. "Revisitando a espanhola: a gripe pandêmica de 1918 no Rio de Janeiro." *História, Ciência, Saúde—Manguinhos* 12, no. 1 (Jan.–April 2005): 101–42.

O governo presidencial do Brasil, 1889–1930: guia administrativo da Primeira República: Poder Executivo. Brasília: Senado Federal, Pró-Memória; Rio: Fundação Casa de Rui Barbosa, 1985.

Graham, Maria [Dundas], [Lady Calcott]. *Journal of a Voyage to Brazil and Residence There During Part of the Years 1821, 1822, 1823*. London: Longman, Hurst, Rees, Orme, Brown, and Green, 1824.

Graham, Richard. *Britain and the Onset of Modernization in Brazil, 1850–1914*. London: Cambridge University Press, 1968.

Graham, Sandra Lauderdale. *House and Street: The Domestic World of Servants and Masters in Nineteenth-Century Rio de Janeiro*. Cambridge: Cambridge University Press, 1988.

Green, James N. *Beyond Carnival: Male Homosexuality in Twentieth-Century Brazil*. Chicago: University of Chicago Press, 1999.

Gregory, Frederick L. "Roberto Burle Marx: The One-Man Extravaganza." *Landscape Architecture Magazine* 71, no. 3 (1981): 346–57.

Grin, Mônica. "O desafio multiculturalista no Brasil: a economia política das percepções raciais." PhD diss., Instituto Universitário de Pesquisas do Rio de Janeiro, 2001.

Guanabara, Govêrno Carlos Lacerda. *Mensagem à Assembléia Legislativa: análise econômica, aspectos gerais, 1961–1965*. Rio: n.p., [1965].

Guia do Districto Federal (para o serviço de policiamento). Edited by José da Silva Pessoa. Rio: Typ. da Policia Federal, [1921].

Guia do viajante no Rio de Janeiro, accompanhado da planta da cidade, de uma carta das estradas de ferro do Rio de Janeiro, Minas e São Paulo e de uma vista dos Dois Irmãos. Rio: G. Leuzinger & Filhos, B. L. Garnier, and H. Laemmert, 1884.

Guia official do trafego: Rio de Janeiro. Rio: n.p., [1934].

Guimarães, Lúcia. "Henrique Fleiüss." In *Dicionário do Brasil Imperial, 1822–1889*, edited by Ronaldo Vainfas, 335–36. Rio: Objetiva, 2002.

Guinle, Jorge, with Mylton Severiano da Silva. *Um século de boa vida: memórias de um brasileiro que nunca trabalhou*. São Paulo: Globo, 1997.

Gunn, Simon, and Robert J. Morris, eds. *Identities in Space: Contested Terrains in the Western City since 1850*. Aldershot, UK: Ashgate, 2001.

Hahner, June E. *Poverty and Politics: The Urban Poor in Brazil, 1870–1920*. Albuquerque: University of New Mexico Press, 1986.

Hanchard, Michael. "Black Cinderella? Race and the Public Sphere in Brazil." *Public Culture* 7, no. 1 (Fall 1994): 164–85.

Hansen, Devon. "Shades of Change: Suntanning and the Twentieth-Century American Dream." PhD diss., Boston University, 2007.

Hassan, John. *The Seaside, Health and the Environment in England and Wales since 1800*. Aldershot, UK: Ashgate, 2003.

Hertzman, Marc A. *Making Samba: A New History of Race and Music in Brazil*. Durham, NC: Duke University Press, 2013.

Heynemann, Cláudia. *Floresta da Tijuca: natureza e civilização*. Rio: Secretaria Municipal de Cultura, Departamento Geral de Documentação e Informação Cultural, 1995.

Hitchcock, Alfred, dir. *Notorious*. Hollywood: RKO, 1946.

Hoffmann-Harnisch, Wolfgang. *O Brasil que eu vi: retrato de uma potencia tropical*. Translated by Huberto Augusto. São Paulo: Melhoramentos, n.d. [German ed., 1938].

Holanda, Guerra de. "O Barão de Lucena e o escravo Romão." *Boletim da Cidade e do Porto do Recife* 19–34 (Jan.–Dec. 1946–49): n.p.

Holloway, Thomas H. *Immigrants on the Land: Coffee and Society in São Paulo, 1886–1934*. Chapel Hill: University of North Carolina Press, 1980.

———. *Policing Rio de Janeiro: Repression and Resistance in a 19th-Century City*. Stanford, CA: Stanford University Press, 1993.

Horwood, Catherine. "'Girls Who Arouse Dangerous Passions': Women and Bathing, 1900–39." *Women's History Review* 9, no. 4 (2000): 653–73.

Hudson, Strode. *South by Thunderbird*. New York: Random House, 1937.

Huntsman, Leone. *Sand in Our Souls: The Beach in Australian History*. Melbourne: Melbourne University Press, 2001.

Ipacom Travel. *Insider's Guide to Rio de Janeiro*. http://ipanema.com/ (accessed on 3.3.2012).

Jaguaribe, Beatriz. "A Barra da Tijuca e as estéticas do consumo." In *Fins de século: cidade e cultura no Rio de Janeiro*, 135–66. Rio: Rocco, 1998.

Jesus, Gilmar Mascarenhas de. "Construindo a cidade moderna: a introdução dos esportes na vida urbana do Rio de Janeiro." *Revista Estudos Históricos* 13, no. 23 (1999): 17–39.

Johnson, Harold B., Jr. "A Preliminary Inquiry into Money, Prices, and Wages in Rio de Janeiro, 1763–1823." In *Colonial Roots of Modern Brazil: Papers of the Newberry Library Conference*, edited by Dauril Alden, 70–89. Berkeley: University of California Press, 1973.

Jordan, André. *O Rio Que Passou na Minha Vida*. Rio: Leo Christiano Editorial, 2006.

Jordan, Thomas Marshall. "Contesting the Terms of Incorporation: Labor and the State in Rio de Janeiro, 1930–1964." PhD diss., University of Illinois at Urbana-Champaign, 2000.

Kane, Robert S. *South America: A to Z*. New York: Doubleday, 1962.

Karasch, Mary C. *Slave Life in Rio de Janeiro, 1808–1850*. Princeton, NJ: Princeton University Press, 1987.

Kaz, Roberto. "Das coxias ao palco: a transformação da praia em um centro de lazer." *Revista de História da Biblioteca Nacional* 17 (Feb. 2007): 23.

Kaz, Stela. *Um jeito copacabana de ser*. Rio: Ed. PUC-Rio; Reflexão, 2014.

Kehl, Renato. *Formulario da belleza*. Rio: Francisco Abreu, 1927.

Kehren, Mark Edward. "Tunnel Vision: Urban Renewal in Rio de Janeiro." PhD diss., University of Maryland, 2006.

Kessel, Carlos. *A vitrine e o espelho: o Rio de Janeiro de Carlos Sampaio*. Rio: Prefeitura da Cidade do Rio de Janeiro, Secretaria da Cultura, Departamento Geral de Documentação e Informação Cultural, Arquivo Geral da Cidade do Rio de Janeiro, Divisão de Pesquisa, 2001.

Kidder, Daniel P[arish]. *Sketches of Residence and Travels in Brazil, Embracing Historical and Geographical Notices of the Empire of Brazil and Its Several Provinces*. 2 vols. Philadelphia: Sorin & Ball; London: Wiley and Putnam, 1845.

Kidder, D[aniel] P[arish], and J[ames] C[ooley] Fletcher. *Brazil and the Brazilians, Portrayed in Historical and Descriptive Sketches*. Philadelphia: Childs & Peterson, 1857.

Kipling, Rudyard. *Brazilian Sketches*. Bromley, Kent, UK: P. E. Waters, 1989.

Kobel, W. H. *The Great South Land: The River Plate and Southern Brazil of To-day*. London: Thornton Butterworth, 1919.

Koifman, Fábio. *Quixote nas trevas: o embaixador Souza Dantas e os refugiados do nazismo*. Rio: Record, 2002.

Kraay, Hendrik. "The 'Barbarous Game': *Entrudo* and Its Critics in Rio de Janeiro, 1810s–1850s." *Hispanic American Historical Review* 95, no. 3 (Aug. 2015): 427–58.

La Berge, Ann. *Mission and Method: The Early Nineteenth-Century French Public Health Movement*. Cambridge: University of Cambridge Press, 1992.

Lago, Bia Corrêa do, ed. *Praias do Rio: 25 ensaios fotográficos—Beaches in Rio: 25 Photographic Essays*. Rio: Capivara, 2005.

Landseer, Charles. *Charles Landseer: desenhos e aquarelas do Brasil, 1825–26*. Edited by Leslie Bethell. São Paulo: Instituto Moreira Salles, 2010.

Langsdorff, E. [Victorine Emilie de Sainte-Aulaire] de, Baronne de. *Diário da Baronesa E. de Langsdorff: relatando sua viagem ao Brasil por ocasião do casamento de S.A.R. o Príncipe de Joinville, 1842–1843*. Translated by Patrícia Chittoni Ramos and Marco Antônio Toledo Neder. Florianópolis: Editora Mulheres; Santa Cruz do Sul: EDUNISC, 1999.

Lanna, Ana Lúcia Duarte. *Uma cidade na transição: Santos, 1870–1913*. São Paulo: HUCITEC; Santos: Prefeitura Municipal de Santos, 1995.

Lavinas, Lena, and Luiz César de Q. Ribeiro. "Imagens e representações sobre a mulher na construção da modernidade de Copacabana." In *Imagens urbanas: os diversos olhares na formação do imaginário urbano*, edited by Célia Ferraz de Souza and Sandra Jatahy Pesavento, 43–56. Porto Alegre: Editora da UFRGS, 1997.

Leclerc, Max. *Cartas do Brasil.* Translated by Sérgio Milliet. São Paulo: Companhia Editora Nacional, 1942.

Leff, Nathaniel H. *Development and Underdevelopment in Brazil.* 2 vols. London: Allen & Unwin, 1982.

Leithold, Theodor von. "Minha excursão ao Brasil, ou Viagem de Berlim ao Rio de Janeiro e volta, acompanhada de numerosa descrição dessa capital, da vida na corte e de seus habitantes, bem como conselhos para os que buscam melhorar sua sorte no Brasil." In *O Rio de Janeiro visto por dois prussianos em 1819*, translated by Joaquim de Souza Leão Filho, 1–121. São Paulo: Companhia Editora Nacional, 1966.

Lemos, Luiz Henrique Carneiro. "Posição social, consumo e espaço urbano: um estudo sobre a dinâmica sócio-espacial nas áreas nobres do Rio de Janeiro." PhD diss., Universidade Federal do Rio de Janeiro, 2008.

Lenček, Lena, and Gideon Bosker. *The Beach: The History of Paradise on Earth.* New York: Penguin, 1999.

———. *Making Waves: Swimsuits and the Undressing of America*. San Francisco: Chronicle Books, 1989.

Léry, Jean de. *Journal de bord de Jean de Léry en la terre de Brésil, 1557*. Edited by M.-R. Mayeux. Paris: Éditions de Paris, 1957.
Lessa, Carlos. *O Rio de todos os Brasis (uma reflexão em busca de auto-estima)*. Rio: Record, 2001.
Lesser, Jeffrey. *Welcoming the Undesirables: Brazil and the Jewish Question*. Berkeley: University of California Press, 1995.
Levine, Robert M. *The Brazilian Photographs of Geneviève Naylor*. Durham, NC: Duke University Press, 1998.
Lévy, Maria Bárbara. *História da Bolsa de Valores do Rio de Janeiro*. Rio: IBMEC, 1977.
Lima, Henrique Carlos da Rocha. *Do emprego da hydrotherapia no tratamento das moléstias chronicas*. Rio: Typ. Universal de Laemmert, 1869.
Lima, Ivana Stolze. *Cores, marcas e falas: os sentidos da mestiçagem no Império do Brasil*. Rio: Arquivo Nacional, 2003.
Lima, Rogério Barbosa. *O antigo Leblon: uma aldeia encantada*. 2nd ed. Rio: R. B. Lima, 1999.
Lobo, Eulália Maria Lahmeyer. *História do Rio de Janeiro (do capital comercial ao capital industrial e financeiro)*. 2 vols. Rio: IBMEC, 1978.
Lopes [Ferreira], Thomaz [Pompeu]. *A vida*. Rio: Livraria Garnier e Irmãos, [1911].
Love, Joseph L. *São Paulo and the Brazilian Federation*. Stanford, CA: Stanford University Press, 1980.
Luccock, John. *Notes on Rio de Janeiro, and the Southern Parts of Brazil; Taken During a Residence in that Country, from 1808 to 1818*. London: Samuel Leigh, 1820.
Macedo, Joaquim Manoel de. *Memorias da Rua do Ouvidor*. Rio: Typographia Perseverança, 1878.
Machado, Helena Cristina Ferreira. *A construção social da praia*. Guimarães: IDEAL, 1996.
[Maciel], Antônio [Arthur Antunes]. *Memórias de um rato de hotel*. Note by Plínio Doyle, Article by João do Rio, and Afterword by João Carlos Rodrigues. 2nd ed. Rio: Dantes, 2000 [1912].
Mackaman, Douglas Peter. *Leisure Settings: Bourgeois Culture, Medicine, and the Spa in Modern France*. Chicago: University of Chicago Press, 1998.
MacLachlan, Colin A. *A History of Modern Brazil: The Past against the Future*. Wilmington, DE: Scholarly Resources, 2003.
Madden, Annette. *In Her Footsteps: 101 Remarkable Black Women, from the Queen of Sheba to Queen Latifa*. Berkeley, CA: Conari Press, 2000.
Maio, Marcos Chor. "Costa Pinto e a Crítica ao 'Negro como espetáculo.'" In *O negro no Rio de Janeiro: relações de raças numa sociedade em mudança*, edited by L[uiz de] A[guiar] Costa Pinto, 2nd ed., 17–50. Rio: Editora UFRJ, 1998 [1953].

Malamud, Samuel. *Recordando a Praça Onze*. Rio: Kosmos, 1988.
Marcílio, Maria Luiza, ed. *Família, mulher, sexualidade e Igreja na história do Brasil*. São Paulo: Edições Loyola, 1993.
Marras, Stelio. *A propósito de águas virtuosas: formação e ocorrências de uma estação balneária no Brasil*. Belo Horizonte: Editora UFMG, 2004.
Martínez-Echazábel, Lourdes. "O culturalismo nos anos 30 no Brasil e na América Latina: deslocamento retórico ou mudança conceitual?" In *Raça, ciência e sociedade*, edited by Marcos Chor Maio and Ricardo Ventura Santos, 107–24. Rio: FIOCRUZ/CCBB, 1996.
Martins, Luís. *Noturno da Lapa*. 3rd ed. Rio: José Olympio and Biblioteca Nacional, 2004 [1966].
Matschat, Cecile Hulse. *Seven Grass Huts: An Engineer's Wife in Central and South America*. New York: Farrar & Rinehart, 1939.
Mauad, Ana Maria. "Sob o signo da imagem: a produção da fotografia e o controle dos códigos de representação social da classe dominante, no Rio de Janeiro, na primeira metade do século XX." PhD diss., Universidade Federal Fluminense, 1990.
Maul, Carlos. *O Rio da bela época*. Rio: Livraria S. José, 1967.
Máximo, João. *Cinelândia: breve história de um sonho*. Rio: Salamandra, 1997.
McCann, Bryan. *Hard Times in the Marvelous City: From Dictatorship to Democracy in the Favelas of Rio de Janeiro*. Durham, NC: Duke University Press, 2014.
McCann, Eugene J. "Race, Protest, and Public Space: Contextualizing Lefebvre in the U.S. City." *Antipode* 31, no. 2 (1999): 163–84.
Meade, Teresa A. "'Civilizing' Rio de Janeiro: The Public Health Campaign and the Riot of 1904," *Journal of Social History* 20, no. 2 (Winter 1986): 301–22.
———. *"Civilizing" Rio: Reform and Resistance in a Brazilian City, 1889–1930*. University Park: Pennsylvania State University Press, 1997.
Meireles, Cecília. *Rute e Alberto*. Edited by Virginia and Eunice Joiner. Boston: D. C. Heath, 1945 [1938].
Mello, Joaquim Pedro de. *Generalidades a cerca da educação physica dos meninos*. Rio: Typographia de Teixeira, 1846.
Mello, José Justino de. *Do emprego da hydrotherapia no tratamento das molestias chronicas*. Rio: Typ. do *Apostolo*, 1870.
Melo, Hildete Pereira de. "A trajetória da industrialização do Rio de Janeiro." In *Um estado em questão: os 25 anos do Rio de Janeiro*, edited by Américo Freire, Carlos Eduardo Sarmento, and Marly Silva da Motta, 219–48. Rio: Editora FGV, 2001.
Melo, João Batista de. *Memórias de um João Ninguém: o farofeiro de Ipanema*. Valença: Ed. Valença, 1994.
Melo, Victor Andrade de. *Cidade sportiva: primórdios do esporte no Rio de Janeiro*. Rio: Relume Dumará and FAPERJ, 2001.

Melosi, Martin. *The Sanitary City: Urban Infrastructure in America from Colonial Times to the Present*. Baltimore: The Johns Hopkins University Press, 2000.

Melville, Herman. *White Jacket; or The World in a Man-of-War*. New York: Grove Press, [1850].

Mendes, António Lopes. *América Austral: um viajante português no Brasil, 1882–1883: carta*. Rio: UNIPAR, 1998

Mendonça, Alberto de. *Historia do sport nautico no Brazil: ligeiro esboço*. Rio: Sociedade Brazileira de Sociedades do Remo, 1909.

Mertz, Elizabeth. "Beyond Symbolic Anthropology: Introducing Semiotic Mediation." In *Semiotic Mediation: Sociocultural and Psychological Mediation*, edited by Elizabeth Mertz and Richard J. Parmentier, 1–19. Orlando, FL: Academic Press, 1985.

Mesquita, Cláudia. *De Copacabana à Boca do Mato: o Rio de Janeiro de Sérgio Porto e Stanislaw Ponte Preta*. Rio: Ed. Casa de Rui Barbosa.

Miller, Shawn William. *The Street Is Ours: Community, the Car, and the Nature of Public Space in Rio de Janeiro*. Cambridge: Cambridge University Press, 2018.

Moncorvo Filho, Arthur. *A cura pelo sol*. Buenos Aires: Las Ciencias, 1924.

———. *Em favor das creanças: a cura pelo sol*. Rio: Typ. Besnard Frères, 1924.

———. *Historia da protecção á infancia no Brasil, 1500–1927*. Rio: Imprensa Graphica Editora, 1927.

———. *Os primeiros ensaios de heliotherapia no Brasil (trabalho do Dispensario Moncorvo)*. Rio: Typ. Besnard Frères, 1917.

Motta, Manoel Pinto da. *Que influencia tem tido sobre a saude publica da Capital os banhos de que usa sua população?* Rio: Typographia Litteraria, 1852.

Motta, Marcelo Paiva da. "O centro comercial do Rio de Janeiro na segunda metade do século XIX—uma interlocução com a noção de área central." In *Rio de Janeiro: formas, movimentos, representações, estudos de geografia histórica carioca*, edited by Maurício de Almeida Abreu, 106–127. Rio: Da Fonseca, 2005.

Motta, Marly Silva da. "A fusão da Guanabara com o Estado do Rio: desafios e desencantos." In *Um estado em questão: os 25 anos do Rio de Janeiro*, edited by Américo Freire, Carlos Eduardo Sarmento, and Marly Silva da Motta, 19–56. Rio: Editora Fundação Getúlio Vargas, 2001.

Nascimento, Álvaro Pereira do. "Um reduto negro: cor e cidadania na Armada (1870–1910)." In *Quase-cidadão: histórias e antropologias da pós-emancipação no Brasil*, edited by Olívia Maria Gomes da Cunha and Flávio Gomes dos Santos, 283–314. Rio: Editora FGV, 2007.

Needell, Jeffrey D. "The *Revolta Contra Vacina* of 1904: The Revolt against 'Modernization' in *Belle-Époque* Rio de Janeiro." *Hispanic American Historical Review* 67, no. 2 (May 1987): 233–69.

———. *A Tropical Belle Époque: Elite Culture and Society in Turn-of-the-Century Rio de Janeiro*. Cambridge: Cambridge University Press, 1987.

Niemeyer, Conrado Jacob. *Questão technica: estudos da* [sic] *Ferro-Carril Copacabana: justificativa*. Rio: Lombaerts, 1884.

Nina, Marcello Della. "Jorge Guinle e o Copa: entrevista. . . ." In *Copacabana, cidade eterna: 100 anos de um mito*, edited by Wilson Coutinho, 39–44. Rio: Relume Dumará, 1992.

Nohara, W.K. *Brasilien Tag und Nacht*. Berlin: Rowalt, 1938.

Nossa Sociedade 1946. Rio: O Construtor, [1946].

Novaes, Carlos Eduardo. "Cem anos de praia." In *Copacabana, cidade eterna: 100 anos de um mito*, edited by Wilson Coutinho, 51–53. Rio: Relume Dumará, 1992.

Octávio, Laura Oliveira Rodrigo. *Elos de uma corrente: seguidos de novos elos*. 2nd ed. Rio: Civilização Brasileira, 1994.

O'Donnell, Julia Galli. *A invenção de Copacabana: culturas urbanas e estilos de vida no Rio de Janeiro (1890–1940)*. Rio: Zahar, 2013.

———. "Um Rio atlântico: culturas urbanas e estilos de vida na invenção de Copacabana." PhD diss., Universidade Federal do Rio de Janeiro, 2011.

Oliveira, Cláudia de, Mônica Pimenta Velloso, and Vera Lins. *O moderno em revistas: representações do Rio de Janeiro de 1890 a 1930*. Rio: Garamond and FAPERJ, 2010.

Oliveira, Edmundo de. *Fossas e exgottos de Copacabana*. Rio: Typ. Besnard Frères, 1906.

Oliveira, Flávia Santos de. "O *habitus* no lugar e o lugar da Tijuca." MA thesis, Universidade Federal do Rio de Janeiro, 2001.

Oliveira, Lenice Pulice de, and Vera Lúcia de Menezes Costa. "Histórias e memórias de pioneiros do vôlei de praia na cidade do Rio de Janeiro." *Revista da Educação Física* 21, no. 1 (1st Trimester 2010): 91–113.

Oliveira, Márcio Piñon de, and Nelson da Nóbrega Fernandes, eds. *150 anos de subúrbio carioca*. Rio: Lamparina, FAPERJ, EdUFF, 2010.

Orazi, Angelo. *Rio de Janeiro and Environs: Traveller's Guide*. Rio: Guias do Brasil, 1939.

———. *Rio de Janeiro e arredores: guia do viajante*. Rio: Guias do Brasil, 1939.

Ouseley, W[illiam] Gore. *Description of Views in South America from Original Drawings Made in Brazil, the River Plate, the Parana, &c. &c., with Notes*. London: Thomas McLean, 1852.

Owensby, Brian P. *Intimate Ironies: Modernity and the Making of Middle Class in Brazil*. Stanford, CA: Stanford University Press, 1999.

Oxford English Dictionary. 2nd ed. 10 vols. Oxford: Clarendon Press, 1989.

Pack, Sasha D. *Tourism and Dictatorship: Europe's Invasion of Franco's Spain*. New York: Palgrave Macmillan, 2006.
Paiva, Eugenio Carlos de. *Como se deve proceder a uma autopsia jurídica. . . .* Rio: Typ. Universal de Laemmert, 1851.
Paiva, Vitor. "A história do pier de Ipanema, ícone da contracultura e do surf no Rio dos anos 1970." *Hypeness* (Jan. 2017), www.hypeness.com.br/.
Pandolfi, Dulce. "Os anos 30: as incertezas de um regime." In *O Brasil republicano*, 4 vols., edited by Jorge Ferreira and Lucília de Almeida Neves Delgado, 2:13–37. Rio: Civilização Brasileira, 2003.
Paranhos, José Maria da Silva, Viscount of Rio Branco. *Cartas ao amigo ausente*. Edited by José Honório Rodrigues. Rio: Ministério de Relações Exteriores, Instituto Rio Branco, 1953.
Parente, José Inacio, and Patrícia Monte-Mór, eds. *Rio de Janeiro: retratos da cidade*. Rio: Interior Produções and Banco do Brasil, 1994.
Pastoriza, Elisa, ed. *Las puertas del mar: consumo, ocio y política en Mar del Plata, Montevideo y Viña del Mar*. Buenos Aires: Biblos, 2002.
Pastoriza, Elisa, and Juan Carlos Torre. "Mar del Plata, un sueño de los argentinos." In *Historia de la vida privada en la Argentina*, 3 vols., edited by Fernando Devoto and Marta Madero, 3:49–78. Buenos Aires: Taurus, 1999.
Peck, Anne Merriman. *Round about South America*. New York: Harper & Bros., 1940.
Peck, Annie S. *The South American Tour*. New York: George Doran, 1916.
Pedro II. *D. Pedro II e a condessa de Barral, através da correspondência íntima do imperador*. Edited by R. Magalhães Júnior. Rio: Civilização Brasileira, 1956.
Peiss, Kathy. *Hope in a Jar: The Making of America's Beauty Culture*. New York: Metropolitan Books, 1998.
Peixoto, Mário, Carlos Eduardo Barata, Claudia Braga Gaspar, and Marilúcia Abreu. *Villa Ipanema*. Rio: Novo Quadro, 1994.
Peixoto, Mário, with the assistance of Marcelo Câmara. *Ipanema de A a Z*. Rio: A. A. Cohen, 1999.
Penha-Lopes, Vânia. "A racialização do espaço: o caso dos shoppings." *Afro-Press* (28.11.2007), https://www.afropress.com/a-racializacao-do-espaco-o-caso-dos-shoppings/ (accessed by editors on 5.8.2021).
Pereira, Cristina Schettini. "Sexo e humor para (alguns) homens." *Nossa História* 1, no. 7 (May 2004): 47–51.
Pereira, Leonardo Affonso de Miranda. *Footballmania: uma história social do futebol no Rio de Janeiro, 1902–1938*. Rio: Nova Fronteira, 2000.
Pereira, Simone Andrade. "Os anos dourados: Copacabana e o imaginário urbano dos anos 50." MA thesis, UFRJ, 1991.

Perlman, Janice E. The *Myth of Marginality: Urban Poverty and Politics in Rio de Janeiro*. Berkeley: University of California Press, 1976.
Perrotta, Isabella. "Desenhando um paraíso tropical: a construção do Rio de Janeiro como destino turístico." PhD diss., Fundação Getúlio Vargas, Centro de Pesquisa e Documentação de História Contemporânea do Brasil, 2011.
Phelps, Gilbert. *The Lost Horizon: A Brazilian Journey*. 2nd ed. London: Charles Knight, 1971 [1964].
Pickard, Christopher. *Rio: The Guide*. Rio: Zylon, 1995.
Pierson, Donald. *Negroes in Brazil: A Study of Race Contact at Bahia*. Chicago: University of Chicago Press, 1942.
Pimenta, Tânia Salgado. "Terapeutas populares e instituições médicas na primeira metade do século XIX." In *Artes e ofícios de curar no Brasil*, edited by Sidney Chalhoub, Vera Regina Beltrão Marques, and Gabriela dos Reis Sampaio, 307–30. Campinas: Ed. da UNICAMP, 2003.
Pimentel, Joaquim Galdino. *O Sr. Ministro das Obras publicas e os carris de ferro da Copacabana: artigos publicados no Jornal do Commercio*. Rio: Typ. de J. Leuzinger & Filhos, 1883.
Pinheiro, Eliane Canedo de Freitas, and Augusto Ivan de Freitas Pinheiro. *Encantos do Rio*. Rio: Salamandra, 1995.
Pinheiro, Maria Terezinha Gama. "A fundação do Balneário Cassino ao final do século XIX e sua expansão e transformação no decorrer do século XX." MA thesis, Universidade Federal de Santa Catarina, 1999.
Pinho, Ana Madureira do. "O bonde da história." In *Circuito Copacabana*. CD-ROM. Rio: Col. Circuitos do Rio, 2002.
Pinho, [José] Wanderley [de Araújo]. "Cinqüenta anos de vida social, 1895–1945: alguns aspectos da evolução da alta sociedade." *Sul América* (Jan.–June 1945): 35–41.
Pinto, L[uiz de] A[guiar] Costa. *O negro no Rio de Janeiro: relações de raças numa sociedade em mudança*. 2nd ed. Rio: Editora UFRJ, 1998 [1953].
Pochmann, Márcio, Ricardo Amorim, and Alexandre Guerra, eds. *Atlas da exclusão social*. 5 vols. São Paulo: Cortez, 2003–2005.
Poerner, Arthur. *Leme*. Rio: Relume Dumará, 1998.
Porto, Sérgio. *A casa demolida*. Rio: Ed. do Autor, 1963.
Pravaz, Nathasha. "The Tan from Ipanema: Freyre, Morenidade, and the Cult of the Body in Rio de Janeiro." *Canadian Journal of Latin American and Caribbean Studies / Revue canadienne des études latino-américaines et caraïbes*, no. 67 (2009): 79–104.
Rago, Margareth. *Os prazeres da noite: prostituição e códigos da sexualidade feminina em São Paulo (1890–1930)*. São Paulo: Paz e Terra, 1991.
Rainho, Maria do Carmo Teixeira. *A cidade e a moda: novas pretensões, novas*

distinções—Rio de Janeiro, século XIX. Brasília: Editora Universidade de Brasília, 2002.

Ralston, Tyler Andrew. "Social Change and Populist Politics in Brazil: The Baixada Fluminense and the Legendary Tenório Cavalcanti, 1945–1964." PhD diss., University of Arizona, 2013.

Randle, Henry W. "Suntanning: Differences in Perception throughout History." *Mayo Clinic Proceedings* 72, no. 5 (1997): 461–62.

Rangel, Cynthia Campos. "As Copacabanas no tempo e no espaço: diferenciação socioespacial e hierarquia urbana." MA thesis, Universidade Federal do Rio de Janeiro, 2003.

Reid, William. *Seeing South America: Condensed Facts for Prospective Travelers*. Washington, DC: Pan American Union, 1931.

Reis, João José. *A morte é uma festa: ritos fúnebres e revolta popular no Brasil do século XIX*. São Paulo: Companhia das Letras, 1991.

Reis Filho, Nestor Goulart. *São Paulo e outras cidades: produção social e degradação dos espaços urbanos*. São Paulo: HUCITEC, 1994.

Renault, Delso. *O dia-a-dia no Rio de Janeiro segundo os jornais, 1870–1889*. Rio: Civilização Brasileira; Brasília: INL, 1982.

———. *Rio de Janeiro: a vida da cidade refletida nos jornais (1850–1870)*. Rio: Civilização Brasileira; Brasília: INL, 1978.

Ribas, Martha, Silvia Fraiha, Tiza Lobo, and Giovanna Hallack. *Botafogo e Humaitá*. Rio: Fraiha, [2000].

Ribeiro, Luiz Cesar de Queiroz. *Dos cortiços aos condomínios fechados: as formas da produção da moradia na cidade do Rio de Janeiro*. Rio: Civilização Brasileira, IPPUR, UFRJ, FASE, 1997.

Rio, João do. *A alma encantadora das ruas*. Edited by Raúl Antelo. São Paulo: Companhia das Letras, 1997 [1909].

———. *Crónicas e frases de Godofredo de Alencar*. 2nd ed. Porto: Livraria Chardron; Rio: Livraria Francisco Alves, 1920 [1916].

———. *João do Rio: um escritor entre duas cidades*. São Paulo: Instituto Moreira Sales; Poços de Caldas: Casa da Cultura de Poços de Caldas, 1992.

———. "A parada da ilusão." In *Dentro da noite*, edited by João Carlos Rodrigues, 128–137. São Paulo: Antiqua, 2002.

Rio de Janeiro. Instituto de Planejamento Municipal (IPLANRIO). *Anuário estatístico da Cidade do Rio de Janeiro*. Rio: IPLANRIO, 1991.

———. Prefeitura da Cidade, Empresa Municipal de Informática e Planejamento. *Anuário estatístico da Cidade do Rio de Janeiro*. Rio: IPLANRIO, 1993.

———. Secretaria Municipal de Cultura, Turismo e Esportes. *Urca: construção e permanência de um bairro*. Rio: Secretaria Municipal de Cultura, Departamento

Geral de Documentação e Informação, Departamento Geral de Patrimônio Cultural, 1990.
———. Secretaria Municipal de Cultura, Turismo e Esportes, Departamento Geral de Documentação e Informação Cultural. *Bairro Peixoto: o oásis de Copacabana*. Rio: PCRJ, Secretaria Municipal de Cultura, Turismo e Esportes, 1992.
———. Secretaria Municipal de Planejamento e Coordenação Geral. *Informações básicas da Cidade do Rio de Janeiro—1981/1982*. [Rio]: n.p., [1983].
———. Secretaria Municipal de Urbanismo, Centro de Arquitetura e Urbanismo do Rio de Janeiro. *Guia da arquitetura Art Déco no Rio de Janeiro*. Rio: Index, 1997.
———. Secretaria Municipal de Urbanismo, Centro de Arquitetura e Urbanismo do Rio de Janeiro. *Guia da arquitetura eclética no Rio de Janeiro*. Rio: Index, 2000.
Rios Filho, Adolfo Morales de los. *O Rio de Janeiro imperial*. 2nd ed. Rio: Topbooks and Editora UniverCidade, 2000.
Rito, Lucia, and Jair de Souza, eds. *Zona Norte: território da alma carioca*. Rio: Shopping Norte, 2001.
Rodrigues, João Carlos. *João do Rio: uma biografia*. Rio: Topbooks, 1996.
Rose, R. S. *Uma das coisas esquecidas: Getúlio Vargas e o controle social no Brasil—1930–54*. Translated by Anna Olga de Barros Barreto. São Paulo: Companhia das Letras, 2001.
Rosenthal, Anton. "Spectacle, Fear, and Protest: A Guide to the History of Urban Public Space in Latin America." *Social Science History* 24, no. 1 (Spring 2000): 33–73.
Rotherby, Agnes. *South America: The West Coast and the East*. Boston: Houghton Mifflin; Cambridge, MA: Riverside Press, 1930.
Rugendas, João Mauricio [Johann Moritz von]. *Viagem pitoresca através do Brasil*. Translated by Sérgio Milliet. 2 vols. São Paulo: Livraria Martins, 1940.
Sá, Hernane Tavares de. *The Brazilians: People of Tomorrow*. New York: John Day, 1947.
Sá, José Marques de. *Structura das carpellas em relação á fecundação. . . .* Rio: Typ. Universal de Laemmert, 1850.
Saliba, Elias Thomé. "*Belle époque* tropical." *História Viva* 2, no. 13 (Nov. 2004): 80–84.
Sampaio, Gabriela dos Reis. *Nas trincheiras da cura: as diferentes medicinas no Rio de Janeiro Imperial*. Campinas: Ed. da UNICAMP, 2001.
San Martini, Lindita, ed. *Copacabana—1892–1992: subsídios para a sua história*. Rio: RIOTUR, 1992.
Sansone, Livio. "Nem somente preto ou branco: o sistema de classificação racial no Brasil." *Afro-Ásia*, no. 18 (1996): 165–87.

Santos, [Francisco Agenor de] Noronha. *Meios de transporte no Rio de Janeiro: historia e legislação.* 2 vols. Rio: Typ. do *Jornal do Commercio*, 1934.
Santos, Joaquim Ferreira dos. *Um homem chamado Maria.* Rio: Objetiva, 2005.
Santos, Jocélio Teles dos. "De pardos disfarçados a brancos pouco claros: classificações raciais no Brasil dos séculos XVIII–XIX." *Afro-Ásia*, no. 32 (2005): 115–37.
Schetino, André Maia. *Pedalando na modernidade: a bicicleta na transição do século XIX para o XX.* Rio: Apicuri, 2008.
Schlichthorst, Carl. *O Rio de Janeiro como é, 1824–1826 (huma vez e nunca mais).* Translated by Emmy Dodt and Gustavo Barroso. São Paulo: Getúlio Costa, 1943.
Schpun, Mônica Rais. *Beleza em jogo: cultura física e comportamento em São Paulo nos anos 1920.* São Paulo: Boitempo/SENAC, 1999.
Schultz, Kirsten. *Tropical Versailles: Empire, Monarchy, and the Portuguese Royal Court in Rio de Janeiro, 1808–1821.* New York: Routledge, 2001.
Schwarcz, Lilia Moritz. *As barbas do imperador: D. Pedro II, um monarca nos trópicos.* São Paulo: Companhia das Letras, 1999.
———. *O espetáculo das raças: ciências, cientistas, instituições e questão racial no Brasil, 1870–1930.* São Paulo: Companhia das Letras, 1993.
Schwartz, Rosalie. *Flying Down to Rio: Hollywood, Tourism, and Yankee Clippers.* College Station: Texas A&M University Press, 2004.
Scobey, David. "Anatomy of the Promenade: The Politics of Bourgeois Sociability in Nineteenth-Century New York." *Social History* 17, no. 2 (May 1992): 203–27.
Sedrez, Lise Fernanda. "'The Bay of All Beauties': State and Environment in Guanabara Bay, Rio de Janeiro, Brazil, 1875–1975." PhD diss., Stanford University, 2004.
Segrave, Kerry. *Suntanning in 20th-Century America.* Jefferson, NC: McFarland, 2005.
Sérgio, Renato. *A alma da cidade: reminiscências e lorotas, lugares, fatos e personagens cariocas.* Rio: Ediouro, 2000.
Sevcenko, Nicolau. "A capital irradiante: técnica, ritmos, e ritos do Rio." In *História da vida privada no Brasil*, 4 vols., edited by Fernando Novais, 3:513–619. São Paulo: Companhia das Letras, 1998.
———. *A Revolta da Vacina: mentes insanas em corpos rebeldes.* São Paulo: Brasiliense, 1984.
Seyferth, Giralda. "Os paradoxos da miscigenação: observações sobre o tema imigração e raça no Brasil." *Estudos Afro-Asiáticos*, no. 20 (1991): 165–85.
Silva, Antonio de Moraes e. *Diccionario da lingua portuguesa.* 3rd. ed. 2 vols. Lisbon: Typ. de M. P. de Lacerda, 1823 [1789].
Silva, Antonio José Bacelar da. "The Indexing of Race: The Case of *Moreno* as a

Referent for Racial Distinction." Unpublished manuscript (cited by permission of the author).
Silva, Carlos Leonardo Bahiense da, and Victor Andrade de Melo. "Fabricando o soldado, forjando o cidadão: o doutor Eduardo Augusto Pereira de Abreu, a Guerra do Paraguai e a educação física no Brasil." *História, Ciências, Saúde—Manguinhos* 18, no. 2 (April–June 2011): 337–54.
Silva, Eduardo. "Law, Telegraph, and Festa: A Reevaluation of Abolition in Brazil." In *Pour l'histoire du Brésil: hommage à Katia de Queirós Mattoso*, edited by François Crouzet, Philippe Bonnichon, and Denis Rolland, 451–62. Paris: L'Harmattan, 2000.
Silva, Maria Laís Pereira da. *Os transportes coletivos na cidade do Rio de Janeiro: tensões e conflitos*. Rio: Secretaria Municipal de Cultura, Turismo e Esportes, Departamento Geral de Documentação e Informação Cultural, Divisão de Editoração, 1992.
Silva, Nelson do Valle. "Cor e o processo de realização sócio-econômica." In *Estrutura social, mobilidade e raça*, edited by Carlos Hasenbalg and Nelson do Valle Silva, 144–163. São Paulo: Vértice; Rio: IUPERJ, 1988.
———. "Morenidade: modo de usar." *Estudos Afro-Asiáticos*, no. 30 (Dec. 1996): 79–95.
Skidmore, Thomas E. *Black into White: Race and Nationality in Brazilian Thought*. New York: Oxford University Press, 1974.
Slenes, Robert W. "The Great Porpoise-Skull Strike: Central African Water Spirits and Slave Identity in Early-Nineteenth-Century Rio de Janeiro." In *Central Africans and Cultural Transformations in the American Diaspora*, edited by Linda M. Heywood, 183–208. Cambridge: Cambridge University Press, 2002.
Smith, Virginia. *Clean: A History of Personal Hygiene and Purity*. New York: Oxford University Press, 2007.
Soares, Luiz Carlos. *O "povo de Cam" na capital do Brasil: a escravidão urbana no Rio de Janeiro do século XIX*. Rio: FAPERJ and 7 Letras, 2007.
The South American Handbook. London: South American Publications, 1925–41.
Sousa, Gabriel Soares de. *Notícia do Brasil*. Edited by [Frederico Adolfo de] Varnhagen, Pirajá da Silva, and [Frederico G.] Edelweiss. São Paulo: n.p., 1974 [1587].
Souza, Augusto Fausto de. *A bahia do Rio de Janeiro: sua historia e descripção de suas riquezas*. 2nd ed. Rio: Typographia Militar de Costa & Santos, 1882.
Souza, Sílvia Cristina Martins de. *As noites no Ginásio: teatro e tensões culturais na Corte, 1832–1868*. Campinas: Editora da UNICAMP, 2002.
Stein, Stanley. *Vassouras: A Brazilian Coffee County, 1850–1890*. 2nd ed. New York: Atheneum, 1976 [1957].
Stepan, Nancy Leys. *The Hour of Eugenics: Race, Gender, and Nation in Latin America*. Ithaca, NY: Cornell University Press, 1999.

Stephens, Thomas M. *Dictionary of Latin American Racial and Ethnic Terminology*. 2nd ed. Gainesville: University of Florida Press, 1999.
Sterngass, Jon. *First Resorts: Pursuing Pleasure at Saratoga Springs, Newport, and Coney Island*. Baltimore: Johns Hopkins University Press, 2001.
Stoler, Ann. "Racial Histories and Their Regimes of Truth." In *Political Power and Social Theory*, vol. 11 edited by Diane E. Davis, 183–206. Greenwich: JAI Press, 1997.
Stovall, Tyler Edward. *Paris Noir: African Americans in the City of Light*. Boston: Houghton Mifflin, 1996.
Sweigart, Joseph Earl. "Financing and Marketing Brazilian Export Agriculture: The Coffee Factors of Rio de Janeiro, 1850–1888." PhD diss., University of Texas at Austin, 1980.
Táti, Miécio. *O mundo de Machado de Assis (o Rio de Janeiro na obra de Machado de Assis)*. 2nd ed. Rio: Secretaria Municipal de Cultura, Turismo e Esportes; Departamento Geral de Documentação e Informação Cultural, Divisão de Editoração, 1991.
Taunay, Alfredo d'Escragnolle, Viscount of. *Memórias*. Rio: Biblioteca do Exército, 1960.
Tavares, Flávio. *O dia em que Getúlio matou Allende e outras novelas de poder*. Porto Alegre: L&PM, 2014.
Taylor, Edwin, ed. *Insight Guides: Rio de Janeiro*. London: APA, 1996.
Teixeira, Manoel Pereira. "Sobre as causas provaveis da frequencia do hydrocele nesta Cidade do Recife; modo de as remir ou minorar, e melhor fórma de curar dita enfermidade: contendo a historia da molestia nesta mesma Cidade desde trinta annos a esta parte." *Annaes da Medicina Pernambucana* 1, no. 2 (Feb. 1842): 63–75.
Telles, Edward. *Race in Another America: The Significance of Skin Color in Brazil*. Princeton, NJ: Princeton University Press, 2004.
Thalassotherapia, ou a cura pelo banho de mar. Santos: Typ. do Instituto Esthetica Rosa, 1921.
Théo-Filho [Manoel Theotonio de Lacerda Freire Filho]. *Praia de Ipanema (romance)*. Rio: Editora Livraria Leite Ribeiro, 1927.
———. *Ao sol de Copacabana: romance*. Rio: G. Costa, 1946.
Thompson, E. P. *Customs in Common: Studies in Traditional Popular Culture*. New York: New Press, 1993.
———. *The Making of the English Working Class*. Harmondsworth, UK: Pelican Books, 1980 [1963].
Thorp, Rosemary. "Reappraising the Origins of Import-Substituting Industrialisation." *Journal of Latin American Studies* 24, Quincentenary Supplement (1992): 181–95.

Tollenare, Louis-François de. *Notes dominicales prises pendant un voyage en Portugal et au Brésil en 1816, 1817 et 1818*. Edited by Léon Bourdon. 3 vols. Paris: Presses Universitaires de France, 1971–1973.
Touring Club of Brazil, *Rio de Janeiro in a Few Hours: A Guide Book for Tourists*. [Rio]: n.p., 1938.
Travis, John. "Continuity and Change in English Sea-bathing, 1730–1900: A Case of Swimming with the Tide." In *Recreation and the Sea*, edited by Stephen Fisher, 8–35. Exeter, UK: University of Exeter Press, 1997.
Trevisan, João Silvério. *Devassos no paraíso: a homossexualidade no Brasil, da Colônia à atualidade*. 3rd ed., rev. and enl. Rio: Record, 2000.
Urbain, Jean-Didier. *Sur la plage: moeurs et coutumes balnéaires, XIXe–XXe siècles*. Paris: Éditions Payot & Rivages, 2016.
[United Nations], PNUD [Programa das Nações Unidas para o Desenvolvimento—Brasil]. "A distribuição de renda na cidade do Rio de Janeiro." *Rio Estudos*, no. 10 (April 2001), portalgeo.rio.rj.gov.br (accessed by editors on 5.8.2021).
Valladares, Licia do Prado. *A invenção da favela: do mito de origem à favela*. Rio: FGV, 2005.
Vallotton, Henry. *Brésil, terre d'amour et de beauté*. Lausanne: Librairie Payot, 1945.
Vargas, João H. Carlos. "Apartheid brasileiro: raça e segregação residencial no Rio de Janeiro." *Revista de Antropologia* 48, no. 1 (2005): 75–132.
Vaz, Lilian Feschler. *Modernidade e moradia: habitação coletiva no Rio de Janeiro, séculos XIX e XX*. Rio: 7Letras, 2002.
Velho, Gilberto. *A utopia urbana: um estudo de antropologia social*. 5th ed. Rio: Jorge Zahar, 1989.
Veríssimo, Érico. "Passeios por aí. . . ." In *Rio de Janeiro em prosa & verso*, edited by Manoel Bandeira and Carlos Drummond de Andrade, 68–71. Rio: José Olympio, 1965.
Veríssimo, Francisco Salvador, and William Seba Mallmann Bittar. *500 anos da casa no Brasil: as transformações da arquitetura e da utilização do espaço de moradia*. Rio: Ediouro, 1999.
Veríssimo, Francisco Salvador, William Seba Mallmann Bittar, and Maurício Alvarez. *Vida urbana: a evolução do cotidiano da cidade brasileira*. Rio: Ediouro, 2001.
Vianna, Hermano Vianna. *O mistério do samba*. Rio: Ed. UFRJ Zahar, 1995.
Vianna, Luiz Fernando. *Rio de Janeiro: imagens da aviação naval, 1916–1923*. Rio: Argumento, 2001.
Vieira, José Luiz. *Quaes as modificações que o toro floral pode oferecer. . . .* Rio: Typ. do *Diario* de A. & L. Navarro, 1852.

Vigarello, Georges. *Le propre et le sale: l'hygiène du corps depuis le Moyen Âge*. Paris: Seuil, 1985.

Villaça, Nízia Maria Souza. "Points do Rio: uma semiologia corporal." *Brasilis: Revista de História sem Fronteiras* 1, no. 1 (July–Aug. 2003): 29–37.

Wadsworth, James. "Moncorvo Filho e o problema da infância: modelos institucionais e ideológicos da assistência à infância no Brasil." *Revista Brasileira de História* no. 37 (July 1999): 103–24.

Walkowitz, Judith. *City of Dreadful Delight: Narratives of Sexual Danger in Late Victorian London*. Chicago: University of Chicago Press, 1992.

Walton, John K. *The English Seaside Resort: A Social History, 1750–1914*. Leicester, UK: Leicester University Press; New York: St. Martin's Press, 1983.

———. "Health, Sociability, Politics, and Culture: Spas in History, Spas and History, an Overview." *Journal of Tourism History* 4, no. 1 (2012): 1–14.

———. "Policing the Seaside Holiday: Blackpool and San Sebastián, from the 1870s to the 1930s." In *Comparative Histories of Crime*, edited by Barry Godfrey, Clive Emsley, and Graeme Dunstall, 145–58. Cullompton, Devon, UK: Willan Publishing, 2003.

Walvin, James. *Beside the Seaside: A Social History of the Popular Seaside Holiday*. London: Allen Lane, 1978.

Wehrs, Carlos. *O Rio antigo de Aluísio Azevedo*. Rio: n.p., 1994.

Welch, John H. *Capital Markets in the Development Process: The Case of Brazil*. London: Macmillan, 1993.

Wilberforce, Edward. *Brazil Viewed through a Naval Glass: With Notes on Slavery and the Slave Trade*. London: Longman, Brown, Green, and Longmans, 1856.

Wiltse, Jeff. *Contested Waters: A Social History of Swimming Pools in America*. Chapel Hill: University of North Carolina Press, 2007.

Wolfe, Joel. *Autos and Progress: The Brazilian Search for Modernity*. Oxford: Oxford University Press, 2010.

Woodcock, George, and Ivan Avakumatov. *The Doukhobors*. Toronto: Oxford University Press, 1968.

Index

Page numbers in *italic* text indicate illustrations.

CPSIA information can be obtained
at www.ICGtesting.com
Printed in the USA
LVHW040311190222
710941LV00003B/5

9 780826 363633